FRENCH Sociology

Johan Heilbron

CORNELL UNIVERSITY PRESS
Ithaca and London

First published 2015 by Cornell University Press
First printing, Cornell Paperbacks, 2015
Printed in the United States of America

Library of Congress Cataloging-in-Publication Data

Heilbron, Johan, author.
  French sociology / Johan Heilbron.
    pages cm
  Includes bibliographical references and index.
  ISBN 978-0-8014-5382-3 (cloth : alk. paper)
  ISBN 978-0-8014-5663-3 (pbk. : alk. paper)
  1. Sociology—France. I. Title.
  HM477.F8H45   2015
  301.0944—dc23   2015003479

Cornell University Press strives to use environmentally responsible
suppliers and materials to the fullest extent possible in the publishing
of its books. Such materials include vegetable-based, low-VOC inks
and acid-free papers that are recycled, totally chlorine-free, or
partly composed of nonwood fibers. For further information, visit
our website at www.cornellpress.cornell.edu.

Cloth printing   10 9 8 7 6 5 4 3 2 1
Paperback printing   10 9 8 7 6 5 4 3 2 1

FRENCH
Sociology

Contents

Figures and Tables

Figures

Tables

Acknowledgments

This study about the development of sociology in France is based on a variety of sources. In addition to the usual research in libraries and archives, I have relied on a database that I put together, as well as on interviews and observations. The database contains biographical and bibliographical information about some six hundred social scientists and philosophers. The information comes from the usual biographical sources, many of which can now be readily consulted in the biography department of the Bibliothèque nationale de France (BNF). Additional information came from obituaries and biographical notes in sociological and other academic journals, and from yearbooks, *Annuaires*, of institutions like the École pratique des hautes études (EPHE), the Association des élèves de l'École normale supérieure (ENS), the École des hautes études en sciences sociales (EHESS), and the Collège de France. I have also used various biographical files that Victor Karady kindly made available to me.

Over the years I have also interviewed French social scientists. Some of the forty scholars I interviewed were students in the 1920s and 1930s and were able to give me their views on academic life from the interwar years up to the 1980s; members of the youngest generation were students in the 1960s and 1970s and started their career shortly afterward. Most of the interviews are in chapters 4 and 5; these are complemented by more recent interviews in chapters 6 and 7. The interviewees included: Raymond Aron, Philippe Besnard, Luc Boltanski, Pierre Bourdieu, François Bourricaud, Lucien Brams, Jean Cazeneuve, Louis Chevalier, Jean-Claude Combessie, Pierre-Henri Chombart de Lauwe, Lewis Coser, Michel Crozier, Eric de

Dampierre, André Davidovitch, Yves Delamotte, Henri Desroche, Alain Desrosières, Mikel Dufrenne, Joffre Dumazedier, Henri Gouhier, François Isambert, Viviane Isambert-Jamati, Victor Karady, Jacques Lautman, Michel Leiris, Claude Lévi-Strauss, Edgar Morin, Francine Muel-Dreyfus, Émile Poulat, Robert Pagès, Denise Paulme, Clémence Ramnoux, Paul Rendu, Jean-Daniel Reynaud, Monique de Saint Martin, Jean Stoetzel, Jean-René Tréanton, Paul Vignaux, and Pierre Vilar.

I have also drawn on my own observations as a foreign student in Paris beginning in 1979–80. Although these observations and experiences are more difficult to assess, they have no doubt been essential, both for what I was able to observe and understand and for what has remained beyond my comprehension. Coming from a quite different academic background in the Netherlands, I was at once intrigued and baffled by the French intellectual scene. My first serious scholarly interest, when still a student at the University of Amsterdam, was in historical epistemology (Bachelard, Canguilhem). In part because this tradition was then barely known outside of France, it seemed worthwhile to conceive a study about its development—a study that I envisioned in the historical sociological tradition that Johan Goudsblom and Abram de Swaan taught me in Amsterdam. But as the grant for which I applied was declined, and having in the meantime discovered the work of Pierre Bourdieu, I found another way to study in Paris. Following a considerable number of courses and seminars (Foucault, Vuillemin, and others), either out of curiosity, personal interest, or just to get a sense of this peculiar intellectual universe, the primary locus of my study during that year was Pierre Bourdieu's seminar at the École des hautes études. It was perhaps the best place in Paris to understand something of French intellectuals and academics, and, beyond the specific interests one might have, it was an incomparable sociological workshop. After an exhilarating year I returned to the Netherlands, and when in the mid-1980s Bourdieu gave me the opportunity to return to France, I did some of the work that has found its way into this book. Interrupted by other projects and academic peregrinations of various kinds, I returned to France many years later and rejoined Bourdieu's center in 2000. There I eventually picked up my work on French sociology where I had left it many years earlier. In one of Bourdieu's early seminars I attended, he once ironically remarked that the researcher shouldn't disappear in the object of her or his study. In a sense, though, that is what happened to me; I have become part of what this book is about. Neither outside observer nor seasoned insider, this study is inevitably also the sediment of that particular experience.

This book was for the greatest part written when I was a fellow at the Netherlands Institute for Advanced Study (NIAS) in Wassenaar. I am very grateful to the staff who helped to make my stay as enjoyable as it was productive. In particular I thank Petry Kievit-Tyson, Dindy van Maanen, Erwin Nolet, and Eline van der Ploeg. Prior to my stay at NIAS, Anaïs Bokobza and Christine Michel helped me with certain parts of the data collection and analysis. After my stay I profited from the comments of Nic van Dijk, Christian Fleck, and Marc Joly, who read parts of the manuscript, and from two anonymous reviewers. I owe a great deal to French colleagues and friends, who over the years have in various ways helped me to understand the peculiar universe that this book is about. Regrettably some of them—Philippe Besnard, Alain Desrosières, Michael Pollak—are no longer there to discuss the result; my greatest debt is to Pierre Bourdieu, without whom this book would not exist.

FRENCH
Sociology

INTRODUCTION

✕✕✕

"No science can be truly understood independent of its own history."
—Auguste Comte

Sociology is a French invention and, just like the essay and photography, is undoubtedly among the country's most lasting export products. Ever since the late 1830s, when Auguste Comte proposed the word "sociology" for the new science he envisioned, the term has found acceptance in academic institutions around the world. Although first elaborated in France, sociology spread more rapidly in Britain and it had its earliest success in the United States. Around 1900 the discipline obtained a place in university courses in Western countries, and its expansion accelerated after the Second World War when the social sciences became full-fledged academic disciplines. By 2000, as the *World Social Science Report* (2010) has documented, sociology, like other social science disciplines, was practiced in virtually all regions and countries around the globe.

French sociologists have not only been among the discipline's most notable pioneers but their collective efforts also represent a particularly rich tradition up to this very day. Some of the classic and contemporary figures are well known, and French social scientists figure prominently among the most-cited scholars in the world. In 2009, for example, the *Times Higher Education Supplement* published a list of most-cited book authors in the social and human sciences.[1] Twenty-nine of them published their major works after World War II and were cited more than five hundred times in a single year. With one exception—Edward Said—all were from Western countries and all except Judith Butler and Hannah Arendt were men. More surprising were the geographical distributions and disciplinary affiliations. The scholarly hit parade was headed by three Frenchmen (Foucault, Bourdieu, Derrida) and among the top ten, half were French (including Deleuze and Latour); the other five were Canadian (Bandura, Goffman), British (Giddens), German (Habermas), and American (Butler). No less striking were their disciplinary affiliations. Representatives of the largest disciplines in terms of students and staff, which are also the disciplines with the greatest impact on citation scores—economics, management, psychology—are virtually absent from the list. The most-cited authors were scholars from relatively small disciplines with a more intellectual profile, a fairly strong theoretical orientation, and a sizeable audience outside of their own research specialties. About half were affiliated with philosophy, nearly a third with sociology; all other disciplines had a much smaller share.

Although this citation ranking attests to the exceptional prominence of French authors, bibliometric studies have rightly emphasized that their recognition tends to be restricted to a very small number of stars whose work is widely translated.[2] In contemporary social science, books and journals that are not available in English have become more or less invisible outside the language in which they have been published. The United States is the predominant power in international social science and English has become its lingua franca, but although French work has lost some of its standing, it has at least retained some of its originality. Part of the notoriety of French sociology, in particular, is that it is less of a narrowly defined research domain than it is the component of a more broadly conceived intellectual culture. Raymond Aron, Pierre Bourdieu, and Bruno Latour belong to successive generations, they represent quite distinct intellectual programs and styles of work, but all embody a more intellectual way of practicing sociology in which sociological inquiry is related to other intellectual endeavors and in which not merely specialized academic questions are addressed but broader public issues as well. Whether this larger conception of sociology is admired or objected to, it is often seen as typically French.

Understanding French Social Science

Because knowledge of the French language and French publications has become rare and the level of translations in the social sciences is low, French scholarship increasingly appears as an exotic brand.[3] What is called "French theory," for example, is associated with a more adventurous type of theorizing that is marked by a rather peculiar literary-philosophical writing style that deviates from the standards of Anglophone social science. Often, however, this perception of French work is curiously selective, ignoring the context in which it is actually carried out, and even when celebrated it tends to be poorly understood. What is subsumed under the label "French theory" is more often than not an arbitrary selection of authors, people who have little more in common than being French, or writing French, and who in one way or another seem to depart from the conventions of the Anglo-American mainstream.[4]

Given the selective and rather superficial knowledge of French social science, this study of sociology in France is, first, intended to document and clarify its development and to uncover historical patterns that are little known. As such I will try to correct certain misapprehensions, recall forgotten episodes, and clarify the work of main figures and groups. In several cases I will propose interpretations that differ from current thinking. In doing so I will, more broadly, try to demonstrate that sociology, like any other intellectual tradition, is best understood by means of historical sociological inquiry. Since this book is about scholars and scholarship, it focuses on the producers of sociological knowledge, the groups and networks they have formed, and the conditions under which they have done their work. As far as it seemed relevant, I have also, albeit less systematically, paid attention to the teaching of sociology, to the demand for sociological knowledge and its uses, and to its modes of professional organization.

To understand scientific knowledge, the first requirement is to properly *historicize* its production. In contrast to the presentism and the lack of historical awareness that obscure many debates, the social sciences not only deal with historical realities but the way they account for them is itself a historical process. Reflecting on the social sciences, on their virtues and their flaws, thus needs to be historicized, without, however, falling into the trap of historicism in which the search for historical detail obscures more general patterns and discourages sociological analysis of how knowledge is produced, circulates, and evolves.

For this historical-sociological view I have adopted a long-term perspective in order to uncover patterns of continuity and change that would have otherwise remained hidden. Several aspects of contemporary French sociology—its position in the Faculty of Letters, for example—can be understood only by going back in time much further than is commonly done. The development of sociology in France will be covered for almost two centuries, from its beginnings in the early nineteenth century until about 2000, when the long-term trend of expansion seems to have come to an end and the discipline is confronted with a series of new challenges, notably those resulting from the rise of vocational studies and increasing internationalization.[5] The present book is the sequel to *The Rise of Social Theory* (1995), which was concerned with the "predisciplinary" history of sociology up to the mid-nineteenth century. As an attempt to account for two centuries of sociology in France, I have focused on the structure of its development, that is, on the most crucial episodes and dominant trends, even if some of these may have fallen into oblivion.

Such a long-term perspective, however, cannot be limited to ideas, theories, and research practices, nor can it be restricted to the paradigms, epistemes, or other deep structures that would define the conditions of possibility of knowledge in a given period. In whatever way ideas are defined, they cannot be understood in and by themselves. Intellectual outcomes, on which historians of ideas concentrate their work, are the result of the work that is done by those who produce such ideas, and that work is enabled or obstructed by particular social conditions. Understanding ideas is not merely about concepts, theories, and assumptions—however important they are—it simultaneously raises issues about how such ideas come into being, how they are mobilized in research and other intellectual enterprises, and how they have, or have not, spread beyond the immediate circle of producers. Understanding intellectual products, to put it simply and straightforwardly, cannot be divorced from understanding their producers and the conditions of production. Intellectual history, in other words, needs to be combined with social history, and that is best achieved within the larger framework of historical sociology. The broader objective of this study, then, is to integrate historical inquiries about sociology not so much into a specialty of historical erudition, but into historical sociology, and as such to contribute to a historical sociology of the social sciences.[6]

As compared with the approaches that are known as "social studies of science"—or more specifically "actor-network theory"—historical sociology has, it seems to me, distinct advantages. Social studies of science tend to focus on the present and have not paid systematic attention to the historical development of scientific practices. In the dominant approaches the production of knowledge is observed in local settings, laboratories, and other research sites, and understood by describing and dissecting the microprocesses that underlie the social construction of knowledge. Although this has significantly improved our understanding of scientific practices, it has occasionally also had the effect of omitting more structural conditions and their historical transformation from the analysis. The microdynamics of intellectual networks is no doubt crucial for understanding processes of knowledge production, but the conditions under which such networks emerge, function, expand, or disintegrate should not be eliminated from an account of how knowledge is produced.

For doing justice to these more structural dimensions of intellectual practices, the field theoretical approach of Pierre Bourdieu provides a fruitful framework. In the chapters that follow, my aim has not been to apply field theory as rigorously as possible to the case of sociology in France, but rather to use it as a heuristic model or, more modestly, as a sensitizing framework. Field theory indicates the most significant analytical dimensions to take into account, even when the material that I gathered often remained too fragmentary to allow a full-fledged field analysis. But in spite of such shortcomings, a field theoretical perspective derives its value mainly from its comparative advantage. It enables understanding individual trajectories and the microdynamics of groups and networks as part and parcel of broader field structures. Fields are relatively autonomous social spaces in which actors, individually and collectively, compete for specific stakes. The relations between these actors—to summarize the basic model very succinctly—are defined by the position they occupy in the field in question, by the volume and composition of resources they dispose of, and by the dispositions that orient the ways they are inclined or disinclined to mobilize their resources. One of Bourdieu's working hypotheses is that there is a homology between the space of intellectual products and the space of their producers. Understanding intellectual work thus consists of relating to each other two sets of relations, the "space of works or discourses taken as differential stances, and the space of the positions held by those who produce them."[7] In other words, a specific set of academic practices, that is, a particular configuration of intellectual approaches, specialties, or styles, tends to be structured in such way that it corresponds to the social relations among its producers.

Since fields are only relatively autonomous, internal struggles depend on the broader context as well. The academic field has a structure and dynamics of its own, but its functioning depends on state policies with regard to higher education, on the social and economic demand for expert knowledge, and on the workings of the publishing industry and the book market. Rather than choosing either a macro perspective, which systems theorists or Marxists have traditionally adopted, or a micro approach, which is predominant in social studies of science, a field approach allows one to articulate distinct and irreducible levels.[8]

Using a field approach has a few basic implications. The most important one is that individual practitioners or specific institutions cannot be artificially divorced from their relations to other practitioners and institutions, both within the domain of sociology and between sociology and other endeavors. Rather than isolating sociology from other intellectual enterprises, its changing relationships to the sciences, philosophy, and literature should be an integral part of study. This broader constellation is structured, first and foremost, by the power relations of the academic field at large. It is useful, therefore, to recall at the outset that the French academic field has a few general characteristics that have continuously shaped the country's social science production.

Academic and intellectual production, first, tends to be centralized in Paris, where the most important institutions have been concentrated (schools, libraries, archives, journals, research institutes, publishers). Intellectual work is strongly affected by this dominant center, where intellectual activity is particularly dense and competitive. This centralization produces a peculiar center-periphery dynamics. Groups or departments in the periphery can only escape their fate of being in the margins of the system by concentrating their activities in certain niches or, more boldly, by challenging the center with new programs: Durkheim developed his sociological program in Bordeaux, the *Annales* school of history took off in Strasbourg.

Not only is the French system centralized, but it is, second, strongly hierarchical as well, with small and selective elite schools, *grandes écoles*, and competitive national *agrégation* exams at the top. Graduates from elite schools and those who have successfully passed the selective annual *agrégation* exams, *agrégés*, dominate the intellectual scene.[9] Graduates from the École normale supérieure, *normaliens*, have traditionally played a particularly prominent role; many of the best-known social scientists were educated at the boarding school in the Parisian rue d'Ulm, where, for example, all three of the most cited scholars referred to earlier—Foucault, Bourdieu, and Derrida—studied in the late 1940s and early 1950s. The geographical center in Paris is thus reinforced by this concentration of intellectual resources, networks, and ambitions in and around elite institutions. This particular educational structure reproduces hierarchical relations and well-established patterns of domination. Those who have not made it into an elite school and have only a regular university education have fewer chances and will be inclined to accept less ambitious tasks or revert to outsider strategies, that is, to provoke the academic establishment by prophetic discourses or radically different points of view. This elite system, which institutes a dividing line between the selected few and all others, also implies that intellectual competition is marked by particular rivalries among these selective schools, between *normaliens* and *énarques*, for example, that is, between graduates from the traditionally more intellectual École normale supérieure (ENS) and the École nationale d'administration (ENA)—the training school for the country's political and administrative elite.

The French academic field is, third, marked by a relatively clear-cut separation between teaching and research. Alongside universities and other teaching institutions, research schools and research institutes have developed, in which much of the research is concentrated. Institutions like the Centre national de la recherche scientifique (CNRS) and the École des hautes études en sciences sociales (EHESS) house a large part of the more prominent French social scientists, research seminars, journals, and book series. This duality, and the tensions between research and teaching, are in a sense continuations of the old division between ecclesiastic universities, where canonical knowledge was transmitted and degrees were granted, and national academies, the membership of which consisted of the most eminent practitioners of the arts and sciences.

Although the French academic field is obviously also structured by disciplines and departmental structures, which are not unlike those in other countries, this mode of academic compartmentalization takes very specific forms owing to the above-mentioned cleavages. A Parisian *normalien* who is a university professor in sociology has quite a lot in common with a Parisian *normalien* in philosophy or classical letters. Their shared background and a common training in writing essays on general topics, *dissertations*, facilitate communication across disciplines and research specialties. Their joint background also helps to explain why this centralized and hierarchical academic field, with its relatively outspoken division between teaching and research, is more closely interwoven with the intellectual field than in many other countries. Because of the prestige it offers, the intellectual field and the figure of the public intellectual have exercised a particular attraction in France. Literary models, from Voltaire to Sartre, continue to exert their influence, cultural and intellectual journals for more general audiences have remained a relevant medium for social scientists up to this very day, as has writing books, editing book series, and participating in intellectual and public debate.

French social scientists are not only tempted to cross the boundaries of their own discipline and department, but they are also inclined to look beyond the national border. Science and scholarship have at the highest level always been an international affair. Focusing on the embeddedness of sociologists in the national, academic and intellectual field therefore needs to be complemented by both a comparative and transnational perspective. Brief comparisons with other national traditions will be made whenever possible in order to get a better sense of the peculiarities of the French tradition. But comparisons of this kind risk replicating national categories and national modes of understanding if they are not simultaneously combined with studying cross-national transfers and the transnational circulation of scholars and ideas. Against the illusion of autarky and the idea that national traditions need to be understood within their national context only, I will therefore also make use of a transnational perspective. Key individuals and research groups will be examined from the perspective of their transnational connections, thus giving particular weight to the international circulation of ideas. The French sociological tradition owes much of its continuity to an enduring set of constraints and opportunities on the national level, but these national structures are shaped, reinforced, undermined, or transformed by the transnational relations of which they are an integral part.[10]

Outline of the Book

Since sociology emerged in a context in which other social sciences already existed in one form or another, the first chapter is concerned with the structure of nineteenth-century French social science. Studies that are focused on a single discipline often fail to see how much a discipline owes to its relations to other disciplines. Sociology is no exception. After the short-lived experiment during the revolutionary years to institutionalize the social sciences, a national institution emerged with the Academy of Moral and Political Sciences (1832). Although its role has been largely forgotten, the Academy was a pioneering effort to institutionalize the social sciences and represented the dominant institution in France until the end of the nineteenth century. Only during the last third of the nineteenth century did the center of the social sciences shift from the official academy to expanding universities. This institutional shift was accompanied by a corresponding change from a unified conception of social science in the service of governmental institutions to more varied and autonomous disciplines. Social science production shifted from a centralized national regime to a more decentralized field based on university disciplines. With the exception of political science and economics, the other social sciences (sociology, ethnology, psychology) were now instituted in the Faculty of Letters, thus engendering an enduring dependence on the humanities and philosophy—its "crowning discipline," as Jean-Louis Fabiani has called it.

Chapters 2 and 3 reveal how sociology obtained a position within this emerging field structure. Chapter 2 is concerned with the invention of sociology as a new science of human society. As conceived by Auguste Comte, sociology was neither a continuation of the ideas about "social science" that had triumphed during the revolutionary years nor a form of "moral science" for governing modern nations. Comte's sociology represented a profound yet widely misunderstood renewal, which took shape outside of and in opposition to the established academies. Reflecting on the state of the sciences after the Revolution and the Napoleonic reforms, Comte's theory of the sciences allowed him to reconceptualize the relations among the various sciences, to redefine the status of the social sciences, and to propose the new science of sociology as one of its major consequences. Although Comte's theory would eventually have considerable impact in both the life sciences and the social sciences, sociology virtually disappeared after Comte's *Cours de philosophie positive* (1830–42). Migrating to Britain, its resurgence in France occurred during the first decades of the Third Republic (1870–1940) in the context of expanding universities and as a response to sociology's more favorable reception in Britain. This response was carried by heterodox positivists outside of the university and philosophers within the Faculty of Letters. Whereas the first failed to obtain academic recognition, members of the new generation of university philosophers succeeded in transforming sociology from a stigmatized extra-academic enterprise into a legitimate university endeavor.

Building on the work of this small group of university pioneers, the number of sociological studies multiplied rapidly between the 1880s and the outbreak of the First World War. Sociology became a subfield of its own, with its own journals and associations, and shaped by fierce competition between two rival networks: one led by René Worms, the other by Émile Durkheim. The shaping of university sociology and the antagonisms between Worms and Durkheim form the subject of chapter 3. Rather than focusing on biographical details or canonical ideas, the analysis is primarily concerned with the inseparably social and intellectual competition between these two networks. Out of this rivalry Durkheimian sociology emerged as the preeminent form of sociology in France. Durkheim's sociology, it is argued, was essentially a critical continuation of the Comtean conception of the social sciences. It is shown in some detail how Durkheim elaborated this position in opposition to both organicist conceptions and psychological approaches, and how he transformed it into a research program and formed a school around his journal *Année sociologique.*

While the Durkheimian group eclipsed its competitors and obtained considerable scholarly prestige, sociology did not fare very well institutionally. Sociology was too general a science for academic specialists and too laboriously scientific for philosophers. By 1920 sociology's institutional position was limited to four chairs. During the interwar years, as is shown in chapter 4, sociology underwent a double transformation. The first was linked to the development of the Durkheimian group and the growing split between university teachers and research scholars. The research scholars belonged to the world of relatively small and specialized research schools. Through their work, sociology entered a wide variety of scholarly domains and contributed to a range of intellectual innovations. The university professors, on the other hand, represented the more official brand of sociology and were close to the dominant forms of idealist philosophy and the republican educational establishment. The other defining change during the interwar years was related to the transmission of sociology and generational discontinuities. The university successors to the Durkheimians rejected not only certain forms of Durkheimianism, but its very aim and style as well. That Durkheimian sociology survived as a scientific tradition was due to the research wing of the network, but as such it subsisted mainly in disciplines other than sociology.

After the Second World War, sociology expanded again, first in a newly created research institute, and after 1958, when an autonomous bachelor degree (*licence*) in sociology was created, in the universities as well. Although the growth of sociology may appear as a continuous process, the actual development can be divided in distinct and only slightly overlapping phases. Chapter 5 focuses on the rise of empirical research between 1945 and 1960 at the first research institute in sociology. To understand the functioning of this center, it is shown how the center was embedded in broader field structures and how these affected the research carried out. Sociological work came to be caught up in a configuration that was defined by two antagonistic poles: an intellectual pole dominated by existentialist philosophy and a policy research pole in state institutes. In spite of their apparent autonomy, sociologists were in fact caught in a double bind. In the theoretical and political concerns that dominated the intellectual field and that were defined by philosophers around Jean-Paul Sartre and the journal *Les temps modernes*, sociology was considered a suspicious enterprise, associated with American-style empiricism in the service of the ruling classes. On the other hand, neither did sociology have an established position in policy research. By responding to the policy demand for applied research, the researchers obtained some funds and gradually enhanced their professional experience. By presenting the results of their work as being about the needs and conditions of the working classes, they attempted to gain a certain intellectual recognition as well. The microdynamics of the research practices can thus be understood only when taking the broader field structure into account.

Central in chapter 6 is the second institutional breakthrough of the discipline. The first had occurred at the end of the nineteenth century with the establishment of the first chairs, journals, and learned societies. The second breakthrough occurred between 1960 and 2000 and brought unprecedented growth to all of the social sciences. For each of the disciplines, expansion implied more autonomy and the creation of professional universes with their own degrees, career structures, publication outlets, and modes of professional association. Starting as a small and divided subfield, sociology became an organized university discipline. In order to understand the structural dynamics of this long phase of growth, two cycles of expansion are distinguished. The first was concentrated in the 1960s and the beginnings of the 1970s, when opportunities for social scientific work improved drastically and the human sciences gained an intellectual and public acclaim that was unprecedented. In France this was the era of "structuralism" and the flowering of new theoretical programs ranging from structural anthropology and structuralist versions of Marxism and psychoanalysis, to Foucauldian archaeology and Derridaen deconstruction. After a decade of lower levels of funding, diminishing recruitments, and a politically and scientifically divided academic community, the social sciences went through a second cycle of expansion from 1985 to the beginning of twenty-first century. This time, however, the expansion was limited to universities, while the research sector stagnated or declined and the social sciences were intellectually and politically contested. Instead of primarily challenging the classical humanities, as had been the case in the 1960s and 1970s, the social sciences now had to compete with disciplines that were attuned to the market sector, that is, with economics, which became the dominant social science in academia as well as in policy circles, and with a host of vocational disciplines, which promised students opportunities on the labor market that the classical social sciences lacked.

After analyzing the changing field structure and its consequences, chapter 7 seeks to understand how some of the most prominent research groups maneuvered within this changing structure and exploited the opportunities it provided. The figures selected—Alain Touraine, Michel Crozier, Raymond Boudon, and Pierre Bourdieu—all produced an internationally recognized body of work. The groups they led developed in mutual competition and occupied particular positions in the academic and the intellectual field, but had a defining significance for the discipline as a whole.

One of the questions touched on regularly in these chapters is whether sociology in France can be seen as "French" sociology. Is it still meaningful to speak of national traditions in the social sciences? In the epilogue I will come back to the question and argue that the justified critique of "methodological nationalism" should not lead us to abandon the study of national structures and traditions as relevant categories of inquiry. Even in times of internationalization and globalization national institutions retain much of their weight, and the different forms and meanings of internationalization can be properly understood only by simultaneously rethinking the question of national traditions in the social sciences.

CHAPTER 1

The Establishment of Organized Social Science

Organized social science, however fragile and contested, was the outcome of the democratic revolutions of the late eighteenth and early nineteenth centuries. The intellectual origins of the social sciences can be traced much further back in time, to the renewed secularization of thought during the Renaissance, the intellectual consequences of the Scientific Revolution, and the fervor of the Enlightenment, but it was only when the institutional structures of the old regime were swept away that the social sciences obtained their place as a distinct and organized branch of scientific inquiry. The knowledge that these new sciences promised to deliver was expected to provide guidance to national elites that could no longer rely on the dogmas of divine right and the structures of absolutist rule.[1] What kind of economic, social, and political processes could be expected to emerge under conditions of political liberty? And how might these be regulated and controlled by the authorities? The institutional recognition of the social sciences took the form of a national and centralized institution that was preoccupied with the issues raised by governing a society that was founded on political rights and civil liberties.

The Politics of Social Science

The institutionalization of the social sciences was in France part and parcel of the country's revolutionary transformation. The abolished royal academies were in 1795 replaced by the newly founded national institute. It was divided into three classes that symbolized the intellectual order of the new era: the natural sciences formed the First Class, the "moral and political sciences" the Second Class, and literature and the fine arts, suspected to have been aristocratic pastimes, the Third Class. The Institut de France thus exemplified Wolf Lepenies's characterization of the modern intellectual world as a constellation of three cultures, with the social sciences situated somewhat uncomfortably between science and literature.[2]

The origins of the newly instituted social sciences can be traced back to the first efforts to reflect on the art of government. For centuries the Aristotelian tradition of practical philosophy, with its threefold structure of politics, ethics, and economics, provided the matrix for such issues in the curricula of European universities. In the early modern period, cameral or state sciences had emerged alongside the universities as a response to the formation of national states, while a plurality of secularizing moral, political, and economic writings had come into being around learned societies, which had expanded since the Renaissance. But whatever their precise standing and significance, the early modern approaches to the social world were only loosely connected to one another, and they lacked the institutional autonomy that had been granted to the natural sciences, literature, and the fine arts.

As a consequence, discourses on human society had been strongly bound to the doctrines of the clergy and the doxa of political rulers. Learned societies, for example, could not discuss religious, moral, and political questions unless they were treated in accordance with the "authority of the king, the government, and the laws of the monarchy."[3] Plans for an academy of political studies had existed in France ever since the latter part of the seventeenth century, but they had been systematically thwarted by the absolutist monarchy for fear of political dispute and opposition.[4] In such a sensitive domain, it was more desirable to have individual councilors and governmental services than to rely on an academy, which would elect its own members and publish its own proceedings. Governmental services, on the other hand, were under direct control of state officials and the knowledge they produced generally remained confidential. In the late 1770s an anonymous author noted: "All over I see academies for all branches of knowledge, but nowhere do I see one for the moral and political sciences. What could the source of this exclusion be?"[5]

If the Enlightenment has been seen as a formative period for the social sciences, it was fundamentally because a secular intelligentsia now explicitly claimed and effectively exercised the right to analyze any subject matter, however controversial, independently of official doctrines.[6] No longer was any domain to be excluded from rational inquiry and public deliberation. Writings on political, moral, and economic issues flourished as never before, and they attained a level of public interest that was unprecedented. One of the symptoms of this movement of renewal was the introduction of new terms and categories. A marked shift occurred from the older frameworks of moral philosophy and natural law to more specialized, and often more scientific, designations like political economy, economic science, political science, ethnography, and anthropology. At the same time, new expressions emerged as a common denominator. The expressions *sciences de l'homme* and *sciences humaines* spread gradually after 1770; the notion of *sciences morales et politiques* came into use at about the same time. The expression *science sociale* was coined during the revolutionary turmoil by Sieyès and other members of the circle around Condorcet to indicate a broadly conceived new science of government.[7]

Although the institutionalization of the "moral and political sciences" during the revolutionary period was the outcome of changes that had been underway for some time, it represented an innovation of considerable significance. For the first time were the social sciences recognized institutionally as constituting a distinct branch of scientific knowledge that was formally treated on an equal footing with that of the other sciences. The social sciences were no longer reduced to being merely practical arts or crafts, as in the Aristotelian tradition, but came to form an organized and publicly acknowledged scientific domain in its own right. Similar to the natural sciences, the moral and political sciences of the Institut de France would deliver scientific expertise for the government. In the latter half of the 1790s, the members of the Second Class played a key role in public debates about educational reform, legislation, health policy, and economic affairs. Among them were philosophers, political economists, jurists, and historians, most of whom were committed to the objective of stabilizing the revolutionary changes.[8] Their pioneering role, however, was short-lived. After clashes with the government, Napoleon dissolved the Second Class in 1803, and its members were relocated in one of the two remaining classes. It was not until the fall of the Napoleonic Empire and the end of the Restoration (1815–30) that the Second Class was reestablished on a more permanent basis. The national Académie des sciences morales et politiques (1832) became the official center for moral and political studies under the constitutional regime of the July monarchy (1830–48). Although curiously absent from standard histories of the social sciences, the Academy of Moral and Political Sciences was the dominant social science institution in France until the end of the nineteenth century; it was also the leading example for social science organizations that emerged in other countries.

Although hardly any of the Academy's studies have gained a place in the canon of the social sciences, the Academy played a pivotal role in the early development of the social sciences. As the first public institution in the world devoted to this relatively new scientific domain, it provided a national infrastructure for the social sciences and concentrated, coordinated, and controlled previously dispersed efforts. The historical significance of the Academy is well illustrated by the fact that, by the end of the nineteenth century, representatives of the emerging university disciplines conceived their work in explicit opposition to the Academy. The formation of economics, psychology, and sociology as university disciplines arose primarily out of a struggle against the doctrines and practices of the Academy, and the very success of these university pioneers is the main reason why the Academy has virtually disappeared from collective memory. Academicians lost their supremacy to university professors, on the one hand, and to new policy experts, on the other. It became increasingly rare to pursue a scholarly career while simultaneously having political and administrative responsibilities. The fields of higher education and politics became more autonomous social universes with their own criteria of recruitment and career advancement, thus separating what the Academy had typically combined for the major part of the nineteenth century.

France fulfilled a pioneering role in this relatively long first phase in the institutionalization of the social sciences that was characterized by the emergence of a national coordinating body. In other advanced countries comparable institutions emerged somewhat later, generally after the revolutions of 1848 and in relation to growing concerns about the social consequences of industrialization. While countries such as Belgium, Italy, and Spain followed the French example of establishing an institute for "moral and political sciences," another model developed in Britain, the United States, and Germany.[9] In Britain, the National Association for the Promotion of Social Science (1857), just like the French Academy of Moral and Political Sciences, bore the mark of reform-oriented liberals. French and English liberals opposed conservative elites and radical workers' movements alike, but the British organization was an associational structure that functioned in a more decentralized manner than the French academy.[10] Driven by an explicit concern for legislative and administrative reform, and carried by a broad alliance of social reformers, the British Association was remarkably effective in proposing social reforms. Contemporaries described it as an "outdoor parliament" that focused on policy solutions for the "social question," yet showing little interest in theoretical or academic issues and with hardly any connections to the universities. The American Social Science Association (1867) followed the British model without ever achieving its political effectiveness; the German Verein für Socialpolitik (1873) was also closer to the British than the French model, although it didn't match its British equivalent in reform success either.[11]

Moral Science in Government Service

As a meeting place for senior civil servants, politicians, and scholars, the Academy of Moral and Political Sciences embodied a peculiar form of a science of government or, more broadly, of governance. Continuing the centralized French state tradition and reacting to the trauma of the French Revolution, liberal political elites in France were above all committed to ensuring the stability of the national state. According to the principle of their leader Royer-Collard, authority had to be established first, then liberties could be introduced as counterweights. This peculiar form of state liberalism was not primarily market oriented, but was rooted in a broad, historically oriented political outlook.[12] Like Montesquieu and his inheritors, it considered political questions in relation to the morals and manners of the nation, but within a framework that was more historically grounded than Montesquieu's with the French Revolution at its center. The philosophical stance of this state liberalism was eclectic, intending to neutralize or overcome postrevolutionary antagonisms, while at the same time remaining uncompromisingly "spiritualist" or idealist in its conception of human beings and human science.

The vast majority of academicians belonged socially to the liberal factions of the upper classes.[13] They differed in their politics from conservative Catholics and nostalgic noblemen, while resisting the demands of emerging workers movements. In keeping with their *juste milieu* views, academicians read memoirs, organized prize contests, published proceedings, and commissioned research into the conditions of the urban poor and the working classes. The Academy had been founded by intellectuals who belonged to the liberal opposition under the Restoration, notably the historian François Guizot and the young philosopher Victor Cousin. Their objective was to put an end to the ongoing battles between conservative defenders of the absolutist monarchy and their revolutionary opponents. In Guizot and Cousin's view only a moderate, constitutional regime could provide a stable basis for the future of the French nation. When Guizot became a minister in 1830, he advised the king to reestablish the class of moral and political sciences in the form of a national academy. Promising to provide "an indirect but useful support" to the new government, Guizot argued that the moral and political sciences were an "indispensable intellectual force." In no other nation and in no other era had these sciences acquired such importance and gained so much public esteem. Furthermore, for the first time in history, the moral and political sciences had become "truly scientific" in that they were founded on "facts" and promised to be applicable and useful. Since the new constitutional government guaranteed the "union of the interests of the government with those of society," the moral and political sciences were henceforth in a position to "sustain what they had previously shaken."[14]

Guizot's proposal was intended to reconcile liberal intellectuals with the political and administrative needs of the new government. In this sense the Academy instituted a long tradition of administrative research and reflections on the art of statecraft, which in France had been carried by the *noblesse de robe* and upper-level state officials.[15] However, unlike the Second Class of the Institut de France, the Academy of Moral and Political Sciences proved a lasting achievement. Up to this day, its characteristic mixture of state officials, professors, and other dignitaries represents the social sciences in its most official guise. Of the national French academies, the Academy of Moral and Political sciences was the one closest to the state and the state nobility. The vast majority of its members, nearly three-quarters, held a political position as parliamentary deputy, senator, or minister, a proportion that was much higher than in any other national academy (it was 16 percent for the Academy of Sciences, 3 percent for the Academy of Fine Arts).[16] Links with the state apparatus were reinforced by the social background of the academicians; three-quarters of them came from families belonging to the "notables," whereas only a minority had middle-class backgrounds.[17]

The Academy of Moral and Political Sciences was comprised of five sections: philosophy, history, morals, political economy and statistics, and legislation. Each section had six regular members plus a number of correspondents and foreign associates made up of a characteristic mixture of diplomats, statesmen, and scholars (among the latter were Thomas Malthus, James Mill, Adolphe Quételet). The best way to understand the role of the Academy is to consider the actual work that was carried out. Between 60 to 80 percent of the academic lectures, book reviews, and prize contests during the first three decades were devoted to policy matters, many of them related to issues of public order.[18] Most frequently addressed were problems of crime, poverty, and public health among the working classes. Studies of these issues were complemented by statistical surveys of specific populations, which, in turn, informed local and national elites about the dangers they faced, while prudently suggesting how these could be dealt with.[19] Besides themes related to public order, more technical issues were addressed concerning juridical and economic questions; they were often related to the work of parliamentary commissions.

Within the Academy there was not only a thematic division of labor, which corresponded to the different sections, but also a specific balance between policy needs and more academic concerns. The most urgent policy issues were dealt with by three sections in particular: morals, legislation, and political economy; they had the highest proportion of senior civil servants as well. The philosophy and the history sections, on the other hand, were more involved in scholarly matters, although they did fulfill political and civic functions as well. The philosophers provided a general outlook on the issues that the Academy dealt with, whereas the historians offered a historical perspective on such matters.

One of the most prominent and active members of the Academy was the leading figure of the philosophy section, Victor Cousin, an orator and public figure of great renown. A graduate of the École normale supérieure, the young Cousin had made a name for himself with his Sorbonne lectures of the 1820s. In these public courses, which were attended by large audiences, he elaborated a spiritualist philosophy that would eventually be taught in every lycée and university in the country. This doctrine implied a firm rejection of the "materialist" philosophy of the late Enlightenment and the revolutionary period. Because man is a "spiritual being," endowed with a soul and consciousness, Cousin considered the methods of the natural sciences to be wholly inappropriate for the human sciences. Philosophy, he argued, should be concerned with universal standards of truth, beauty, and virtue. These eternal truths are not specific to any philosophical doctrine in particular, and Cousin's philosophy was also referred to as eclectic. Cousin and his associates thus favored a position that was "secular and yet not irreligious, liberal and yet not revolutionary."[20]

This philosophical stance fulfilled a dual function. On the one hand, it defined the national program for philosophy teachers in the lycées and the universities by combining a spiritualist psychology with an eclectic understanding of philosophical doctrines and their history. This eclectic spiritualism was taught in the Faculty of Letters, which had been separated from the Faculty of Science since the Napoleonic reforms. Besides providing a general orientation for professional philosophers, Cousin insisted that his spiritualist creed also represented an appropriate basis for the civic spirit of the modern constitutional regime.[21] Its central principles—the existence of God, free will, and objective standards of good and evil—were considered necessary values for a stable and orderly modern nation, resting ultimately on the common sense of its citizens. Cousin's philosophy therefore not only provided a mandatory doctrine for philosophy teachers, but it simultaneously defined the unity of the different sections of the Academy and the Academy's relationship to the postrevolutionary nation-state.

Within the section for "general and philosophical history," the historians were in a position quite similar to that of the philosophers. Leading figures like Guizot, Mignet, and Thierry were closely connected with both the political elites and the universities. Their work was categorized as "general and philosophical" because it was distinct from the more specialized historical research that was the domain of another academy: the

Académie des inscriptions et belles-lettres. Much of the work of the historians at the Academy of Moral and Political Sciences was concerned with the national past in relation to historical and political justifications of the postrevolutionary constitutional regime. Just as Cousin had outlined the framework for a more or less official philosophy, Guizot and his associates set the standards for the dominant liberal view on the history of the French nation.[22]

The morals section focused on what the Academy consistently defined as an issue of morals and morality, but what opponents called the "social question." The growing misery of the working classes and the urban poor was viewed by the academicians as a question of immorality, of failing moral standards and lack of character. Because of the possible threats to public safety, the danger the poor represented was investigated in considerable detail. The level of concern is illustrated by the fact that the Academy's morals section was the first to award a prize for the best answer to the following question: "Which are, according to exact observation of the facts, the elements that in Paris, or in any other big city, compose the part of the population that forms a dangerous class because of its vices, its ignorance, and its misery? Which means could be employed by the Administration, the rich or prosperous men, and the intelligent and laborious workers to improve this deprived and miserable class?"[23]

This twofold question was offered up to the public 1833, but the prize was not awarded because the submitted reports were judged to be insufficient. However, one *mémoire* written by an employee of the Parisian prefecture, Frégier, was awarded with a fee; it was eventually published under the title *Des classes dangereuses de la population des grandes villes, et des moyens de les rendre meilleures* (1840). Research was also done on prostitution, prison reform, pauperism, and on the physical and moral state of the working classes.[24] One of the best-known works was written by Villermé, a medical doctor and author of the *Tableau de l'état physique et moral des ouvriers employés dans les manufactures de coton, de laine et de soie* (1840).[25] In his capacity as minister, Guizot had commissioned Villermé to do the work after the urban upheavals of 1831 and 1834. An important part of his research concentrated on the dangers of epidemics, which after the cholera and typhus epidemics of the early 1830s were perceived to be another major threat to public order.[26]

Although this growing corpus of research described the living conditions of the laboring poor in alarming detail, it led to hardly any legislation during the first half of the nineteenth century. Political repression and private charity were the dominant modes of dealing with the social question. Ruling elites in France, in contrast to their British equivalents, refused to consider the social question as a matter for public or "legal charity."[27]

According to Tocqueville, for example, the legislative reforms in Britain were a typically Protestant solution, inappropriate for France.[28]

The section of political economy and statistics was known for its members' staunch defense of free trade and laissez-faire politics. There were only two chairs for political economy during the first half of the nineteenth century and the members of this section were less interested in scientific issues than in propagating laissez-faire politics. The economists formed a relatively dense social network characterized by intermarriage and close family connections, and directly related to a publishing house (Guillaumin), the Société d'économie politique (1842), and the *Journal des économistes* (1841). The network consisted of politicians, publicists, and merchants or entrepreneurs, often trained in law, but more frequently related to business circles than to scholarly institutions. Both the Société d'économie politique and the *Journal des économistes* were committed to the idea that political economy was a "practical science" representing a set of more or less fixed doctrines "beyond which there is little to improve."[29] Their convictions derived from the work of Jean-Baptiste Say, who held the first chair in political economy in France and had codified the classical economics of Adam Smith in various textbooks. Being a pressure group or a "lobby" rather than a learned society, the leading political economists were obsessed by the dangers of socialism, hostile to any method other than deduction (whether historical, mathematical, or monographic), and rejected the theoretical innovations of Cournot, Walras, and Marshall.[30] Marx typically considered their work a brand of "vulgar economics"; Schumpeter similarly qualified them as ultraliberals whose work remained analytically sterile.[31]

The work that was published, commissioned, or supported by the Academy rested broadly on two basic principles. First, it was characterized by a unitary conception of the moral and political sciences. All these sciences were defined as moral sciences, founded on a spiritualist psychology, and as such not only distinct from but also explicitly opposed to the models and methods used in the natural sciences.[32] Victor Cousin's philosophical doctrine provided its general orientation, and its different branches were considered to be philosophical sciences. The central categories of this philosophical outlook are well summarized in the official *Dictionnaire des sciences philosophiques* (six volumes, 1844–52). The concept of "society," for example, is based on three conditions: liberty, property, and the family. All three conditions are said to rest on the moral nature of man and presume the "religious dogmas of Providence and a life hereafter."[33] In contrast to this liberal Christian creed, socialism was merely referred to as those doctrines that "directly or indirectly" deny these conditions.

The second principle underlying the Academy's work was its consistent focus on policy issues and the idea that the social sciences should be practiced as sciences of government and governance. Academic studies were considered legitimate insofar as they focused on problems of government, paying particular attention to issues of public stability and moral order. Academicians frequently called to mind the irresponsible nature of revolutionary theories that were caused by the attempts to separate social theorizing from actual political responsibility. Academicians accused writers and publicists of having been "lost in abstractions" and "seduced by utopias" instead of devoting themselves to useful and applicable studies. To counter this trend, the Academy set out to unite the sciences and to direct them toward a "common center," toward the study of *verités d'application*.[34] This theme of practical and applied truths was vital for scholarly statesmen like Guizot, as well as for more research oriented members like Villermé. It is equally prominent in the work of Tocqueville, who went to the United States on an academic mission to study the prison system, and whose critical analysis of uprooted intellectuals was central to his understanding of the French Revolution. Tocqueville's conception of the political sciences was directly related to his critique of men of letters who under the Old Regime had acquired political influence without having political responsibility. Of noble origin and only slightly younger than Guizot and Cousin, Tocqueville described his own work as belonging to that "great science of government," the objective of which is to "understand the general movement of society, to judge what passes in the mind of the masses, and to foresee what will result of it."[35]

The notion of "moral and political sciences" was an apt description of the outlook that the Academy embodied. Using the concept of "moral sciences" sustained the lineage of classical moral philosophy, while their various branches were practiced in order to contribute to policymaking and governance. The alternative expression "social science" was avoided, as it was associated with the scientism of the revolutionary period: Condorcet's "social mathematics," Cabanis's physiological science of man, and the work of "utopian" reformers like Saint-Simon, Charles Fourier, or Robert Owen, who continued using the notion "social science." The particular objective of the Academy was to replace this revolutionary tradition with a liberal view aimed at ensuring the stability of France's institutions. By establishing a national infrastructure for these studies, the moral and political sciences came to be more firmly separated from the natural sciences and more closely allied to the Faculties of Law and Letters as well as to a variety of governmental agencies. The work of Auguste Comte and Augustin Cournot, for example, who were both trained in the physical sciences, typically developed outside of the circles of the Academy and was ignored by the academicians.

The Invasion of the Positive Sciences

Since the Academy was a national institute that significantly overlapped with the ruling elite of the July monarchy, it was vulnerable to changes in the political conjuncture. After the revolution of 1848 and the coup d'état of 1851, the academicians and their allies were forced to reconsider their position. Confronted with the repressive Bonapartist government of the Second Empire (1851–70), there were conflicts about elections and procedures and the formal autonomy of the Academy was violated frequently.[36] Liberal professors were deprived of their chairs, some went into exile, and in educational matters the Catholic Church was favored once again. The 1850s was the decade during which Flaubert's *Madame Bovary* (1857) was prosecuted for obscenity and Baudelaire's *Les fleurs du mal* (1857) sentenced for offending religion and public decency.[37] Only in the 1860s were more liberal policies reintroduced. Both the establishment of the imperial regime and the growing left-wing opposition since the revolution of 1848 undermined the confidence of the liberals. In his memoirs of the 1860s, Guizot observed the "fatal influence" of a host of new doctrines. Whether they were called republican, democratic, positivist, socialist, or communist, all the new ideas, Guizot noted, opposed the established order. And they all had a "radical vice" in common: although each of them contained a grain of truth, they isolated and exaggerated this truth to an "enormous and detestable error."[38]

No less important for Guizot and Cousin's disillusionment with the course of events was the manifestation of a new generation of intellectuals. In the 1860s, Ernest Renan and Hippolyte Taine gained intellectual notoriety by attacking the very principles of the academic establishment. Both men, born in the 1820s, had experienced the revolution of 1848 and the coup d'état of 1851 as the end of the dreams of the preceding generation. In the name of a more demanding conception of philosophy and science, their criticism was directed against the reestablished clerical powers and simultaneously turned against the metaphysics of Cousin's school, which appeared outdated and incapable of competing with the scientific advances in Britain and Germany. Renan wrote his *L'avenir de la science* in the wake of the revolution of 1848, displaying a nearly religious belief in the sciences and their promise to understand the history of humanity. He deplored Cousin's lack of method, his superficial appeal to common sense, as well as his religious assumptions. Impressed with German scholarship, Renan advocated historical and philological erudition as a science with a philosophical goal: the science of the products of the human mind.[39] Becoming a member of the more specialized Académie des inscriptions et belles-lettres, he wrote historical studies and critical essays; his *Vie de Jésus* (1863) provoked one of the great scandals that marked the last decade of the Second Empire.

Taine, a philosopher trained at the École normale supérieure, but whom his spiritualist teachers had failed for the *agrégation* exam, gained public attention with a devastating polemic, *Les philosophes français du XIXe siècle* (1857). The "official philosophy" taught at the university and in the lycées had, according to Taine, contributed next to nothing to the scientific advances of the century. Divorced from the analytical and experimental spirit of the sciences and reduced to rhetorical exercises and deist morals, French philosophy had become sterile. Tracing this tradition from the beginning of the nineteenth century up to Cousin, Taine argued that philosophy would have to be allied again to the sciences. In the moral sciences one had to proceed like naturalists. These sciences were nothing else than a kind of "botany" that dealt with the works of men rather than plants. Such a view, Taine stated, was in line with the general movement in which the moral and the natural sciences were converging. Every science studies "facts" and investigates their "causes," no matter whether the facts are physical or moral.[40] Taine expressed this naturalist view in provocative phrases ("vice and virtue are products, like vitriol and sugar") suspect of the very materialism Cousin had so energetically combated. In his *Histoire de la littérature anglaise* (1863) Taine proposed his conceptual trinity, *la race, le milieu,* and *le moment,* as the explanatory factors for the study of moral phenomena. In *De l'intelligence* (1870) he outlined a naturalist psychology that radically rejected Cousin's speculations about the soul and its attributes.[41]

Besides Taine and Renan, a few other intellectuals played a prominent role in the emerging alliance against the spiritualist liberals and the clerical party.[42] Among them was Émile Littré, the most authoritative follower of Auguste Comte. After studying medicine and working as an assistant to a celebrated Paris physician, Littré gave up medicine for private tutoring, journalism, and translation, thus becoming a private scholar. For Littré, Comte's greatness was to have conceptualized modern science and used that understanding to conceive of the first true science of history.[43] As a philosophically minded *érudit,* the translation of the complete works of Hippocrates had won Littré a seat in the Académie des inscriptions et belles-lettres; his studies of the history of medicine and a new edition of Nysten's *Dictionnaire de médecine* ensured him membership in the Academy of Medicine as well. Alongside his long-term encyclopedic projects, Littré was one of the main editors of a nonsocialist republican newspaper and took an active part in the revolution of 1848. Like Comte, with whom he founded the Société positiviste (1848), Littré believed that the "critical phase" of the revolution was over and that the "organic" phase, which would reconcile order and progress, could at last begin. Opposed to "retrograde" or simply "stationary" doctrines, the positivists were no less critical of revolutionary ones. Although they were close to socialism in certain respects, socialism could become synonymous with progress only if it took the "sociological path," that is, if socialists submitted to the teachings of positive knowledge and abandoned their revolutionary articles of faith: the metaphysics of popular sovereignty, the illusion of equality, and the doctrine of class struggle.[44]

The writings of young philosophers like Taine and Renan and somewhat older but somewhat marginal scholars like Littré forcefully suggested that the whole conception of the moral sciences lacked a scientific basis and owed its authority merely to the fact that it was an official doctrine. Their plea for modern scholarship and more rigorous scientific study was part of a broader movement of opposition to both clerical authorities and the older generation of spiritualist philosophers. When the liberalization of the imperial regime during the 1860s gave rise to a host of oppositional newspapers and journals, a polarization of the intellectual field ensued. A series of affairs and polemics illustrated the battle between a clerical and an anticlerical camp. When Littré, for example, presented his candidacy for the Académie française, this so horrified the academician Dupanloup, bishop of Orléans, that he wrote an *Avertissement à la jeunesse et aux pères de famille sur les attaques dirigées contre la religion par quelques écrivains de nos jours* (1863). Four authors—Littré, Taine, Renan, and Maury—were identified as atheists who, refusing to respect the country's religion, had fallen into the old revolutionary errors of materialism, fatalism, and pantheism. To demonstrate the worrying proportions that atheism had taken, Dupanloup compared the earlier edition of Nysten's *Dictionnaire de médecine* with the new edition of the positivists Littré and Robin, explaining how key entries (soul, mind, philosophy) had fallen under the deleterious influence of atheism and materialism. Littré's competitor for the seat in the Académie française won the election, but the dispute it gave rise to extended far beyond the usual conflict over a seat in the Academy and brought Littré great renown.

The spiritualist philosophers, who still reigned supreme at the Sorbonne and the Academy of Moral and Political Sciences, were generally convinced that Dupanloup's concern was justified, and they replied to the critics by restating their beliefs. The best-known spiritualist philosopher of the time, Elme Caro, professor at the Sorbonne and the École normale supérieure, member of several academies, and a powerful orator, published an eminently orthodox defense of Christian spiritualism, *L'idée de Dieu et ses nouveaux critiques* (1864). A decade later, he still deplored what he saw as "the invasion of the positive sciences into the moral sciences."[45] Paul

Janet, like Caro a philosophy professor at the Sorbonne but more sensitive to the new movement, had published a voluminous textbook, *Histoire de la philosophie morale et politique* (1858), and acknowledged the situation in an essay on *La crise philosophique* (1865). Whereas spiritualism had had no serious rival during the first half of the century, it suffered a profound crisis ever since. Discussing the work of Taine, Renan, and Littré, Janet observed that the spiritualist school no longer dominated enlightened opinion and that the "spirit of the positive sciences" advanced with incalculable speed.[46] After a wave of brochures and books attacking or defending the position of Dupanloup and his allies, Dupanloup clarified his views in *L'athéisme et le péril social* (1866), which was an inventory of the movement of impiety and its harmful consequences. Dupanloup identified positivism (Comte, Littré), pantheism (Hegel, Renan), and materialism (Büchner, Vogt) as the main forms of atheism, but in the end deplored the polemic, which had given rise to well over a hundred articles in newspapers and reviews.

In this atmosphere of intellectual polarization, the clerical party, supported by the political Right and some of the spiritualist philosophers, found themselves up against an intellectual opposition whose forces readily became more numerous. Alongside individual figures, several groups and societies were formed. In the Société d'anthropologie (founded 1859) free-thinking physicians interested in physical anthropology and the natural history of man came together around Paul Broca.[47] The positivists formed two groups: orthodox partisans of integral positivism around Pierre Lafitte, and heterodox positivists around Littré. Young "scientific materialists" based their work on German materialists (Büchner, Vogt, Haeckel, not Marx) and were uncompromising in intellectual as well as political matters. The most renowned intellectuals met in Parisian salons; other meeting places were the free-thinking associations, which developed in the 1860s, and Masonic lodges, which were moving toward positions close to the republicans and expanded in the last years of the Second Empire. If the Third Republic (1870–1940) was the first republican regime in France that lasted, it was in part because the networks of opposition to the Second Empire had allowed the socialization of new elites who would provide the new Republic's leadership personnel.[48]

Opposition to the Academy of Moral and Political Sciences thus came from different quarters. During the 1860s scholars like Renan, Taine, and Littré became the intellectual avant-garde of the day, making a lasting impression on the intellectual youth. Generally from the small and peripheral research sector of higher education, they were allied to a small group of *érudits*, mainly historians, linguists, and philologists, as well as to natural scientists. Renan was a long-standing friend of the chemist Marcellin Berthelot, Littré collaborated with the biologist Charles Robin, Taine was well acquainted with several naturalists and medical doctors. Their intellectual interactions were marked, furthermore, by contacts with writers like Flaubert and the Goncourt brothers, whose struggle for a more autonomous literature, expressed in the doctrine of *l'art pour l'art*, challenged the Académie française in a similar way as Renan and Taine had challenged philosophical academism. This convergence of interests, vividly discussed in certain salons and intellectual societies, occurred entirely outside of the Academy of Moral and Political Sciences and the Faculty of Letters, but gained a prophetic function during the early years of the Third Republic.

Republicanism, Science, and the Research University

The major changes during the last third of the nineteenth century were all directly or indirectly related to the consequences of the Franco-Prussian War. Within weeks after the French emperor's declaration of war in 1870, eighty thousand of his men were taken prisoner. The news led to the downfall of the Second Empire and the proclamation of the Third Republic, and the new government was forced to accept Bismarck's conditions for a peace treaty. While the power of the German state had become an inescapable reality, insurrections of urban workers continued and eventually culminated in the Parisian Commune, which was crushed by the army. Both the humiliating military defeat and the bloodshed of the Commune led to a reconfiguration of political forces.

The early years of the Third Republic have been famously characterized by Daniel Halévy as the end of the notables. Whereas previous governments had rested on either conservative or liberal factions of the notables, the Third Republic became a more democratic regime. Civil liberties were guaranteed and the parliamentary system became well established; in 1884 France was the first country with universal male suffrage. At the same time public education expanded and secularism advanced. Both the increasing autonomy of different social fields and new patterns of recruitment weakened the position of the notables. As a consequence of this process, the political, economic, and intellectual elites became more clearly differentiated from one another than ever before.[49]

These changes had been brought about by the interplay of international and national developments. With the increasing force of the unified German Empire, international rivalries became more acute. While the World Fairs and the spread of international organizations symbolized the cosmopolitan airs of the more advanced nation-states, new forms of nationalism and protectionism accompanied the steady growth of international exchanges.

International trade had risen strongly since 1820, and the last part of the nineteenth century is considered to have been a period of economic globalization, rather similar to the one that occurred at the end of the twentieth century. But the rising tide of international exchange was accompanied by mounting nationalism. Questions of national identity and nationhood were central to the political movement in France, to republican patriots as well as to conservative nationalists. In 1882 Renan gave his famous lecture *Qu'est-ce qu'une nation?* Taine spent the years after 1870 working on the volumes of *Les origines de la France contemporaine*. During the Boulanger crisis of the late 1880s and the Dreyfus Affair somewhat later, violent nationalist reactions sprang up, and the nationalist revival gained momentum in the beginning of the twentieth century.[50] But despite acute crises and ultranationalist mass movements like the Action française, landowning notables and other conservative forces did not succeed in overthrowing the bourgeois republic.

The main challenge for the republican governments was to find an answer to both the powerful German Empire and popular revolts and uprisings like the Commune. Educational reform thus became the cornerstone of republican politics. The new educational system was designed to integrate larger segments of the population and bring them under more direct control of the French state. Fierce opposition to the new policies came from the church. The Faculties of Catholic Theology were removed from the university in 1885, and although private Catholic schools and institutes continued to exist and expanded, in 1905 the definitive separation of church and state was instituted by law. Driven by anticlerical movements, the expansion of public education was simultaneously seen as a reply to German superiority, since the power of the German Empire was widely held to be based on its scientific and educational advance. "In 1870," wrote Émile Zola, "we were beaten by the scientific spirit."[51] Republican politicians and many intellectuals shared this view.

Expanding the system of public education was thus considered a vital condition for the "regeneration" of the French nation. Reason and science became fundamental values for the secular regime, which appealed to neither God nor king, and a form of pedagogical idealism became characteristic of French republicanism.[52] Reforms of higher education were an integral part of educational policies. Projects for reform originated in the 1860s. Following a decade of censorship and repression, scholars like Renan and Taine had voiced severe criticism of French higher learning. The first result of their campaign for renewal had been the establishment of the École pratique des hautes études (1868), a relatively small school for the training of researchers that was independent of the universities and elite schools; following the German example, teaching was done in seminars. Its first three sections were devoted to the natural sciences, the fourth one to the historical and philological sciences.

During the 1870s and 1880s the movement for university reform spread through the academic community, which was eager to improve its position.[53] It was promoted by pressure groups like the Association française pour l'avancement des sciences (1872), which was founded by leading scientists on the model of a similar British association. With its motto *par la science pour la patrie*, it sought to increase public interest, state support, and private funding for the sciences. It had well over four thousand members at the end of the 1880s.[54] The Société de l'enseignement supérieur (1878) pursued similar objectives. The society was founded by a small group of scholars, very few of whom had followed the classic career pattern. Many had close connections with German scholars. Among them were Taine and Renan, leading historians (Fustel de Coulanges, Monod, Lavisse), philologists and linguists (Michel Bréal, Gaston Paris), and natural scientists like Pasteur and Berthelot. University professors massively joined the society, which had more than five hundred members in 1880. This powerful reform movement was allied to the republican elite, which believed that university reform would serve the needs of the secular republican state. The expanding public sector demanded more teachers and administrators and the reform policies gained some support from the private sector as well. Among the sponsors of the Société de l'enseignement supérieur were representatives of the most dynamic sectors of the French economy, especially banking and railroad interests. Protestant and Jewish bankers were especially prominent; traditional French elites, however, showed little interest in public education.[55]

The actual reforms, from the end of the 1870s to the beginning of the twentieth century, fundamentally altered the size and structure of higher education. Stimulated by the introduction of scholarships, the number of university students multiplied from ten thousand in 1875 to forty-two thousand in 1914. The expansion was concentrated in the Faculties of Science and Letters. They had had very few students until about 1880—each of them less than three hundred in 1876—since their role was practically restricted to offering public lectures and grading the final secondary school exam (the *baccalauréat*). Following the proposals of the reform movement, the republican administration not only stimulated the growth of the faculties but it also encouraged scholarship and research, which would redefine the role of professors. Travel grants were made available, junior staff positions created, chairs established for new fields of research, and public lectures for worldly audiences were dropped in favor of teaching full-time students. The Faculties of Science and Letters were thus transformed into more research-oriented institutions, and scholarly publications became a key component for a successful university career. Before 1840, theses for the doctorate of letters were hardly ever longer than 100 pages. After 1880 the vast majority of theses was more than 300 pages, reaching an average of 510 pages in 1900.[56] A thorough monograph based on original research became a precondition for a professorship. Parallel to the transformation of the university, a publishing industry arose for scholarly journals and books, often directed by people like Félix Alcan who were graduates from the same elite schools as the members of the new professoriate.[57]

In a few decades, professors in the Faculty of Letters thus became more numerous and more scholarly professionals (see table 1.1). Increasingly recruited from intellectual families of the middle classes, they were often graduates of the selective École normale supérieure. Inevitably their extra-academic activities diminished. The presence of university professors in the Senate and the National Assembly decreased, and by the end of the century it had become rare for a university professor to simultaneously pursue a political career.[58] The public visibility of professors decreased as well; journalism, public lecturing, and composing essays for general periodicals gave way to more scholarly work and a corresponding lifestyle.[59] Since university professors became specialists, primarily engaged in teaching and scholarly publishing, many democratic ideals of the educational reforms eventually proved disappointing. The promise of social integration

TABLE 1.1
Demography of the Faculty of Letters (1870–1914)

	Number of students	*Licence* degrees	Doctorats	Teaching positions
1870–74	–	129	10	90
1875–79	–	142	16	133
1880–84	1,021	244	17	211
1885–89	2,358	272	18	261
1890–94	2,632	296	23	268
1895–99	3,248	412	25	312
1900–04	4,134	475	30	358
1905–09	5,877	537	33	368
1910–13	6,383	476	35	387

Sources: For the student numbers 1880–89, A. Prost, *L'enseignement en France, 1800–1967*, Paris, Colin, 1968, p. 243; for the student numbers for the other years, degrees, and doctorates: *Annuaire statistique de la France* (1939 and 1966); for teaching positions: *Annuaire de l'instruction publique* (1875–1913).

Note: The numbers are five-year averages, except for the years 1910–13 and the number of teaching positions. The number of teaching positions concerns the last year of the indicated period and includes the University of Algiers and vacancies, but excludes free courses, honorary positions, and replacements.

through public education had been one of the key factors behind the political support for university reform. But its impact turned out to be far less significant than expected.[60] In the wake of the Dreyfus Affair the broad movement of "people's universities" came closest to the ideals of the republican movement, but their existence was short-lived.[61]

Disciplinary Frontiers

With the rise of the research university and the transformation of the intellectual field after 1870, the center of the social sciences shifted from the Academy of Moral and Political Sciences to university faculties. The Academy lost its dominant role, becoming a largely honorific institution, and both the expression and the concept of "moral and political sciences" lost their appeal and became outdated. The centralized group of moral and political sciences split up into more autonomous disciplines, each with its own chairs, scholarly journals, and professional associations. Disciplinary social science now became the predominant mode of teaching, research, and publishing.[62] University-based disciplines gained a greater degree of autonomy not only with respect to the national Academy but also vis-à-vis governmental agencies and lay audiences. Establishing professional autonomy in its different guises—conceptually, socially, and institutionally—was the main preoccupation of the representatives of the university-based disciplines. This characteristic holds true for the university pioneers in psychology and sociology; it also applies to the economists who introduced political economy in the Faculty of Law.

Seen in a comparative perspective, the conflicts between younger representatives of university disciplines and the Academy were not specific for France. In other advanced nation-states a comparable structural opposition manifested itself between a younger generation of university professors and an older generation of more policy-oriented scholars. Although there were no national academies as in France, the British National Association for the Promotion of Social Science (1857), the American Social Science Association (1867), and the German Verein für Socialpolitik (1873) experienced a similar decline as the Academy of Moral and Political Sciences, giving way to more scholarly university disciplines, on the one hand, and to new ameliorative initiatives and policy agencies, on the other.

The fundamental shift from a monopolistic regime based on national social science organizations to a more differentiated field of university disciplines was shaped by more regular transnational connections.[63] Two closely related institutions provided the framework for such exchanges: the international scientific conference and the international scientific association.

Both are distinctly modern forms, which emerged only in the second half of the nineteenth century. Covering the major social science disciplines, international organizations not only provided meeting places, offering occasions for communication across national borders, but they also functioned as interest groups, stimulating the international spread of disciplinary knowledge. The emergence of international social science organizations during the second half of the nineteenth century was related to the more general flourishing of international organizations, which were thought of as a new phase in the relations among the advanced nation-states.[64] Effective collaboration across national borders, however, remained infrequent. Information sharing, diffusion, and intellectual diplomacy were more important than actual collaboration. Only after the Second World War, when new international social science organizations were founded under the auspices of UNESCO, did more regular transnational flows of people and ideas emerge.

One of the first models of the international social science organizations were the international congresses of statistics, which were founded in 1853 by the Belgian statistical entrepreneur Adolphe Quételet. Every two or three years they brought together hundreds of participants, both academic and administrative statisticians, to discuss the technical, scientific, and organizational progress of their work. The proceedings of the congress represented the international state of the art. These periodic international congresses, which generally preceded the formation of international associations, typically led to the establishment of an International Institute of Statistics in 1883.[65] In the anthropological sciences, including both physical and social anthropology, international congresses were held since 1865, while in political science and psychology the temporal and the organizational pattern was similar. Sociology was only slightly different; since the Institut international de sociologie was founded in Paris in 1893, together with the *Revue internationale de sociologie* (1893), it preceded the establishment of national journals and associations.

One of the main consequences of the existence of international organizations was the more regular circulation of disciplinary knowledge across national borders and the strengthening of disciplinary identities. In other respects, the consequences were more variable. In some fields, such as statistics, they played a key role in the standardization of technical and administrative tools for producing authoritative knowledge. In other cases, such as the Institut international de sociologie (1893), international conferences resembled a diplomatic order, with occasions for polite encounter and exchange, but of limited significance for actual research. In still other cases, especially after the First World War, the actual effect may have been the opposite of what was officially intended, reinforcing national rivalries and fuelling struggles for international domination.

The Tripartite Division of French Social Science

While roughly the same set of social science disciplines was established in universities of the core countries in the Western world between the 1870s and the 1920s, national peculiarities remained and some of them even became more pronounced. Having entered national systems of higher education, the social sciences became more strongly bound to national educational systems (curricula, exams, administrative divisions, and hierarchies) and to related national differences in intellectual style. The new professoriate, furthermore, was commonly inclined to support patriotic causes because the national policies of expanding the university system had created feelings of loyalty among those who had profited from the expansion. Growing international tensions reinforced national identifications, in particular because the appearance of the German Empire had upset the balance of power between the leading imperial powers, Britain and France.[66]

Beyond the establishment of specific disciplinary structures, the new social science disciplines in France came to form a relatively stable tripartite structure.[67] Research in the social sciences was practiced either as "political science," "economics," or "human science." These three groups no longer formed a unified set of "moral and political sciences," but, on the contrary, a constellation of disciplines marked by structural differences. That French social science has clustered around these three poles is best illustrated at the institutional level.

The political sciences came to be taught at the École libre des sciences politiques (1871), a private and relatively expensive professional school, close to the state administration but separated from the university faculties. The school trained many generations of upper-level civil servants by preparing them for the competitive exams by which they are recruited. The founder of the school, Émile Boutmy, had an ambitious research agenda as well, but his scientific objectives were very soon abandoned in favor of preparing his pupils for their exams.[68] The "political sciences" represented a flexible combination of different disciplines, mainly law, history, and economics, taught from the point of view of public administration but without any significant research practice. While in a sense forming a profession, the political sciences acquired the characteristics of a discipline only well after the Second World War when the École libre was transformed into the Fondation nationale des sciences politiques (1945) and a growing number of institutes for political studies were founded in the major cities of the country. At about the same time the Association française de science politique (1949) and the *Revue française de science politique* (1951) were created. In addition to this new disciplinary infrastructure, the teaching of political science was gradually also incorporated into the Faculty of Law.[69]

For well over a century the political sciences remained an eclectic subfield, deprived of a recognizable research tradition, located at the margins of the intellectual field, and institutionally divided between a professional school and the Faculty of Law. Tocqueville, for example, entered the canon of the political sciences but was not considered a sociologist until Raymond Aron included him in his *Main Currents in Sociological Thought* (1965).[70] This structural division between the political and the other social sciences was still prevalent in the 1970s. Among the many schools and disciplines that Pierre Bourdieu included in his analysis of elite schools and the field of power, political science students were closest to the students of the École nationale d'administration (ENA) and a business school.[71] Their social background was significantly higher than that of the students at the Faculty of Letters, whereas their school results compared unfavorably with students of the intellectual elite schools like the École normale supérieure. Fernand Braudel, the historian and institution builder, remarked in 1969 that the political sciences had yet to become properly scientific disciplines.[72] A decade later the political scientist Jean Leca similarly observed that French political science—contrary to other human sciences—had no presence to speak of in the intellectual field, that it was peripheral with regard to other social science disciplines, and that it hardly even constituted a scientific subfield of its own.[73]

At the opposite pole of the political sciences were the human sciences, located in the Faculty of Letters, which trained people for careers in teaching, research, and related intellectual activities. These *sciences humaines* represented the intellectual pole of the spectrum and included both the classical humanities and new disciplines like psychology, sociology, and ethnology. Both the proximity of the social sciences and the humanities and their mutual dependence on philosophy as the dominant theoretical discipline account for some enduring characteristics of French social science: the presence of a more literary and essayistic style of expression, a slow acceptance of quantitative research methods, and a certain craving for theoretical and conceptual abstractions. Whereas these features may be obstacles to scrupulous research and scientific rigor, as some of the most eminent French social scientists (Durkheim, Lévi-Strauss, Bourdieu) have repeatedly argued, they also discourage simple empiricism, facilitate communication across specialties and disciplines, and allow for the regular presence of social scientists in the public debate.

Economics, representing the third pole, was located in between the professional school for political studies and the more intellectually oriented disciplines of the Faculty of Letters, since it entered the Faculty of Law. Political economy became a compulsory subject for law students in 1877. The decree created an immediate need for establishing chairs and recruiting teaching staff, which increased from a single, experimental chair established in 1864 to about forty teaching positions around 1900.[74] With the creation in 1895 of a PhD for the economic and political sciences, and of a yearly nationwide *agrégation* exam for selecting economics professors in 1896, the economics curriculum acquired a substantial degree of disciplinary autonomy. Although economics was also taught in business schools and at some technical and engineering schools, the economics professors of the Law Faculty became the core group of the discipline. They founded a scholarly journal, the *Revue d'économie politique* (1887), which presented itself as "exclusively scientific" and as a forum for various schools of economic thought. Both objectives were explicitly directed against the monopoly of the laissez-faire orthodoxy that controlled the Academy, the Société d'économie politique, and the *Journal des économistes*. The *Revue d'économie politique* operated as a "war machine" against the bastion of orthodox liberals and published articles by French as well as foreign scholars, which were often more favorable to state intervention than those of their opponents.[75]

By entering the Faculty of Law, economics not only became a more scholarly, less doctrinal, and more varied discipline, but it also became more dependent on students and teachers within a juridical setting. Gide and the *Revue d'économie politique* were keen to publish the new work in mathematical economics by Léon Walras, but owing to their position in the Faculty of Law, the mathematization of the discipline was slow and statistical research relatively rare. Walras, who was trained as an engineer, was a relative outsider in France. Interested in economics as a "pure science" and calling himself a socialist were sufficient reasons to exclude him from the circles of the liberal orthodoxy. Obtaining a chair in Switzerland, he wrote devastating comments on "official" French economics and gave tactical advice to Gide on how to run his journal and fight the "tyranny" of the Academy of Moral and Political Sciences.[76]

Besides the advocates of laissez-faire and new generations of economists in the Law Faculty, France has also known a small but significant tradition of engineer-economists. In the course of the twentieth century, and especially since the great depression of the 1930s, graduates from elite engineering schools like the École polytechnique and the École des mines entered the discipline in growing numbers. Similar to the political sciences, which were torn between the professionals from the École libre and professors of the Faculty of Law, economics became divided between graduates from the Faculty of Law and mathematically trained engineers. The latter group, traditionally well represented among state technocrats, became ever more important, first in the expanding state institutions of statistics, economic research, and economic planning, and eventually also in the universities.[77]

The Literary Opposition

The growth and transformation of the university and in particular of the Faculty of Letters did not take place without provoking a powerful reaction. Writers and publicists outside of the educational system, lacking the autonomy of the professoriate and dependent on work for the press and a wider audience of readers, turned against the increasingly specialized scholarship and what they saw as the decline of literary and cultural values. The "new Sorbonne" became their chief target.[78] In their attachment to the classical virtues of the humanities—style, intuition, originality—and their mistrust of detailed research and systematic scholarship, many of them became religiously involved, eventually converting to Catholicism (Paul Claudel, Léon Bloy, Joris-Karl Huysmans), and increasingly stressing the virtues of faith and fatherland.[79] This literary, traditionalist, and often Catholic revival sprang up during the first period of anticlerical reforms; it gained strength in the 1890s and became a major cultural and political force during and after the Dreyfus Affair.

The novels and poetry associated with this revival depicted the fatal consequences of the scientism that prevailed in the new Sorbonne, not only in new disciplines like sociology or pedagogy but also in classical disciplines such as history and philosophy, and even in literary studies.[80] One of the first novels in which the conflict between scientific determinism and faith-based morality was portrayed was Le disciple (1889), written by the former naturalist writer Paul Bourget. A determinist philosopher, Adrien Sixte, seduces the sister of a pupil of his. Upon discovering his unromantic motives the girl commits suicide. The widely discussed novel raised the question of whether scientism and determinist doctrines that were associated with the "positive sciences" as opposed to the "moral sciences" could be held responsible for immoral consequences. Weren't the positive sciences and the related philosophical outlook in reality immoral sciences? The leading literary critic, Ferdinand Brunetière, took up the issue some years later. After a visit to the Vatican, Brunetière published a much-discussed article in which he attacked Taine, Renan, and various natural scientists. Religion, according to Brunetière, had reconquered part of its prestige, and if science was not totally discredited, it had at least lost much of its appeal.

His 1895 article provoked a vivid polemic on the "bankruptcy of science."[81] Some of the social background of the polemic was evoked in another novel, *Les déracinés* (1897), in which Maurice Barrès described the vicissitudes of a few young men who had left their native province to study in Paris. Uprooted from their homes and traditional upbringing, they too came under the spell of a philosophy teacher at the lycée. Like Bourget, to whom *Les déracinés* was dedicated, Barrès used Taine's theories of heredity and milieu, not as an analytical scheme for understanding moral phenomena but to prove the necessity of tradition and the attachment to local roots. Whereas Taine had proposed these notions for a broader understanding of art and literature, Bourget and Barrès gave them a different meaning by arguing for an uncompromising return to the values of the family and the land.[82]

It was in this same corpus of texts that the negative stereotype of the "intellectual" appeared. The new term designated people affiliated with the university and secular schools; they were uprooted, pale and book-ish, and had a special inclination for positivist narrow-mindedness and abstract views on morality and truth.[83] When the term became a catch-word during the Dreyfus Affair, the opposition between scholars and writers had become one of the main dimensions of the conflict.[84] The themes initially explored by a small group of novelists became the subject of heated polemics in the years prior to the First World War. Agathon, the pen name of Henri Massis and Alfred de Tarde, the son of the sociologist Gabriel Tarde, published *L'esprit de la nouvelle Sorbonne* (1911). The conservative nationalist Pierre Lasserre, a leading figure of the Action française, launched an even more violent attack in *La doctrine officielle de l'université* (1912). The complaints concerned the decline of French and Latin in the secondary-school curriculum, and the ominous replacement of style and elegance by narrow specialization and Germanic "erudition." Among the professors singled out were the historian Charles Seignobos, the literary scholar Gustave Lanson, and the sociologist Émile Durkheim—the last one was particularly important since he gave the required course on pedagogy for secondary-school teachers.[85]

The revolt against "positivism" and "scientism" was carried out by literary intellectuals, publicists, and journalists, who were often excluded from the career openings offered by the expanding educational system. Their cultural capital had been devalued by modern methods of research and many of them increasingly allied themselves with the Catholic Church, whose educational role had been reduced by the anticlerical reforms. The attacks on the "new Sorbonne" represented a pressing challenge to the university community. In philosophy, for example, new forms of idealism questioned the limits of science and elaborated on the inadequacies of determinism. Proposing new frameworks for the outdated metaphysics of Cousin, neo-Kantianism became one of the main tools for critically investigating the limits of science and reasserting the centrality of transcendental values. Discussing these trends in a survey of philosophy, Alfred Fouillée published a study he entitled *The Idealist Movement and the Reaction against Positive Science* (1896). Bergson's philosophy echoed the same themes, opposing intuition and imagination to the methods of scientific inquiry. His lectures at the Collège de France became exceptionally popular and he acquired a kind of public role that had become extremely rare for a university philosopher.[86] For other circles outside of the university, Nietzsche offered an even more crushing analysis of scientific masquerades and illusions of progress.[87]

For the emerging social sciences, the literary opposition and new forms of philosophical idealism proved a similar challenge. Social scientists responded to the attacks not merely by defending their craft but also by proposing alternative views on the central issues of the debate: specialization versus *culture générale*, method versus intuition, individual versus collective values, and secular versus religious beliefs.[88] In Durkheim's work, for example, all of these themes play a major part. His study on the division of labor demonstrated that increasing specialization does not necessarily lead to social disintegration, but can, on the contrary, produce new forms of social cohesion. In his contribution to the debate on the "bankruptcy of science," Durkheim replied to Brunetière that "individualism" was neither the pathology produced by the loss of religious faith nor the narrowly conceived utilitarianism of liberal economists, but the shared belief system of highly differentiated societies.[89] In his work on pedagogy, he developed a critical analysis of the traditional forms of pedagogy in French education, which had relied on literary rhetoric rather than on critical thinking. Although supportive of the policies of secular reform, Durkheim made religion into a central object of sociological study, eventually even becoming the paradigm for understanding the entire class of "collective representations." But Durkheim's role in these public debates can only be properly understood after considering the peculiar way in which sociology entered French universities.

CHAPTER 2

✖✖✖

An Improbable Science

As the youngest, the least specialized, and perhaps the most ambitious of the social sciences, sociology occupies a peculiar position in the world of higher learning. From its inception, it was an improbable science. When Auguste Comte publicly came up with the term "sociology" in the late 1830s, it sounded awkward.[1] The impure etymology, an unusual compound of Latin (*socius, socialis*) and Greek (*logos*), offended language purists, who dismissed the word as a horrible hybrid. To many, the very idea of a new and encompassing science of society seemed ill founded and over-ambitious. Comte's proposal lacked proper historical antecedents, since it was rooted neither in the classical tradition of "practical philosophy" nor in any of the early modern systems of moral philosophy and natural law. In comparison with existing specialties, the novel science seemed devoid of a well-circumscribed object-matter and it had no clear-cut position in the academic division of labor; quite to the contrary, it contested well-established divisions and pretended to overcome them. And the whole idea had been proposed in a private course outside of the academic institutions. In conflict-ridden postrevolutionary France, Comte's idea had the air of an idiosyncratic enterprise of a reform-minded scientist engaged in elaborating yet another theoretical system. Some of his contemporaries were impressed by the scope of his knowledge and his mastery of different sciences; others were reminded of some of the grand schemes that had flowered during the revolutionary era but had fallen into disrepute. Few, however, perceived the originality of his work; no one foresaw its eventual impact.

Reconceptualizing Social Science

Although the aim of scientifically studying human societies seems simple and straightforward, the very terminology was controversial. The generic notion of "society" and the adjective "social" gained currency only in the latter part of the eighteenth century, mainly in France and Scotland. The terms were used by scholars for whom the prevailing political, moral, and economic idiom had become too restrictive. Focusing on "human societies" as the unit of analysis represented both a more general and a more egalitarian way of thinking. "Societies" were units whose members were not considered sinners or subjects owing obedience to the lord and the ruler, but rather associates or companions, as in the Latin expression *socius* ("companion") and in the smaller companies and associations for which the term "society" was used.[2] The adjective "social" had spread in France in particular since Rousseau had given it a critical meaning in *Du contrat social* (1762), arguing that the political contract between ruler and ruled had to be replaced by a "social" contract. Instead of delegating power to the sovereign in exchange for protection, the social contract would be based on the free association of equals. The emerging vocabulary of the "social" became a favorite mode of speech during the revolutionary years, when it was enriched, among others, with the expression "social science," *science sociale*. For Sieyès, Condorcet, and other members of the *Société de 1789*, "social science" referred to the wide-ranging science of government that was required for the new era.[3] Social science would be an overarching science, subdivided into different branches—primarily law, morals, economics—and serving as the foundation for an applied social art, an *art social*, which was a kind of public policy concerned with the rational improvement of the new society. The novelty of the expression *science sociale* is well indicated by the fact that it took three decades before it was properly translated into English as "social science" (instead of as "moral science").[4] The introduction in the German-speaking countries took longer still, although it gradually took hold there as well.[5]

The expression "social science" appeared in all likelihood for the first time in the famous revolutionary tract by Sieyès, *Qu'est-ce que le Tiers État?* (1789). The author, fond of neologisms, experimented with other terms as well. In unpublished manuscripts, he even playfully uses the words "sociology" and "socialism," which would appear in print only in the 1830s.[6] But as far as the social sciences were concerned, the revolutionary experiments were short-lived. They were dismissed by Napoleon and his immediate successors, who favored more traditional modes of governance. The revolutionary heritage was, in part, also rejected by the liberal intellectuals who founded the Academy of Moral and Political Sciences.

Deliberately avoiding the expression "social science," the academicians preferred to frame the issues they discussed in the more traditional languages
of philosophy, morality, law, and history. Comte's sociology was thus at
odds with the prevailing idioms. Although the word "sociology" recalls
the revolutionary notion of "social science," which had been taken up by
autodidact reformers like Henri de Saint-Simon, Charles Fourier, and Robert Owen, Comte went well beyond his predecessors. His sociology was
distinct from the original meaning of "social science" as well as from its
later uses by Saint-Simon and Fourier. Comte rejected the existing theories,
either because they were too narrowly conceived or because they were compromised by metaphysical thinking.

Historically, Comte argued, it is quite understandable that various specialties had evolved for dealing with questions about human society. That
political and moral questions had been treated separately, for example,
was typical of the social organization of the old regime. Once the equal
rights of citizens are recognized and the "common interest" prevails, such
a separation no longer makes sense. It becomes apparent, as Condorcet had
convincingly demonstrated, that political and moral issues both have to be
studied in relation to the development of human society and civilization.[7]
A similar argument applied to the study of commerce and industry. Comte
had expressed his admiration for some works of Adam Smith, but rejected
Jean-Baptiste Say's plea for studying the economy independently of other
institutional structures of society. Instead of separating economics from
other social sciences, it had to be incorporated in the encompassing framework of a genuine science of society.

Acknowledging the fundamental interdependence of human society that
Comte expressed with terms like "connectivity," "consensus," and "solidarity" implied a general ambition that was well captured by the term
"sociology." In his earliest writings, Comte continued to use the term
"social science." Rethinking the relationship to the other sciences, and
rejecting Condorcet's mathematical approach, he then preferred the expression "social physics." This did not refer to "physics" as the discipline to
be emulated, as is commonly assumed, but to the older meaning of the
word "physics," which covered the general notion of "empirical natural
science." The term was comparable to the concept of "natural philosophy,"
which was prevalent in Britain. To speak of physics in this older, general
sense was a way to avoid the more specific notions of "social mathematics," "social mechanics," or "social physiology," which were associated
with Condorcet, Laplace, and Cabanis, and which had flowered during the
revolution. Physics in this overarching meaning was divided by Comte into
two branches, inorganic and organic physics, each of which was in turn
subdivided. In the *Cours de philosophie positive*, the terminology shifted

again. Comte dropped the overarching notion of physics as well as the more specific notions of "organic physics" and "social physics." In accordance with the ongoing process of discipline formation, physics henceforth referred to the discipline that was to be distinguished from mathematics, astronomy, and chemistry. Comte thus replaced the term "organic physics" with "biology" and the term "social physics" with "sociology."[8] The "science of sociology," a term coined by analogy to biology, was defined as the "positive study of the totality of fundamental laws that are specific of social phenomena."[9] Just as biology as the general science of life had unified the previously separated domains of botany, zoology, and medicine, sociology would integrate the study of politics, morals, and economics into a fundamental science of human society.

Comte made it clear, furthermore, that the new science could not come into being by simply applying the methods of other sciences. Sociology was to become an uncompromising positive science that would rigorously break with theological and metaphysical thinking, yet he simultaneously rejected the attempts to define it as a form of "social mathematics" or "social physiology." Trained as a scientist strongly attached to the scientific ethos, Comte was nonetheless highly critical of the existing models for the scientization of the social sciences.[10] Advocating an approach that would do justice to the specific complexities of human society, he elaborated a theory in which sociology was neither opposed to nor derivative of the established sciences. That line of argument was a fundamentally new way of conceptualizing the relationships between the sciences. While remaining within a naturalistic framework, Comte's strategy opposed emulating the established sciences and was explicitly antireductionist. His differential approach inaugurated a specifically French tradition, which would have considerable impact in both the life sciences and the social sciences. The program of the *Société de biologie* (1848), the first learned society specifically devoted to the study of biology, was drawn up by a pupil of Comte, Charles Robin, and was directly based on Comte's interpretation of the life sciences.[11] Nearly a quarter of a century later the first sociological society in the world, the *Société de sociologie* (1872), was founded by another follower of Comte, Émile Littré, who similarly followed Comtean principles.

Comte and the Second Scientific Revolution

Comte's work can be properly understood only if it is related to the transformation of the scientific field of his time and to the unprecedented role the sciences acquired during the revolutionary era, when Paris was not only the political but also the scientific capital of the world. Comte's *Cours de philosophie positive* (1830–42) is best understood as a theory of the second scientific revolution. The first scientific revolution is generally associated with the mathematization of the physical sciences (and in particular with classical mechanics), with the rise of national academies like the Royal Society and the Académie des sciences, and with the accompanying belief in "natural philosophy" as an overarching view of nature and natural science. In the period between the 1770s and 1830s leading scientists and their allies had the chance to expand and reorganize the scientific world by creating a host of new institutions, which were based on disciplinary structures. This second scientific revolution, as it may be called, was characterized primarily by the institutionalization of a regime of disciplines.[12] The founding of separate journals, chairs, and other institutional arrangements for the various sciences brought about a much stricter division of labor between mathematics, physics, and chemistry, while simultaneously including biology as a general science of life and the formation of the social sciences as an organized field of inquiry of its own. What the *Cours de philosophie positive* achieved was nothing less than a theory of this new scientific constellation.

As a student of the École polytechnique, Comte shared many of the aspirations of his schoolmates, but he was tempted neither by engineering nor by specific research issues in mathematics or the physical sciences. Interested in more general questions of science and society, Comte became increasingly critical of the unlimited claims some of his fellow scientists made. When during the conservative regime of the Restoration Comte and other pupils were expelled from the École polytechnique, he involved himself with oppositional groups, worked for the prophetic Saint-Simon, and wrote his first articles and essays. What distinguished him from Saint-Simon and other political reformers was that he continued to pursue his study of the sciences in order to find a truly scientific basis for reform. Decisive in this quest for a new science of society was his appreciation of the life sciences, where, thanks to early theorists of biology like Bichat and Blainville, he encountered different methods of inquiry and other modes of thinking than those of the mathematical and physical sciences in which he was trained. His understanding of the life sciences would eventually provide the intellectual impetus for both his theory of the sciences and his reconceptualization of the social sciences.

The critical core of what Comte encountered in the life sciences was a scientifically based critique of mathematics. That encounter allowed him to rethink his own training, to oppose the leading paradigm in mathematical physics, and to eventually elaborate a more general theory of the sciences. What may loosely be called "vitalism" played a strategic role in this process. Vitalists assumed that living organisms have properties that are irreducible to mechanics. On the basis of these irreducible features (such as irritability and sensibility), doctrines had emerged in the latter half of the eighteenth century that assumed the existence of vital principles or life forces. The unitary view of nature, commonly expressed in mechanical metaphors, thus gave way to a dichotomy of inanimate and animate bodies, of matter and life. The common properties of living organisms were subsequently defined as the object-matter of the new science of "biology"—the term was coined in the 1790s.

One of the consequences of the rapid intellectual and institutional differentiation of the natural sciences occurring around 1800 was that it undermined the unitary conception of natural philosophy. Representatives of the life sciences, in particular, had fought their battle of independence against mechanist and reductionist programs, of which the Laplace school was the prime example in physics and chemistry. In the first decades of the nineteenth century, then, a shift was recognizable from a unified conception of natural philosophy with various branches toward a division in more autonomous scientific disciplines.[13] Encompassing terms such as "nature" and "reason" lost some of their appeal and the notion of philosophy underwent a similar change. Philosophy tended to become a discipline as well, a superior one perhaps, but a discipline nonetheless. From designating a general notion of systematic knowledge, philosophy was redefined as a specialty for transcendental analysis (Kant) or for analyzing ideas (as in Destutt de Tracy's *idéologie*).

This process of discipline formation transformed the legacy of the Enlightenment and raised the question of unity and difference in science in an entirely new manner. This, then, was the central problem of the *Cours de philosophie positive*. As Comte explained in the first lesson, it is a philosophical illusion to define knowledge in an a priori manner, independent of its actual historical development. The production of knowledge needs to be seen as a historical process that develops in successive stages: the theological, the metaphysical, and the scientific stage. In the positive or scientific stage, knowledge is concerned merely with laws or law-like regularities. Since laws are "relations of similarity and succession," positive knowledge can be acquired neither of the intimate nature of the phenomena (essences, substances) nor of their first or final causes.

Referring to this idea of laws as the common characteristic of positive science, Comte is generally remembered for his obsession with invariable regularities and, more in particular, for his unfailing belief in having discovered the law of human society. This reputation, however, is too restrictive and in an important sense misleading. What the six volumes of the *Cours de philosophie positive* actually contain is not an elaboration of the first but of the second lesson, amounting not so much to a unified but, on the contrary, to a differential theory of science.[14] This differential theory of science was a positive response to newly emerging sciences such as biology and social science, as well as to recent developments in physics (Fourier, Fresnel, Ampère) that had diverged from the reductionist program of Laplace (for whom celestial mechanics was the model for all branches of physics and chemistry).[15] During the years when Comte worked with Saint-Simon and was involved in various other projects, he gradually developed the ambition of constructing a theory of science in an age of differentiation. That theory would provide a proper foundation for the social sciences and a sound basis for political and social reform. Saint-Simon and others lacked the scientific competence and the rigor this would require and mistakenly gave priority to social and economic reform. Scientists like Condorcet or Cabanis, on the other hand, who had tried to create a social science derived from the natural sciences, had also failed because they typically overestimated the validity of their own discipline.

The theoretical message of the *Cours* was, briefly put, that the sciences share the ambition of uncovering laws, but that they do so in various ways, using different methods. The argument is worth recalling in some detail because—with few exceptions—it is widely misunderstood. Considering the positive sciences in their increasing diversity, Comte argued, there is no way they could be reduced to one basic type, neither to mechanics, as the Laplacians had defended, nor to some form of general physiology, as some of the biologists had suggested. Instead of following a uniform model and a single method, each fundamental science has its own methods and research procedures, and necessarily so because the degree of complexity of its object-matter varies significantly. Astronomers study the geometry and mechanics of celestial bodies. Physics is already a more complex and less unified science: it cannot be reduced to mechanics, although physical phenomena (light, heat, electricity, magnetism) are simple enough for mathematical description. Chemistry studies matter at the level of molecular composition and decomposition. In addition to the laws of mechanics and physics, these processes are also subject to specific chemical regularities ("chemical affinities"). Biologists study beings whose conduct cannot be explained by physical forces or chemical affinities, since conduct depends primarily on the "organization" of the body. Human societies, finally, represent an order of even more complex interdependencies.

The sciences, in this view, constitute a series of increasing complexity and decreasing generality. The laws of physics are relatively simple and are valid for all natural phenomena, large and small, animate and inanimate. Chemistry is both more complex and less general: there are many physical phenomena without chemical effect, but no chemical phenomena without physical effect. The laws of biology are again more complicated and their validity is restricted to living organisms. The laws of human societies are still more complex and less general; human beings thus represent the smallest subset of all natural phenomena.

The main thrust of the *Cours de philosophie positive* is that recent developments in the sciences are best understood in terms of this scheme of increasing complexity and decreasing generality. Contrary to widespread anachronisms, the central issue of the *Cours* is neither how science should be demarcated from metaphysics nor how a logical or methodological foundation might be constructed for the unity of science. Comte's analysis had a quite different purpose. It explained in great detail how and why different methods prevail in the various sciences: the experimental method in physics, the comparative method in biology, the historical method in sociology. As a consequence of this view—and in contrast to widespread misunderstandings—Comte rejected the use of mathematics in biology and sociology. Whereas in chemistry mathematics is still of some use, in biology the "enormous numerical variations" of the phenomena and the "irregular variability of effects" make mathematical techniques useless.[16] This argument applies even more strongly to the social sciences, and Comte accordingly rejected the social mathematics of Condorcet and Laplace and ridiculed Quételet's social physics, which was nothing more than "simple statistics" anyhow.

Emphasizing the relative autonomy of the sciences, as it would later be called, Comte elaborated an ingenious and pioneering differential theory of science. Instead of founding the social sciences on one of the natural sciences, he demonstrated that it was more fruitful to indirectly follow the example of biology. As a distinct science of life, the constitution of biology had suggested both a differential understanding of the natural sciences and a program for reconceptualizing the aims and claims of social science. As vitalists had done for biology, Comte founded sociology on the specific and irreducible properties of its object-matter. Because human animals have the capacity to learn, the progress of knowledge is the basis of the development of human society, and the law of the three stages the core of sociology.

Although the *Cours de philosophie positive* thus presented a new theory of science and an ambitious program for reviving and reorienting the social sciences, it did not obtain the recognition Comte expected. His exceptional mastery of the various sciences and his perseverance were rewarded in 1832 with his appointment as tutor at the École polytechnique, somewhat later followed by the nomination as examiner. Efforts to obtain a professorial chair or a seat in the Academy of Sciences, however, proved in vain, and the reception of the *Cours de philosophie positive* was extremely disappointing. The first French review, written by Émile Littré, appeared fourteen years after the publication of the first volume and two years after the completion of the sixth and last one. For Comte that was too late. In the very year that Littré published his extensive and enthusiastic review, Comte lost his position as examiner at the École polytechnique and fell hopelessly in love with a young woman, Clotilde de Vaux, whose affection promised a "sacred compensation" for his misfortune.

The *Cours de philosophie positive*, which is undoubtedly one of the great intellectual achievements of the nineteenth century, was the result of a peculiar social dynamic. It was the work of a scientist, trained at the most advanced school in mathematics and physics in Europe, who had become increasingly critical of his own education and of the unlimited claims made by leading mathematical physicists of the time. When the École polytechnique was closed during the Restoration and Comte and others were expelled, he started to work on two, apparently disconnected, projects. With Saint-Simon and other opponents of the Restoration, he dedicated himself to questions of social reform and social science. At the same time he worked on a book about mathematics, which was intended to understand both the power and the limits of mathematical formalization. Decisive for the development of both these projects was his encounter with the emerging science of biology. Theorists of biology gave Comte an incisive and systematic insight into the limits of mathematization and mechanical models of causality. The specific characteristics of the life sciences suggested a differential understanding of the natural sciences, while simultaneously providing a clue for reconceptualizing the social sciences. On the basis of the distinction between varying levels of complexity, social science could be conceived as being to biology what biology was to physics.

In elaborating these insights into a general theory of the sciences, Comte relied on the scientific capital he had accumulated and profited from the fact that he did not belong to any scientific group or institution in particular, neither in the physical or the life sciences nor in the social sciences. But as the reception of his work tragically shows, that independent position was extremely vulnerable and in the end unsustainable. Within the academic field of his time, Comte's theory was too broad in scope for the increasingly specialized scientists at the Academy of Sciences and was too critical of the leading model of mathematical physics, whereas it was too scientific for the Academy of Moral and Political Sciences. Gradually turning away from the academic establishment, Comte famously stopped reading scientific books, started to enjoy music, and increasingly identified with women and workers as the true carriers of change. His "second career" developed under the sign of the needs of the "heart." Elaborating on the implications of the "subjective method" that he had unjustly neglected during his first career, Comte's new project culminated in a secular religion, the religion of humanity, which represented the ultimate synthesis of scientific understanding, social organization, and emotional fulfillment.

Although the revolution of 1848 and the founding of the Société positiviste (1848) had given him a new audience, Comte's political support of the Second Empire (1851–70) provoked a split among his newly won followers. Émile Littré, who was one of his most talented disciples, rejected Comte's new political stance, unambiguously preferring the constitutional, pacific regime to Bonaparte's military dictatorship.[17] After Comte's death in 1857, the orthodox wing of the positivists continued the diffusion of integral positivism by public lecturing, civic initiatives (such as petitions for statues of scientists and republican leaders), occasional religious ceremonies, and the publication of the *Revue occidentale* (1878–1914). A heterodox and more prestigious group gathered around Littré and his journal *La philosophie positive* (1867–83). Applying the precepts of positive philosophy to the political, scientific, and cultural issues of the day, Littré refused any allegiance with the "subjective method" and the religion of humanity, and evolved in a more political direction.[18]

It has been suggested, among others by Durkheim, that in the decades after Comte's *Cours de philosophie positive* (1830–42) no Frenchman made any significant contribution to sociology, not Comte himself, not his immediate disciples, not Le Play or any other intellectual. The new science had no sooner come into existence than it disappeared from the horizon, an eclipse that, according to Durkheim, lasted nearly forty years.[19] But that judgment is too rash because it ignores various attempts to construct a social science outside of the universities. Whereas the orthodox positivists indeed paid little attention to sociology, which was merely one branch of the positivist worldview, the efforts of Littré and his companions were among the first activities explicitly presented as sociological. But their version of the Comtean heritage was a response to challenges that had occurred mainly in England. After the publication of the *Cours*, the idea of "sociology" migrated to Britain; Comte and his immediate followers in France were too busy carrying out their educational, political, and religious tasks. When sociology reemerged in France, first with the group around Littré, then in various other circles outside as well as inside the universities, it was to a considerable degree as a response to the reception of British sociology, and in particular to the work of the towering figure of Herbert Spencer.

The British Evolution of Sociology

In the context in which Charles Babbage's *Reflections on the Decline of Science in England* (1830) expressed a widespread feeling among English men of science, British scholars had become particularly receptive to French scientific achievements. Determined to catch up, they founded the British Association for the Advancement of Science (1831), which became a major force in the scientific life of the country. Compared with the reception in his home country, the reviews of Comte's *Cours* in Britain were earlier and more favorable. This occurred by and large outside of the English universities, which were ecclesiastical and generally conservative institutions. In 1838, when Comte's *Cours* was halfway completed, the well-known Scottish physicist David Brewster, who was one of the cofounders of the British Association for the Advancement of Science, wrote a lengthy and highly complimentary review. But Comte owed his reputation in Britain mainly to John Stuart Mill and the members of his circle. Mill read the first volumes of the *Cours* in the 1830s and expressed his admiration in a letter to the author in 1841. An extensive correspondence ensued, and in 1844 Mill organized financial support for the former examiner. Comte's reputation in England and the United States was initially based on Mill's discussion in his widely read *System of Logic* (1843), in which the Frenchman was lauded as the most important contemporary philosopher. Mill toned down his praise in later editions, and when he eventually broke off contact, his role as a prominent intermediary was taken over by George Henry Lewes. In the same year that Harriet Martineau published her condensed English edition of the *Cours*, Lewes published his *Comte's Philosophy of the Sciences* (1853); later he renamed his popular biographical history of philosophy *History of Philosophy from Thales to Comte* (1867).

In the 1850s and 1860s, positive philosophy and positivism provoked innumerable discussions in Britain. Criticism first came from religious quarters. At regular intervals, Comte's English admirers urged him to be more cautious in his statements on the *canaille théologique*. Mill, Lewes, and Martineau raised objections mainly to Comte's later work. Scientists like Herschel and Huxley, however, expressed reservations suggesting that in spite of appearances, Comte's *Cours* might not have such a solid scientific foundation after all. With his *Auguste Comte and Positivism* (1866), some thirty years after he had first come across the *Cours*, Mill felt it was time to take stock. He was harsh about Comte's personality, his political views, and his later writings. Comte's rejection of psychology was a "big mistake" and his opinions on political economy were "extraordinarily superficial." When it came to sociology, however, Mill was favorable, considering that the term was a "convenient barbarism" and that Comte's views on the historical development of society were sound and stimulating.

The various topics of atheism, philosophy, and modern science were in the British context soon overshadowed, however, by the question of evolutionism, which became the single most important scientific issue in the second half of the nineteenth century. Conceptualizing progressive change over longer periods of time was rooted in two distinct intellectual traditions: philosophical history and natural history. One of the central texts was Condorcet's posthumously published *Outline of an Historical View of the Progress of the Human Mind* (1795), which was a tribute to human perfectibility through the advancement of knowledge. Widely read as a heroic testament of the Enlightenment, Condorcet's work was not only the basic reference for Saint-Simon's and Comte's ideas of progress, but it had also provoked Malthus's strongly anti-utopian *Essay on the Principles of Population* (1798). Attacking Condorcet's optimistic vision of perfectibility, Malthus argued that instead of leading to progress, the operation of natural laws in reality tended to produce misery and starvation. Because of the sexual appetite of man, populations tend to grow at a geometrical rate, whereas food supplies increase only arithmetically. The imbalance made starvation and poverty natural phenomena, and a permanent feature of the human condition. Just as Malthus's image of population development provided Darwin with a clue for his theory of natural selection, other historical works similarly contributed to the historicization of natural history, while the new conceptions of natural history in turn reinforced the historicization of the social sciences.[20] Developmental and evolutionary theories in the broad sense became the prevailing form of social science in the nineteenth century. After the American and the French Revolutions, and with ongoing industrialization and urban growth, more general social theories were all fundamentally concerned with the deep-seated causes and consequences of these transformations. Comte and Tocqueville, Buckle and Spencer, Marx and Maine all grappled with the historical characteristics of modern society, its principles of change and its future direction. In that sense all were evolutionary thinkers, although few of them were evolutionists proper.

The best-known representative of evolutionism, and probably the most widely read and translated European intellectual of the latter half of the nineteenth century, was Herbert Spencer.[21] After having worked as a railroad engineer and briefly as an editor of the *Economist*, a family inheritance allowed him to pursue scholarly interests and become a prolific writer. For Spencer, who became an evolutionist before Darwin, progressive change was the common denominator of all natural processes. From the maturation of an embryo to the development of human society and the evolution of the solar system, all things evolve from the simple to the complex through successive differentiation. Evolution, in other words, is the natural and necessary process of change from incoherent homogeneity to coherent heterogeneity. Because differentiation leads to higher levels of integration and coordination, evolution was practically synonymous with progress. The idea that development means progress through differentiation combined

Adam Smith's view of the division of labor with notions from embryology (where the terminology of homogeneity and heterogeneity was current). Spencer's view of evolution was thus much broader than both Comte's sociological and Darwin's biological theory. It had the status of a cosmic law and formed the core of his all-embracing system of synthetic philosophy. The outline of this universal philosophy of evolution was presented in his essay "Progress: Its Law and Cause" (1857), which appeared two years before *The Origin of Species* (1859) and was systematically developed in his *First Principles* (1862). From there, after a short text explaining his Reasons for Dissenting from the Philosophy of M. Comte (1864), followed the series of multivolume books in which Spencer applied the model successively to biology, psychology, sociology, and ethics.

Spencer's sociology, outlined in his famous essay "The Social Organism" (1860), was first elaborated in his *Study of Sociology* (1873). It was intended as a preliminary book but became one of his most popular works. It was followed by *The Principles of Sociology* (1874–96) and a series of factual inquiries gathered in *Descriptive Sociology* (1873–1934). Spencer's sociology was cast in the organic idiom. The features of social organization result neither from divine Providence nor from worldly government; they are the consequences of the ever-growing social organism. Spencer and many organicists after him took the analogy quite literally and worked out detailed correspondences between human society and other organisms. Social change, according to Spencer, was linked especially to the transition from military to industrial society. In the first type of society integration derives from a controlling center, in the latter it is the spontaneous effect of individuals cooperating on the basis of a division of labor. For Spencer market exchange was the paradigm of the advanced type of integration. Since social evolution was a natural and spontaneous process with an immanent tendency to higher levels integration and coordination, Spencer favored the radical laissez-faire view of politics that he had already put forward in his *Social Statics* (1851). Although this liberal stance against government intervention is commonly identified with social Darwinism, Spencer's own faith was more in natural growth and evolutionary progress than in selection or the elimination of the unfit.

The Return of Sociology in France

In France sociology reemerged and spread during the last third of the nineteenth century. During the 1860s, there were hardly any publications that were explicitly presented as sociological. The change occurred in the course of the 1870s and 1880s, when the meaning of the term "sociology" was still highly variable. Since sociology was initially associated with the positivist movement, the term could refer to Comte's original conception, to his later writings on reform and the religion of humanity, or, more generally, to the notion of social reform based on social science. Those in the Comtean tradition used the term "sociology," as did some reformers of a different persuasion.[22] Others, however, preferred the seemingly less partisan expression "social science." Herbert Spencer's *Study of Sociology* (1873), for example, was translated into French as *Introduction à la science sociale* (1874).[23] Although the rapid impact of Spencer's work in France in the 1870s made it clear that sociology was not restricted to followers of Comte, French scholars were reluctant to present their work as sociological. This was particularly true for the members of the new generation of university philosophers, who preferred to speak of "social science."

The place of sociology in the emerging constellation of social science disciplines is well indicated by the increase in the number of its publications (books, brochures, journals). From the 1870s to the First World War, social science publications show a pattern of strong growth for nearly all relevant bibliographical rubrics (see Table 2.1).[24] The increase, related to the expansion of higher education and to the growing demand for social science expertise, is much stronger than that of publishing in general. Within the larger corpus of the human and social sciences, sociological publications were listed in the rubric "socialism, social science," which underwent a particularly rapid growth (multiplying by a factor 6.7). This heterogeneous

TABLE 2.1
Number of publications* in the human and social sciences (1876–1915)

Rubric	1876–85	1886–95	1896–1905	1906–15
Socialism-social science, of which:	87	331	478	585
Sociology-social science(s)	7	44	103	115
Philosophy	142	279	363	467
Morals	107	189	233	292
Psychology	72	135	235	336
Political and social economy	108	181	179	240
Anthropology**	49	82	90	133
Ethnography	66	28	38	54
Statistics	10	16	13	52

Source: Sébastien Mosbah-Natanson, *La sociologie est à la mode: Productions et producteurs de sociologie autour de 1900*, Thèse de doctorat, Université Paris-Dauphine, 2007.

*Publications include books, brochures, and journals.
**Anthropology refers to physical anthropology and is distinguished from ethnography.

rubric contains all publications that use the adjective "social" or its derivatives: "sociology" and "social science" as well as "socialism." This curious mixture is probably because this rubric was originally conceived as a residual category, a section that would list all publications that did not fit the official categories in use by the Academy of Moral and Political Sciences. Containing several subgenres, Sébastien Mosbah-Natanson identified a total number of 269 properly "sociological" publications for the period 1876–1915. About three-quarters is explicitly sociological; one-quarter refers to "social science(s)" but can be considered to belong to sociology.

The sociological production is smaller than that of more established disciplines and categories (philosophy, morals, political economy, and psychology). But in relative terms, its growth has no equivalent and is part of the strong growth of publications about the social question, a development that was supported by the broad movement for social reform between 1880 and 1914. The main differentiation within the sociological corpus is between authors who are located inside higher education and those outside of it. The members of the positivist networks, for example, had very few connections to the university. Members of the more prominent network of Littré were typically journalists, administrators, and politicians, often with a background in medicine or law, but hardly ever engaged in a university career. The social research and reform movement instigated by Frédéric Le Play was much larger in size, but similarly had few connections to university. The group of aspiring sociologists who worked in public education, secondary schools, and universities, on the other hand, was connected to the Faculty of Letters, especially to philosophy, although for a while there was a significant group of legal scholars as well. In order to understand how this sociological movement evolved, I will first consider the sociological or parasociological production outside of the university; in the next chapter I will turn to the university scholars.

Positivist Politics

When Émile Littré founded his journal *La philosophie positive* in 1867, the scientific and philosophical works that he and his collaborators discussed were primarily British. There were reviews and discussions of Mill and Lewes, of Bain, Buckle, Spencer, Darwin, and Huxley. In the last years of the Second Empire, eminent French scientists like Claude Bernard and Louis Pasteur had expressed concern about the state of French science as compared with the recent advances in Britain and Germany. They were joined by philosophers like Taine and Renan, and by many other scholars in the humanities. Under these conditions of heightened international competition, Littré's journal defended the heritage of French "positive philosophy," including Comtean sociology. In one of his earliest articles on sociology, Littré recalled the advantages of Comte's approach. Arguing against the attempts to conceive of societies as organisms, Littré also turned against German materialists (Büchner, Moleschott, Vogt) and their French admirers in the Société d'anthropologie (1856). On the basis of Comte's theory of the sciences, Littré's article "On the Essential Condition that Separates Sociology from Biology" (1868) presents an articulate defense of the specificity and autonomy of sociology.[25] Since humans have the capacity to learn, the "gradual, continual influence of human generations on each other" is the specific property of human societies. Historical evolution was not so much a biological fact ("the views of Lamarck and Darwin have not yet emerged from the status of a hypothesis") as the sociological reality par excellence. As the science of social evolution, sociology had to employ the historical method and, in doing so, was in need of a specific sociological vocabulary. Borrowing biological notions, as Spencer and others had started to do, was misleading: "Every application of a biological term in sociology is either a simple analogy or a metaphor. Neither organs nor functions are in sociology what they are in biology. Some of the confusion and error comes from this transfer of meaning. This cause of misunderstanding must be promptly removed. As soon as sociology has its own technical language, we will get used to thinking sociologically."[26]

Littré thus proposed a series of technical terms, but they remained a dead letter and the pioneering sociological treatise he announced was never published.[27] The reason was not so much that he abandoned sociology, but that after 1870 Littré and his companions were drawn into the political life of the Third Republic (1870–1940). Their journal published more on political issues than on any other topic, and its leading figures nearly all were involved in political and administrative careers. Littré himself, who became a member of parliament and a lifetime senator, redefined sociology along political lines.[28] In his essay "On Sociological Method," published in 1870 in the midst of a new and particularly "unstable" phase of national history, Littré argued that it was time to reconsider the role and nature of the social sciences. It followed from Comte's epistemology, he argued, that the more complex a science is, the more alien and resistant it is to deductive reasoning. In mathematics, the possibilities of deduction are unlimited; in biology deduction is rather suspect as long as its results have not been confirmed. Since social science is the most complex science of all, deductive reasoning is least applicable and it is least possible to construct coherent "systems" from which predictions can be derived.[29] The consequences of this view were far reaching. Observing that in France revolutions had followed one another "in vain" and that predictions of the course of events had proven futile, Littré maintained that recent historical experience implied that instead of relying on general theories, it was necessary to rethink both political action and sociological understanding. It had to be admitted that what enables social situations to advance is the "empirical wisdom" of publicists and statesmen. Social change is gradual and progressive, social situations develop "little by little, step by step, always taking the present as their point of departure." Contrary to utopian visions, a priori arguments, and deductive reasoning, political practice, according to Littré, confirms the methodological specificity of sociology. Political practice is in fact none other than the sociological method "in action," or at least "the empirical confirmation of its truth and power."

Littré's reorientation had political as well as scientific implications. Politically, he called for a more prudent political practice, one that would be attentive to the details of the issues at stake and more sensitive to the "opportunities" of the moment. In the second edition (1879) of his *Conservation, révolution et positivisme* (1852), he spelled out the mistakes of his earlier writings and self-critically commented on the illusions of predicting the future of European societies. With his new commitment to a sense of measure and prudence, imposed by the complexities of human history, Littré was politically close to reformist republican leaders like Ferry and Gambetta, of whom he was a prominent adviser.[30] Parallel to this political stance, Littré reconsidered the task of sociology. No longer concerned with sociology as the fundamental science of human societies, Littré called for a "practical" or "contemporary sociology," a sociology that was to be carefully used for understanding the specific political and social questions of the moment.

In light of this double revision, Littré founded the Société de sociologie (1872–74); it had twenty-six members, two foreign associates (John Stuart Mill, Eugène de Roberty), and was the first sociological society in the world. Although more a political club than a learned society, two diverging conceptions of sociology emerged among its members and associates. Littré and some of his closest companions developed a reinterpretation of positive philosophy wherein the political dimension was central, and their republican commitments generally extended into a political-administrative career in the Third Republic. Nine of the society's members, nearly a third of its membership, attained high political office: six were parliamentary representatives, three became ministers. Occupying positions in the political field outside the university, they insisted on the difficulties of uncovering laws and the futility of abstract principles. Having become indifferent to sociology as a fundamental science, their "practical sociology" was the positivist version of a form of political pragmatism or "opportunism" (the term didn't have the pejorative meaning it has today). Since their views were more liberal and democratic than those of the late Comte, the revision stimulated a rapprochement with other political currents, resulting in their integration into the republican establishment of the time.

A few other members of Littré's network continued to be mainly interested in general theoretical questions. They did not occupy university positions either, but had fewer political resources, did not live in Paris, and were, in fact, peripheral in Littré's network. Although their publications were part of the very first sociological publications of the 1870s and early 1880s, none of them did any empirical research or succeeded in elaborating positive theories. Among them, the Russian scholar Eugène de Roberty was the best known. After having taught in private schools in Brussels and Paris in the 1890s, he returned to Russia in 1904, where he held one of the first chairs in sociology. If the meetings of the Société de sociologie lasted barely two years, Littré's political engagement after 1870 may well have determined both the origin of the society and its early end: its origin because the Société de sociologie was conceived more as a political club than as a learned society; its end because the theoretical papers on classification and taxonomy read during the society's first sessions all suffered from the abstractness and *esprit de système* that Littré had so resolutely criticized in his 1870 text on the proper "method" in sociology.

Social Reform and Social Research

In his articles on the early development of sociology in France, Durkheim mentioned neither Littré's journal nor his Société de sociologie, although it was in this network of heterodox positivists that the first debates about the nature and future direction of sociology took place. Durkheim implicitly based his judgment on the fact that these efforts were situated outside of the institutions of higher learning and remained the work of "amateurs." Such a polemical selection was also at work with regard to other currents like the research movement of Frédéric Le Play or socialist theorists. Working outside of the university system, they were treated critically by members of the professoriate, who were eager to draw a clear line of demarcation between the alleged rigor and objectivity of their work and the multiple forms of social research and social thinking that were part of reform movements and that spread through the country during the last decades of the nineteenth century. The various reform initiatives came to form a social universe of its own, distinct from the political as well as the economic field, transcending the existing ideological cleavages, and socially more inclusive than the associations of the old-style notables.[31]

Given the political and social circumstances after 1870, the successive governments of the Third Republic were favorable to reform and could rely on a growing resistance to the social consequences of industrialization and laissez-faire politics. Besides established social Catholic groups, Protestant reform societies, and private philanthropies, new reform currents emerged. Social liberals sought ways to alleviate the harsh conditions of the working classes without interfering with the market economy. The current of "solidarism," which became a sort of official philosophy of the more prominent republican groups, was a form of social liberalism focused on how social integration could be achieved without restricting individual liberties.[32] This intermediary way between liberal individualism and socialist collectivism typically stimulated mutual aid societies, cooperatives, and new forms of professional corporations.

One of the earliest and largest movements of social research was founded by the young engineer Frédéric Le Play. The empirical monographs he promoted were in many respects a continuation of the social research tradition that had emerged in Britain and France during the first half of the nineteenth century. Le Play's founding study, *Les ouvriers européens* (1855), appeared during the Second Empire and was supported by governmental departments and published by the official imperial press. The massive work, containing thirty-six detailed case studies of working-class families, inaugurated a school of social research and reform that would last until well into the twentieth century. During his frequent travels in France and abroad as an expert in metallurgy, Le Play was time and again confronted with the social consequences of industrialization. While holding the chair for metallurgy at a leading engineering school, the École des mines, he started to undertake case studies—"monographs," as he called them—of the living conditions of working-class families. Interested in comprehensive descriptions of individual cases, Le Play disliked abstract theories and was skeptical about statistical generalizations. Statisticians, he wrote, can compare populations and the relative power of states, but they cannot properly comprehend the moral and intellectual condition of working-class families. Instead of compiling numbers and calculating averages, Le Play advocated "direct observation" as the only method that could lead to rigorous conclusions. Since he considered families to be the "genuine" social unit, he focused on different aspects of family life, for which he designed standardized schemes for observation.[33]

Although these observational devices included a broad range of practices, Le Play's interest as a convinced Catholic led him to focus on the moral capacity of the families he studied. While recognizing that his studies could help shape public policies and the reorganization of factories, Le Play was most strongly committed to a religiously inspired moral perspective. Contrary to liberal economists who relied on market forces and opposed to socialists who favored state legislation, the central issues in improving the conditions of workers were for Le Play moral well-being and social harmony. That perspective led him to focus on the way children were raised, intergenerational relations, inheritance practices, the family's capacity to save money, and its susceptibility to living by the rules. To improve the condition of the masses, the necessary reforms would have to be exercised at the level of morals and morality, not by coercion but by "the force of opinion." This moral force, which could "restrain egoism" and prevent the wealthy from renouncing their duty, was to be found in religion.[34]

Although Le Play refers to the need for generalization on the basis of observations, his habit of multiplying detailed case studies made that difficult to realize. There was no idea yet of representative sampling, Le Play did not like Quételet's averages, and he was surprisingly reluctant to use the comparative method. The main obstacle to formulating more general insights and proposing a theoretical account of his findings was probably that Le Play himself saw little or no need for it. In his model study *Les ouvriers européens* he remarks that in thoroughly analyzing facts, "social science furnishes essentially the same conclusions as morality."[35] Deeply convinced that there was not much to discover beyond the universal truths of the scripture, Le Play's social science was to morality what the metallurgy he taught was to physics: more an applied form of belief than a fundamental science. His monographs were moral exemplars rather than attempts at examining variation that could be related to explanatory principles.

Under the Second Empire Le Play profited from the support of the emperor. He held official positions, became a member of the state council, the Conseil d'État, and was general commissioner of the Parisian World Fair in 1867. After publishing *Les ouvriers européens*, Le Play founded the Société d'économie sociale (1856). Within ten years the association had 360 members, organized regular conferences, and over a period of more than half a century published 126 detailed monographs, the very last one in 1930.[36] The society formed the core of Le Play's movement. Its leaders were local notables, high civil servants, and members of the learned professions (engineers, priests, lawyers, doctors). Some taught at private Catholic schools or at the École libre des sciences politiques, a few of the best known belonged to the Academy of Moral and Political Sciences, but very few had connections to the public universities.[37] During the Third Republic, when Le Play gave up his official functions and membership in his association slightly declined, the journal *La réforme sociale* (1881–1931) continued publishing research monographs and political and social commentary. The reform initiatives were carried by the Unions of Social Peace, which were launched after the Paris Commune and included up to 3,000 members in the 1880s.[38] After Le Play's death in 1882, a schism occurred and two of his followers founded their own journal, *La science sociale* (1886), focusing more on research issues and claiming to be open to revising Le Play's ideas.

Another form of social thinking that was closely related to social reform was Marxism. Compared to the heterodox positivists around Littré and the leaders of Le Play's movement, Marxist theorists like Jules Guesde and Paul Lafargue were in a more disadvantageous position. Excluded from the university, they were isolated from the political and administrative elites as well, a situation which they resolved polemically by arguing against bourgeois intellectuals and politicians, avoiding opportunities for debate and discussion with their bourgeois enemies, and seeking comfort in the role of the "party intellectual" as the guardian of the doctrine of scientific socialism.[39] The Marxist tradition in France, as a consequence, did not have the theoretical sophistication it had in Germany. Durkheim considered socialist thinkers to be important, not for their insight into the mechanisms of class conflict and exploitation but for representing a symptom of social crisis. Socialism in Durkheim's view was not a science but a belief system, and had to be treated as such. Compared with Max Weber and other German sociologists, the French group around the *Année sociologique* paid relatively little attention to socialist thought, despite the fact that Durkheim was a personal friend of the reformist socialist Jaurès and many of his younger collaborators were active members of socialist groups.[40] Rejecting political partisanship and economic determinism was for the Durkheimians sufficient reason to simultaneously reject the scientific challenge that Marxism represented for Weber.

Although the positivist, Le Playist, and socialist literature was tied to particular doctrines and partisan groups, the broadening movement for social reform at the end of the nineteenth century also included ecumenical initiatives. Most were focused on certain sectors (public health, education, prisons); some had a more general ambition. The Musée social (1894), for example, was a kind of private think tank, offering a meeting ground for industrialists, politicians, engineers, academics, and moderate labor leaders. Focused on finding solutions for the social question, it was in the forefront of reexamining the role of the state and proposing schemes for pension legislation and urban-planning policies.[41] Private teaching institutions like the École libre des sciences sociales (1895) and the École des hautes études sociales (1900), both founded by the journalist, writer, and organizer Dick May, did not offer any degrees but were intended to educate the public and diffuse social science knowledge.[42] Much like the people's universities, their appeal was carried by the political and social struggles in the wake of the Dreyfus Affair.

Despite the brief and unsuccessful effort of Littré and his companions, sociology proper had no more than a peripheral presence in this broadening movement for social research, social reform, and social science teaching. Any role it did play was the result of the work of university philosophers, who started taking up sociology in the 1870s and who would soon monopolize legitimate sociological production.

CHAPTER 3

❊ ❊ ❊

Sociology and Other Disciplines
in the Making

The main impetus for sociology in the last third of the nineteenth century did not come from any particular school of social thought outside of the university, but from a small number of university philosophers who took up sociology during the 1870s and 1880s and transformed it from a stigmatized positivist project into a legitimate university endeavor. These university pioneers belonged to the younger generation of the academic elite, that is, students from the École normale supérieure and *agrégés*. They introduced new disciplines such as experimental psychology, pedagogy, and sociology and succeeded in imposing a profound reorientation in established disciplines like philosophy and history. The opportunity for their collective effort was provided by the expanding universities, which offered a widening range of career possibilities and a larger degree of autonomy from governmental institutions.

The Two-Front Struggle of the Professoriate

Regardless of the specific issues at stake in each of these disciplines, the movement for academic renewal can be understood more generally as a struggle on two fronts.[1] On the one hand, its members opposed the monopoly of the Academy of Moral and Political Sciences and combated the outdated spiritualism of Cousin and its presumptions about the "moral sciences." This battle implied a critical stance toward conventional philosophical and literary rhetoric and was articulated in the name of a more demanding conception of "experimental" or "positive" science. The aspiring professors were, on the other hand, equally critical of the intellectual exponents of the reform movements that had developed outside of the university (positivists, socialists, Catholic reformers like Le Play). Here they opposed a more professional scholarly ethos to the doctrinal character of reformers, critiquing their uncritical combination of normative commitment and scholarly pretension. In this two-front struggle, they relied heavily on contemporary foreign scholarship, essentially British and German, which was seen as the most advanced of the time and was depicted as representing an urgent challenge to the French scholarly community.[2]

In the center of this tension-ridden field of relations stood a new type of publication: the disciplinary journal. Specialized university journals were the main vehicle for the scholarly claims of the new generation, who thus distinguished themselves from general intellectual reviews like the *Revue des deux mondes* and from doctrinal outlets such as the positivist journals, the liberal *Journal des économistes* or the periodicals of Le Play's movement. In addition to the *Revue d'économie politique* (1887), founded by young professors in the Faculty of Law, these disciplinary journals included the *Revue historique* (1876), *Revue philosophique* (1876), *Revue pédagogique* (1878), *Année psychologique* (1895), *Revue internationale de sociologie* (1893), and *Année sociologique* (1898). The journals were based in the Faculty of Letters and produced by publishing houses close to the professoriate. The similarity in journal titles was underpinned by affinities in intellectual style and academic strategy. The founders of the *Revue historique* typically declared that they would adopt a "strictly scientific point of view" that adhered to the principles of "positive science." Contributors were asked to observe "strictly scientific methods of exposition": each generalization or conclusion was to be accompanied by proof, source references, and quotations; "vague generalities and rhetoric" were excluded, yet the literary character of historical writing should be respected.[3]

Of central significance in this scholarly movement was the *Revue philosophique*, the first university journal in philosophy, which became the leading periodical for philosophy as well as for many newly emerging disciplines.[4] The journal was launched by the thirty-six-year-old Théodule Ribot, who had withdrawn from teaching to start his own journal and who became known as the founder of experimental psychology in France. Ribot presented his undertaking as a professional scholarly journal, open to all philosophical schools, provided that the contributors did not simply restate what was already known. The brief declaration distinguished the journal from the best-known doctrinal periodicals: Littré's *La philosophie positive* (1867–83) and Renouvier's neo-Kantian *La critique philosophique* (1872–89). Contrary to their "sect-like spirit," as Ribot said in private correspondence, his journal would be a "neutral" and professional medium. The positivist Wyrouboff reacted immediately by recalling that this neutrality was precisely what he and his companions had rejected all along. Their positivist review, *La philosophie positive*, had no ambition to be neutral: it was the expression of a worldview, it combated rival doctrines and opposed the narrow-mindedness of specialists who had abandoned general questions. The very idea of a specialized, professional journal was dismissed by Wyrouboff as a "chimera"; it would "never produce anything serious." Philosophical schools had no desire to be reconciled with one another: "quite the contrary, they can only endure and be fruitful if they remain consistent and pure."[5]

In a more subtle way, Ribot's declaration was a warning for the dominant spiritualist school as well, since it attacked the monopolistic practices of the Academy and proclaimed that articles would be rejected if they had nothing new to offer. In an essay for the British journal *Mind*, Ribot was more explicit. Cousin's philosophy was a doctrine "without originality," which had "shamefully" developed aloof from the "discoveries of science." Although it was still the official philosophy, and the Academy of Moral and Political Sciences was the "sanctuary of philosophical orthodoxy," there was in France after 1870 less liking for "verbiage and eloquence" and more for "facts, thorough study, and scientific culture."[6] The newly founded *Revue philosophique* was a sign of change since it was open to different currents, regularly published foreign authors, had a critical section for book reviews, and contained bibliographical information that was to be as "complete as possible."[7]

The most frequently discussed authors and areas of inquiry indicate the orientation of Ribot's journal (tables 3.1 and 3.2). While Cousin disappeared as a major figure, the most widely discussed philosopher was now Kant, who allowed members of the new generation, like Boutroux, to break away from the old spiritualism yet resist the invasion of the empirical sciences. Observing that among philosophers Kantianism was replacing spiritualism, Ribot commented that this was an "honest way" to leave the old doctrines behind, even if Kantianism was in reality just another brand of spiritualism: the "good God replaced by duty."[8] Impressed by a range of British and German authors, Ribot published widely read overviews of experimental psychology in Britain and Germany, *La psychologie anglaise contemporaine* (1870) and *La psychologie allemande contemporaine* (1879). With Charcot he founded a learned society for physiological psychology and eventually returned to higher education to teach the first courses in experimental psychology at the Sorbonne and the Collège de France.[9] After Kant, the most frequently discussed figures in the *Revue philosophique* were Herbert Spencer and Wilhelm Wundt, who ranked

TABLE 3.1
References to major authors in the *Revue philosophique* (1876–1905)

	1876–87	1888–96	1896–1905
Kant	72	28	77
Spencer	32	13	23
Wundt	36	20	8
Plato	23	11	24
Spinoza	13	10	10
Descartes	11	12	9
Leibniz	9	12	9
Darwin	21	2	5
Aristotle	10	13	2
Comte	5	6	13
James	12	4	6
Hegel	8	4	9
Cousin	1	–	2
Littré	3	–	–

Source: The number of references does not refer to citations, but to references included in the indexes of the tables of the *Revue philosophique* for the indicated decades. Included are articles by or about the author, as well as book reviews about the author.

TABLE 3.2
References to extra-philosophical areas of inquiry in the *Revue philosophique* (1876–1905)

	1876–87	1888–96	1896–1905
Anthropology	6	2	14
Biology	8	3	34
Ethnology	3	1	26
Mathematics	12	14	26
Physics	14	14	13
Psychology	144	235	391
Sociology	12	62	321

Note: The number of references refers to areas of inquiry indexed in the tables of the *Revue philosophique*.

higher than canonical philosophers from Plato and Aristotle to Descartes, Spinoza, or Leibniz. The most prominent extra-philosophical area of inquiry was psychology, at the end of the century joined by sociology, which came close to being as popular a topic as psychology (table 3.2).[10] The decline of the old spiritualist philosophy, the rise of new disciplines, and the prominence of figures like Spencer and Wundt were identified by commentators as a profound "crisis" of philosophy.[11]

University Pioneers

Ribot's closest collaborator was his fellow *normalien* and friend Alfred Espinas, who tried to do for sociology what Ribot did for psychology.[12] Together they translated Spencer's *Principles of Psychology*, which impressed them deeply, and they kept up a regular correspondence; among other matters they discussed the tactics of the *Revue philosophique*. Parallel to Ribot's overviews of experimental psychology in Britain and Germany, Espinas wrote a survey of experimental philosophy in Italy. The French defeat of 1870 and the Parisian Commune led Espinas to the study of society, and in particular to the question of whether there are laws of societal development that would allow for predictions.[13] Based largely on the work of Spencer, whose evolutionary theory he accepted while rejecting his political stance, Espinas wrote his doctoral dissertation on animal societies. Its critical point was the distinction between two forms of social cohesion or "solidarity": organic cohesion characteristic of lower organisms and more conscious forms of cohesion made possible by the use of signs and intelligence. Advanced animal societies were characterized by more conscious modes of cohesion, by a "collective consciousness" and more voluntary forms of "solidarity."[14] Contrary to individualist presumptions about competition and metaphors about the war of all against all, social solidarity was nothing but the continuation of the solidarity found in the animal kingdom. Sociology, according to Espinas, could only become a positive science by starting from what biologists know about organisms and their evolution and by conceiving the new science as an "enlargement" of biology. In the long introduction to his dissertation, he traced the history of this naturalist view, opposing it to the artificialist conception, according to which human societies are the product of an original contract. Espinas's PhD thesis, defended in 1877, became a notorious cause not only because it was the first doctoral dissertation in sociology but also because the spiritualist members of the jury found the discussion of Auguste Comte in the introduction inadmissibly heretic. Refusing to eliminate the offensive passages, Espinas removed the entire introduction and published it only in the second edition.

In the first decade of its existence, the *Revue philosophique* published articles about sociology by mainly three authors: Spencer, Espinas, and Fouillée. The journal also published review essays and numerous book reviews, which are particularly telling because they reveal how younger philosophers defined what in their view was the legitimate way of practicing sociology. The publications of the three main sociological contributors were extensively and favorably reviewed, the evolutionary organicist work of Spencer and Espinas as well as the attempts by Fouillée to combine positive social science with idealist philosophy. Espinas's doctoral thesis, for example, was twice reviewed by Ribot, both the first and the second edition, and lauded for its "very good method" and "scientific spirit."

Alfred Fouillée, another young philosophy *agrégé*, won two prizes of the Academy of Moral and Political Sciences, wrote his dissertation on *Liberty and Determinism* (1872), and taught briefly at the École normale supérieure. Applying an eclectic method of reconciling opposites, he used his capacity for "integral synthesis" to bridge the gap between spiritualist philosophy and Spencerian sociology. Central to his work was the notion of *idée-force*, which captured the causal role of ideas in social life and formed the core of his notion of societies as "contractual organisms," that is, units in which causality and teleology were joined in a higher order.[15] Instead of rejecting the positive sciences and their naturalist assumptions, Fouillée argued that it was possible to accept their results without having to give up the most cherished articles of philosophic idealism. In *La science sociale contemporaine* (1880) he proclaimed that the constitution of the social sciences was the primary task of the century. Every philosophical and moral question was a social question as well, and philosophers should help to understand how the tensions this produced between liberty and determinism and between contractual and organic relations could be overcome by the concept of a "contractual organism," of which "consciousness" or "will" was the very center.[16]

Other sociological publications than the ones by Spencer, Espinas, and Fouillée, however, failed to meet the standards of the *Revue philosophique*. Guarin de Vitry and Roberty, both contributors to Littré's positivist journal, were judged to work in an a priori manner contrary to the scientific method. The book series by Paul von Lilienfeld, *Gedanken über die Sozialwissenschaft der Zukunft* (1873–81), was considered to be "deprived of any originality." Charles Letourneau's *La sociologie d'après l'ethnographie* (1880) was found to be unoriginal and superficial, to which Ribot in a private letter added: "bad collection of facts, uncritical, and without general ideas."[17] The publicist Gustave Le Bon was judged to be a *touche-à-tout* and little more than an opinioned "popularizer." The retired engineer Léopold Bresson, author of *Idées modernes: Cosmologie, sociologie* (1880) and *Études de sociologie* (1888), suffered a similar fate: he was also qualified as a "popularizer," albeit an "honest" one.[18]

The reviews, articles, and books of the small group of collaborators of the *Revue philosophique* had a threefold effect on the reputation of sociology. First, it transformed sociology from a stigmatized extra-academic endeavor associated with followers of Comte into a worthy subject of reflection for university philosophers. This was brought about largely by a sort of Spencer effect, since it was by and large the outcome of translating, discussing, and applying the work of Spencer, who left all other sociologists far behind. Second, a distinction was established between this academically legitimate form of sociology and merely popular or wholly "unscientific" enterprises. By disqualifying most of the early sociological publications as either "unoriginal" or not properly scientific, the *Revue philosophique* separated a small body of legitimate scholarly work from vulgarization and worse. This demarcation typically coincided with the boundaries of the Faculty of Letters. Espinas, Fouillée, and several other reviewers were professional philosophers with positions in secondary and higher education, whereas the critically reviewed authors were not and found themselves disqualified as amateurs, even if they may have had a thorough training in other fields. Philosophers claimed a monopoly on defining the legitimate forms of sociology, a claim that proved to be remarkably successful in comparison with the competing claim of legal scholars at the Faculty of Law. Third, some of these philosophers, Fouillée in particular, enhanced sociology's emerging legitimacy by reconciling it with the legacy of spiritualist philosophy. That effort contributed to a change in the attitude of the official Academy of Moral and Political Sciences as well.

The Academy had for decades not merely ignored Comte and his conception of sociology, but it also actively combated the various forms of naturalism, positivism, and materialism that had spread after 1848. True to that tradition, Elme Caro characterized Ribot's doctoral dissertation as a "600-page provocation," while dismissing Espinas's work on animal societies as mere zoology.[19] By then, however, the balance of power between the spiritualist elite in the Academy and the younger generation of philosophers was already changing in favor of the latter. Indicative of this change, Spencer's *First Principles* (1863) was appreciated by certain spiritualist philosophers for its metaphysical qualities.[20] Spencer's oeuvre, which was rapidly translated into French during the 1870s, had considerable impact in a wide range of disciplines and could no longer be ignored, and Spencer couldn't be suspected of any socialist sympathies. Fouillée, furthermore, was appreciated by the academic establishment, and his plea for reconciling philosophical idealism and social science won the support of more liberal academicians, who were prepared to reconsider their hostility to sociology.[21]

Around the time Espinas defended his controversial doctoral dissertation, the academicians discussed a proposal for the Bordin prize contest of the Academy. The indomitable question proposed was officially adopted in 1879, but for unknown reasons withdrawn: "Examine and discuss the systems that from the eighteenth century up to the present have denied or limited in the extreme human freedom and the role of the individual in history."[22] A few years later, in 1883, the Academy reformulated the question and finalized the contest. The Bordin prize that year would go to a manuscript that critically examined "the principles and foundations of the theories that are nowadays designated under the name of sociology." In a brief explanation, it was asked whether these theories contained anything new as compared with "social morals, natural law, political science, and political economy? Do they contain elements that may be considered well established and that can be integrated in the science of philosophy?"[23]

Only a few years later, when the prize contest was renewed, did the Academy finally receive a manuscript. It was written by a pastor from Geneva, Louis Wuarin, who would teach the first sociology course in Switzerland. Wuarin discussed two sociological schools, one descending from Comte, the other from Spencer. Although sociology had been born out of the erroneous belief that a natural science of society was possible, Wuarin wrote that the discipline had an object of its own, human society, and a program that several scholars had started to execute. There was no longer any reason to denigrate the new science, although its extreme ideas and exaggerations had to be combated, and the influence of reason and ideals in social life more clearly acknowledged.[24] Wuarin was awarded the prize, so by 1885 the Academy of Moral and Political Sciences had given up its outright rejection of sociology.

On the other side of the divide, among groups outside higher education, sociology's emerging recognition was met with skepticism and resentment. Orthodox positivists noted that Espinas's dissertation was the first university study that paid satisfactory tribute to Comte, but did not fail to note that Herbert Spencer was treated as the most significant sociologist.[25] The more general process of discipline formation, however, provoked a stern rejection. When the editors of *La philosophie positive* were forced to suspend their publication in 1883, this attested to the declining interest in precisely the kind of "general ideas" they wanted to promote. And they observed: "We are disappearing, then, in the face of a general indifference to general questions. Writers and readers are busy with quite different things, which have little to do with great scientific syntheses."[26] With the growth and differentiation of the university system, more specialized research and disciplinary affiliations were acquiring greater weight—diminishing that of the grand doctrines and worldviews, which had dominated the intellectual field for the major part of the nineteenth century.

An Emerging Subfield

While sociological publications expanded substantially during the 1880s and 1890s, philosophy remained the primary context for university publications and academic debate. The *Revue philosophique* continued to publish articles by Espinas and Fouillée, as well as by several foreign sociologists, most notably Spencer. They were gradually joined by a widening circle of aspiring sociologists, including Gabriel Tarde, Jean-Marie Guyau, Émile Durkheim, and Gaston Richard.[27] The ongoing growth of university positions and scholarly publications eventually led to a further differentiation. Young philosophers created a second periodical, the *Revue de métaphysique et de morale* (1893), which included a special review section for sociology.[28] During the next decade, when two psychology and two sociology journals were established, both disciplines acquired a larger degree of autonomy and a dynamics of their own. Internal competition became more prevalent and the major sociologists all attempted to stake out a position within the newly emerging subfield.

The subfield of sociology, which included actors related to both the Faculty of Letters and the Faculty of Law, has been described as a ménage à trois consisting of the prolific outsider Gabriel Tarde, the omnipresent organizer René Worms, and the more scholarly and rigorous Émile Durkheim.[29] Belonging to different generations and pursuing diverging strategies, their work marked the contours of the emerging subfield of sociology from the 1880s until the outbreak of the First World War. All three typically published sociological monographs as well as programmatic statements about the discipline, its methodology and its relationship to other sciences. Tarde advocated a psychologically oriented form of sociology focused on "intermental" processes. Belonging to the generation of Espinas, he had studied law, didn't have a doctorate, and was a provincial magistrate, not a professional philosopher; he only started publishing in the *Revue philosophique* after unsuccessful attempts at publishing his first books. Durkheim and Worms were, respectively, fifteen and twenty-six years younger. Durkheim, trained as a philosopher at the École normale, was selected to teach the first university course in sociology in 1887, although it was not officially called sociology. His efforts developed into a vast research enterprise, but by the time Durkheim had published his first books and was considering creating a journal, the younger René Worms had already founded a sociological journal of his own and two professional associations. Trained in both law and philosophy, Worms owed his position primarily to his work as an academic entrepreneur who created an international infrastructure for the discipline. Since Tarde joined Worms's organizations, university sociology was primarily shaped by the competition between the networks of Worms and Durkheim. Older sociologists (Espinas, Fouillée) joined Worms's organizations; members of the younger generation were more attracted to Durkheim's enterprise.[30]

From Psychology to Sociology

Descended from a family of provincial nobles in a small town in the Dordogne, Gabriel Tarde received a classical education at the local Jesuit college.

Like his father, who died when he was seven years old, he studied law, became a magistrate, and for the major part of his career lived the life a provincial notable, far removed from the effervescence of the capital. He married the daughter of a local magistrate, tried his hand at writing philosophical texts, and participated in the social life of the region, among others things by writing comedies and vaudeville acts. Tarde's work developed in opposition to the naturalist schools, which highlighted biological and physical factors in understanding social life. At the root of this opposition was a long-standing interest in mental phenomena. As a young man Tarde had known prolonged periods of forced introspection due to temporary blindness caused by an eye illness. Like the philosopher Maine de Biran, one of his favorite authors, he kept a diary in which he commented on his interior life and the working of the mind. The new psychological literature of the 1860s and 1870s enhanced Tarde's interest in psychology and led him to focus on the intermental phenomenon of imitation, on which he built his entire sociology.

Tarde's first publications were general psychological essays about the role of "belief and desire" in inner life and human behavior. Critically discussing physiological accounts, he simultaneously raised questions about the analogies between individual and collective psychology.[31] When "social science" was becoming a topic in the *Revue philosophique*, Tarde's interest shifted to questions of criminology and sociology. His work on crime was related to his professional expertise, while his first articles on "social science" continued his psychological interests. In these studies Tarde identified "imitation" as the most elementary and characteristic fact of social life. He considered it a state of mind comparable to "suggestion" and "hypnosis," topics that were attracting considerable attention. A social group could be defined as a collection of individuals who "imitate one another" and who—beyond actual imitation—look alike, because their common characteristics are the result of earlier mimetic behavior. Unconcerned with the empirical grounding of this idea, Tarde's earlier texts boldly assert that "society is imitation."[32] Everything in social phenomena "that is not vital or physical, in its similarities as well as in its differences, has imitation as its cause."[33] Based on this principle, he erected a system of thought he exposed in his classic *Les lois de l'imitation* (1890), which was his bid for a "pure and general" sociology. In subsequent books he extended, refined, and popularized the idea, spelled out its metaphysical consequences in *L'opposition universelle* (1897), and illustrated it for multiple social domains (art, law, politics, power, the economy).

The Tardean approach of an "interpsychological" sociology was based on the transposition of psychological ideas about "suggestion" to the realm of social relations, thereby challenging naturalist approaches as well as juridical and economic assumptions about the rationality of human behavior. This transposition was accompanied and justified by an epistemological argument. Following the philosopher and scientist Antoine Cournot, to whom *Les lois de l'imitation* was dedicated, Tarde held that science studies patterns of phenomenal repetition. For sociology to become a science, then, it had to define a central principle of repetition, which would be the equivalent in the domain of social relations of "heredity" in biology and "ondulation" in the physical sciences. Imitation, according to Tarde, was precisely that principle. Following this argument, Tarde broke not only with evolutionary and organicist theories but also with the Comtean conception, which Littré had tried to revive and in which human society is conceived as a relatively autonomous and particularly complex order. Contrary to this "positivist prejudice," Tarde held that societies are far more transparent than Comte and his followers assumed, and are in reality "far less complex than organisms."[34] The pattern of inventions that are subsequently imitated is a relatively simple social mechanism—a "key that opens all locks," as Tarde liked to say.

Although written by a magistrate from a small town in southern France, *Les lois de l'imitation* (1890) was widely reviewed and discussed. Recognized as a fresh approach to sociology, Tarde quickly gained the reputation of an original thinker. Adopting the style of the philosophical essay, his prose was vivid and accessible, unburdened by extensive footnotes, scholarly digressions, and tedious research details. In 1894 he was offered a position as the head of the statistical bureau of the Ministry of Justice and moved to Paris. Although he never held a university position, he became a well-known lecturer at private institutions and was often described as a "charming causeur," although his reputation in university circles was less secure.[35] In 1900 he was elected to the chair of modern philosophy at the Collège de France and became a member of the Academy of Moral and Political Sciences.

During his lifetime Tarde was undoubtedly the best-known sociologist in France. His *Lois de l'imitation* (1890) brought him a reputation well beyond academic circles, and when he moved to Paris he became a well-known public figure as well. From the publication of Durkheim's dissertation on the *Division of Labor* (1893), which Tarde reviewed, until Tarde's death in 1904, Durkheim and Tarde kept up a pungent exchange. Tarde fundamentally objected to Durkheim's "social realism," which he qualified as "metaphysics": social life consists merely of individual actions and interactions.[36] Durkheim criticized not only Tarde's psychological mode of explanation, but he also rejected the simplicity of his explanatory scheme and was severe about its lack of empirical grounding. With the exception of his more empirical work in criminology, the Durkheimians generally considered Tarde a "clever writer" but not much of a scholar. His

essayistic style was considered inappropriate and his work was at best perceived as "half-literary" and "only semi-scientific," as Lucien Lévy-Bruhl
remarked.[37]

Organizing a Science of Synthesis

About a decade younger than Émile Durkheim, René Worms's presence
nonetheless preceded much of Durkheim's most significant work. In a surprisingly short time span, Worms established a set of international organizations for sociology that included a journal, the *Revue internationale de
sociologie* (1893), an international association, the Institut international de
sociologie (1893), and a book series, the Bibliothèque des sciences sociales
(1894). These accomplishments were all the more noteworthy because their
creator was only in his mid-twenties. The son of a professor of law and
political economy who had withdrawn from his chair in 1882 to dedicate
himself to the upbringing of his son, the precocious René Worms obtained
the highest degrees in three disciplines: philosophy, law, and political economy.[38] For a while he taught philosophy in secondary schools, political
economy in the Law Faculty, and lectured at private schools in Paris and
Brussels. But Worms characteristically refrained from a university career,
apparently because he lacked the discipline to devote himself to a specific
academic domain and because he was uninterested in specialized research.
Instead of taking up a university position, he was for over three decades a
senior civil servant and a member of the prestigious national state council,
the Conseil d'État.[39]

Neither a particularly original theorist nor a researcher, Worms became
a prodigious organizer. As an institution builder and administrator, he
bridged the gaps between disciplines, faculties, and nations, and built an
extensive network of people who were all somehow interested in sociology
or who were at least willing to support his enterprise. François Simiand
later recalled that Worms was an ambitious man who "could do anything"
and "always wanted to start something."[40] After their first meeting, Tarde
described him in his diary as an "omnivorous and ambitious agitator."[41]
Worms's written production corresponds to the profile of a tireless organizer. He wrote easily, had a pedagogical more than a scholarly style, and
besides a continuous flow of overviews and textbooks, typically published
general treatises like *Organisme et société* (1896) and a three-volume
Philosophie des sciences sociales (1903–7). Uninterested in doing or even
organizing empirical research, his work was to coordinate, institutionalize,
and administer across the boundaries of academic disciplines and faculties.
To Worms sociology was a broad, synthetic science rather than a discipline,

an "essentially generalizing" endeavor, which should not be confused with detailed investigations.[42] The articles his journal published fit this conception: they were either general and theoretical studies or informative reports about the international sociological movement.[43]

Worms's strategy was to gain support for sociology by associating eminent personalities from a broad range of disciplines. The *Revue internationale de sociologie* (1893) was presented as a general scientific enterprise, academic and impartial, not be confounded with either political partisanship or attempts at finding solutions for social problems. Because of its general character and uncompromising scope, the journal was open to "all sciences" and "all schools" of thought.[44] Worms engaged a large and heterogeneous group of people whose names and positions were mentioned on the cover of his journal. Nearly all were distinguished figures, but more often professors of law and political economy than professors at the Faculty of Letters. Within this heterogeneous group, there were virtually no younger scholars and only a few were sociologists proper. In addition to academic authorities, Worms was eager to attract men of distinction from other walks of life. Among the forty-one associated editors of the first issue, eight were (former) senators, ministers, or members of parliament. A large proportion of the French members of his international association were likewise nonacademics: judges, senior civil servants, members of the liberal professions. At a time of increasing specialization and academic professionalization, Worms's organizations in a way continued the tradition of learned societies of gentlemen amateurs.

Since the associated editorship was a honorific position, the actual content of the journal was the work of a much smaller and far less international group. Nearly two-thirds of the contributors were French and the most productive authors were nearly all based in Paris, being either French scholars or Francophone Russians.[45] Of the fourteen most frequent contributors, five were sociologists proper, that is, authors who presented a significant part of their work as sociological (Espinas, Tarde, Worms, Duprat, Bernès).[46] Four were well-known representatives of other disciplines: a judge and publicist (Raoul de la Grasserie), a member of the group of physical anthropologists (Letourneau), and two historians (Hauser, Levasseur). Five others were foreigners—with the exception of the Finnish anthropologist Westermarck, all of them Russians temporarily living in France (Kovalewski, Novikow, Roberty, Lilienfeld). Although Worms's *Revue internationale de sociologie* was the first sociology journal, its actual significance was limited. It went against the tendency toward disciplinary specialization, was largely dissociated from empirical research, and its international position was rapidly overshadowed by the creation of national sociology journals in Britain, Germany, and the United States. In his home country, Worms's journal suffered from the appearance of Durkheim's *Année sociologique* (1898), whereas outside of France it appealed more to sociologists in the periphery, who were deprived of their own national journal, than to sociologists from the leading national sociological communities.

The Institut international de sociologie (1893) was in all likelihood a more successful undertaking than Worms's journal. In the years up to the First World War nearly all the major sociologists became either a regular or—like Max Weber—an associated member. The Durkheimians were the only major exception. Among the presidents and vice presidents, for example, were Espinas, Fouillée, Giddings, Gumplowicz, Lilienfeld, Schäffle, Simmel, Small, Tarde, Tönnies, Veblen, and Ward. They shared their board membership with scholars from other social and human sciences, in particular law and political economy. Although the members were concentrated in Europe and sociologists from the United States were underrepresented, both the composition of the executive board and the membership of the association were far more international than the contributors to Worms's journal.[47] Prior to the First World War eight international conferences were held, where commonly fifteen to twenty-five papers were presented for an audience that included between twenty and forty members and a much larger number of outside participants.[48] The international conferences allowed scholars to share information, exchange ideas, and establish personal connections across national borders. Because the conferences were public events, covered by the press and attended by up to a few hundred interested listeners, they also generated publicity for the new discipline and contributed to the spread of sociological ideas well beyond the discipline.

International conferences often resembled a diplomatic setting: they were occasions for polite encounters but had limited significance for actual collaboration. One of the members of the International Institute, Casimir de Kelles-Kraut, observed that participants commonly presented their own individual work but did not work together.[49] Comparing the international conferences with the meetings of the newly founded German sociological society, Robert Michels observed a striking contrast. The German gathering was typically a "working conference," an *Arbeitskongress*, deprived of an official address and without the participation of public officials; the representative of the mayor of Berlin had even been asked to refrain from taking the stand. There were, furthermore, no official greetings, "no party, no reception, no banquet, no excursion. Nothing, nothing but concentrated and absorbing work."[50] Although Worms's international conferences followed the more diplomatic model, many had a central theme, which allowed for discussion and debate. The papers published in the proceedings contain strongly diverging views.[51] A notorious case was the 1897 conference on organicist thought; it opposed proponents like Novikow and Worms to a considerable group of critics, with Tarde as their most articulate spokesman. Worms himself, partly on the basis of Tarde's criticisms, eventually revised his views and moved away from his organicist view of societies toward a more eclectic stance.

One of the most tangible results of the international conferences was, paradoxically, that they stimulated the founding of national sociological societies. Within a decade after the founding of the International Institute, national sociological associations appeared in seven countries.[52] The Société de sociologie de Paris (1895) was the Parisian branch, with Tarde as its first president and monthly meetings that were attended by up to two hundred people. Membership eventually went up to more than three hundred persons, most of them nonacademics who, according to some observers, brought the discussions down to an "abysmally low level."[53]

The Durkheimian Program

Among the major sociologists at the end of the nineteenth century, Émile Durkheim was the challenger. Early on he proposed a sociological program of his own and his postdoctoral work evolved in systematic opposition to the existing approaches. Born in 1858, Durkheim was raised in a traditional Jewish family from Alsace-Lorraine in the eastern part of the country.[54] His father was a rabbi, just like his grandfather and great-grandfather, and Émile was probably destined for the rabbinate himself. His school success gave his life different turn. An outstanding student, he passed his secondary school exams in Letters (1874) and Sciences (1875) and left his native Épinal to prepare for admission to the École normale supérieure. His years of study in Paris coincided with the conflict-ridden first period of republican reforms, the launching of numerous scholarly journals, and the first wave of publications in new disciplines like experimental psychology and sociology.

Although his Parisian years of study were difficult, socially as well as intellectually (he failed the entrance exam of the École normale twice), once admitted to the École Durkheim enjoyed the school's intense intellectual life. Becoming a lifelong friend of the future socialist leader Jean Jaurès, he was a staunch supporter of the anticlerical reforms and the establishment of a national system of secular education. Among his teachers, he most admired the philosopher Émile Boutroux and the historian Fustel de Coulanges, to whom he dedicated one of his books. In their own way, they embodied the scholarly rigor to which Durkheim was much attached. Like several of his fellow students, he was also taken by the work of Charles Renouvier, who was an influential outsider trained in the sciences and a central figure in redirecting philosophical reflection toward questions of science, republican politics, and secular morality.[55]

After passing the *agrégation* exam in 1882, Durkheim followed the usual path of teaching philosophy in secondary schools in the provinces. At about the same time, he started working on his doctorate, which was related to fiercely debated political and social questions of the early Third Republic. It started out as a study of the relations between "individualism and socialism," which was reformulated as the relationship between "individual personality and social solidarity." The question figured prominently on the philosophical agenda and led Durkheim to a vast literature on the division of labor in disciplines ranging from biology and political economy to history, anthropology, and sociology. After studying in Germany for a year and having published his first articles and reviews, the twenty-nine-year-old student was selected to teach the first sociology course in the country, although the word "sociology" was prudently avoided in the official title of the course, "social science and pedagogy." In the same year he married Louise Dreyfus, daughter of a Parisian entrepreneur, and moved to Bordeaux, where he was welcomed by Espinas, who was dean of the Faculty of Letters. He would stay there for fifteen years until he returned to Paris in 1902.

In his opening lecture and in a more dispersed manner in his early review essays, Durkheim outlined a distinctive sociological program. Various aspects of it were not yet worked out, but the direction he indicated was unambiguous and consistent. It may be summarized by three closely related points.[56] First, social science was to be strictly independent from philosophy and had to be founded on the search for laws and law-like regularities. This principle of "determinism" had been extended to the study of societies by political economists and a host of other social scientists from Saint-Simon and Comte to Spencer and Schäffle. Here Durkheim sided with the proponents of the "experimental" or "positive sciences," as they were called, not only against advocates of the "moral sciences" but also against those who, like Fouillée, sought solutions in a comprise between idealist philosophy and positive science.

Second, sociology was to become not only an uncompromising positive science but also an autonomous and a specific science. Sociology needed to be independent of the physical and the life sciences because its object—human societies—represents a specific, irreducible, and particularly complex level of reality. Instead of conceiving sociology as an enlargement or a continuation of biology, it was necessary, Durkheim argued, to "return to the conception of Comte" and to recognize that sociology should establish its own modes of conceptualization and research.[57] Rejecting the predominant forms of organicism of Spencer and Espinas, Durkheim explicitly adopted the principles of Comte's differential epistemology. He had encountered Comte's work in the courses of his teacher Boutroux and read (parts of) the *Cours de philosophie positive* when still at the École normale.[58] In *De la contingence des lois de la nature* (1874), Boutroux had used Comte's theory of the sciences for his philosophy of contingency. For Boutroux the scientific search for laws does not imply the end of human liberty. Reality is made up of different levels (physical, biological, psychological, sociological) and in the relationships between them there is contingency, not necessity. Biological phenomena cannot be derived from physical or chemical processes: they have their own laws and characteristics. This contingency, furthermore, increases with the level of complexity: the more complex the level, the more contingent the phenomena one encounters. On the basis of this Comtean reasoning, Boutroux concluded that necessity is a concept of logic rather than of science, and that the development of the sciences had confirmed rather than refuted the role of human freedom and moral responsibility.

Durkheim was indifferent to the argument about liberty and necessity; he considered it a metaphysical issue, which the positive sciences "can and should" ignore.[59] But it was undoubtedly through Boutroux that he had become familiar with Comte. As he later recalled: "Boutroux often repeated to us that each science must explain by *its own principles*, as Aristotle put it: psychology by psychological principles, biology by biological principles. Very much impressed by this idea, I applied it to sociology. I was confirmed in this method by reading Comte, since for him sociology is irreducible to biology . . . , just as biology is irreducible to the physico-chemical sciences."[60] Comte's theory of the sciences thus provided Durkheim with an analytical tool to break away from organicist and psychological modes of conceiving sociology and to stake out a position of his own.

Third, Durkheim did not entirely follow a Comtean strategy because he was very critical of another aspect of Comte's work. Although his relation to Comte is often described as ambiguous, Durkheim's position was clear and consistent: he accepted Comte's differential epistemology but rejected his conception of sociology. Comte had looked for a fundamental law of the development of human society. But it is erroneous, Durkheim wrote, to assume that human evolution is everywhere "identical" and that societies are all but "variations" of one and the same type.[61] Comte's law of the three stages, which was the core of his whole sociology, had condemned him to "vague generalities" that wrongly assumed that in the social realm knowledge of the whole has an absolute priority over knowledge of its parts. As much as Durkheim praised Comte for his theory of the sciences, this was Comte's "fundamental error": "These general views of which he speaks are vague representations with which science cannot contend itself. Analysis imposes itself in sociology as elsewhere. These confused syntheses are the beginning of scientific knowledge, not its result. So if one decomposes social phenomena, one will find that they are divided in economic, artistic, intellectual, moral, juridical, and political facts. Each one of these grand classes represents a social function. Each of these functions has its organ."[62]

This criticism of "generalities" and the insistence on decomposing societies into various classes of phenomena, which have to be investigated empirically, was the third ingredient of the Durkheimian program. In his inaugural lecture in Bordeaux he proclaimed that the "era of generalities" was over and that sociology had to be subdivided in well-defined research branches.[63] His early reviews make very much the same point. Durkheim lauded Wundt's concentration on "precise and restricted problems" and his avoidance of "vague generalizations and metaphysical possibilities." He similarly praised the "laborious and patient work" of Schäffle, which was full of "erudition, details, and observations" and lacked the superficial "simplicity" of most French authors. Espinas's work on animal societies was an exception in this regard because it was among the first to have studied a specific class of social facts in order to "construct a science of them rather than to preserve the symmetry of a great philosophical system."[64]

As a consequence of his critical assessment of general theories of society and his insistence on identifying definite problems and specific research areas, Durkheim valued an organicist author like Espinas to the extent that he had contributed to a more precise understanding of a particular question. The social realm escapes biological investigation and is in need of proper sociological explanations, but analogies can be a "precious instrument for scientific research" once they are treated as heuristic tools in well-focused research projects. Rejecting monism as well as physical or biological reductionism, and vigorously defending the autonomy of sociology, Durkheim nonetheless felt free to use certain contributions from organicist theories while rejecting their basic assumption that societies had to be understood as organisms.[65]

Durkheim's early work, then, critically took up the Comtean conception of the sciences and proposed to do what Comte's followers had been incapable and unwilling of doing, namely, to transform it into a viable sociological research program. Durkheim called it a "naturalist" approach in the sense that it adopted the same mental attitude to its object as natural scientists. But he added that it was not naturalist in the sense of "absorbing the social realm into other realms of nature." Quite the contrary: it was the task of sociology to account for the "specificity" and "originality" of its object.[66] The approach was well captured by his famous dictum that social facts need to be explained by other social facts (and not by biological or psychological facts). The consequence of this position was that different orders of facts had to be delineated, that the sociological domain had to be subdivided into well-defined research areas, and that sociologists would have to confront established specialists in each of these areas. Over the years he proposed several ways to accomplish this, encountering the problem most acutely when he started his own journal.

Aside from the need to find a feasible division of sociological labor, two other consequences followed from the program he laid out. One was that the proper construction of sociology was a collective task. The "heroic age" of grand sociological systems was over and progress could only be made by dividing the tasks and coordinating the work in a "collective effort."[67] Although sociology had been an affair of grand personalities, it had to be become a collective, even "impersonal" task.[68] The other consequence, following from his reappraisal of Comte against the predominant forms of organicism, was that sociology was actually more of a "French science" than was generally assumed. The long hostility to Comte in France and the recent favor of British and German scholars had produced amnesia with regard to the French origins of sociology.[69] Because of Comte's centrality for his own program, and later undoubtedly also to counter the attacks of right-wing nationalists, Durkheim more and more presented sociology as an "essentially French science."[70]

Following the program he had laid down, Durkheim taught courses and worked on a series of issues such as the family, crime and punishment, suicide, education, and pedagogy.[71] His first major work was his doctorate on the division of labor, which identified key issues for sociological analysis within a broad-ranging analysis of industrial societies. Having started from the question about the relations between individual personality and social solidarity, Durkheim contrasted two types of society and social solidarity. "Mechanical solidarity" is prevalent in small-scale societies, which are organized in homogenous segments with a high degree of resemblance in social positions. In this case one observes a pervasive "collective consciousness" and a strong collective authority. With population growth and increasing differentiation, "organic solidarity" prevails. Based on the division of labor, it is characterized by another type of regulation and morality. As indicated by juridical norms, sanctions become more restitutive than repressive; cooperative, not penal, law is the dominant mode of juridical regulation; and collective beliefs and sentiments become highly individualized.

In contrast to conservative theorists, Durkheim made it clear that social solidarity is not restricted to traditional, small-scale communities. At the same time, and in opposition to liberal economists, he insisted that the consequence of the division of labor was not simply to increase productivity, but to create a new social and moral order. The division of labor is not restricted to the economy and advanced societies cannot function solely on the basis of the market mechanism. Beyond the appropriate juridical and political arrangements, there are "noncontractual elements in contracts," which represent forms of moral regulation. Such obligatory moral codes are essential in making contracts binding and, more generally, fulfill the function not of suppressing competition, but of moderating it and restraining the unlimited pursuit of self-interest. The rising number of suicides and crimes was therefore indicative not of modern societies per se, but of inadequate social and professional organization and a lack of binding moral rules or "anomie."

Durkheim's study on the social division of labor was a foundational contribution. It outlined an evolutionary transformation of human societies, indicating a basic mechanism of change (population growth and social differentiation) and reconceptualizing several sociological problems (social solidarity, collective consciousness, modes of regulation, anomie). In the course of time, certain aspects of this model were reformulated, but Durkheim stuck to the most basic features of his analysis of social differentiation.[72] Neither Durkheim himself nor his immediate collaborators would systematically take up the issue of societal evolution again, but some version of the evolutionary transformation Durkheim had outlined was a common reference. The interest in ancient societies, for example, which was of central importance in the *Année sociologique*, was directly informed by Durkheim's early work on the division of labor and different types of social integration and moral regulation.[73]

Antagonistic Competition

In the five years between the publication of his well-received doctorate and the founding of the *Année sociologique* (1898), Durkheim accelerated and intensified his work. In the short time span between 1893 and 1895, the young René Worms had launched the first sociology journal and founded an international and a French sociological association. The sociological landscape suddenly looked quite different. Since Durkheim considered Worms to be a person with little scientific credit and the "reputation of a joker," as he said in a private letter, he did not want to compromise himself by collaborating with Worms's journal.[74] The proliferation of sociological essays and books more generally upset Durkheim. Much of what was suddenly presented as sociology was premature at best and instead of contributing to the new discipline risked discrediting it. The only way forward was not to show any complaisance for these "improvised sociologists" who "compromise a science that is all too easily compromised."[75] Durkheim thus chose to focus on an accelerated and systematic elaboration of his own program in explicit opposition to others. Engaged in this dynamic of antagonistic competition he sharpened his views, refocused his own research program, and opposed what he saw as a rigorous and truly scientific sociology not only to his direct competitors but also to the growing number of "amateurs" and "dilettantes."

The polarization of sociological perspectives that ensued was accompanied by diverging methods of responding to public demand. Worms used the popular interest in sociology to build up his organizations; Durkheim did the opposite: he founded a rather austere scholarly journal, which was ostensibly of no immediate interest to the fashionable themes of the day.[76] Only after the first volume of the *Année sociologique* had been published did Durkheim return to more diplomatic tactics. The publication of his article "Individual and Collective Representations" (1898), for example, was an attempt to pacify offended philosophers (social life is characterized by a "hyperspirituality") and those who preferred psychology to sociology (sociology is described as "a psychology, but a psychology sui generis").[77]

The characteristic first step in this process of antagonistic competition was the series of articles that led to *The Rules of Sociological Method* (1895). The *Rules* is a kind of demarcation manifesto. If sociology is to become a science, Durkheim stated, it is not enough to separate it from philosophy and other forms of intellectual speculation; its method has to be specified. With the single exception of a chapter written by Comte, this had never been done. The neglect was understandable because the great sociologists had hardly gone beyond "generalities" about the nature of human societies, the relations between sociology and other sciences, and the "general march of progress."[78] This judgment about his predecessors was far more polemical than earlier, more nuanced statements. Pursuing his attempt to define a rigorous sociology, Durkheim first delineated the object of sociology: social facts form a reality sui generis, to be distinguished from the realms of biology and psychology. Social facts can be defined as being capable of exercising an "external constraint" over the individual. Studying social facts scientifically means that they have to be "treated as things," that is, as an objective reality to be observed and investigated without any "prenotions." Observing social facts can lead to establishing various orders of facts or "types," which are to be explained either causally or functionally. Facts that are generally considered reprehensible, like a certain level of crime, can sociologically be considered "normal"; only when the aggregate level is above a certain average can they be treated as "pathological."

Shortly after having laid down these "rules," he exemplified the approach in *Le suicide* (1897), which is written in the same incisive style as the *Rules*. Durkheim first proposes an "objective definition" to prevent "arbitrary exclusions" and "deceptive comparisons." Instead of focusing on the individual act of ending one's life or on the moral questions associated with it, Durkheim presents suicide rates as the proper object for a sociological study. On the basis of extensive statistical documentation—Marcel Mauss classified more than twenty-five thousand individual cases of suicide for his uncle's study—Durkheim first identifies various nonsocial causes. By closely comparing suicide rates across different groups and societies, he demonstrates that race, heredity, and climate all have insignificant or unproven effects. Physical factors like climate and temperature do correlate with levels of suicide, but these are in reality causally related to a social factor, namely, the intensity of social interactions. A special chapter of his critical examination is dedicated to "imitation," which, Durkheim argues, has no appreciable effect on suicide rates and merely reinforces other, more important social factors. The idea of imitation, he concludes, has never been demonstrated empirically for "any order of social facts." It has been enough to "state the idea in the form of an aphorism, resting on vague metaphysical notions." And he adds: "sociology cannot claim to be considered a science until those who practice it are no longer allowed to propagate this sort of dogma while so manifestly evading the normal obligation to provide proof of what they say."[79]

After having eliminated nonsocial factors, Durkheim presents his own analysis. The main explanatory factor is the degree of social integration. "Egoistic suicide" occurs when the integration of the group is weak. Because the Catholic Church, for example, is a more strongly integrated community than Protestant churches, Catholics have a lower chance of committing suicide than Protestants. The same applies to domestic groups. Marriage and the presence of children in a family are factors that enhance social integration and protect against suicide. The opposite form of "altruistic suicide" occurs when social groups are so tightly integrated that individual self-destruction can be an honorable and even obligatory act, as in military groups after a defeat. Aside from these opposite types, Durkheim distinguishes "anomic suicide," which is related to modes of regulation rather than to the degree of integration, and which occurs in periods of temporary instability and disruption, or when a more chronic lack of regulation occurs, as was the case in France at the end of the nineteenth century.[80] In the final part Durkheim addresses some of the implications of his study. The "abnormal rise" in voluntary deaths indicates a collective suffering and malaise for which neither the family nor local communities or the state can offer a solution. More people could attach themselves to ends that effectively transcend them by participating in professional groups. In the preface to the second edition of *The Division of Labor* he elaborated this idea of strengthening professional corporations as a remedy for anomie.

Le suicide was not instantly recognized as a classic, quite the contrary. Its reception was mixed at best and Durkheim himself was "profoundly discouraged."[81] While preparing the launch of his own journal, he had hoped that his monograph would produce a better understanding of his position and take away the reservations that had been expressed about the *Rules*. But that was not the case. Publishing the book was like the "stroke of a sword in the water," as he wrote to Mauss, it did not change anything.[82] There were some benevolent reviews, but even several of his future collaborators were critical, including Gaston Richard in the review he published in the first volume of Durkheim's own *Année sociologique*.[83] It took a long time before the reputation of the book changed and it would become a classic. In comparison with his other books, *Le suicide* remained "misrecognized" and "even forgotten" for about half a century, both in France and abroad; the English translation appeared only in 1951.[84]

The objections against the book stemmed partly from the way Durkheim presented certain arguments. Entangled in a process of intense competition and driven by the will to rigorously distinguish his own position from that of his competitors, Durkheim no doubt overstated certain aspects of his approach. The radical demarcation of sociology from psychology, which was the most controversial issue, was directly linked to his rivalry with Tarde. It was not only criticized by many reviewers, but it would also deprive Durkheim of certain questions and research procedures that could have otherwise proved fruitful. Durkheim and his collaborators were very suspicious, for example, about survey research because it collected individual opinions instead of studying collective representations.[85]

Durkheim's desire to establish a rigorous empirical science and to keep amateurs at a distance also led him to draw a much more strict line between science and normative commitments. He did not expect his program to attract a numerous clientele, he wrote in the *Rules*, but this was not his goal anyway: "We believe, on the contrary, that the time has come for sociology to renounce worldly successes, so to speak, and take on the esoteric character which befits all science. Thus it will gain in dignity and authority what it will perhaps lose in popularity."[86] This seems a far cry from his contention only two years earlier that sociology was not worth an hour's trouble if it had merely speculative interest.[87] And it does not correspond with Durkheim's active role during and after the Dreyfus Affair either. From 1898 onward, Durkheim continued to separate scientific work from political commitments, but only to reconnect them in certain ways. If social scientists participate in political life like other citizens, they would merely elaborate "common ideas" without much originality and without profiting from their specific competence. Sociologists should therefore base their public role on their knowledge of particular questions. Refusing party politics as well as academic retreat, Durkheim's manifold public activities and interventions testify to his conception of what would much later be called the "specific" intellectual.[88] His involvement in the Dreyfus Affair, for example, not only implied numerous practical activities (like setting up the Ligue des droits de l'homme, of which he was the secretary, in Bordeaux), but he also wrote an important essay on "individualism and intellectuals" as a reply to Brunetière's assault. Attacking the "individualism" of the intellectuals, Brunetière had defended the competence of the military leadership and refused to grant "intellectuals" any authority. Beyond the factual evidence, Durkheim argued, defending Dreyfus is indeed an expression of "individualism," not the individualism of the utilitarians but the individualism in which the human individual represents the highest moral value. Not only does this moral individualism not lead to anarchy, as Brunetière suggested, but it is also the only belief system capable of assuring the "moral unity" of the country. With an advanced division of labor, all that is left for human beings to collectively honor and love is the human individual itself.[89]

The *Année sociologique*

Convinced that constructing sociology was a collective task, Durkheim's refusal to collaborate with Worms implied that he would have to seek other forms of collaboration. After the *Rules* and while still working on *Le suicide*, he corresponded with several philosophy students who had obtained their *agrégation* and were interested in sociology. In the course of these exchanges, especially with Célestin Bouglé, who had returned from Germany, Durkheim decided to start his own journal.[90] Following the examples of the review section "L'année sociologique" in the *Revue de métaphysique et de morale* (1893) and a review journal like the *Année psychologique* (1895), the new journal would be a bibliographical yearbook containing a few articles, but mostly critical reviews of significant publications in other scholarly fields. This formula was chosen "to fight the still widespread conception according to which sociology is a branch of philosophy, treating questions only in their most general aspects and tackling them without any special competence."[91]

From his correspondence it is quite clear that neither Durkheim nor anyone else had the intention of founding a "school" in the sense of a group united around a definite theoretical program. Given the critical reception of his own work by several of his future collaborators—Bouglé, Lapie, as well as Simiand—Durkheim could have hardly expected to recruit devoted followers. What he did want to engage were well-qualified "workers," *travailleurs*, as he liked to say, who were prepared to participate in the collective enterprise of reviewing the scholarly literature in a certain area in order, so to speak, to build up sociology from below. One of the implications of this undertaking was that Durkheim recruited young scholars at the beginning of their career who were prepared to execute the not very gratifying task of review writing. In contrast with Worms, Durkheim's collaborators were promising students rather than distinguished professors. When the first issue of the *Année sociologique* appeared (1898), Durkheim was forty years old, Gaston Richard two years younger, and all others were in their twenties. Over the years very few of them ended their collaboration, and they were joined by a steadily increasing group of talented youngsters. As a consequence, the average age of collaborators remained relatively low: thirty-one years for the first volume (1898), thirty-six for the twelfth and last volume (1913).

The first principle that seems to have attracted Durkheim's collaborators and created a certain unity among them was the striving for scholarly excellence, intended to counter the popular sociology of the day. Sociology, Durkheim wrote to Bouglé, has been compromised by "charlatans" who have exploited its premature fashionableness: "It is important to separate ourselves from those who are a discredit to sociology, so as to shield it from well-founded arguments in the attacks it will undergo."[92] Given the educational qualifications of Durkheim's coworkers, scholarly distinction must have been a common ambition and a shared expectation. The core group consisted of philosophers from the École normale (Durkheim, Richard, Bouglé, Simiand, Halbwachs) and the academic standing of the larger group is well illustrated by the fact that the nineteen most frequent collaborators were all, except one, *agrégé*, fourteen of them having an *agrégation* in philosophy.[93] The *Année sociologique* was the work of the younger members of the academic elite of the Faculty of Letters, primarily philosophers, but including a small number of historians, linguists, and legal scholars.

This academic profile contrasts with that of competing networks. The members of the Le Play movement, who were often Catholic notables, had few connections to the public universities. René Worms's organizations had a more academic recruitment, but its academic members came predominantly from the Faculty of Law; very few of them had a position in the Faculty of Letters, and Worms's network included a sizeable group of nonacademic publicists as well.[94] In addition to the generational differences mentioned above, the rivalry between the networks of Durkheim and Worms thus had an institutional basis in the strained relationships between the more intellectual Faculty of Letters and the more professionally oriented Faculty of Law.

A second principle about which Durkheim was eager to establish some degree of agreement among his coworkers was the recognition of what he called the "specificity of social facts." Sociology, he repeatedly explained in exchanges with future collaborators, could not be derived from biology or individual psychology, it had to be practiced "sociologically."[95] The principle of doing sociology sociologically obviously distinguished Durkheim from his main rivals Worms and Tarde, but for his collaborators this demarcation was far from unproblematic. Bouglé and Lapie were interested in psychology and had a far more favorable opinion of Tarde than Durkheim did. In the process of founding the journal, Durkheim seems to have at least neutralized some of their reservations, among other ways by reformulating his position ("in sociology I see only a psychology, but a psychology sui generis").

A largely unanticipated third factor of group integration, finally, was neither doctrinal agreement nor the veneration of Durkheim, but the political conjuncture of the Dreyfus Affair. Virtually all of Durkheim's collaborators were active Dreyfusards and were implicated in the numerous civic and political activities that sprang up in its aftermath: the people's universities, the journal Notes critiques—sciences sociales (1900–1906), the socialist newspaper L'humanité (1904).[96]

The coherence of the group around Durkheim was based on objective features that distinguished it from other groups, but it was also the outcome of the interactions and the work that was done together. The Année sociologique was not a review journal in the conventional sense. It is not our aim, Durkheim wrote to Mauss, to "distribute praise and blame, good and bad points."[97] The central task was to extract sociological insights from the most advanced scholarship in other disciplines, in "the history of law, of morals, of religion, moral statistics, economic science, etc." Of special significance in this respect were the "historical and ethnographical schools" in Germany and Britain.[98] Durkheim insisted on carefully selecting the books and articles to be reviewed (it is "useless to waste a page by saying that a book is bad"), invariably with the aim of highlighting either sociologically interesting facts or sociological ideas. The length of the reviews would be proportionate to the sociological significance of the reviewed work, varying from a few lines to twenty or more pages. Sociology could thus be built up on the basis of methodical analyses of the best scholarship in other fields. In the beginning, as Durkheim recalled in a letter, it was important "to demonstrate to scholars and specialists that we were not ignorant, to make sociologists feel their ignorance, and to give the public a sense of what they are entitled to expect from work that calls itself sociological."[99] That strategic objective hardly changed. What is needed, Durkheim wrote to Hubert, is "that scholars and specialists, while respecting us, know that we do something different, and that the sociologists, while fearing us, sense that we do the same thing, but differently."[100]

One of the leading devices for appropriating material and ideas from other disciplines was the use of a thematic classification that differed from the division of disciplines. The classification implied reviewing studies about, for example, religious ritual in one and the same rubric or subrubric, regardless of whether the reviewed studies were historical, theological, or ethnographical. The classification forced collaborators to specialize in certain areas, although the central members of the group contributed to various sections. Instead of restricting sociology to the most general aspects of social life, as Worms did, the Durkheimians specialized in particular areas without giving up the ambition that sociology was, in fact, a general social science. The working principles by which this was achieved were those of genetic understanding and analytical comparison. Social facts could be understood either by tracing their origins or by comparing them across different societies.

The classificatory framework used for this purpose was relatively stable over time, although some adjustments and rearrangements were made in every volume. The first but relatively small section was about "general sociology."[101] It concerned social philosophy and general sociological theory, fell under the prime responsibility of Bouglé, but was not particularly appreciated among the Durkheimians. Many considered it the old-fashioned, nineteenth-century way of doing sociology. The core of the journal consisted of four other sections. The largest and according to Durkheim most important one was about the sociology of religion. It was the responsibility of Durkheim's nephew Marcel Mauss and his companion Henri Hubert. The internal structure of the section followed an evolutionary scheme, which went from the earliest "primitive" religions to national and universal religions. The third and fourth sections were concerned with moral and legal rules, concentrating respectively on their genesis (third section) and on their actual functioning, as measured, for example, by moral statistics (fourth section). The most active contributors were Durkheim, Richard, Lapie, Fauconnet, and the two jurists of the group (Huvelin, Lévy). The following section covered "economic sociology" and was directed by Simiand, aided by the Bourgin brothers and Halbwachs. The last two sections were smaller and less prominent. One was entitled "social morphology" and focused on studies about the substratum of social life: size, distribution, density, and migration of populations (what was conventionally classified as demography and human geography). The last, miscellaneous section treated language, technology, and art.

The classification was comprehensive and had well-defined core areas. Aside from the important economic sociology section and ethnological studies of the most "simple" and "earliest" forms of religion, morality and law were a predominant feature.[102] Mauss and Hubert, who were the main figures in this respect, had a classical training in philosophy (Mauss) and history (Hubert), but continued their studies in more exotic areas: Mauss in Sanskrit and other oriental languages, Hubert in folklore and European prehistory. Both obtained positions at the specialized École pratique des hautes études, where Mauss officially taught the "history of the religions of noncivilized peoples" and Hubert taught "primitive European religions."

Although comprehensive, the classification of the *Année* did have a major lacuna. The study of politics and the state never obtained a definite place and was present only in a very fragmentary manner.[103] Political studies were concentrated at a private school, the École libre des sciences politiques, and were not considered to be a serious scholarly field from which one could draw material in the same way as from history, ethnography, or economics. Another reason for the absence of political sociology was that Durkheim was keen not to compromise the precarious scholarly status of sociology.[104] Insisting on the objective and methodical study of social facts, he wished to avoid any impression of political partisanship. The political commitments of his younger collaborators could all too easily spill over in their analysis of political institutions, thus jeopardizing the scientific credibility of the journal. Most Durkheimians, including Durkheim himself, therefore wrote on political matters in another journal, *Notes critiques—sciences sociales* (1900–1906), which was directed by François Simiand and was the organ of Dreyfusard intellectuals and Jauresian socialists.[105]

The relationships among the collaborators are best understood on the basis of their relative share of articles and reviews, their area of specialization, and their personal connections. As the founding editor and senior member of the group, Durkheim was obviously the central figure; he also contributed the largest number of papers: 6 articles, 15 introductions, and almost 300 reviews longer than a printed page, to which he added another 370 reviews of less than a page.[106] The magnitude of this review labor is clear: an average of 54 reviews per annual volume. Linked to this central position were three subgroups with relatively strong internal connections and much weaker ties between them (see figure 3.1). The first was the group around Mauss and Hubert, responsible for the sociology of religion, institutionally based at the École pratique des hautes études, and mockingly described by Bouglé as the "taboo-totem clan." Mauss and Hubert came very close to Durkheim in productivity. Because of the large number of short review notices (less than six lines), Mauss was, in fact, the most dedicated reviewer of group, writing an average of 76 reviews per yearly volume. Durkheim, Mauss, and Hubert together wrote nearly half of all the reviews. The second subgroup centered on economic questions and was headed by Simiand, who—averaging 49 reviews per volume—was only slightly less productive. The third subgroup formed around Bouglé, who was responsible for the section on "general sociology" and had been instrumental in the launching of the journal, but was more peripheral within the group as a whole. It included Lapie and Parodi, who had a strong interest in psychology as well, were somewhat ambivalent about sociology, and remained more attached to philosophy. Other members of the group were individually linked to Durkheim rather than to any particular subgroup; among them were Durkheim's own students (Aubin, Hourticq, Hertz, Davy) and his contemporary Gaston Richard.

What made the immense review work all the more demanding was that the reviewed publications were mainly foreign titles. The proportion of publications in French was small, less than 30 percent and decreasing over time.[107] In this respect the *Année* contrasts with Worms's *Revue internationale de sociologie*, which paradoxically reviewed primarily French books (more than two-third of the reviews). In the *Année*, publications in German were the most important category, increasing from 38 percent of the reviews in the first volumes to 46 percent in the last. Literature in Italian decreased over time (from 16 to 4 percent), whereas literature in British and American English increased from 17 to 22 percent.

Although the *Année sociologique* published few articles by foreign authors (only by Simmel, Steinmetz, and Ratzel) and came to be known as the "French school" of sociology, it had a decidedly international orientation. The qualification not only applies to the linguistic diversity of the publications reviewed, but it is also apparent in its regional scope, systematically covering areas far beyond the boundaries of the French Empire and Europe and ranging from Australian aborigines to the ancient civilizations of Egypt, India, and China. In the last issue of the *Année*, Durkheim and Mauss, well aware of the limitations of political boundaries, proposed "civilizations" as a specific object of sociological study, not civilization in the singular, they explained, but "civilizations" in their actual diversity.[108]

The review process, including all the practicalities involved (demanding review copies, corresponding with publishers and reviewers, editorial work, indexing), was a cumbersome burden for the central members of the group and delayed their individual work. Durkheim himself did not succeed in publishing his courses on the family and on socialism, and his long-awaited study on religious life, *Les formes élémentaires de la vie religieuse* (1912), appeared long after the 1894–95 lecture course, which marked the beginning of his studies on religion. Many younger members of the group had trouble finishing their doctoral dissertations and other individual projects. More remarkable than these recurrent difficulties was that the *Année* lasted, and that in the course of its fifteen years, the sense of participating in a meaningful collective enterprise increased. The crises the journal went through were all overcome, and of the total forty-six collaborators, only

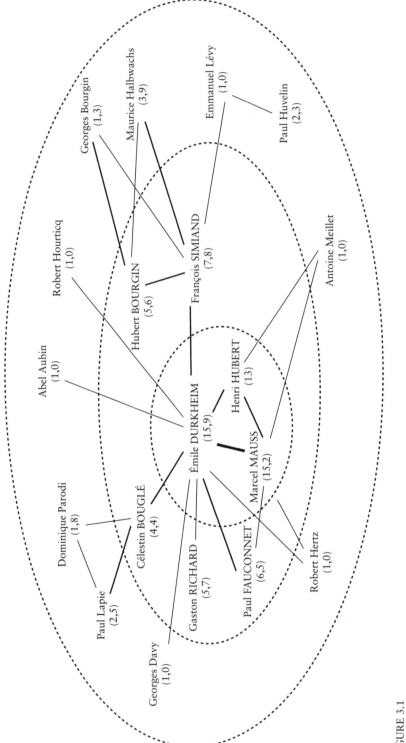

FIGURE 3.1
Network of the most productive collaborators of the *Année sociologique* (1898–1912). The most productive collaborators are those who contributed at least 1% of the full book reviews. The numbers in parentheses indicate the percentage of the total number of reviews written by the individual in question. The inner circle (Durkheim, Mauss, Hubert) thus wrote 44.1% of the reviews, the second circle 30%, the third circle 17.8%. The visualization of the network is based on Philippe Steiner, *La sociologie de Durkheim*, Paris, La Découverte, 1994.

one, Gaston Richard, broke with the group. After having resolved the crisis of 1902, Durkheim wrote to Simiand that in the beginning he had not dared to hope for the "intellectual homogeneity" that had emerged: "I thought only of making the *Année* a collection where, to enter, it would suffice to be scientifically honest."[109] The collective endeavor, which resulted from prolonged interaction and intense collaboration, was described by Mauss as the most characteristic feature of his whole scientific career.[110]

When Durkheim's *Les formes élémentaires de la vie religieuse* (1912) was published, it was received as a major study that effectively revised his earlier theory of mechanical solidarity and collective consciousness. Based on recent and far more detailed ethnographic evidence of Australian tribes as well as on the collective work that was published in the *Année*'s section on religion, Durkheim examined the earliest forms of religion and linked them not only to the social morphology of tribal societies but also to periodic ritual and ceremonial practices. In addition to his interest in ritual and mechanisms of "collective effervescence," he also paid more attention to the cognitive dimension of collective representations. The analysis of the earliest forms of religion allowed him to propose an account of the social origins of general categories of thought (notions of "force" or "cause") and of systems of classification.

The twelfth and last volume of the *Année sociologique* appeared in 1913. The First World War mobilized virtually all members of the group, who for the most part discontinued their scholarly activities. Durkheim did continue his teaching, but was involved in numerous activities and government committees related to the war effort. Other members of the group worked for ministries and younger members of the group were sent to the front. Durkheim's last publications were two obituaries, one of Robert Hertz, the other of his son André, who had passed the *agrégation* just before the war and would be the linguist of the group. Devastated by his death, Durkheim withdrew into a "ferocious silence"; he resumed his work briefly but died in 1917.

Defining a Specialty of Generalists

Made possible by republican politics to expand the universities and catch up with British and German science, the rapidly increasing sociological production at the end of the nineteenth century was primarily shaped by the rivalries between the networks of René Worms and Émile Durkheim. Both networks had their own institutional base, a distinct social and intellectual profile, and promoted a specific conception of sociology. Worms, who never made a university career, built up a large and heterogeneous network by associating with distinguished personalities. They occupied positions within as well as outside the university; the French members were most often affiliated with the Faculty of Law, where the hostility to sociology proved far greater than in the Faculty of Letters.[111] Continually maneuvering to defend sociology and to bridge the gaps between disciplines, faculties, and countries, Worms conceived of sociology as a science of synthesis that was more a philosophy of the social sciences than an empirical discipline. Including the older generation of French sociologists (Espinas, Fouillée, Tarde), the most important members of Worms's network had no university position (Worms, Tarde), or when they did, it was not in sociology. For many of them the sociological engagement was but a side activity. Although Worms's organizations survived the First World War, it was characteristic that none of their members succeeded in carving out an institutional niche and establishing a recognizable sociological tradition.

The rival group around Émile Durkheim consisted of well-qualified younger scholars, predominantly philosophers, who combined their theoretical interests with empirical work in various domains. Far from being a sign of its intellectual weakness, the vivid controversies about Durkheimian sociology—like the well-documented disputes with philosophers, historians, and economists—were indicative of its recognition as a considerable scholarly challenge to the established disciplines.[112] Because the Durkheimian program eclipsed that of its competitors and obtained considerable intellectual recognition, sociology in France did not enter the university as a science of "leftovers," as Albion Small said about American sociology. Durkheimian sociology, quite the contrary, represented a challenging and rigorous program to scientifically study crucial questions about morality, religion, and other collective representations, their historical evolution and institutional underpinnings. But in spite of their scholarly accomplishments, the institutional success of the Durkheimians was limited. By 1920 only four chairs in the Faculty of Letters were recognized to be at least partly sociological; all of them went to members of the Durkheim group. This relatively precarious position was matched by a virtual absence of sociology in other academic institutions. Several Durkheimians (Mauss, Hubert, Simiand) made careers in specialized schools like the École pratique des hautes études, but none of their positions was in sociology. A sociology chair at the Collège de France was created only in the 1930s, and although Tarde had been elected to the Academy of Moral and Political Sciences, the sociology section that Émile Worms—René's father—proposed to create in 1899 was never established.[113] And yet, in spite of its limited institutional success, French sociology was widely perceived as the international center of the discipline. It was in France, as Lester Ward observed in 1900, that "sociology has taken the firmest hold on the thinking classes, and it is there that we find the largest annual output."[114]

By entering the university and becoming a discipline, sociology was reshaped and both its external and internal boundaries were redrawn. As compared with the all-encompassing systems of Comte and Spencer, the sociological domain was redefined in accordance with the structures of national academic systems and implied a divergence of national traditions.[115] The dominant form of sociology in France avoided studying the state and politics, was cut off from psychology, and analytically focused on issues of collective representations, which were related to the battle for legitimacy with philosophers.

CHAPTER 4

※ ※ ※

The Metamorphoses of
Durkheimian Scholarship

The development of Durkheimian sociology is often depicted in a "rise and fall" pattern, as if it followed a quasi-natural cycle of growth and decay. Considering sociological production in the more restricted sense, there is indeed some evidence of this. After the flowering of the Durkheimian group around the *Année sociologique*, the First World War caused a dramatic break in production: scholarly work was interrupted, publications came to a near halt, and many younger members of the group died on the front. Two new volumes of the *Année* finally materialized only in 1925 and 1927. They opened with obituaries of seventeen people who had died during or shortly after the war. Among them were Émile Durkheim, his wife Louise, and their only son André. Not yet mentioned in this long list was Henri Hubert, the close companion of Marcel Mauss and one of the most productive members of the group; he died in 1927, when the second volume was just in press. "The greatest setback of my scientific life," Mauss wrote, "was not the work lost during the four-and-a-half years of war . . . , nor even my helplessness brought about by the premature deaths of Durkheim and Hubert, it was the loss of my best students and friends during these painful years. It could be said that it was a loss for this branch of French science; for me, everything had collapsed."[1]

In addition to the losses of the war, few younger scholars were in the interwar years attracted to sociology, and hardly any one of them was tempted by the Durkheimian example. The rejection of Durkheimian sociology was such that just about any other intellectual orientation seemed more attractive and exciting than the outdated sociology à la Durkheim. Raymond Aron turned to German philosophy of history and Max Weber,

Georges Friedmann became interested in Marxism and the critical analysis of labor relations, and several others, Jean Stoetzel among them, started importing empirical research techniques from the United States. As a result, Durkheimian sociology declined and its abandonment was nearly general in French sociology in the years after 1945.

Upon closer inspection, however, this apparent "rise and fall" pattern is a superficial and inadequate characteristic, based on a too narrow and, in fact, anachronistic view of sociology. For purely descriptive purposes, it is misleading because the overall number of scholars who were interested in Durkheimian approaches was not at all in decline. In a remarkable number of scholarly fields, Durkheimian ideas flourished and contributed significantly to innovative research. The French school of anthropology around Marcel Mauss is the best-known example, but there are many others. The historians around the *Annales d'histoire économique et sociale* (1929) of Marc Bloch and Lucien Febvre, the comparative studies of Indo-European mythology by Georges Dumézil, the structural analysis of kinship by Claude Lévi-Strauss, substantive work in economics as well as in economic history, the "historical anthropology" of ancient Greece and Rome, numerous studies in social or "collective psychology," all were unthinkable without the inquiries and the active involvement of Durkheimians. The "rise and fall" scheme thus obscures a considerable body of work that was not only of great vitality but of far-reaching significance as well, as would become clear in the 1960s when "structuralism" became fashionable and its most authoritative representatives (Dumézil, Lévi-Strauss) turned out to be heirs to Durkheimian concepts and in particular to the work of a largely forgotten Durkheimian: Marcel Granet.[2] The "rise and fall" description is unsatisfactory also because it does not suggest any sociological explanation, neither for the apparent rupture within sociology nor for the remarkable flourishing of the Durkheimian legacy in other scholarly fields.

For a more adequate understanding of the paradoxical fate of Durkheimian sociology in the interwar period, two sets of questions have to be considered. The first concerns the peculiar position of the Durkheimians in the academic field at large, the conditions under which their work evolved and was transmitted, and the gradual divergence of their work and their orientation. The second set of questions concerns the crisis in recruiting young sociologists, their break with Durkheimianism and the consequent redefinition and reorientation of sociology.

The Contours of Sociology

Sociology after the First World War was no longer as vast and promising an intellectual project as the first series of the *Année sociologique* had been, nor was it a well-established discipline. Institutionally, it was a somewhat marginal specialty, but one that had an uncommon degree of intellectual legitimacy, this being the primary feature of what Victor Karady called Durkheim's "semi-failure."[3] In 1920, sociology began to be taught officially in the framework of a *certificate* in "morality and sociology" that represented one-fourth of the bachelor (*licence*) degree in philosophy (the other *certificates* were the general history of philosophy, psychology, and general philosophy and logic). In most universities there was no sociology chair, so the subject was taught by philosophy professors. For half a century, from 1910 to about 1960, only four university chairs were specifically known or recognized as "sociological," although the official title did not always correspond and administrative discontinuities were legion. Durkheim's chair at Bordeaux was held successively by Gaston Richard, Max Bonnafous, and Jean Stoetzel. The Strasbourg chair was created in 1919 for Maurice Halbwachs, who was succeeded by Georges Gurvitch and Georges Duveau. The other two sociology chairs were at the Sorbonne. After Durkheim's death, one was successively held by Paul Fauconnet and Albert Bayet; the other by Bouglé, Halbwachs, and Georges Davy.[4] With the exception of Marcel Mauss's chair at the Collège de France, these four chairs represented the near totality of "sociological" positions in higher education. In institutional terms sociology was thus a minor academic specialty taught in the Faculty of Letters for and primarily by philosophers for whom sociology was specifically linked to the study of morality.

The prestige of sociology was derived largely from the work of the Durkheimians, which had eclipsed the rival group around René Worms's *Revue internationale de sociologie* (1893–39). Some scholars had trouble in even imagining a non-Durkheimian sociology.[5] Durkheim's authority was recognized by his competitors as well, who often defined themselves simply as the opponents of Durkheimian sociology, while occasionally proposing "reconciliation." The best-known members of Worms's network were no longer alive (Tarde died in 1904, Espinas in 1922), and when Worms himself died in 1926, his successor was Gaston Richard, who had broken with the Durkheimians and by then was already sixty-six. With only a few exceptions (René Maunier, Daniel Essertier), the *Revue internationale* continued to function separately from the Durkheimians, maintaining its international orientation and its eclecticism (illustrated among other things by its reviews of novels). The recruitment crisis seems to have hit the Worms group harder than the Durkheimians, because the only young collaborators of some importance were Gaston Bouthoul and Roger Bastide. The Institut international de sociologie experienced a similar decline: only two international conferences were held in more than twenty years (1918–40), compared with eight during the decade before 1914.

The judgment of two members of Worms's network taking stock in the 1930s leaves no doubt as to the supremacy of the Durkheimians. Achille Ouy, a lycée teacher of philosophy, noted the demise of the organicism that the young Worms had promoted and the lack of followers for Tarde's psychologism even among individualist thinkers. The "independent" sociologists, he concluded, had little more in common than their opposition to "Durkheimian imperialism." Guillaume Duprat, a professor of sociology and social economy in Geneva, remarked that Worms's "eclecticism" had next to no partisans,[6] in contrast with the Durkheimians, whom Ouy described as follows: "Durkheim's school, on the other hand, has assembled a *pléiade* of scholars and researchers, mainly in France. Their many, often remarkable studies have received much attention and are authoritative on more than one point."[7]

The most visible effect of the prestige of the Durkheimians was the expansion of their network and the diversification of exchange with scholars working in a wide variety of disciplines. Of the collaborators on the second series of the *Année sociologique* (1925, 1927), nearly 40 percent were newcomers. Later, in the *Annales sociologiques* (1934–42), the vast majority of the collaborators, nearly three-quarters of them, had not contributed to the first series of the *Année*.

But the majority of the newcomers belonged to the same generation(s) as the Durkheimians, as is indicated by the average age of the collaborators, which went up from thirty-three to around fifty (table 4.1); they had similar positions in the academic hierarchy and often shared the same political experiences, namely, the struggles during and after the Dreyfus Affair to defend the Republic against attacks from the nationalist right. The Durkheimian network was thus part of the new academic establishment, as is indicated by the educational background and academic positions of the contributors to Durkheimian journals (table 4.2).

An important factor of differentiation among the members of this network was the academic discipline to which they belonged, and in this

TABLE 4.1
Average age of the members of the Durkheimian network

	Année sociologique	*Année sociologique*	Institut français de sociologie		*Annales sociologiques*
	1898–1913	1925	1931	1933	1938
Average age	33.6	45.8	51.8	52.2	47.4
N	46	38	43	63	46
Unknown	—	1	—	1	2

Note: For the first series of the *Année sociologique*, the figure is the average of the average age of each of the 12 volumes; for the *Annales sociologiques*, the average age is the age of the collaborators in 1938.

TABLE 4.2
Academic credentials of the members of the Durkheimian network

	Année sociologique (1898–1913)		Année sociologique (1925)		Annales sociologiques (1934–42)	
		unknown		unknown		unknown
% normaliens	52%	—	56%	—	46%	—
% agrégés	82%	—	89%	2%	79%	6%
% PhDs	54%	—	73%	2%	69%	4%
	(n = 46)		(n = 38)		(n = 46)	

respect the Durkheimian network was highly dispersed. Its heterogeneous composition reflects both sociology's prestige and sociologists' dependence on recognition from neighboring disciplines. Among its members, the Institut français de sociologie counted prominent psychologists (C. Blondel, G. Dumas), historians (Marc Bloch, A. Piganiol), linguists (Antoine Meillet, Marcel Cohen), ethnologists (M. Leenhardt, René Maunier, Paul Rivet), a political scientist (André Siegfried), and many jurists and economists.[8] The best indication of the intellectual credit of Durkheimian sociology is probably the degree to which it had penetrated the Faculty of Law. Among the members of the Institut français de sociologie there were as many professors from the Faculty of Law as from the Faculty of Letters (twelve). Legal scholars were also well represented among the collaborators of the *Annales sociologiques*; 25 percent of them had a PhD or their *agrégation* in law (twice as many as in the first series of the *Année sociologique*).

To understand this process of dispersed diffusion, it is necessary to consider the various uses of sociology. Scholars generally used sociological studies to renew or bolster their position within their own discipline. Transferring sociological concepts and modes of thought implied a process of selection and reinterpretation, which in turn also affected the image of sociology. The dominant image of sociology at the time was in all likelihood close to the image that existed in the dominant disciplines. Within these disciplines sociology underwent a reinterpretation in which the rejection of "sociological imperialism" was often used to reassert their own supremacy.

This occurred most strikingly in philosophy. In his *History of Modern Philosophy in France* (1899), Lucien Lévy-Bruhl wrote that sociology was far from being a positive science in the way psychology was.[9] Twenty years later, Dominique Parodi devoted an entire chapter of *La philosophie contemporaine en France* (1925) to "Émile Durkheim and the sociological school," whereas J. Benrubi allotted 12 percent of *Les sources et les courants de la philosophie contemporaine en France* (1933) to sociology. This tendency was even stronger in Émile Bréhier's *Transformation de la philosophie française* (1950), in which the "Durkheimian initiative" was allotted twice as many pages as eminent philosophers like Bergson or Brunschvicg. But this remarkable recognition was accompanied by an interpretation of sociology that was quite remote from the actual work of the Durkheimians. This is clear even from the judgment of Parodi, who had himself been a contributor to the *Année sociologique*. As he saw it, Durkheim's influence consisted in a kind of "idealism toward which, in our opinion, the various tendencies of contemporary thought should now converge."[10] Durkheim's "positivism," on the other hand, could incur anti-intellectualism because of his "exclusive and somewhat superstitious concern for scientific rigor."[11] Without discussing any empirical studies, Parodi went on to say that the sociologists made up for their positivism by their "respect for duty and sense of morality," which was "deep and lofty."[12] The philosophers' recognition of sociology came down to attributing a philosophical bent to Durkheim, which corresponded to the "triumphant renewal" of what Parodi called that "great French idealist thinking." Bréhier similarly claimed that Durkheim was working to "save spiritualism." The defense of spiritual values against the diffusion of materialism gave rise to a "neospiritualism that took many forms . . . : Bergsonian intuition, which was knowledge of the spirit as such; Durkheim's social mystique; Laberthonnière's 'intuition on the labor' of charity."[13] Academic philosophers appropriated sociology as a contribution to a new kind of spiritualism or, as Bouglé put it, a kind of "modern idealism."[14] In addition to this idealist reinterpretation, the presented image of sociology was exclusively French and hardly up to date: one of the few foreign sociologists mentioned was Herbert Spencer (frequently quoted by both Parodi and Benrubi), while Max Weber and Pareto were absent.

This mixture of intellectual recognition and radical reinterpretation was absent in more peripheral disciplines and research specialties, where the reference to sociology served instead as a means of acquiring greater scientific legitimacy. This was the case in the "debutant science" of religion. It was "only through sociology" that this domain became a "social science."[15] Even in a field like international relations, where the Durkheimians had published next to nothing, sociology was considered "essential" because the *Année sociologique* contained "the sociological bases that would provide a foundation for the study of international relations."[16] Statements such as these were based not only on the appreciation of a sociological point of view but also on a widely shared respect for the scholarly ethos of the Durkheimians, for their rigor and their achievements in analytically reviewing an enormous scholarly literature in several languages.

The spread of Durkheimianism was complicated by the political uses that were made of sociology, such as in the *Année politique française et étrangère* (1925). "The eminent master, Emile Durkheim" and "the admirable scientific example" of the *Année sociologique* here served as an intellectual guarantee for "the development of a new political philosophy" inspired by republican patriotism, a philosophy whose partisans were alarmed by the "material and moral effacement of France" up against "the Anglo-Saxon mystique" and the German and Russian regimes. The primary vice of the French political system, as they saw it, lay in "an insufficiently inculcated public spirit. The spirit of the public has not yet been sufficiently infused with the extremely precise teachings of the contemporary social sciences . . . which have taught us that a society is not composed exclusively of individuals."[17] This political philosophy, close to the views of the so-called Radical Party,[18] was also what inspired the introduction of "sociological notions applied to morality and instruction" in the training schools for primary school teachers (the *écoles normales primaires*) in 1920. These changes in national educational programs were introduced by a sector of the republican administration, which had ties to some of the Durkheimians.

The End of a Collective Enterprise

In 1927 Célestin Bouglé summed up the position of the Durkheimians by saying that "its center is nowhere, its circumference everywhere."[19] "Spontaneous sociology" seemed omnipresent, but "methodical sociology," sociology in the proper sense of the word, was a problem.[20] Sociology's prestige greatly facilitated connections and exchanges with scholars in other disciplines, while its low level of autonomy actually made those contacts necessary. For example, the Durkheimians heavily depended on nonsociological journals to have their texts published: only three of the thirty-four articles published by Maurice Halbwachs after the First World War were published in a sociological journal.[21] Because the Durkheimians' position involved a dispersed recognition, they could not readily pursue a strategy of autonomization, thus preferring interdisciplinary exchange and abandoning the "imperialist" claim that sociology constituted the "corpus" or "system" of the social sciences. The Institut français de sociologie functioned as a meeting place for scholars interested in sociology; typically the word "sociology" did not even figure in the learned society's statutes. Its stated aim was merely "to bring together specialists in the various social sciences, the union of these sciences constituting the science of man living in society." Sociological "imperialism" had yielded ground to the desire for rapprochement, which brought in new members and led to productive debates and exchanges. The style of the institute's gatherings was consistent with that of the first series of the *Année sociologique*. In contrast to other learned societies, the Institut was an "exclusively scientific, closed society"; its membership was limited and its sessions were characterized by a deliberate sobriety: no "worldly" or political matters had a place there.[22]

Paradoxically, this peculiar mode of academic recognition also contributed to the disintegration of the group. The publishing history of the *Année sociologique*—the journal was the principal means by which the group constituted itself—is the best indicator of the changes in internal relations. The first volume was eventually published in 1925 with the same classification of research areas and nearly all the major collaborators from the first series. The annual periodical was directed by Marcel Mauss, who was by far the most productive author, followed by Halbwachs and Simiand. The second volume, incomplete in that it was without book reviews, was published in 1927.[23] A third volume was announced but never came out. Its successor, the *Annales sociologiques* (1934–42), was no longer a regular and coherent periodical: it was published in five separate series, edited by different persons, for a total of nineteen issues. These publications marked the end of the collective undertaking. Several of the former collaborators no longer participated and others, such as Mauss, disinvested considerably. Halbwachs remained very active, especially after 1935 when he was appointed to a professorship in Paris; he became the journal's main figure. As Mauss recognized, the Durkheimian group gradually disintegrated, as did the coherence of the Durkheimian project: "The sociological *oeuvre* ceased being systematic and generalizing. We had not entirely lost contact, but we were not marching together . . . it was necessary to relinquish what were premature systematizations."[24] To account for what became of the Durkheimian group, it is important, however, to look beyond external constraints and changing opportunities, in part because these reinforced internal differences. The point of departure of the disintegration of the group was the existence of three subgroups within the original group.

The first subgroup, centered around Marcel Mauss and Henri Hubert, was institutionally based at the École pratique des hautes études (EPHE), where its members' careers advanced relatively quickly. They were specialized in such fields as the history of religions (Mauss), prehistory (Hubert), and sinology (Granet). The second subgroup centered around Bouglé, Paul Lapie, and Dominique Parodi, who worked primarily for the "general sociology" section of the journal and were quick to obtain university posts (Bouglé, Lapie) or made careers as administrators in the educational system (Parodi and later Lapie). On the basis of their institutional position and approach, they may be grouped together with other members who also made university careers (Georges Davy, Paul Fauconnet) and with para-Durkheimians like Albert Bayet and René Hubert, who began publishing in the *Année sociologique* after the First World War. The third subgroup was composed of Simiand, Halbwachs, and the Bourgin brothers and specialized in statistics and economics. After obtaining doctoral degrees in the Faculty of Law, Simiand, Halbwachs, and Hubert Bourgin had no choice but to follow the trajectory of either the first or the second subgroup. Halbwachs also defended a doctorate in the Faculty of Letters and pursued a university career, while Simiand taught at the École pratique des hautes études. Hubert Bourgin's situation illustrates the particular difficulties of this subgroup: despite the titles of *normalien* and *agrégé* and doctorates in both law and letters, he remained a lycée teacher all his life.

The unity of the first series of the *Année sociologique*, owing to several factors of integration and a favorable academic and professional context (university expansion, the Dreyfus Affair), in a way masked the internal differences, which after the First World War took the form of a split between university teachers and research scholars. That opposition was not solely an effect of the institutional position they occupied; it was also related to differences in their intellectual investments and scholarly dispositions.

Institutionally, sociology could only be taught in connection with another discipline. For university teachers, that discipline was philosophy, for research scholars it was a specialized domain taught at one of the specialized scholarly institutions. The trajectory of university sociologists can be explained in part by the fact that their only training was in philosophy (Bouglé, Fauconnet, Lapie, Parodi, René Hubert) or letters (Bayet). Only Georges Davy had been formally enrolled also at the École pratique des hautes études, but his work did not obtain the recognition of the research scholars. In a very unusual internal polemic, Marcel Granet harshly and publicly criticized Davy's PhD thesis, *La foi jurée* (1922)—a clear indication of the distance that gradually separated the two groups and the corresponding forms of Durkheimianism.[25] Within university education, sociology was linked to the philosophical study of morality and, by implication, with the republican establishment. In this regard too, the university teachers differed systematically from the research scholars. Whereas the research scholars had no important administrative responsibilities that were not directly related to research, nearly all the university professors did, often early in their careers and for long periods of time, serving as inspectors, deans, or university rectors.[26] This close relationship with the public bureaucracy was accompanied by a systematic difference in political affiliations: the university teachers were not affiliated with socialist groups, whereas nearly all research scholars were or had been socialists (Mauss, Simiand, Halbwachs, Henri Hubert, Granet, Gernet, Hertz). Instead they belonged to the more moderate Radical Party (Bouglé, Bayet) or had affinities with that party (Davy, René Hubert, Lapie). Fauconnet was the only university professor to have had links with the socialists. This difference, while of secondary importance in the years of the Dreyfus Affair, played a more significant role in the interwar period.

The primary difference between both groups lies probably in the fact that the university teachers did not seek to acquire qualifications other than their initial training. They seem to have had a somewhat less "critical" relationship to the educational system. Being of slightly higher and not as marginal social origin (not Jewish, for example), they were more at ease within the educational system and were probably tempted to rely on their short-term educational success rather than make longer-term investments of uncertain outcome.

Célestin Bouglé, born into a Breton family of military officers, "had gifts that promised brilliant success: comfortably articulate, a ready talker, a virtuoso speaker of the *normalien* variety." According to all accounts, he was "a sparkling orator and conversationalist" with a "rapid intelligence" and a turn of mind that was neither "anxious nor tormented." Moreover, he had "charm," in part physical because as a "sportsman" (tennis player) he "stayed young and handsome." He cared for neither solemnity nor obscurity, and "anything hermetic or too specialized seemed to him to bear the mark of futility." His educational and cultural ease and social capital predisposed him to teaching and to academic and epistemological diplomacy rather than slow-moving, discreet research. He was the link between the Durkheimians and the *Revue de métaphysique et de morale*, and he defended sociology "in all milieus, to all audiences." According to Halbwachs, he probably encountered "the greatest resistance, either hidden or overt," within the Durkheimian group itself.[27]

Paul Fauconnet, the other sociologist who long dominated teaching at the Sorbonne, was a different personality than Bouglé, but not in all ways, as is indicated by the following account of a lycée friend: "He was abreast of all that happened in the world; he occasionally spent evenings out at the family of friends and he was greatly appreciated as a dancer—all at age sixteen, also at age twenty. He had a whole social life I knew nothing about, meanwhile he was winning the *prix* in history, the *prix* in letters, then the *prix* in philosophy and still other *prix*—before completing his university studies, from *licence* to *agrégation*, in the space of two years."[28] It is probably not insignificant that among the Durkheimians, Bouglé was the youngest doctor (obtained at age twenty-nine) and Fauconnet the youngest *agrégé* (age twenty-one).

There are no such glowing accounts of the major research scholars, though they too were very good students. Simiand, for example, the son of a provincial primary school teacher, was ranked first in the *agrégation* in philosophy (like Bouglé), but was never described as "brilliant": there was something "slow, forced, hesitant" about his conversation. When he was young his behavior was "aloof and even rather harsh," while in the view of others this was more a matter of "embarrassment or timidity." Very early on, this "relentless worker" denounced the sociology that was in fashion, and all his life he "persistently refused" to "concede anything in his lectures or books to scientific popularization because he was so repelled by the idea of making a science, whose complexities and uncertainties he was only too familiar with, appear easy."[29] An important aspect of these somewhat ideal-typical differences between Bouglé and Simiand was their respective relation to language and style. Bouglé had a talent for being "eloquent while remaining simple," and his clarity earned him recognition as a "pedagogue and educator" of the first order. Simiand was identified with the other extreme: some praised the "fine austerity" of his style,[30] which others regretted: "he readily adopted an abstruse, heavy, graceless style in his books that was a major obstacle to dissemination of his thought—to the regret of those who liked him."[31]

Conflicting Interpretations

The university professors did not produce much original research. Their writings were primarily overviews, textbooks, and texts of popularization, which were often linked to the social uses of sociology. All of Bayet's works focus on moral questions, Fauconnet's only book is on responsibility, René Hubert published texts on pedagogy, and Bouglé wrote a great deal on social issues and current political events—the echo of which is present in his scientific work (his thesis was on egalitarian ideas).[32] The way they defined and defended sociology engendered rivalries with the research scholars. The absence of major external competitors implied that the struggle about defining sociology became an internal struggle. The opposed interpretations of Durkheim's work provide a clear indication of the split between the two groups.

The texts on Durkheim written by research scholars like Mauss, Halbwachs, and Granet are dominated by a kind of scientific pragmatism: "Durkheim's ideas should be judged on their yield."[33] Of Durkheim's unpublished courses on pedagogy, the history of doctrines, and his scientific courses, Mauss deemed the latter "naturally the most important."[34] In the sociology of religion, Granet presented Durkheim as a scholar, a *savant* who had "proved" something "through analysis of facts."[35] Halbwachs wrote that Durkheim's research might have provided "an original solution" to certain problems in philosophy and morality, but this research

had nothing to do with "social metaphysics"; and "a good number of principles, of the sort that may be believed a priori, are in fact the result of
the long positive studies he did, but could not always present the details
of."[36] To have proceeded this way, "Durkheim, like many innovators, had
had to position himself through opposition."[37] He had to defend sociology
against the "simplisms" of Tarde and Spencer and against "metaphysicians
of morality and religion,"[38] while being "greatly concerned about rescu-
ing the fields of religion, law, etc. from the oversimplified philosophical
essay and the moralist's merely literary description."[39] The research scholars insisted on Durkheim's scientific aspirations and on the difficulties of
producing new knowledge, but they were largely uninterested in its philosophic or moral aspects. The only philosophical approach Mauss attributed
any importance to was pragmatism, and Durkheim's courses on this subject were, in his opinion, the "crowning philosophical achievement" of his
oeuvre.[40] But Mauss also affirmed that these courses were "no longer philosophy"[41]: "I would go so far as to say that complete anthropology could
replace philosophy because it would comprise precisely the same history of
the human spirit that philosophy presupposes."[42] And he defended a similar
view when it came to sociology: "It is not particularly useful to philoso-
phize about general sociology when we have so much to know and so much
to do in order to understand what we know."[43]

The interpretations of the university teachers were, on the contrary,
organized around the philosophical thrust and the social implications
of Durkheim's sociology. They placed much emphasis on the philosophical tradition—which, in their view, Durkheim's thought was continuous
with—than on his scientific innovations. Davy affirmed that "despite
appearances," Durkheim was situated "entirely within the philosophical
tradition. Like Socrates, his aim was to define, and like Descartes, to explain.
And this method, which he developed by means of a long meditation on
rationalist thought, became in his view the right method for both science
and philosophy, to which he ascribed one and the same spirit."[44] Early on,
Davy had professed his interest in "a philosophical sociology,"[45] and he saw
sociology in France as characterized by an "ampler, more philosophical,
and more humane" approach.[46] In his view, Durkheim had moved in the
direction of "idealism." For Bouglé, Durkheimian sociology represented
"an effort to found and justify spiritualist tendencies in a new way."[47] To
the university professors, the cast of mind of the man whom Mauss, Halbwachs, and Granet described as a "scholar" and "researcher" was first and
foremost philosophical, and his "temperament" was, as Parodi asserted,
"decidedly metaphysical."[48]

These philosophical affinities also informed the posthumous editing of Durkheim's works. Bouglé edited a book he entitled *Sociologie et
philosophie* (1924) to show "how and to what degree sociology renews

philosophy." For it he chose three of Durkheim's articles, omitting ones that were more critical of philosophy, such as "L'enseignement philosophique et l'agrégation de philosophie (1895)." In his preface he stressed sociology's "antimaterialist tendency," stating that Durkheim had concentrated on "moral problems" and refounded spiritualism "in a new way." Bouglé's attitude and approach were the same in his editing of the discussion that followed Durkheim's 1906 lecture to the Société française de philosophie, "La détermination du fait moral." That is, Bouglé reduced the discussion, which obviously had included interruptions and objections, to six statements presented under such headings as "Individual reason and social reality" and "Philosophy and moral facts," at some points without even indicating his deletion of one of Durkheim's own questions or comments. The published fragments create an impression quite different from what actually occurred, if only in that Durkheim sometimes referred to Kant or Socrates in answering a question that Bouglé omitted. Nor can the reader understand from Bouglé's volume that by presenting himself as a scholar, a *savant*, Durkheim was assuming a critical stance with regard to philosophy and philosophers: "I use the word *savant* not to designate a mandarin caste but to characterize a mental attitude toward the questions we are discussing." Durkheim refused to answer certain questions—"[that] question falls outside my concerns"—and he reformulated others, occasionally responding in a sharply polemical tone: "What we have here is a question of fact. Let me tell you that you don't know the slightest thing about it. The most rudimentary scientific precaution requires us to. . . ." His audience got few concessions from him: philosophers "were to some degree precursors of the science of moral facts that we are trying to create, just as alchemists were precursors of chemistry. But they lacked everything needed for scientifically conducting this study." He also at one point in the discussion refused to accept "an apparent point of agreement due in fact to a misunderstanding or equivocation."[49] Bouglé published none of these passages. His version remains the only one available, however, and was translated into numerous languages.

The importance that the university teachers attached to philosophy was linked to their position in an academic field where philosophy was the dominant discipline. Like the research scholars who situated themselves in a universe dominated by specialized scholarly studies, university teachers reinterpreted Durkheimianism in terms amenable to university philosophy. The particularity of that version of philosophy was that it was philosophy in its most official guise, that is, a philosophy dominated by the question of secular morality, its foundation and intellectual justification.

According to Bouglé, Durkheim's studies were "all concerned more or less directly with moral sociology." His "supreme purpose was to reach practical conclusions and indicate directions for social action."[50] And as Bouglé saw it, beneath Durkheim's "scientistic" attitude was "an ardent moralist of the firmest convictions."[51] Durkheim's moralism was close to what was seen by some as his conservatism and his obsession with social order. According to Davy, he was "passionately" attached to "the essential virtues of order and discipline, the only ones capable of ensuring stability."[52] The difference in both content and form between the university teachers and the research scholars' interpretations is apparent if we compare a text by Davy with one by Halbwachs on the same question and published at practically the same moment:

Maurice Halbwachs

Durkheim's sociology brought into full relief the difference between an approach in terms of knowledge and an approach in terms of action. From the outset he dismissed all teleological considerations, treating social facts like any *savant* handles the facts of his science, precisely because he intended to explain rather than judge them. And indeed, when he spoke of a science of morality, he meant the science of moral facts, which is something quite different from studying to determine what complies with what philosophers call morality. We can no doubt conceive of the results of sociological science being taken up by an art whose intention is to regulate and guide the practices of men. But the conditions in which the individual finds himself called on to act morally are too complex, and the science of moral facts is not at all sufficiently advanced for us to be thinking already of applying it. In any case, this is not at all the direct focus of social science.[53]

Georges Davy

The man was driven and sustained by a single idea: to accomplish the duty he felt and knew to be his. Likewise his work was driven and guided by a single idea: to determine the foundations of duty for all; in one gesture to endow man and society with a set of rules for conduct, and to justify it rationally, so that it could finally impose itself without provoking challenge or protest, so that it could serve as guiding principle in morality and politics. . . . Durkheim never published a single work during his lifetime on morality strictly speaking . . . it is nonetheless true that his constant preoccupation and the aim of all his research was morality—morality that would extend into political life, for a man's internal virtue and strength are quite naturally realized in civic action. . . . Given that this is so, we would condemn ourselves to understanding nothing of his work if we failed to realize that morality was at the very center of it, its very aim.[54]

It is hardly surprising, then, that there was no consensus among the Durkheimians regarding sociology courses in the training schools for primary school teachers, the *écoles normales primaires*. The discipline was introduced in 1920, probably at Bouglé's instigation.[55] Lapie applauded "the close union between science and morality" and expressed his hope in the emergence of "a type of morality founded on sociology."[56] Along the same lines, Bouglé argued until the end of his life in favor of teaching sociology to primary school teachers, and Paul Fauconnet was convinced that sociology would ultimately provide a "rational basis" for secular morality.[57] But when this educational program, which was being attacked by the political Right, was debated within the Institut français de sociologie, the only decision its members made was to communicate the content of the debate to the rector of the Sorbonne and the director of primary education, "without formulating any express wishes."[58] In the discussions, Simiand came out in favor of eliminating the program, and Halbwachs, Granet, and Mauss were also very critical, though they did not go as far as requesting an end to it publicly. Mauss expressed his skepticism as follows: "Anxious crowds are wondering whether sociology, a new science, is going to provide solutions to the problems of morality, politics, the economy, life itself. If they take certain so-called sociological declamations too seriously, . . . they could well turn against us too, mistaking us for charlatans when in fact we are making no such claims. . . . It is for the future of our science that we have to protest against all such possible confusion and confess we know very little about either the past or the present. . . ."[59]

To Profess or to Inquire?

The research scholars' stance in this conflict derived from a concern to increase their scientific credibility by refusing to be involved in activities that might compromise their work. They had no important administrative functions, rarely made important public appearances, and since they were generally not brilliant orators they did not have access to several of the perquisites enjoyed by the most eminent professors. When Mauss was appointed to the Collège de France he explicitly requested a small lecture hall. As mentioned, the work of the research scholars was relatively specialized, and to varying degrees they mistrusted philosophical interpretations of sociology and the idea of drawing moral or political conclusions from it. In Raymond Lenoir's view, they showed "exaggerated scruples"[60] with regard to the teaching of sociology. During the discussion of a sociology course developed by Fauconnet, Granet argued energetically against the concepts of both Bouglé and Fauconnet: the "very last thing" he wanted was "for sociology as a whole to be reduced to what M. Bouglé has called the sociological point of view."[61] In Granet's understanding, their version of sociology seemed to reduce it to a parade of illustrated theories, whereas "nothing seems less scientific to me—and above all less interesting—than an illustrated theory, however well illustrated it may be. Illustration is not demonstration, and it certainly doesn't teach how to demonstrate, let alone how to do research."

To Granet, the "encyclopedic" course Fauconnet was proposing had the additional disadvantage of appearing "dogmatic" at a time when sociologists were already often reproached with being part of a "closed" and "dogmatic" school. It was extremely important to avoid giving an impression of dogmatism, since sociology programs in the primary teacher training schools fostered an image of sociology as nothing more than a justification of institutions, morals, and ways of life, which appeared old-fashioned to many young teacher trainees. The idea that sociology could be "reactionary" or "conservative" had made its appearance and taken hold, and it was important that this fear "not appear founded." Like Simiand, who remarked that it was important not only to teach the results of sociological research but also to train sociological "workers," Granet preferred a program that would elicit a sense of "vocation" in potential researchers, that would be "exciting" rather than "complete." Since sociology was a science *à faire* rather *faite* (yet to be made rather than made), it was important to deal with specific questions, to show the progress sociologists had made on this or that problem—suicide, for example, in studies by Durkheim and Halbwachs—or how they discovered new problems, such as the "potlatch" Mauss wrote about in his essay on the gift.

Once again, a professorial university model stood in contrast to one characteristic of a small research school such as the École pratique des hautes études, and since not even minimal agreement could be reached on how sociology should be taught, "the great scientific textbook," as Mauss called it, never came to be. Parodi effectively summed up the philosophical and political orientation one finds in nearly all texts written by university teachers: "Political rationalism tended to be defined as a kind of idealism. It involved introducing moral considerations into the study of social questions, and this is precisely the substance of its opposition to the amoralist realism of rightist traditionalists. It was from this moral viewpoint that proponents of political rationalism defended the rights to free thinking and to science in modern society; that also explains the importance attached to the role of education."[62]

Bayet, Bouglé, Davy, Lapie, Parodi, and to a lesser degree Fauconnet and René Hubert, reinterpreted Durkheim's sociology in this sense, and it is Bouglé who formulated the most systematic version of it in his *Leçons de sociologie sur l'évolution des valeurs* (1922), a work that according to Davy was nothing less than "a synthesis of contemporary sociology."[63] Beginning with the postulate that "the existence of a society is first and foremost spiritual," Bouglé defined sociology's "essential object" to be "values," and thereby was able to return to philosophical spiritualism, the dangers of socialism (which threatened to create a nation within the nation), and "the hope" of helping to orient "the consciousness of educators." This position could be qualified as rationalist, he added, but on condition that this type of reason be recognized as "something singularly richer and more flexible than the reason the scientist or the scholar uses when he demonstrates or verifies."[64] Bouglé's understanding, which was opposed to "narrow" and "superstitious" positivism (as his friend Parodi put it), is clearly illustrated by the text in which he expounds his vision of society. The move from narrow to broad sociology is expressed in these terms: "Society is not a sort of block weighing down on the individual; it is a flame that burns and rises toward the heavens: society is the guardian of values."[65]

Clearly, then, the opposition between research scholars and university professors also produced different versions of Durkheimianism. Stiffening the oppositions somewhat, it could be said that one group used the concept of "collective representations" in an approach focused on "values" and "ideals" in connection with issues of social integration and consensus. It specifically related these notions to questions about morals and morality, which were contested especially in the domain of public education. The research scholars, on the other hand, used the focus on collective representations to study questions of symbolic classifications in relation to institutional structures and social morphology in different societies. Philosophically, the first position was linked to neospiritualism, wherein everything—including scientific research itself—tended to be perceived from a moral viewpoint.[66] The other position was marked instead by a form of scientific pragmatism, oriented toward establishing a comparative research program and "real, practical relations" (Mauss) between various disciplines and research areas. Mauss's concept of a "total social fact" served such a purpose, Simiand and Halbwachs's use of statistical series similarly allowed for various forms of transdisciplinary exchange and collaboration.

This systematic opposition was not symmetrical, however. Among other reasons, the researchers' network was broader in scope because it developed around two subgroups of the initial team: one around Mauss, the other around Simiand. Institutionally concentrated in the fifth section of the École pratique des hautes études, where Mauss, Hubert, and Granet worked, with links to the fourth section (Simiand) and the École des langues orientales (Granet, M. Cohen), the research scholars had ties with and in some cases were members of the Institut d'ethnologie, the Collège de

France (Meillet, Isodore Lévy, Mauss, Simiand), and learned societies such as the Société française de psychologie, of which Mauss was vice president in 1923, and the Société statistique de Paris, of which Simiand was president in 1921.

The network of university teachers, concentrated in the Faculty of Letters, had particularly strong links to the Centre de documentation sociale (1920–40) of the École normale supérieure, headed by Bouglé. And Bouglé himself, with his close contacts with the Société française de philosophie and government administrations, was the central figure of it. Fauconnet, somewhat off to the side in part because of fragile heath, was the member of this group most closely linked to the research scholars. The position of the university teachers within the Durkheimian group was more peripheral. The learned society of the Durkheimians, the Institut français de sociologie, was clearly dominated by research scholars—as indicated by its name, forged by Mauss to avoid "kinship" with the Société française de philosophie and to mark its affinity with the Institut français d'anthropologie (1911). There are many other examples of these tensions; the connotations and allusions they involved may seem rather opaque today. For example, it is not transparent why Mauss speaks of "the hollow philosophy of the radicals" in his introduction to Durkheim's book on socialism without being aware of the gradual splitting up of the Durkheimians.

The divergence of the Durkheimians in the interwar years retrospectively recalls different ways of adhering to the sociological enterprise and highlights some of the ambiguities of Durkheimian sociology itself. Durkheim himself had fought on different fronts and occasionally followed a strategy to concede all so as to win acceptance for the essential. This is perhaps why he was often perceived as ascetic, scrupulous, disinterested, and simultaneously as a major manipulator at the New Sorbonne, highly skilled in the academic power game. Durkheim himself, in any case, was occasionally unable to refuse the "lesser evil" policy, in contrast to Mauss or Simiand, who pursued careers that were more marginal, although as "consecrated heretics," to use Bourdieu's term, they ultimately obtained chairs at the Collège de France.

The impossibility of attaining the unity that had characterized the first series of the *Année sociologique* was thus linked to conditions that in turn explain why the differentiation between university professors and research scholars took the form of a rather systematic opposition. The most important reason the split has not appeared overtly is that the "generation of 1930" revived the polemical image of the Durkheimians as a dogmatic, closed, and powerful school that right-wing publicists (Agathon, Lasserre) had propagated at the beginning of the century, an image that then somehow made its way into intellectual common sense.

Recruitment Patterns

An approximate idea of generational differences may be obtained by looking at how the collaboration of graduates from the École normale supérieure
on the Durkheimian journals evolved (table 4.3). Recruitment of *normalien*
contributors began to decrease before the First World War, probably in
connection with the lack of career possibilities. This trend continued after
the war, although it was compensated for by recruiting persons in the same
age groups as the Durkheimians from different disciplines.

Among the fifteen new collaborators on the second series of the *Année
sociologique*, eleven had finished their training before the war, and many
of these seem to have been recruited by Mauss. Three of the four youngest
newcomers were *normaliens* and *agrégés* in philosophy recruited by Bouglé
(Marcel Déat, Max Bonnafous, Jean Laubier). The other was a female student of Henri Hubert, Françoise Henry, who was the first women to join
the Durkheimian group. The age structure of the second series was thus
virtually the opposite of what it had been for the first: very few collaborators under thirty and a high number of men forty and over. Moreover, the
young contributors' commitment was weak, since none of the four young
recruits continued to contribute to the *Annales sociologiques*.

Recruitment for the *Annales sociologiques* reflects both the dispersion
of the sociological network and the breaking up of the Durkheimian group.
Five separate series were composed by loosely linked teams headed by a few
central Durkheimians. Thirty-seven of the forty-six collaborators worked
on only one series (eight collaborated on two series; Halbwachs contributed
to four). A majority (twenty-seven out of forty-six) had not collaborated on
the first or second series of the *Année sociologique*. The "general sociology" series (A series), directed by Bouglé, was handled by philosophers
Bouglé recruited from the Centre de documentation sociale at the École
normale (Raymond Aron, André Kaan, Henri Mougin, Raymond Polin,
Jean Stoetzel) and by those who had ties to the Centre (Valentin Feldman,
Robert Marjolin). The first issues in Mauss's sociology of religion B series
included only one long study by Granet on kinship relations in China (which
would provide the major source for Lévi-Strauss's analysis of the elementary structures of kinship).[67] Only the fourth and last issue included book

TABLE 4.3
Number of *normaliens* collaborating on the *Année sociologique* (1st and 2nd series) and
Annales sociologiques by year of their promotion

Prior to 1893	1893–1903	1904–14	1918–29	1930–42
8	16	8	7	3

Note: No *normalien* who graduated in 1915, 1916, or 1917 collaborated on the journals.

reviews, written by Mauss's students (Michel Leiris, Anatole Lewitzki, Jacques Soustelle). The C series, directed by Jean Ray, covered law and morality and involved two types of collaborators: legal scholars (Emmanuel Lévy, Henri Lévy-Bruhl) and Durkheimians with a university position interested in issues of morality (Bayet, Bouglé, Fauconnet, René Hubert). The economic sociology series D brought together well-established specialists (Simiand, Georges Bourgin, Halbwachs) and a few newcomers (Robert Marjolin, Georges Lutfalla, Philippe Schwob). Halbwachs's E series handled nearly all the other themes: aesthetics (Charles Lalo), linguistics (Marcel Cohen, Lucien Tesnière), social morphology (Demangeon, Jules Sion), and statistics (Pierre Depoid), supplemented by contributions from a few of Halbwachs's colleagues from Strasbourg (Gabriel Le Bras, Pierre Montet). Recruitment for the *Annales sociologiques* was thus quite similar to what it had been for the second series of the *Année*: many newcomers but few young ones. The only series with a high number of young collaborators was Bouglé's (table 4.4).

Before looking more closely at the recruitment pattern, it is important to note that the same aging phenomenon was observable for other academic journals. In philosophy, for example, the average age of collaborators in two main journals, the *Revue philosophique* and the *Revue de métaphysique et de morale*, went up from over forty in 1905 to slightly over sixty in 1935.[68]

The younger generation, often referred to as the "generation of 1930," was defined first and foremost by an attitude of revolt.[69] In 1932 the *Nouvelle revue française* published a register of demands, a *cahier de revendications*, with contributions by Paul Nizan, Henri Lefebvre, Emmanuel Mounier, and others, and an introductory text by Denis de Rougemont. Observing a phenomenon that was allegedly "quite new" among intellectuals, Rougemont suspected that it might even give rise to a "new French revolution": "Solidarity in the face of peril is creating a unity among us that neither masters nor doctrines were able to create: we are united in our rejection of the appalling misery of a period when everything a man may love and desire is cut off from its living source, withered, denatured, inverted,

TABLE 4.4
Average age of the collaborators on the *Annales sociologiques* by series

	Series A	Series B	Series C	Series D	Series E
Average age	38.6	50.6	53.3	50.1	53.3
n	14	8	14	12	10
unknown	—	—	—	2	—

sabotaged."[70] This revolt gave rise to the proliferation of little groups and journals, some within existing organizations, like the "young Turks" of the Radical Party or Marcel Déat's "neosocialists," but most outside the established institutions, around small journals ranging from the fascist Right to the extreme Left: *Je suis partout* (founded in 1930), *Réaction* (1930), *Esprit* (1932), *Combat* (1935), *Revue marxiste* (1929), and *Critique sociale* (1931). These "neo" or simply "anti" or "ultra" initiatives were related to the growing number of students in a period of shrinking job possibilities (table 4.5).

The steady increase in student numbers, bachelor degrees (*licence*), and PhDs was accompanied by a general stagnation in the number of teaching positions (the increase in teaching positions between 1910 and 1920 is explained by the creation of the University of Strasbourg). This phenomenon was particularly marked for the Faculty of letters, which received an increased proportion of university students, in large part because of the increasing proportion of female students. The overproduction of university degree-holders, momentarily attenuated by the effects of the First World War, became manifest after the financial crash of 1929. Unemployment rose steadily, also for holders of a university degree, and even the best qualified had difficulty in finding a job. Between 1922 and 1935, for example, there were approximately 180 vacancies yearly for teaching literature, while the number of candidates increased from 830 to 2,060.[71] Alarming reports spoke about an "intellectual proletariat" and one of the well-known young authors, Denis de Rougemont, published *Diary of an Unemployed Intellectual* (1937).

TABLE 4.5
Demography of the Faculty of Letters (1900–1940)

	Number of students	% of women	% of all students	*Licence* degrees	PhDs	Teaching positions
1900–1904	4,134	13	13	463	25	312 (1900)
1905–09	5,877	26	15	535	34	
1910–13	6,382	35	15	482	35	368 (1910)
1920–24	8,887	43	17	680	25	402 (1920)
1925–29	14,297	49	22	678	44	436 (1929)
1930–34	19,489	49	23	1,243	55	
1935–39	17,853	50	25	1,312	48	459 (1939)

Sources: *Annuaire statistique de la France: Résumé rétrospectif, 1966.* The number of teachers (including those at the Université d'Alger) is based on the *Annuaire de l'instruction publique et des beaux-arts* (1900, 1910) and, for the interwar years, on O. Dumoulin, *Profession historien, 1919–1939: Un métier en crise?,* PhD thesis, Paris, École des hautes études en sciences sociales, 1983, p. 72.

Note: Five-year averages unless otherwise indicated.

The overall stagnation in teaching positions in the Faculty of letters, which had been preceded by a strong expansion (1880–1910), explains the increased age of collaborators on sociological and philosophical journals, as well as students' feelings of revolt against the steadily aging university establishment. Careers in higher education were blocked, and this stimulated aspiring academics to abandon risky disciplines (such as sociology) and adopt the alternative strategy of innovating within the more established ones (such as philosophy or history) or changing professional plans altogether and reconverting their educational capital in other sectors. Intellectual innovation involved importing a wide range of new theoretical programs (phenomenology, philosophy of history, Marxism), while strategies of reconversion concerned domains such as politics, journalism, and literature.[72] Many future sociologists of this generation were indeed tempted by itineraries at least partially outside higher education. Georges Friedmann, the *normalien* and philosopher, published three novels and was involved in many other cultural activities before starting to do research at the Centre de documentation sociale.[73] Georges Duveau worked as a journalist and edited a small literary review, *L'oeuf dur*, before cofounding the journal *Esprit* (1932). Jean Stoetzel created the Institut français d'opinion publique (1938) as a private institute for public-opinion polling.[74] Two of Bouglé's other recruits, Déat and Bonnafous, who were considered to be the more promising members of the new generation, started out as neosocialists but moved to the right and ended up as collaborators of the Vichy regime.[75] And the Collège de sociologie (1937–39), founded by Georges Bataille and Roger Caillois with the purpose of transgressing the boundaries of academic sociology and establishing ties with literature and experiences of the sacred, may be considered a particular case of this general tendency to turn away from a closed and steadily aging academic establishment.[76]

Nearly all young collaborators on the sociology journals were, furthermore, engaged in significant political activities. This holds for the "neosocialists" (Déat, Bonnafous), Marxist or Marxian philosophers (Friedmann, Feldman, Mougin), socialist students (Lévi-Strauss), and those close to the Socialist Party (Aron, Marjolin). Political commitments often played a major role in redefining scholarly work, as indicated for example by Raymond Aron's interpretation of Weber. For the young Aron, Max Weber was not so much a historical and comparative sociologist as someone who had combined scholarship and politics in a new manner: "Weber's originality and grandeur derive first and foremost from the fact that he was and wanted to be both a politician and a scholar, or rather that he both separated and united politics and science."[77]

The necessity of finding or creating other possibilities, reinventing intellectual work rather than preparing to pick up where the masters had left off, was reinforced by the specific experiences of the generations in question. The Durkheimians had been trained in the atmosphere of the struggle to establish and expand secular republican institutions, and their careers developed in part thanks to the republican policy of expanding the educational system. Young people who began their studies after the First World War had not experienced the Dreyfus Affair, the *universités populaires*, the fight for the separation of church and state, nor had they directly benefited from republican educational policies. Born around the turn of the century, they were too young to be mobilized for the war and in general had a different relation to the republic and the "fatherland." Experienced from a distance, the war was more likely to be perceived as "tragic" or "absurd." References were regularly made to the "the war generation," and there is reason to suppose that the war experience instated a split, experienced by the young as a "distancing" that in some cases elicited feelings of "disgust" or "hatred" that could readily be directed against veterans' associations.[78] Bouglé was not the only one to have pointed out that the former pupils of the republican schools had "cut a fine figure" at Verdun.[79] Paul Nizan, one of the more articulate spokesmen of the new generation, remarked that his professors "displayed their dead as if they were proofs. Those dead were *their* dead. Those victories, their victories. M. Bergson saw the French victory as his own. And it was Boutroux's victory. Émile Durkheim's victory. To M. Brunschvicg the Marne seemed a stunning confirmation of his philosophy."[80]

In the mocking humor of young students a certain pessimism and sense of impatience transpires in opposition to the calm and reasonable optimism of their professors. One effect of this generation gap was that it synchronized development of the various fields and subfields, and this in turn worked to create the "unity of rejection" and a spontaneous sympathy for anything that went against the *idées reçues*.[81] With the exception of a few artistic movements, consciousness of this break dates from the early 1930s, and there is every reason to believe that it was provoked by the economic downturn following the stock market crash of 1929. The general designation in any case was the "generation of the 1930s" and the "spirit" of the 1930s.

Social Images of Sociology

It is not the least paradox of sociology in the interwar years that the image of the Durkheimian group as a closed and powerful school of thought gained ground precisely as the school itself was falling apart. Durkheimianism became a symbol of all that was being rejected as old-fashioned and conservative, particularly its combination of a positivist approach to science and a secular republican morality. In this respect, Nizan's polemical essay *Les chiens de garde* (*The Watchdogs*, 1932) represents a more typical position than is generally believed. Motivated by "the necessity to attack" and addressing himself to "the newcomers," Nizan wrote to expose the "spiritual comfort and temporal guarantees of that comfort" that his professors enjoyed, especially "state thinkers" like Durkheim and Brunschvicg (different in this sense for Nizan from Catholics like Jacques Maritain and Gabriel Marcel). If sociology occupied such an important position, Nizan claimed, this was primarily because it gave new life to moribund philosophical tendencies such as rationalism and spiritualism. The image he presents of sociology results from a twofold reduction. First, he identifies sociologists with university professors and anyone linked to them. Nizan regularly cites Bouglé, Fauconnet, Lapie, and Parodi, while making no mention at all of Mauss, Halbwachs, and Simiand, although he himself had participated in Simiand's seminar. Behind the university teachers, Nizan perceived Durkheim, and he sided with the attacks of Charles Péguy and Agathon, citing their polemics. Second, he reduced sociology to a "doctrine of obedience" and to social conformism fitting for primary school teachers: "It looks a great deal as though the founder of French sociology wrote the *Division du travail social* to permit obscure administrators to draw up a study program for primary school teachers. The move of bringing sociology into the *écoles normales primaires* marked the state-administrative victory of that morality."[82]

Nizan's essay suggests that the university professors were more visible and better known than the research scholars. Simiand, Halbwachs, and Granet were not unknown, but their works were perceived as "specialized," they were often not immediately thought of as sociologists, and they did not have the academic power of Sorbonne professors. Mauss had published many articles and reviews in a wide variety of scholarly journals, but no individual book, and he seems not to have been very well known, in contrast to Lucien Lévy-Bruhl, who was philosophy professor at the Sorbonne and the most widely read ethnologist. Situated at a distance from the elite schools and the canonical disciplines, the advanced seminars of Mauss, Granet, and Simiand at the École pratique des hautes études attracted relatively few students, though an entire generation of anthropologists was trained by Mauss.

Mauss also taught at the Institut d'ethnologie (1925), which he cofounded with Lévy-Bruhl and Paul Rivet, and at the Collège de France starting in 1931, but the École pratique remained the center of his activities.[83] In the 1930s the École had ties to the new Musée de l'homme, where young researchers deposited the objects they had brought back from their first ethnographic missions and where some found their first employment.[84]

These were often the same persons who attended his courses; with the exception of the Collège de France, they seldom numbered more than twenty. The accounts of his teaching I collected all stress his preference for concrete realities and his great erudition. Moreover, he was not concerned about following the rules of standard pedagogy: "He proceeded by way of shortcuts. He would move easily back and forth between Australians and customs he'd observed in a family in his hometown, Épinal. At times we didn't immediately understand; we had to think about it for a while afterward." A second ethnologist recalled: "He had an extraordinary talent for awakening minds. He would take a Swedish missionary's account of the Papua of New Guinea as his basic text, for example, then look at it page by page, making comparisons, taking out other books—we were watching thought being born."

Mauss's students rarely took the courses given by sociologists at the Sorbonne. Ethnology was becoming a world of its own, at least in the experience of many young students: "It was a tiny circle, and something of a family." Few were *agrégé* or *normalien*; they tended instead to be relative outsiders to the academic world. Maussian ethnology was not, as they saw it, a continuation of Durkheim's sociology, but rather something new, linked to the study of primitive societies, the world of art, to archeology, history of religions, or Oriental languages. For them, whereas Durkheim was perceived as a "harsh, cold, fairly rigid professor, a real schoolmaster," Mauss was different: he was "warm, expansive, he radiated."

University teaching, on the other hand, may be said to have been dominated by the personality of Bouglé, who was a "good teacher" and left Fauconnet, Bayet, and Halbwachs in the shadow. According to the accounts I collected, the others did not have Bouglé's rhetorical talent; they are often described as "boring," even if some were highly respected. Halbwachs, for example, had very few doctoral students; he directed only two doctoral dissertations during his years at Strasbourg (1919–35), both by foreigners.[85] Because it did not involve any specific research effort, university sociology was often a routinized discipline, either related to philosophical problems or reduced to a kind of pedagogy of social facts. A student of Bayet, Bouglé, and Fauconnet recalled: "I turned toward sociology in 1935 or 1936, but the courses were disappointing. Fauconnet looked like a ghost from the past; Bouglé was lively, but his courses consisted in underlining the necessity of studying social life—without teaching how. *Le suicide* was explained as you might explain Plato's *Republic*, and Fauconnet went on and on about responsibility. As sociology, it was dead."

Statistical evidence confirms these testimonies. A decreasing proportion of students at the Sorbonne choose sociology for an optional certificate for the bachelor degree, going down from 1.5 percent in the 1920s to 0.8

or 0.9 percent in the 1930s, thus roughly following the same curve as the number of *normaliens* collaborating on sociology journals.[86] A certain interest in sociology may have subsisted throughout the 1920s, but went down around 1930. The same shift may be observed for doctoral theses. The proportion of *normaliens* among social science PhDs (in sociology, psychology, pedagogy, economics) obtained in Parisian institutions went down from 50 percent for the years 1900–1919 to 16 percent for the years 1920–34, whereas in philosophy, for example, the proportion over the same years went up from 21 to 33 percent.[87] The promise of these new disciplines for the academic elite seems to have faded and many returned to the classical disciplines of philosophy and history, which were also taught in secondary schools.

Students from the École normale graduating in the 1920s mention "a certain interest" in sociology. Others, however, stress that sociology held no "real" interest: "Durkheim was a bit outmoded, turn-of-the-century" (*normalien*, historian). Although it was common practice among Sorbonne students not to attend courses regularly, many mention the absence of "great professors." "We didn't have what Davy and René Hubert had had, a great sociology professor at the Sorbonne. Bouglé explained Comte's texts, Durkheim's, etc., but he wasn't an influential or compelling professor" (*normalien*, philosopher). *Normaliens* often ridiculed Durkheim's prestige. Nizan wrote: "If É. Durkheim would have it be believed that in the final analysis studying menstrual blood in Australian societies is of great assistance in solving social problems, how many primary school teacher trainees will not believe every word of that great founder of sciences?"[88] When sociology had become a subject matter in the *écoles normales primaires*, it lost its attraction for the École normale supérieure.

The Centre de documentation sociale

The Centre de documentation sociale (CDS, 1920–40), attached to the École normale and headed by Bouglé, was surely more important in orienting young *normaliens* toward sociology than the public image or intellectual reputation of the discipline. Funded by a former banker, Albert Kahn, to promote documentation on current political and social issues, it was not a research institute but an information center. It consisted of a library and a reading room for consulting current periodicals and newspapers. It served no formal training function, had few readers, and is in no way comparable to the Institut d'ethnologie (1925) or the Institut de psychologie (1920), where students were trained in research in those disciplines. In addition to *normaliens*, who used it for information on current events, a few Sorbonne students in the higher degree programs visited the center. The secretaries of the CDS occasionally organized lectures, and they assisted Bouglé in preparing the *Année sociologique* and his own books. They shared an interest in current affairs and a preference for a job at the CDS over a teaching post outside Paris.[89]

In the 1930s the CDS became a more important place both for recruiting contributors to the *Annales sociologiques* and introducing new approaches that were distinct and often openly opposed to Durkheimianism. After Albert Kahn was ruined by the 1929 crash, Bouglé obtained a grant from the Rockefeller Foundation that enabled two *normaliens* to do full-time research.[90] The CDS's activities further developed after 1932: regular lectures, some research projects, and publications such as the "general sociology" issues of the *Annales sociologiques* and a series of collective volumes, *Inventaires*, on current political and social problems.[91] Bouglé played an important role in this renewal, as he was "fairly popular" among the *normaliens*, especially compared with his predecessors at the head of the École. He himself was very attached to the school and was *très camarade*: "He was a good director, he was good at getting resources, and he was very devoted to the students" (*normalien*, graduated in the 1930s). Often described as "intelligent" and "lively," he nonetheless had not much intellectual authority among *normaliens*: "We had the best of relations, and personally I really liked Bouglé, but I never talked science with him" (CDS assistant).

The disinterest in or "allergy" to Durkheimianism, as Aron put it, went together with a keen interest in work being done abroad, and more generally in international affairs. This international sensibility, linked to the political atmosphere of the 1930s, was fueled by longer or shorter stays abroad. Professors of the Parisian Faculty of Letters taught abroad far more often than in the years before the First World War.[92] Among the students some went to Germany (Aron, Kaan), many more to the United States (Marjolin, Philip, Schwob, Stoetzel). Book reviews and review essays in the *Annales sociologiques* show an attentive and generally benevolent attitude toward work as diverse as that of Mannheim, Schütz, Elias, Elton Mayo, and Talcott Parsons. The imported themes and approaches were very diverse. Friedmann began studying workers' reactions to industrial rationalization, Schwob worked on concentration in the electricity industry in France, Kaan on Hegel, Stoetzel on the psychology of advertising, Aron on the philosophy of history, and Duveau on workers during the Second Empire. For most, this was their first research work, often in the framework of their PhD. Their highly diverse research topics did have some properties in common because the CDS's activities were focused on current affairs. Bouglé invited political figures to speak, and questions related to contemporary issues were discussed in research seminars and talks, as is indicated by the book series *Inventaires*.

If there was a certain convergence of orientation and research practice, it was due primarily to external conditions. Rockefeller Foundation grants and, to a lesser degree, funding from the Caisse nationale de la recherche scientifique (1935) allowed some promising students to continue their studies. Grants from the Rockefeller Foundation were to be used for "inductive sociological research."[93] The subsidies were increased two years after the first installment, and paid from then on to the University of Paris to be distributed by the new Conseil universitaire de la recherche sociale (1934). The "special aim" of this fund was to organize research projects that would familiarize students with the "observation and working methods required for solving economic, sociological, and political problems."[94] This meant that for young scholars, "modern" disciplines (rather than philosophy and history) and empirical research into contemporary issues were favored.

The grants of the Rockefeller Foundation were effective in large part because they opened up French research to the incipient social demand for such research; that demand in turn stimulated forms of social science research that resembled a more American model. The new demand was related to the economic crisis, the failure of laissez-faire politics, and the diffusion of various forms of planning, approaches that granted the social sciences a role in managing markets and industries. Ideas about economic planning spread among younger business managers and engineers at the École polytechnique. The Centre d'étude des problèmes humains (1936), for example, purported to "apply to human problems the solid knowledge we have acquired of the world of things" and to remedy the "troubling lag" in the human sciences so that man would at last be able to better master his destiny.[95] The Centre was headed by an engineer, Jean Coutrot, and received funding from the Rockefeller Foundation; the demographer Alfred Sauvy and the sociologist Georges Friedmann were among its consulting members.

Although there were some interrelations, there were apparently not many direct contacts between the Centre de documentation sociale and the engineers and consultants who were more oriented toward the rationalization of the private sector. For the most part, the applied social sciences came to be organized within the planning framework that was established during and after the Occupation. But the rising social demand led to a strengthening of the Rockefeller Foundation policy and favored the development of an "inductive sociology" based on field research. Several studies by assistants and regulars at the CDS used this approach,[96] and they were accompanied by innumerable pleas in favor of "surveys"[97] and as many calls to rehabilitate Le Play.[98] Contrasting American research and French sociology, Henri

Mougin noted several obstacles in France: "the rarity of collective studies, a taste for sociological essays on specific notions, preference for interpretive studies rather than research and surveys closer to empirical realities."[99] Though the actual number of empirical studies realized was limited, empirical study became a point of convergence and rapprochement among practitioners otherwise divided by theoretical preferences and political affinities (Le Bras, Friedmann, Mougin, Polin, Stoetzel). For them, sociology was no longer the social science par excellence, but scientific inquiry into the crisis of the contemporary world, legitimated primarily by its possible usefulness to state and business administrations, and implying field work and data collection for which American studies provided the most advanced model. Despite individual variations, this approach predominated in the works of the young researchers. Made up of those who received state fellowships and Rockefeller Foundation grant holders, a new generation of scholars developed at the CDS, which was thus becoming the locus of a redefinition of sociology founded on the break with Durkheimianism. Many of the consequences of these changes would become apparent only after the Second World War when those who started their work in the 1930s obtained influential positions within a profoundly different institutional structure of research and teaching.

The Durkheimian Legacy

Instead of displaying a simple "rise and fall" pattern, French sociology after Émile Durkheim underwent a double transformation. The first was linked to the development of the Durkheimian group and the increasing split between research scholars and university teachers, producing diverging and at times conflicting forms of Durkheimianism. Through the work of Mauss, Hubert, Granet, Halbwachs, and Simiand, Durkheimian sociology entered a wide variety of research fields and contributed significantly to innovative scholarship. Most university professors, on the other hand, were less prominent within the Durkheimian network yet more visible in the academic field at large. They represented the more official brand of sociology and were close to the dominant currents of university philosophy and the republican administration. The second transformation was related to issues of transmission and recruitment of students. The version of Durkheimianism that appeared to be an appendix to neo-idealist philosophy and adapted to fit the demands of secular republican morality disappeared with the conditions that had brought it into being. All four university successors to the Durkheimians (Gurvitch, Stoetzel, Duveau, Aron) rejected not only certain aspects of Durkheimian sociology but its very aim and style as well.

If Durkheimianism survived as a productive research program, it was due to the research wing of the network, and as such in disciplines other than sociology.

This twofold, inseparably social and intellectual transformation has been perceived quite differently from abroad. Two young sociologists—one from Germany, the other from the United States—wrote a strikingly dissimilar appreciation of the state of French sociology in the 1930s. Their reviews exemplify different categories of perception and amounted to opposed judgments. The reviews are all the more interesting since they were written by two major figures in postwar sociology. The young German sociologist René König wrote an extensive overview in 1931–32 in which he highlighted the general "retreat of philosophical work" in favor of "more positive research." He commented on the "astounding scope and depth" that Durkheimian sociology had acquired in spite of the dramatic losses during the First World War. He discussed work by all the major Durkheimians, including studies by Hubert on European prehistory, Granet on ancient China, and Simiand on economic development. In addition to the impressive scope of the issues addressed, König commented on how Maurice Halbwachs's studies of social classes and lifestyle had given a much "greater depth" to the Durkheimian program. After this general characteristic, two special sections followed, one about research in social psychology, discussing the work of Mauss, Halbwachs, Blondel, and Dumas, the other about studies on primitive mentality, among others comparing Lucien Lévy-Bruhl's work with Freud's writings on the subject. König's well-informed account concluded that Durkheimian sociology was developing in the direction of a general theory of the human mind, mobilizing knowledge in numerous specialties and research areas. Instead of making sociology superfluous, the "careful scientific spirit" of Durkheim and his companions had promoted generalizations that were consistently based on rich and varied empirical material. This represented a valuable "protection aid," a *Schutzmittel*, against hastily formulated general theories, which could only discredit sociology in the eyes of serious scholars.[100]

In 1934, shortly after König's two articles had appeared, the young Robert Merton published his assessment of recent French sociology. It was not only different in tone but also presented a picture that contrasted sharply with König's review. Merton's much shorter article acknowledged that a thoroughgoing discussion would have to take into account the "many historians, jurists, economists, philologists, geographers, and psychologists" who had adopted a sociological approach to their respective fields. But because of "exigencies of time" it was not possible to do so. In spite of this cautionary remark, Merton went on to state that in "no other country" was sociological interest so "definitely focused on discernibly few problems."

From Merton's American point of view, which was more strongly bound to a well-established disciplinary division of labor, much of what König perceived as contributing to a general theory of human culture was not immediately relevant for sociology. Noting that "primitive mentality" and the relations between "sociology and psychology" were chief concerns in France, Merton remarked that in addition to the narrow focus of French sociology various issues and approaches were simply missing. The "statistical approach" was eschewed with "an almost studied deliberation." Halbwachs was "perhaps the only statistically-minded sociologist of prominence in France" who had indeed succeeded in an "approximate description of social phenomena." "Inductive investigations" of contemporary society, however, were few in number, and French sociologists seemed "sublimely unaware" of the fundamental circle of "fact-theory-fact." Instead, "theoretic discussions of general methodologic and conceptual problems are being constantly multiplied" and "claim the foreground." In addition to these gaps and fallacies, sociologists in "no other nation" divide so clearly into "distinct schools"; Mauss, for example, was described as an orthodox follower of Durkheim, "avoiding any suspicion of heterodoxy." Whereas König ends his article with a note of praise about how the Durkheimians successfully struck a balance between a broad range of empirical investigations and a general theoretical ambition, Merton ends with a word of advice: "more attention to facts of common experience and less to the elegancies of rarefied theory would do much to increase the fecundity of French sociologic research."[101]

König's well-informed assessment was a plea for a type of sociology that he considered to be unjustly ignored in Germany and that he wished to promote against both purely philosophical theorizing and atheorical empiricism. The French seemed to have succeeded in developing a broad, diverse, and theoretically sophisticated science of human culture that was much discussed in Germany but that remained trapped in philosophical speculation that the French avoided. Merton's more polemical review was written at a time when American sociologists battled over the legacy of the Chicago school, which had long been the leading center. Merton's criticism of French sociology seems to echo some the objections against the Chicago school (such as ignorance of statistics), and it may not have been accidental that the review was written by a PhD student from Harvard and was originally read at a session of the Eastern Sociological Conference, one of the regional associations where the opposition against the Chicagoans was most vivid. The first major victory in the struggle against the supremacy of Chicago was the founding of the *American Sociological Review* (1935), which confirmed that the balance of power was shifting to new centers on the East Coast (Harvard, Columbia).[102]

In its remarkably self-confident style, Merton's paper was also indicative of the changing relationships between Europe and the United States. Shortly after Merton's paper appeared, one of his teachers, Talcott Parsons, published *The Structure of Social Action* (1937). Proposing a theoretical refounding of the discipline, Parsons suggested that the future of sociology was henceforth less dependent on its European roots than on its American merits. As he stated shortly after the Second World War: "Like all branches of American culture, the roots of sociology as a science are deep in Europe. Yet I like to think of sociology as in some sense peculiarly an American discipline, or at least an American opportunity."[103]

CHAPTER 5

✳✳✳

Pioneers by Default?

The development of sociology after 1945 is generally portrayed as a long-awaited break with the past and a vigorous new beginning. Henceforth, based on empirical research and consistently focused on contemporary social problems, sociology would be liberated from the "grip of philosophy" and at last become a "modern" and "empirical" discipline.[1] This reorientation is commonly attributed to the emerging research sector independent of the universities, including the first sociological research institute, the Centre d'études sociologiques (1946). Because virtually all members of the postwar generation of sociologists started their career at the Centre d'études sociologiques, historical studies of the discipline have concentrated on the projects carried out there. In doing so, however, it is too easily overlooked that the research that was undertaken depended on conditions well beyond the Centre itself. Although there is little doubt that the Centre d'études sociologiques formed the center of postwar French sociology, its actual functioning can only be understood by reconstructing its relationships to both the intellectual field and the increasingly important universe of policy research. Sociological work after 1945 was caught up in a constellation that was defined by two antagonistic poles: an intellectual pole represented by existentialist philosophers who dominated the intellectual and much of the academic field and a policy-related research pole in state institutes for statistical, economic, and demographic studies. Many of the difficulties with which the first generation of postwar sociologists grappled can be understood from sociology's precarious position within this broader structure.

Doing sociological research in the 1950s was a troublesome and often awkward affair, not only because the first generation of researchers lacked proper training but also because they had limited access to other resources. In spite of the apparent autonomy of the Centre d'études sociologiques, sociologists suffered from a kind of double exclusion. In the theoretical and political concerns that dominated the intellectual field and that were defined by philosophers around Jean-Paul Sartre and his journal *Les temps modernes*, sociology was seen as an intellectually insignificant and rather suspicious enterprise, mostly associated with American-style empiricism in the service of the ruling classes. At the other pole of the spectrum, in the rapidly growing sector of policy-related research, sociology had no recognized position either. It proved difficult for most researchers in sociology to find their way in a field that was structured by the opposition between politically committed, left-wing intellectuals on the one hand and professional researchers in state institutes on the other. Given the lack of training and material and symbolic means at their disposal, many of the postwar sociologists experienced the beginning of their career as an uncertain and difficult period. Although sociology was not considered an intellectually legitimate endeavor, sociologists could hardly neglect the concerns of the leading intellectual groups. And being involved in empirical research, they could not disregard the nascent sector of policy-related research, although sociology had no position there either. Since sociologists had to cope with this double bind, many of the first research projects undertaken were a hesitant response to the practically insurmountable tensions between Sartre and statistics, between politically committed intellectuals and professional research experts. Researchers had to comply with requirements that were all too often mutually exclusive and that could only be met by restricting the inquiries to descriptive monographs and refraining from more theoretical ambitions. By responding to the demand for applied research, the researchers obtained research funds and gradually enhanced their professional experience. Presenting the results of this work as being about the needs and conditions of the working classes, they hoped to obtain some degree of intellectual recognition.

In order to understand this peculiar social dynamic, I will first outline the structure of this conflict-ridden field of relations and the conditions under which it functioned after the Second World War. I will then turn to sociology at the Sorbonne and in particular to Georges Gurvitch, who was a central figure in postwar sociology. Gurvitch proposed a theoretical renewal of the discipline, which echoed the philosophical themes that dominated the intellectual field, but he didn't succeed in establishing viable connections to either the intellectual world or the emerging empirical research. After discussing Gurvitch's theoretical program and his failed bid to provide an alternative to American functionalism and the structuralism of Lévi-Strauss, I will consider the Centre d'études sociologiques, its main research groups and emerging research specialties. Finally, I will discuss another component of the newly emerging social science research sector, the so-called Sixth Section of the École pratique des hautes études (EPHE). Founded by historians such as Lucien Febvre and Fernand Braudel of the *Annales* journal, the Sixth Section conquered a central position in the social sciences in France. It contributed to a profound reconfiguration of the social sciences and represented an original attempt to provide a new infrastructure for historical and social scientific studies, but here too, sociology's position was relatively weak.

Between Political Commitment and Policy Expertise

In France, the years following the liberation from the German occupation were determined by the demands of economic reconstruction and the desire for a profound social and political renewal.[2] After the economic depression of the 1930s, the calamitous defeat of 1940, and the shameful fiasco of Pétain's collaborationist Vichy regime, a return to the past was excluded. The regimes of the Third Republic as well as its conservative, ultranationalist opponents had been thoroughly discredited. Symbolically, the break with the past came with a referendum in 1945, in which the French voted almost unanimously in favor of a new constitution. The Third Republic was consigned to the past and once-powerful conservative groups like the Action française, which had collaborated with the German occupying forces or with the Vichy regime, had lost their legitimacy. The new political spectrum was dominated by groups linked to the resistance, and the provisional government formed by de Gaulle—made up of left-wing Catholics, socialists, and communists—reflected the new balance of power. The Communist Party emerged from the election as the main winner. With five million votes, it became the largest political force, overshadowing other left-wing parties for many years to come.

The twenty-odd changes of government in the course of the Fourth Republic (1947–58) and the international tensions generated by the Cold War did not fundamentally alter the political situation, and the intelligentsia's postwar mood of quasi-revolutionary fervor lingered on. The former underground newspaper *Combat*, whose contributors included Camus, was subtitled *De la résistance à la revolution*—"from resistance to revolution." In 1951, the left-wing Catholic periodical *Esprit* was still referring to France's "great revolutionary crisis,"[3] and in 1955 its then editor in chief wrote that it was impossible to pursue a left-wing political course without achieving a workable relationship with the Communists.[4] The role of the working classes and the significance of communism became key themes in the debates of the politicized intelligentsia. For a young, bourgeois intellectual like Alain Touraine, the liberation and the postwar years, when the Communists were part of the governmental coalition, had "upset everything."[5]

The widespread urge for renewal and the absence of a restoration of the status quo such as had followed the First World War could, according to Sartre, be explained by the balance of power between generations. After 1918, this had shifted in favor of the older generation, since so many young men had died in the trenches. After 1944, the opposite effect occurred: members of the older generation tended to be replaced more quickly, much old glory was tainted, and "we all quietly forgot about them."[6] Whatever the validity of Sartre's diagnosis, it certainly applied to the new intellectual constellation and to the mood in which Sartre's work was received with unprecedented acclaim. Although France was economically and politically diminished, it was intellectually as confident as ever.[7] And Sartre epitomized the dream that haunts French intellectuals since at least the Dreyfus Affair: he was a writer and philosopher, essayist and critic, independent and politically committed. In comparison with this "total intellectual," others might be worthy scholars, committed writers, or lucid philosophers, but no one combined these various capacities in such a virtuosic manner as Sartre did.[8]

Sartre achieved his position as intellectual par excellence by transcending two historical dividing lines: he was held in high regard both as a philosopher and a writer, and his work was appreciated by both specialized scholars and interested lay readers.[9] For some time, he represented the model that other intellectuals sought to emulate; even academic philosophy and literary studies could not shrug off his example. In an authoritative survey of academic French philosophy published in 1950, he is the author most frequently quoted, ahead of his own masters Husserl and Heidegger.[10]

This unique position stemmed from the particular situation that existed after the Second World War and from Sartre's ability to develop a synthesis between what are generally specialist areas. His concept of "existentialism" was precisely such a synthesis. Its point of departure was an anthropocentric view of human existence. For Sartre, the subject entwined in existential choices was the "universal concrete," with which he reconciled philosophy with literature and ontology with experience.[11] This point of view, which Sartre dramatized in his stage plays, was also the basis of his engagement, his political commitment. According to Sartre, things exist purely in a passive mode, while human beings are condemned to be free: in every situation, whatever the force of circumstances, human beings must chose. That, and that alone, leads to the issues of political and moral judgment, of authenticity and bad faith.

In the first issue of *Les temps modernes*, Sartre argued in a prophetic tone that the impartiality of pure scholarship was just as facile as "art for art's sake." A writer belonged to his time and could not evade responsibility for it: he might write about it, or say nothing about it, but both represented a choice. In opposition to Flaubert, whom Sartre held partly responsible for the bloodbath that had been visited on the Commune because he had not written a single line to prevent it, he posited the creed of *Les temps modernes*: "not to miss anything of our times."[12] The central position occupied by Sartre was underscored by the influential role of the journal *Les temps modernes*, which embraced every genre of intellectual life that counted: literary contributions, philosophical essays, and reflections about art, literature, and current affairs.[13] The other intellectual periodicals reflect a similar involvement with topical political issues. *Esprit* became the mouthpiece of left-wing Catholic intellectuals. Its editor in chief was the personalist philosopher Emmanuel Mounier. *Esprit* had little if any literary pretensions, and theoretically it was overshadowed by *Les temps modernes*. The journal *La nouvelle critique* was linked to the Communist Party and sustained polemics against bourgeois views in the name of a "militant Marxism." Notwithstanding the Communists' political influence, *La nouvelle critique* did not have much intellectual authority.[14] Only the periodical *Critique* adhered to a format different from that of the politically committed periodicals. Founded by the writer Georges Bataille in 1946, it published book reviews in diverse areas. *Critique* kept outside the fray and was original but somewhat isolated from prevailing opinions. Essays by writers such as Bataille and Maurice Blanchot alternated with contributions from the philosophers Alexandre Koyré and Eric Weil, all of whom were in some way atypical among Parisian intellectuals.[15]

In this politicized intellectual field, in which the prewar dividing lines between literature, philosophy, and politics had become blurred, the social sciences were relegated to the margins of the intellectual order. In Sartre's existentialism, the social sciences were stigmatized as objectivist and reductionist undertakings. Just as he regarded materialism as a transparent ploy to rob human beings of their subjectivity, the social sciences were characterized by suspicious claims to objectivity. For Sartre, no social constraint could ever undermine the freedom of choice, which he professed with characteristic fervor: "this area of unpredictability, which is thus disconnected from social forces, is what we call freedom, and a human being is nothing other than his freedom."[16] The aim of identifying laws that determine the course of history had reduced Marxism to a "mindless determinism" and stripped it of its revolutionary potential. The stubborn search for "objectivity" was in reality nothing other than the subjectivity of those who felt ashamed of their subjectivity.[17] In Sartre's intellectual universe, the social sciences scarcely existed. The American social sciences displayed a naive empiricism that could all too easily be co-opted to serve the interests of the establishment. And Durkheim's efforts had long since been written off: "Durkheim's sociology is dead: social facts are not things, they possess significance, and in that capacity they refer to the entity through which meanings enter the world, the human being."[18]

Articles on the social sciences were virtually absent from *Les temps modernes*. The only exceptions were occasional essays about psychology and psychoanalysis, undoubtedly because they represented rival approaches to the themes of existentialism. In *Esprit* too, the social sciences were scarcely discussed, although the journal paid more attention to problems of institutional and political reform than *Les temps modernes*. The editors of *Esprit* viewed the American social sciences with suspicion, but they had more regard for their potential applications than the literary figures and philosophers of *Les temps modernes*.[19] In *La nouvelle critique*, Marxism was mobilized in campaigns against bourgeois social science. The historians of the *Annales* school were the butt of virulent attacks, and sociology was labeled a "police science."[20] Only *Critique*, the least doctrinaire of all the major intellectual journals, regularly included reviews of social science publications. The work of Friedmann and Gurvitch was reviewed, as well as that of Piaget, Merton, Linton, Dumézil, Lévi-Strauss, and numerous economists.

A succinct picture of the intellectual balance of power can be obtained from the reports that appeared in the leading newspaper *Le monde*.[21] Besides literary columns, a spokesman for *Esprit*, Jean Lacroix, wrote a philosophical chronicle, and André Latreille discussed historical studies. There was no separate column for the social sciences, and here too, the only disciplines to receive any sustained attention were psychology and psychoanalysis. Sartre was omnipresent, whereas sociologists were scarcely ever mentioned in the newspaper's columns. On the rare occasions on which sociology was mentioned at all, it was to explain that even in this rather obscure field the value of humanist philosophy was acknowledged. In 1950, Lacroix observed that the French have "no sociological mind," and concluded with the following words: "it is gratifying to see that figures as diverse as Mounier, Gurvitch, Lefebvre, Friedmann, etc. recognize that questions of technology, however important these may be, do not control human progress, but must remain subordinate to a general theory of knowledge, and—in a word—to a philosophy of humankind."[22]

It was in part because of a lack of intellectual status that the demand for applied research came to fulfill a new function for the social sciences.

The growth of applied social science research was produced by the needs of economic recovery and the new role of the state in that respect. After the country's liberation, several banks, insurance companies, and industries were nationalized. In 1946 a system of economic planning came into effect that was key to the economic reconstruction of the country. Supported by political parties, trade unions, and entrepreneurs, the Monnet Plan was the first in a series of democratic and "indicative" five-year plans drafted by committees in which entrepreneurs, trade unions, civil servants, and experts were all represented.[23] Planning became an instrument for economic reconstruction and technological modernization, based on organized consultation and central coordination. A major impetus for the state management of the economy came from the Marshall Plan and hundreds of "productivity missions" to the United States (450 between 1949 and 1956), which contributed to an accelerated import and adaptation of American technology and management models.[24]

The planning system created a growing demand for information and indicators of economic and social trends. Existing services in this area were reformed, new institutes were founded, and only a few years after the country's liberation, a planning structure existed, at the heart of which was the Commissariat au plan. The planning institutes were relatively independent from the volatility of parliamentary politics and were led by engineers from the École polytechnique, who had been trying since the economic depression of the 1930s to construct models of economic development that would avoid the undesirable effects of the free market without degenerating into state *dirigisme*. This "third way" between free-market liberalism and socialist central planning combined elements of Catholic social thought with technocratic views of expertise and rationality. The Monnet Plan displayed distinct similarities, in particular to the proposals that had been elaborated under the Vichy regime. Despite profound political changes, the higher ranks of the civil service had remained much the same as before, so that in several areas initiatives that had been launched during the war—whether or not in relation to the resistance—could be continued.[25] This continuity was most clearly visible in the institutional structure. Institutions such as the Institut national d'études demographiques (INED), the Office de la recherche scientifique et technique d'Outre-Mer (ORSTOM), and the Institut national d'hygiène (later INSERM) were all founded during the war, albeit under slightly different names. The size and financial resources of these institutions enabled them to conduct large-scale research.[26] Although none of these institutions included an official sociology program, there were several relations to sociology and sociologists. The demographic institute (INED), for instance, not only gathered population data but also conducted the first surveys on social mobility and on the social determinants of fertility, choice of marriage partner, and education.[27] The growing significance of this type of research is clear from the fact that several of its representatives eventually also secured positions in the university. The career of Alain Girard is a good illustration. Girard embarked on his research at the Institut français d'opinion publique (IFOP) and the demographic institute INED. He wrote a PhD thesis based on this research and acquired a sociology chair at the Sorbonne in 1964, served on the editorial boards of several sociology journals, and was president of the Société française de sociologie (1972–78).

But the precise consequences of these new structures of policy research for the social sciences depended on the position of the discipline and its protagonists within their field. In order to assess the consequences for sociology, I will first consider sociology at the Sorbonne and then at the research sector.

Sociology at the Sorbonne

In the postwar academic structure, sociology was still a rather marginal phenomenon, a discipline with little prestige that was institutionally no more than a minor for philosophy undergraduates. The leading academics were the two professors at the Sorbonne, Georges Davy and Georges Gurvitch, each of whom presided over his own journal. Davy had succeeded Halbwachs in 1944 and resumed the publication of the *Année sociologique*, assisted by the last survivors of the Durkheimian network. But Davy was more of an administrator than a scholar. Among his many administrative functions, he was dean of the Sorbonne, and as the correspondent of the Rockefeller Foundation noted: "*Monsieur le doyen* is very much a dean, even out of his office."[28] The revival of the *Année sociologique* in 1949 was the last effort of the older generation to preserve the name, if not the fame, of the once-renowned journal.[29] Its structure and layout corresponded roughly to those devised by Durkheim half a century before, but the journal's resemblance to its illustrious predecessor was very superficial. A notice to subscribers announced the need to expand the research area of sociology to include empirical research on contemporary problems, but without overlooking the importance of anthropology and without relinquishing its theoretical orientation. The latter aims contrasted with American sociology, which was thought to be too exclusively focused on contemporary society and too strongly oriented toward understanding current social problems.[30] The editorial board of the revived *Année sociologique* consisted of the last Durkheimians (Davy, Georges Bourgin, Louis Gernet) along with a few others who had been taken on in the interwar years: the legal scholars Henri Lévy-Bruhl and Gabriel Le Bras, the anthropologist Maurice Leenhardt, the economist Georges Lutfalla, and the moral philosopher and sociologist Albert Bayet. Young people were conspicuously absent in the editorial board; by the time the first issue appeared, in 1949, the average age of the editors had reached sixty-four years. It is probably a telling detail as well that until the 1970s the editors in chief were professors of the law faculty (Henri Lévy-Bruhl, Jean Carbonnier). Members of the younger generations saw the *Année sociologique* as a relic from the remote past, although many of them dutifully wrote book reviews for the journal.

Georges Gurvitch was the newcomer. He was appointed at the Sorbonne in 1948 as successor to Bayet and was the founding editor of a new journal, the *Cahiers internationaux de sociologie* (1946). Gurvitch's work was in the academic tradition in the sense that his books largely consist of critical overviews of social and political doctrines; his main interest was in general sociology and he himself did not do any empirical research. But Gurvitch was younger than the Durkheimians, came from a different background, and elaborated a sociology that seemed more in tune with the realities of postwar France. He had grown up in Russia, continued his education in Germany after 1920, and when he eventually settled in France, he published one of the very first books in French on the new German philosophy (Husserl, Heidegger, Scheler). When in 1935 he was appointed associate professor at the University of Strasbourg, he gravitated from social and political philosophy toward sociology.

During the war, Gurvitch worked at the French university-in-exile in New York, the École libre des hautes études, along with Lévi-Strauss and a few dozen other French scholars.[31] He presided over the sociology department and edited the *Journal of Legal and Political Sociology*, which discussed questions of democracy and economic planning in the light of the reconstruction of Europe. In the United States, he built up a network of people who would contribute to his journal, including Moreno and Sorokin, and encountered a mood that was quite alien to Europeans. The idea that a new age had dawned for sociology was not confined to Merton, Lazarsfeld, or Parsons, and this confident optimism impressed Gurvitch. He and Wilbert E. Moore edited the collected volume *Twentieth-Century Sociology* (1945), which reflects this sanguine new mood. The opening statement of his journal, the *Cahiers internationaux de sociologie*, was in the same vein. Sociology had finally come of age; its teething troubles—national traditions and rival schools—had been overcome, and the *Cahiers internationaux de sociologie* was a platform for the international and open-minded pursuit of this discipline.

Gurvitch's own contribution to this program attempted to reformulate the general principles of sociology. Drawing on the young Marx, the French sociological school (Durkheim and Mauss), and American empirical research, Gurvitch devised a framework for a pluralist sociology. In his view, social reality was a complex, living whole, and sociology must be both hyper-empirical and dialectical; it must do justice to individual and contingent facts as well as to relationships and the whole. Sociologists therefore need to adopt a differential working method, and their conceptual frame of reference consists of typologies. Much of Gurvitch's work consists of elaborate typological schemes of different levels of analysis and various aspects of social developments. Many of these typologies successfully avoided reductionisms, but their heuristic value was not always compelling. His sociology of "depth levels," for instance, distinguished ten different layers of society; for an analysis of social groups, he maintained that at least fifteen dimensions must be taken into account.[32] Since these layers and dimensions constituted neither an empirical analysis nor an explanatory model, they appeared to many as arbitrary enumerations rather than heuristic devices.

These classifications and typologies were accompanied by lengthy commentary on the work of classical and contemporary authors, often including harsh verdicts on their shortcomings. Fascinated by the intellectual field and the figure of Sartre, one of Gurvitch's theoretical goals was to rehabilitate human liberty and social vitality. In espousing them, he sought to present himself as a worthy rival to the existentialists, as well as to American-style functionalism and the emerging structuralism of Lévi-Strauss. In addition, Gurvitch argued, sociology must be socially committed, and he liked to define his own efforts as a pedagogy of freedom. In comparison to the *Année sociologique*, Gurvitch's journal was more up-to-date, further removed from scholarship and erudition in small and specialized disciplines, and closer to the intellectual and political debates of the day. *Cahiers* was also more internationally oriented than *Année sociologique*. Since *Année* published mainly book reviews and had lost a recognizable general orientation, it had a low profile. *Cahiers internationaux de sociologie*, on the other hand, published primarily articles and essays. The contributors to both journals formed more or less separate networks. Until 1958, a total of 133 people were involved in producing the new series of the *Année sociologique*, 45 of whom also contributed to the *Cahiers internationaux de sociologie*. Of the 141 people contributing to Gurvitch's journal in these years, 30 were foreigners, many of them Americans whom Gurvitch had met during the war when he lived in New York. Whereas in the *Année sociologique* only 8 percent of the book reviews concerned American studies, in the *Cahiers* this proportion was around 25 percent for both book reviews and review essays.[33]

Gurvitch's program may have, at least for a while, impressed members of the younger generation. The theoretical direction that Gurvith represented—a vigorous renewal of the discipline based on a critical combination of the French tradition, a certain form of Marxism, and empirical American sociology—appealed to more philosophically trained sociologists and anthropologists as well as to some researchers in sociology.[34] But in spite of his pivotal position in postwar sociology, Gurvitch failed to obtain the academic and intellectual recognition he had hoped for. Being sidelined at the Sorbonne by two newly appointed professors in 1955, Raymond Aron and Jean Stoetzel, he became a relatively isolated figure. His way of thinking, writing, and lecturing was rather alien to students schooled in French philosophical and literary studies; his complicated typologies, which had to be reproduced in examinations, were unpopular among students; and both his Russian accent and his sneers about fellow academics like Aron and Lévi-Strauss earned him the reputation of a rather intimidating figure.[35] In an autobiographical text, he remarked that sociologists saw him as a philosopher who had walked into the wrong room by mistake, whereas philosophers had only contempt for him as a sociologist.[36] Meanwhile, sociological research developed largely independently of his work, and Gurvitch did not have a very high regard of empirical studies. Although he published many American authors in his journal, and propagated sociometry as a viable foundation for microsociology, he came to see American surveys such as the American Soldier project—at the time regarded as the standard of methodological sophistication—as "utter failures."[37] US surveys had reached a level that was even below that of Le Play's nineteenth-century monographs, and the younger generation of French researchers did no more than naively copy their errors.[38]

To counter the hegemony of American sociology, Gurvitch founded an international association of French-speaking sociologists, the Association internationale des sociologues de la langue française (AISLF, 1958). The association has had a certain institutional success, regularly organizing international conferences and meetings, although it had difficulty in attracting the most prominent French sociologists and has in the long run perhaps reinforced the international isolation of French-speaking sociologists. By 1960 Gurvitch had lost most of the connections with the younger generation, who were more tempted by the newly appointed Sorbonne professors Aron and Stoetzel. In certain respects, Gurvitch's position was comparable to that of his former compatriot and colleague Sorokin. Both had been involved in the early days of the Russian Revolution and had left their home country, migrating to France and the United States, respectively, where they succeeded in reaching the summit of the academic establishment, the Sorbonne and Harvard. But both were ill at ease in their new habitat and had increasing difficulties in defining a legitimate position of their own. In Gurvitch's case, it was quite typical that even the work of his allies, those, like Balandier and Cazeneuve, who inherited his institutional positions, can scarcely be seen as having fruitfully picked up some of his ideas.[39]

Fieldwork as Vocation?

Although originally intended to foster research in the natural sciences, the Centre national de la recherche scientifique (CNRS), founded in 1939, offered a place to the human and social sciences as well.[40] Unlike the state institutes for economic, statistical, and demographic studies, the CNRS's focus was on fundamental research. Allowing individuals to do full-time research for a number of years, the CNRS also recruited technical and administrative personnel and supported an infrastructure for research by sponsoring conferences, journals, and book publications. The CNRS department for the human sciences was organized on the basis of predominantly disciplinary sections. Disciplines like sociology and ethnology, which had only a marginal existence in the university, obtained a relatively important position in the CNRS. After 1945 sociology was predominantly shaped by the work that was done by CNRS researchers, who outnumbered university sociologists until well into the 1970s. Depending on the institutional structure of the discipline, the CNRS was less important in other fields. The CNRS section for economics, for example, was relatively small because economic research was more often carried out in research institutes related to economic planning.

Sociological research was until around 1960 concentrated almost entirely at the Centre d'études sociologiques (CES, 1946). The work of the CES can be divided into two distinct phases.[41] During the initial phase the CES functioned primarily as a new service available to university professors. Georges Gurvitch, then professor of sociology at the University of Strasbourg, probably initiated the founding of the CES upon his return from the United States. He became the CES's first director, assisted by two professors from the Faculty of Law who had participated in the Durkheimian network: Gabriel Le Bras and Henri Lévy-Bruhl. The large number of books and journals with which Gurvitch returned from New York became the first resources of the CES's library.

The first activities of the CES were not so much to initiate research but to organize lectures. Many conferences were given to stimulate interest in the new social sciences and to combat the widespread indifference toward them. Alongside the lecture program, some professors started studying the social structure of contemporary France, work that they believed would modernize the discipline and enhance its social usefulness. For several of the professors involved, this commitment remained largely verbal, although some seem to have made a genuine effort. Allegedly Gurvitch began working on a study of generational differences, Le Bras continued his sociographic research on French Catholics, Henri Lévy-Bruhl initiated a study of children's rights. Meanwhile the economist Charles Bettelheim, temporarily affiliated with the CES, directed a project on the social life of an average-size provincial city. All these projects used "the method of empirical research," *la méthode des enquêtes*, to quote Henri Lévy-Bruhl, who was still somewhat ill at ease with the new language.[42] To do the work required, the directors of the CES hired "researchers," that is, young people assigned to collect data. The first projects did not produce much in the way of publications. Only Charles Bettelheim and Suzanne Frère's study led to a tangible result: a book on the city of Auxerre, conceived as the French equivalent of Robert and Helen Lynd's well-known study of Middletown.[43]

In 1948–49 the situation at the CES changed. The number of lectures was sharply reduced; the three main directors (Gurvitch, Le Bras, Lévy-Bruhl) had obtained positions at the newly founded Sixth Section of the EPHE, where seminars became the norm for training researchers. Gurvitch, who was simultaneously appointed professor at the Sorbonne, left his position as director of the CES and Georges Friedmann took over with the task of developing the center into a "laboratory," that is, a genuine CNRS research institute. This new policy was linked to the difficulties the CES had encountered and to the possibilities opened up by the CNRS. Neither the lecture program nor the professorial surveys had been very successful, but the CNRS was in a position to hire more "researchers" than in the past. Georges Friedmann recruited many of the new "researchers" and for years his seminar provided a central meeting place. Friedmann's own studies of industrial modernization were related to issues of economic reconstruction and technological modernization; as a well-connected *normalien* and philosopher he had more credit than the other directors of the CES. As one of his former students pointed out: "What really drew me to sociology was attending Georges Friedmann's PhD defense in 1947. *Problèmes humains du machinisme industriel* was one of the first remarkable PhDs after the war. It was inspired by both Marxism and American sociology, which was new at the time, and was primarily focused on the working class (interview)."

Under Friedmann's directorship, three researchers were hired in 1949, nine in 1950, and seven in 1951. By 1955 the total number of researchers at the Centre d'études sociologiques had gone up to thirty-seven and would fluctuate at around forty during the following two decades. The characteristics of the first generation of researchers illustrate the subordinate position of sociological research in the academic world. With few exceptions, the researchers came from the more marginal sectors of the intelligentsia: only two were *normalien* and relatively few had passed an *agrégation* exam (table 5.1). Their distance to the academic world is confirmed by their social origins: very few were from intellectual families; only one, for example, had a father who was a teacher.[44] Those who would play leading roles in the CES tended to have upper-class backgrounds (Chombart de Lauwe and Maucorps came from the military bourgeoisie, Naville was the son of a banker), but most were from fairly modest family backgrounds in the economic sector: shopkeepers, small businessmen, farmers. The profile of this new generation of sociologists thus differed markedly from that of the Durkheimians. The Durkheimian network had a high proportion of members from the academic elite (*normaliens* and *agrégés*), and its central members came from intellectual rather than economic or military family backgrounds.

Curiously enough, it was relatively rare for the researchers who joined the Centre d'études sociologiques to have an explicit interest in sociology. In the interviews I conducted most respondents spoke of "coincidence" or "connections" when asked how they came to join the CES. What the first group of researchers had in common was the Resistance and the values of social and political renewal of the years after the liberation. Of the twelve researchers first hired, five were members of the Communist Party, a few had links to other groups on the left, numerous others were connected to associations of social Catholics such as the "workers-priests" or the movement Économie et humanisme, led by the Dominican Louis-Joseph Lebret.[45] It was by means of information circulating in these groups that several had become aware of the existence of the CES and hiring possibilities: "The CES at the time was a miraculous place, full of people who'd been rejected or excluded somewhere else. There was a dissident Trotskyite, a defrocked priest, a former navy officer who had found grace in psychology, an aviator, etc. My own situation was grim. At a very young age I'd been given high responsibilities in the Resistance; afterward I was nothing—unemployed. I had to start again from scratch. The CNRS could take us in without too much competition because there wasn't any formal sociology training" (interview).

Interest in the working classes was shared by virtually all, regularly accompanied by a certain fascination for Marxism. Among the twenty most often-cited authors in the work of the researchers were Marx, Engels, and Lenin. Aside from the Marxist triumvirate, other frequently quoted

TABLE 5.1
Development of the Centre d'études sociologiques (1950-60)

	1950	1955	1960
Number of researchers of which:	12	37	42
- *normaliens*	2	2	1
- *agrégés*	2	6	2
- women	2	9	10
Average age	33	36	40
Technical and administrative staff	7	19	21

Sources: Administrative documents CNRS, various biographical sources.

authors were classical figures, contemporary patrons, and younger colleagues. The only other authors among the most cited were the American émigrés Paul Lazarsfeld and Kurt Lewin.[46] But more important than
any specific theoretical affiliation was the shared interest for the working classes. For Chombart de Lauwe, for example, who was a left-leaning
Catholic, it was "unthinkable" to study anything other than the predicament of the working class.[47] Henri Mendras, the son of a high military
officer, trained in public administration and a Catholic as well, had been
"scandalized" by the social injustice he observed and by the "misery of
workers."[48] The first studies in the sociology of work were, according to
Alain Touraine, all inspired by a will to improve the situation of the working class.[49] For several of the researchers I interviewed, this implied that
the boundaries between sociological research and political commitment
were blurred: "Personally, I won't hide from you that fact that for a number of years, I . . . well I won't say I wasted my time, but I did spend a lot
of it in union and political activities, and I wasn't the only one." Another
researcher recalled: "Those were learning years. I came from an entirely
different type of training, knew virtually nothing of research techniques or
any real social science theory. And really, I think I spent two or three years
doing little else but learning what a research study is, research technique,
how to construct a research problem, etc."

The working classes and related issues were more than just the dominant focus of interest; they were also a means of obtaining small research
funds and a social legitimacy for the inquiries. Given the strength of the
Communist Party and the trade unions, the attitudes of workers toward
change were of particular concern to the management of firms and the
state agencies involved in modernizing the economy. Since, moreover,
political commitment, engagement, was a major component of the identity of intellectuals, sociological research on the working class could

be presented and debated in the political vocabulary of the time. The researchers enjoyed a fair amount of freedom in this respect. Their job was to conduct empirical studies and their work was assessed by the directors of the CES and the CNRS commission, but they were often free to choose the focus and approach of their studies. The main restriction was probably implicit: the division of intellectual labor had to be respected, meaning that the "big" questions, theoretical and other, were reserved for the professors. This division, engrained in the attitudes and expectations of those concerned, reinforced the separation of theoretical and empirical studies that characterized postwar sociology. There was hardly any connection, for example, between Gurvitch's theoretical system and the various research projects. In fact, the "researchers" were accepted to the extent that they did work that was somewhat beneath the dignity of university professors. In interviews, respondents often use the vocabulary of feudal relations. The professors—some of them, in any case—were described as "lords" whose concern it was to control their fiefs and have "vassals" work for them.

The subordinate position of the researchers was also reflected in their precarious professional status. They only received the protection of a set of professional regulations in 1959, under pressure from the trade union of scientific researchers, but it was not until 1981 that CNRS researchers became full-fledged civil servants.[50] Prior to 1959 researchers were hired on a temporary basis as trainees, *stagiaires*, or as temporary research associates, *attachés de recherche*. Gurvitch had the habit of using the rather condescending term *boursiers* because some had a scholarship to write their PhD. Some researchers typically spoke of themselves as being merely "research technicians."[51]

Assessing the situation in 1955, Alain Touraine observed a near-total separation between university sociology and empirical research. Researchers were isolated, he wrote, and they lacked solid training, research experience, and professional prospects. Their working conditions, furthermore, were poor. The CES had only three study rooms for almost forty researchers and neither the CES nor the CNRS provided research funding.[52] Researchers belonging to this first generation thus experienced similar problems, the most basic ones being a lack of training and material resources. Although these difficulties were rarely expressed in official publications, they occasionally found their way into reports and internal documents. For the most part, however, they were relegated to confidential and private sources.

A vivid example is the unpublished field notes of Bernard Mottez and Jacques Dofny.[53] In the mid-1950s they carried out a well-known research project about the attitudes of workers in the iron and steel industry toward technical change. The research, conducted in 1954 and 1955, was part of an international study funded by the European Agency for Productivity and coordinated by the Organization for Economic Cooperation and Development (OECD). The French study, supervised by the two *normaliens* of the CES, Alain Touraine and Jean-Daniel Reynaud, produced three research reports and an academic monograph that attracted considerable attention among specialists.[54] The scrapbook of Mottez and Dofny shows that many aspects of the research were left out of the published reports, either because the material was too sensitive and controversial (daily management practices, tensions between workers of different nationalities) or because it did not fit the preestablished scheme on which the project was based. The field notes also reveal that the researchers were quite embarrassed about their task. Not only were they permanently afraid of being seen as "cops" by the workers, but they also expressed a skeptical attitude about the project as a whole, and about their own role in particular. The supervisors of the project were designated by the German word *Leiter*, director(s), probably to express the unease with the hierarchical relations of the organization of the inquiry. Basic notions of the project were described in ironic terms, and the researchers depicted themselves as a naive and foolish duo, nicknamed "Gaston and Gaston," a transposition of the Thom(p)sons, the two experts in blunders and misunderstandings who figure in the Tintin comic books by Hergé. The scrapbook was entitled: "Diary of the Mont St. Martin research project by Gaston and Gaston (fieldworkers) (*sogenannte*)." The term "fieldworkers" was in English, the adjective "so-called" (*sogenannte*) in German, both expressing the sense of irony and amused estrangement that runs through the whole text.

Whereas Mottez and Dofny mockingly expressed their doubts and anxieties in confidential field notes, Maucorps, a former naval officer involved in psychometric and sociometric research, had few hesitations in his methodological critique. The researchers, he noted, lacked elementary knowledge of research techniques:

> Some went no further than to construct questionnaires, believing that in so doing they were being sociologists. They accumulated questions in order to ensure that no aspect of the problem could escape them, secretly hoping this would bring unexpected connections to the surface. Gradually increasing the size of their samples, they were soon crushed by the mass of documents they had collected, a mass that was in fact unusable since they had no set of guiding hypotheses. Others took refuge in descriptive monographs. Using an entire arsenal of techniques, from the open-ended interview to character tests and behavior observation, they took it into their heads that the multiplicity and diversity of their observations meant they had resolved a certain number of questions. In fact, they had almost always verified obvious facts or identified singularities due to fortuitous correlations.[55]

Among the researchers, there was no doubt that they needed further training and that the methods and techniques of empirical research had to be imported from the United States. Just as Durkheim and several of his collaborators had gone to Germany to complete their studies, their successors (Friedmann, Stoetzel, Gurvitch) and their students went to America. It was impossible for Communists and fellow travelers to cross the Atlantic Ocean, but noncommunists who had been active in trade unions or in the peace movement also had visa requests refused. It happened to Friedmann in 1950–51, and even a decade later it took an intervention by Raymond Aron to secure visas for François Isambert and Jacques Maître so that they could attend the World Congress of Sociology in Washington.[56] But a considerable group of researchers, especially members of the Friedmann circle, did obtain Fulbright or Rockefeller scholarships and spent longer periods in the United States (Bourricaud, Crozier, Dampierre, Mendras, Reynaud, Touraine, Tréanton). They studied and traveled, learned to do empirical research, some participated in research projects, and they were all impressed by the dynamism of the country and its "unthinkable luxury."[57] Back in France, Mendras translated Merton's *Social Theory and Social Structure*, Bourricaud commented on and translated Parsons, and Crozier introduced the work of March and Simon and studies in the sociology of organizations.[58]

Having been to the United States or not was something of a dividing line. For all those who went it was a significant experience and changed something in their way of conceiving and practicing sociology. Some testimonies state that going to the United States for a French sociologist was like "going to Mecca for a Muslim" (Mendras). While this may have been true for some, others were more ambiguous in their appreciation. All were eager to learn empirical research and were impressed by the functioning of American universities, but several were quite critical of other aspects of American sociology. Central among these criticisms was the one-sided focus on individuals and inter-individual relationships, while ignoring the broader context of social classes and social structures. Some were struck by the poor historical grounding of American sociological studies, and several were surprised or shocked by the uncritical attitude of American sociologists toward large corporations and corporate management.[59] Touraine, for example, experienced Harvard as a refined intellectual world, but also as a place of "false splendor," where "reassuring functionalist theories" were predominant and the level of self-satisfaction was high. What he missed was the capacity for "critical reflection" and the "courage" to look society in the face.[60]

The acquaintance with American sociology solved some of the difficulties the new generation of researchers faced, but it hardly provided a solution for sociology's lack of intellectual legitimacy in France. In his memoirs, Michel Crozier describes his situation in precisely these terms. Since he had no philosophical training and lacked familiarity with Marxism, all he had to his credit was his knowledge of American institutions and American sociology. But in France these were "absolutely not recognized."[61] In a slightly different manner François Bourricaud, the French expert on Talcott Parsons, expressed the same unease: "We had . . . the unpleasant feeling of not being up to our task and not being able to practice our profession correctly . . . or with such difficulty that we wondered if our activity served any purpose, and so ultimately questioned its validity. Many of us felt unable to find any justification for it other than personal tastes and preferences."[62]

This lack of legitimacy, which was related to intellectual hierarchies and exclusions of the time, is well depicted in a novel that was written by a female author who was close to the group of Communists at the Centre d'études Sociologiques. The roman à clef portrays the politicized Cold War atmosphere of the 1950s and relates how the researchers who were Communists or fellow travelers experienced these years. A particular scene is especially illuminating. One evening the heroine and her comrades pass by the crowded café terraces of the fashionable Saint-Germain-des-Prés. The spectacle provokes a sudden emotional outburst: "I had nothing but contempt for the entire lumpen intelligentsia I had been a part of." And immediately afterward the narrator expresses her desire to cry out: "I'm a Marxist!" and "I love Hervé Lefort."[63] The terraces of Saint-Germain-des-Prés, associated with Sartre and the existentialists, evoke an image for the narrator of her own precarious existence. Her desire to identify with this intellectual high life provokes a feeling of disgust for the circle she is part of, and for an instant she imagines herself far above her comrades and colleagues—this "lumpen intelligentsia." But the fantasy is fleeting: she immediately senses the distance between herself and the world of the café terraces. This in turn provokes a desire to bridge the gap that separates them, and to draw attention to herself and her lover. Instead of saying "I'm a researcher!" or "I'm a sociologist!" her imaginary outcry is "I'm a Marxist!," thereby identifying herself with a group that is at least recognized in the intellectual debates of the day. And this self-categorization is immediately followed by a confession: she loves Hervé Lefort, who in the book is a Marxist philosopher and the only character who actually publishes books. Her exclamation is a kind of imaginary offering. What she can offer to the people on the terrace—in exchange for the attention and sympathy she hopes to receive—is her identity as a "Marxist" who is sensitive to existentialist themes (she "loves" a man who is both a "philosopher" and "author" and therefore a legitimate object of such love). Ultimately, however, she does not cry out but merely looks at the people sitting on the terraces and keeps on walking: her sense of reality is stronger than her sudden desire. She realizes that she does not have the means to accede to this enviable world. Indeed, the theme of the novel is the impossibility of accepting her existence as it is. This explains the title of the novel, *Le temps d'apprendre à vivre*, and the epigraph, borrowed from Aragon: "In the time it takes to learn to live, it's already too late."

In the conditions under which the researchers started their inquiries, applied research represented a kind of material and symbolic compensation. Contract research offered both material advantages and a degree of social recognition. Moreover, the research results could be presented as a concrete contribution to knowledge of the living conditions of the working class. In a diffuse and practical manner, a double strategy took shape, making it possible to do applied research without betraying one's leftist political opinions. Indeed, the idea of applied social science met with general approval on condition that it somehow served the interests of the survey respondents. This orientation is well illustrated by the fact that the person who in 1950 coordinated the translation of Lasswell and Lerner's collective volume on *The Policy Sciences* was Maucorps, then a Marxist and member of the French Communist Party. Official documents of the CES similarly expressed the hope of "fertile collaboration" with policy institutions.[64]

Research Groups

The work of Paul-Henri Chombart de Lauwe was one of the earliest forms of research.[65] Like Maucorps, Chombart de Lauwe had been quick to organize a small research team. Chombart de Lauwe was trained as an ethnographer before the Second World War and among the studies his group published, the best known is undoubtedly *Paris et l'agglomération parisienne* (1952). The data for this urban survey were gathered in collaboration with the state institutes of statistics (INSEE) and demography (INED); the Institut national d'hygiène granted a small subsidy, which was prolonged by way of a contract with the Ministry of Reconstruction. The social topography of Paris brought to light by these studies was complemented by interviews and observations. The researchers identified themselves with the working classes and their explicit aim was to acquire knowledge about working-class "needs." Being in direct contact with survey respondents and going out to "see for themselves" was considered an almost moral quality of the work, at odds with academic sociology and purely reflective and professorial activity. The emphasis in Chombart de Lauwe's understanding of sociological work was on collaboration and commitment: researchers spoke of "work comrades," they rejected hierarchical relations within the research group and addressed each other with the more familiar *tu* instead of the usual and more polite *vous*. Their relation to the object of study was defined in a similar manner. Chombart de Lauwe stressed the need for "intimate collaboration" between the sociologist and the group under study: "very often," he wrote, the researcher's only real task is to express the "aspirations" of the group studied. The point was to have the researcher "participate" in the life of that population and the population likewise to participate in the "scientific work," the utility of which they would have to understand.[66]

A particular feature of this communitarian research ethic was its rejection of the academic emphasis on the virtues of detachment and critical reflection. Chombart de Lauwe stressed his particular notion of inquiry in his PhD on the everyday life of working-class families, insisting on the necessity of collaboration between researchers, town planners, and state administrators. Theoretical problems were, as he wrote, "systematically avoided"; the results were thus perhaps less "brilliant" than those of "doctrinal sociology" but "surer."[67] This view put him at odds with his PhD supervisor, Georges Gurvitch, who categorically declared that Chombart would never get a position at the Sorbonne. The conflict was quite typical of the strained relations between university patrons and the new generation of researchers. Chombart de Lauwe deemed that the "researcher" could only do his job by refusing the ambition to be a theorist and suggested that such an approach would produce more "useful" results.

The sociology of religion, which developed around Gabriel Le Bras, had very similar features. Le Bras was a legal scholar, a professor at the Faculty of Law, and specialized in Roman and ecclesiastic law. During the 1930s and 1940s, he had elaborated a sociographic account of the secularization of the country, central to which was a typology of believers that made it possible to measure the "vitality" of Catholicism and to define the most urgent tasks of the church. Le Bras distinguished the pious, the obedient (who confessed regularly), the occasional conformist (who went to church only for important events such as baptism and Holy Communion) from the others (lumping together nonbelievers, apostates, members of other churches).[68] With the help of the parishes, detailed maps could be produced showing how much secularism had advanced. Regions and communities where more than 20 percent of the children were not baptized were defined as "mission areas."[69] The research was coordinated by the Centre catholique de sociologie religieuse (1952), of which Le Bras was president. The cartographic and statistical studies gave fairly precise indications of the degree of adherence to the church and were used to develop new programs for evangelization. On the basis of this program the Groupe de sociologie des religions (1954) was formed at the Centre d'études sociologiques. The group's members, who were generally more familiar with the problems of the Catholic Church than with classical work in the sociology of religion, gradually enlarged the scope of their inquiries and founded the first specialized sociological journal, the *Archives de sociologie des religions* (1956).

Most researchers affiliated with the CES, however, were involved in the sociology of work. Making use of Georges Friedmann's studies as the primary frame of reference and participating in his seminar, the group around Friedmann was the largest research group at the CES (figure 5.1). As compared with the other research teams, the Friedmann circle was best endowed with academic and social capital and dominated the activities

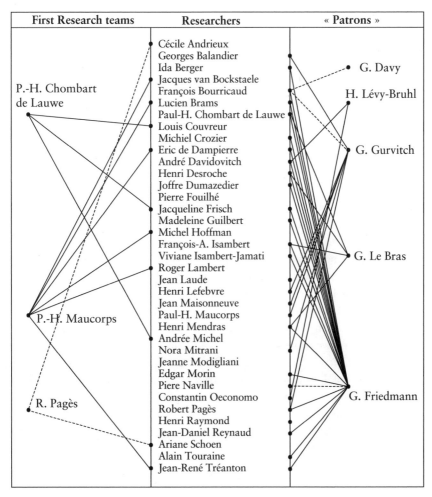

FIGURE 5.1
Network of primary affiliations at the Centre d'études sociologiques in 1955

at the CES. Friedmann's own studies of industrial civilization formed the link between interests of the researchers and the nascent social demand for inquiries into the modernization of the country. The two came together in Friedmann's seminar at the EPHE and during the "evening meetings" he organized where researchers, civil servants, administrators, and union representatives came together. The Institut des sciences sociales du travail (ISST), founded on the initiative of the Ministry of Labor and equipped with a research service funded by the Commissariat de la productivité, functioned as the institutional intermediary between the demand for research and the CNRS. It provided several researchers with their first offices and research funding. Michel Crozier, Jean-Daniel Reynaud, and Alain Touraine, among others, carried out several studies in this setting, later reusing and reframing the results in their PhDs and other academic publications.

What the French systematically called sociology of work, *sociologie du travail*, represented a distinct approach to the labor process. As compared with American studies, it was significantly less often concerned with "human relations," organizational structures, and managerial issues.[70] Work, as Touraine said, was at the "heart of society" and the "structuring category of social relations."[71] As defined by Friedmann, the concept of work focused in particular on technological changes and their effects on the labor process within the broader framework of what he called "technical civilization."[72] In *Problèmes humains du machinisme industriel* (1946), Friedmann had analyzed the development of automated production and its consequences for occupational qualifications and the labor process. On the basis of this analysis he devised a research scheme that was used by Alain Touraine, Viviane Isambert-Jamati, and Maurice Verry in their first studies. Often starting from technological change, they studied manual workers, their working and living conditions, and their attitudes to industrial modernization. Related work focused on trade unions and industrial relations (Reynaud), female workers (Guilbert), employees (Crozier), or on the modernization of the peasantry (Mendras). After the sociology of religion, the sociology of work was the second sociological specialty to dispose of a journal, *Sociologie du travail* (1959); it was a broadly oriented platform for the study of labor processes, professions, and organizations, which remained the largest and most important specialized area of sociological research in France.

No Man's Land

Although the founding and functioning of the Centre d'études sociologiques represented a "turning point" in the history of the discipline, many of the first inquiries were to a certain extent defined negatively. They rarely met the dominant standards of intellectual and academic excellence, nor were they part of the professional research carried out in the state institutes for economic and demographic studies. The dilemmas and anxieties of the first generation of researchers resulted in large part from this twofold exclusion. The Centre d'études sociologiques was located in a sort of no man's land, as Edgar Morin called it. Sociologists were in his view paralyzed by the fear of being either too political and therefore not scientific enough, or not political enough, that is, not sufficiently useful to society.[73] Several researchers described their situation in similar terms, finding it impossible to choose either one and unrealistic to satisfy both. Gregory Bateson introduced the notion of "double bind" to describe just such a situation—that of persons called on to accomplish two tasks that are in fact mutually exclusive. If this was the predicament of sociological research in the 1940s and 1950s, it is easier to understand why their sociological monographs were hesitant and in many ways ambiguous. They tried to respond to the nascent social demand while shunning any attempt to become experts in the service of the state agencies or companies that commissioned their work. Instead, the results of their research were most often presented in the vocabulary that was prevalent among committed intellectuals.

During the first decade of its existence, the research monographs produced at the Centre d'études sociologiques were in many cases limited to what Touraine qualified as "rudimentary empiricism."[74] Their style was that of "synthetic description," oriented toward various forms of fact-finding, generally relying on indigenous notions, and paying scant attention to problems of conceptualization and research methodology.[75] This empiricist style reinforced the distance toward more theoretical disciplines such as philosophy and brought it closer to other descriptive research practices. Researchers, as Edgar Morin explained, "mistrusted" general questions.[76] Being preoccupied with empirical studies, a more ambitious program, such as that of Durkheimian sociology, was, according to Touraine, "out of the question."[77] Durkheimian sociology had become widely associated with philosophical arguments about collective representations and old-fashioned scholarly erudition. With the exception of *The Rules of Sociological Method*, none of Durkheim's books were reprinted between 1945 and 1960.[78] Having only a superficial knowledge of the Durkheimian tradition, several members of the new generation routinely dismissed the Durkheimian tradition as "speculative" and "professorial," but discovered his actual work only during their stay in the United States or when they started teaching sociology in the 1960s.

Postwar sociological research was in a sense caught up in a vicious circle: the discipline's exclusion from the dominant intellectual concerns had the effect of repelling the best-educated and most ambitious students;

the actual research tended to confirm this pattern. According to Pierre Bourdieu, who was a philosophy student at the École normale in the early 1950s, the "contempt" for the social sciences among the elite philosophers lasted until well into the 1960s. Sociology as he and his fellow students perceived it was a rather mediocre enterprise, one "without any theoretical or indeed empirical inspiration behind it." The work of "Jean Stoetzel or even Georges Friedmann, who had written a rather poor book on Leibniz and Spinoza, struck them as being the products of a negative vocation."[79] Because the first empirical inquiries failed to spark great intellectual interest, they tended to reproduce the traditional split between philosophy and empirical research, between noble tasks—general and theoretical—and tedious inquiry. Although representing a break with the past, postwar sociology came to be based on "the illusion of a first beginning."[80] This was indeed the belief that several members of the postwar generation expressed. "We were firmly convinced," Henri Mendras writes in his memoirs, "that we were following in no one's footsteps, there was no inheritance, no tradition; we had to and were going to reinvent social science for the uses of our time."[81]

Reconfiguring the Social Sciences

Sociological research, however, was not exclusively a CNRS affair. In 1947 the historians who edited the *Annales* journal founded a section for the "economic and social sciences" at the EPHE. The plan to create this so-called Sixth Section goes back to the origins of the research school in the nineteenth century.[82] Durkheimians had had positions at the Fourth Section for historical studies (Simiand) and the Fifth Section for the study of religion (Mauss, Hubert, Granet). The Section for economic and social sciences finally took off after 1945 because by then institutional renewals were widely supported and the new section was no threat to the Sorbonne, since it did not have the right to grant university degrees. Having emerged as a relatively marginal and poorly funded institution for the purpose of research and research training, the Sixth Section, as Braudel remarks, turned this restriction into "its strength," into "the basis of its autonomy."[83] A pragmatic openness toward the social sciences and an unorthodox policy of obtaining funds allowed the historians to create a dynamic and original institution. With Lucien Febvre as its first president and Fernand Braudel as its general secretary, the Sixth Section brought various strands of innovative research together. In 1963 they complemented the school with a foundation, the Maison des sciences de l'homme (MSH), which similarly aimed at promoting interdisciplinary research and international exchange.

Together both institutions produced a fundamental reconfiguration of the social sciences.

Unlike the institutional structure of social science disciplines in most other countries, historians occupied the central position in the Sixth Section. The school was led by successive generations of historians and the Centre de recherches historiques (1949) was its first research center and the model for numerous other collective research projects. These research projects made use of up-to-date techniques provided by the school's centers of documentation, cartography, and statistical analysis, which were virtually inexistent in French universities.[84] The long-term economic and social history of Labrousse and Braudel was the leading area of historical inquiry; it was complemented and progressively enlarged with other forms of historical study, most notably cultural history and the history of "mentalities." The broad ambition of Febvre and Braudel was well captured by the new title of their journal, which changed from the original *Annales d'histoire économique et sociale* (1929) into *Annales: Économies, sociétés, civilisations* (1946). Breaking with the traditional modes of narrating political events, the journal was dedicated to a more problem-oriented style of historical inquiry, guided by the aim of unraveling significant historical structures and their underlying processes.[85] The programmatic aim of this type of historical studies was to borrow from the social sciences whatever might be of use. For Braudel, the program of the *Annales* school was quite simply "to go out among the other disciplines, return with the booty, and set forth again the quest of discovery, demolishing obstructing walls at each occasion."[86]

Part of the institutional success of the historians was, paradoxically, that unlike Durkheim, Lévi-Strauss, or others, they were not committed to any strong and specific theoretical paradigm. Their call for exchanges across disciplinary boundaries was easily acceptable for their allies and their conception of interdisciplinarity was marked by a rather pragmatic research ethos. "Exchange of services" was, according to Braudel, "the last and profoundest motto of the *Annales*."[87] The *Annales* journal and the group of historians around it, then, were less a "school" in the common sense of the word than a program for exchange across the boundaries of disciplines and specialties. In this view the Sixth Section was a sort of "common market" with history as its "preponderant power."[88] Around the historians, who formed the predominant minority in the school, the Sixth Section united the "economic and social sciences," which included the most significant empirical disciplines from the Faculty of Letters (geography, sociology, anthropology) and the Faculty of Law (economics). No less characteristic of this policy of selectively concentrating the social sciences in the same institution around history were the disciplines that were excluded. Unlike the

Faculties of Letters, philosophy was not represented at the Sixth Section; there was no room for purely speculative and metaphysical enterprises. The same was true of applied disciplines like political science and public administration. They were not considered sufficiently scholarly endeavors, but merely practical or professional concerns, and were therefore "courteously ignored and secretly despised."[89]

Because of limited funds, the Sixth Section was built up by selecting scholars who already had a position elsewhere and who taught at the school as visiting scholars, so-called *cumulants*. The proportion of people with a full-time position, the *noncumulants*, was only about a third of the teaching staff, and they were often scholars with atypical trajectories: foreigners and others who did not have the qualifications required for a professorship in a French university (École normale, *agrégation*). Among them were East Europeans such as the historian of science Alexandre Koyré, the sinologist Etienne Balazs, the historical psychologist Ignace Meyerson, the sociologist Lucien Goldmann, the social psychologist Serge Moscovici, and the ethnopsychiatrist Georges Devereux. The openness to foreigners and international developments was reinforced in the late 1950s and 1960s when a special division was created for "area studies." It hosted centers for studying countries and regions on just about every continent. The program, cofunded by the Rockefeller and later the Ford Foundation and the French Ministry of Education, was set up by Braudel and Clemens Heller, who was Braudel's right hand. Heller was a cosmopolitan Austrian who had studied at Harvard and had become an American citizen; Eric Hobsbawm described him as "the most original intellectual impresario of post-war Europe."[90] Although cofunded by American foundations, the French program in area studies was not a copy of the American conception. Braudel had criticized North American area studies for their lack of historical and theoretical grounding and in his own policies tried to avoid both of these pitfalls.[91]

During the postwar years Febvre and Braudel supported many initiatives to revive sociology. Georges Friedmann was a member of the editorial board of the *Annales* and became director of studies at the Sixth Section, just as Gurvitch, Le Bras, and Henri Lévy-Bruhl had been. At the end of the 1950s, several members of the younger generation of sociologists also joined the Sixth Section (Chombart de Lauwe, Desroche, Touraine). But with few exceptions the historians were quite skeptical about postwar sociology. The revival of the *Année sociologique* had "disturbed" Lucien Febvre, who—"still grateful" for the *Année sociologique* of his youth—was upset by its lack of coherence and vigor. The new series of the *Année* was merely a "collection" of book reviews, which could have been published anywhere.[92] The emerging research at the Centre d'études sociologiques was not received in a more positive manner.[93] And when Braudel reviewed a book by Gurvitch in 1953, he observed a "sudden and terrible change of times" that profoundly upset him. The fruitful exchanges and debates that historians had had with Simiand, Mauss, or Halbwachs were interrupted. Gurvitch's primary interest, according to Braudel, was in the more superficial levels of social life; he rarely discussed anything but sociological theory and was uninterested in historical processes.[94] Much of postwar sociology was disappointing to Braudel, who contrasted it with the work of the Durkheimians. In his trilogy *Civilization and Capitalism* (1967–79), Braudel was still full of admiration for their achievements, recalling that Durkheimian sociology represented a "Copernican or Galilean revolution, a change of paradigm for social science as a whole," the consequences of which "are still being felt today."[95]

Lucien Febvre held a similar, albeit somewhat more ironic, view. What had counted for him was the critical labor of the *Année sociologique*. The Durkheimian journal had proven that something new and exciting could be constructed by asking the right questions and by critically selecting, interpreting, and combining material from various research areas. That was the model Febvre had in mind when together with Marc Bloch they started the journal *Annales* (1929).[96] The admirable studies by Simiand, Halbwachs, Mauss, and Lucien Lévy-Bruhl, furthermore, had been worthy successors of Durkheim's original enterprise. Whereas the Durkheimians had moved from philosophy to sociology, Gurvitch went in the opposite direction. And yet for all those who had admired the original *Année*, Febvre saw no reason to despair. The Durkheimian heritage "lives on in the work of every one of us, in our personal and in our collective work. I am thinking in particular of the *Annales* because, after all, it is a fine success."[97]

CHAPTER 6

✖✖✖

Cycles of Expansion and Field Transformations

The four decades after 1960 were a period of unprecedented growth for higher education in general and for the social sciences in particular. The expansion included the research sector and the universities, classical social science disciplines as well as a variety of newer and applied fields. For each of the disciplines involved, the growth implied that they became more autonomous and more regulated universes with their own degrees, career structures, publication outlets, and modes of professional organization. From a small and fragmented subfield, institutionally based on a few university chairs and a limited number of ill-defined research positions, sociology became an organized discipline. The changing demography illustrates the magnitude of the process. The number of CNRS researchers in sociology multiplied from about 50 (1960) to a high of 340 during the mid-1980s. After an autonomous bachelor degree (*licence*) was established in 1958, sociology became a full-fledged university discipline as well. Whereas by 1960 the first sociological bachelor degrees were awarded and there was only a handful of university positions, by 2000 the number of yearly bachelor degrees had gone up to 2,200, involving some 670 tenured university positions.[1] By the beginning of the twenty-first century, however, the expansion came to a halt. Research positions in the CNRS were already in decline since the 1990s; university degrees and teaching positions continued to expand for a while, but they were gradually superseded by vocational studies and degrees, which challenged the humanities as well as the classical social science disciplines.

In order to understand the structural dynamics of the discipline during this long phase of expansion and its consequences for practicing sociology, I will consider the institutional development and distinguish between two distinct growth cycles. During the first phase of expansion, from 1960 to the mid-1970s, growth not only favored relatively new disciplines but multiple theoretical programs as well. This was the high tide of "structuralism" and of the intellectual effervescence that is associated with the names of Lévi-Strauss, Barthes, Foucault, Althusser, Lacan, and Derrida. Some of them had started their work well before 1960 and many continued beyond the mid-1970s, but the heart of this period were the years between the end of the 1950s and the mid-1970s. The theoretical fervor corresponded to a conjuncture that offered considerable opportunities for newcomers and for intellectual programs that were relatively indifferent to the boundaries of academic disciplines and that were relatively new (linguistics, semiology, psychoanalysis, Marxism) or, in any case, not fully institutionalized (anthropology, sociology). It was this twofold characteristic, chances for newcomers in a context of strong growth in academic positions within weakly institutionalized disciplines, that created much of the intellectual effervescence of this period.

This period of expanding opportunities and optimism was followed by years of crisis and stagnation from the mid-1970s to the mid-1980s. New recruitments were blocked—both in the research sector and in the universities—and the social sciences were profoundly divided and under attack. Institutional expansion picked up again in the mid-1980s, but growth was now restricted to the universities, whereas the research sector stagnated or contracted. The expanding universities, however, were increasingly specialized and "disciplined," on the one hand, while becoming more attuned to the labor market on the other. The mood of self-confidence and grand ambitions that had swept across the intellectual field during the 1960s gave way to a much more timid atmosphere. Critiques of grand theories became commonplace, increasing specialization and greater scholarly prudence seemed inescapable, and grand-style macroprograms made way for microperspectives. Individualist approaches, including rational choice theories, challenged the encompassing paradigms of structuralism, Marxism, and functionalism. In many disciplines accounts of action and interaction tended to replace the focus on broader topics and more encompassing structures.

I will first provide an overview of the process of institutional growth and its most salient characteristics. Hereafter I will look at the research sector and the universities separately, and highlight the increasing dominance of the latter over the former. I will then consider related changes in the publishing field and, finally, review the attempts at professional organization, which were a collective response to the transformations that had taken place. After this analysis of the changing field structure, I will in the next chapter seek to understand how some of the most prominent research groups emerged within this structure, exploited the opportunities it provided, and produced the work they have become known for.

The Structuralist Boom and After

Although the growth of higher education from 1960 onward is often depicted as a continuous process, and in particular as the belated emergence of a mass university, two cycles of expansion need to be clearly distinguished.[2] The first was concentrated in the 1960s and the first half of the 1970s when the chances to do social scientific work improved drastically and the human sciences gained far more intellectual acclaim and public visibility. This rapid expansion was sustained by high economic growth and by government policies aimed at improving the country's research capacity and enlarging the scope of state planning. More funds were allocated to both fundamental and contract research in a widening range of policy areas, including education, urban planning, and culture, which all emerged as important areas for sociological research. Unsurprisingly, a mood of optimism and self-confidence prevailed. The expanding research sector, the vivid public interest in relatively "new" disciplines such as anthropology, linguistics, or semiology, and the rising student numbers found an intellectual expression in the fascination for "structuralism," which more or less displaced the predominantly philosophic and literary concerns of existentialism. Claude Lévi-Strauss didn't simply supplant Sartre as the leading intellectual, but he certainly represented a rival model that attracted enormous attention. Although there was no longer a central intellectual journal comparable to what *Les temps modernes* had been after 1945, "structuralist" theories and modes of reasoning pervaded the intellectual field. Together with other cultural movements, such as the movies of the *nouvelle vague* and the literary movement around the *nouveau roman*, it contributed to a mood that France was regaining some of its cultural and intellectual grandeur. After the humiliating experiences of the Second World War and difficult years of reconstruction, this mood of confidence was perceptible in the political and economic sphere as well. Under the presidency of de Gaulle, France pursued an ambitious geopolitical agenda of its own and experienced high levels of economic growth and considerable industrial success.

The intellectual scene was, especially after the end of the war in Algeria, dominated by the debates about structuralism. After Claude Lévi-Strauss published *Structural Anthropology* (1958) and was elected to the Collège de France, he spelled out some of the general principles of his work in *The Savage Mind* (1962), in which he explicitly took on Sartre and the existentialists. The controversy was the occasion for the journal *Esprit* to publish a special issue on structuralism in 1963. These first intellectual confrontations between the old and the new guard were followed by a remarkable series of books that appeared more or less synchronically: Althusser's *Pour Marx* (1965) and *Lire le capital* (1966), Lacan's *Écrits* (1966), Foucault's *Les mots et les choses* (1966), Barthes's *Éléments de sémiologie* (1965) and *Système de la mode* (1967), Derrida's *De la grammatologie* (1967), and Braudel's *Civilisation matérielle et capitalisme* (1967). Parallel to this outburst, special issues on "structuralism" appeared in general intellectual journals such as *L'arc* (1965), *Les temps modernes* (1966), and, again, *Esprit* (1967).

The triumph of "structuralism," which was an intellectual mood rather than a systematic approach or a well-defined intellectual movement, basically marked the ascendency of the human sciences over existentialism and the classical humanities.[3] But in spite of the common label and a considerable amount of public attention and intellectual excitement, the affinities among the "structuralists" were rather diffuse, their alliances heterogeneous, and the message they conveyed mixed. As far as structuralist authors shared a common orientation, it was marked by an antisubjectivist stance, directed against the heritage of existentialism and phenomenology, and implied a commitment to some idea of science and objectivism. Those who were labeled "structuralists" no longer wrote about consciousness, choice, and commitment, but about impersonal structures in language, myth, and knowledge. In the fashionable, semiphilosophical language of the day, structuralists proclaimed the "death" of the subject: the death of the speaking subject in structural linguistics, the death of the knowing subject in epistemology, the death of the writing subject in literary theory (Barthes, the journal *Tel Quel*), in short: the "death of man" (Foucault).[4]

Following the example of Lévi-Strauss in anthropology, linguistics provided an analytical model that could be emulated in other domains as well. In psychoanalysis Jacques Lacan advocated an interpretation of Freud by borrowing ideas from linguistics ("the unconscious is structured like a language"). Literary theorists like Roland Barthes turned to semiology, the science of signs that was derived from linguistics and promised to decipher meaning in cultural areas ranging from literary texts and fashion to movies and modern myths. In other areas "structuralism" was less a research program than a new way of reading canonical texts. As specialists in the theoretical reading of theoretical texts, philosophers played a pivotal role in the generalization of structuralist topics and themes and in the accompanying intellectual ferment.[5] Louis Althusser, a philosophy lecturer at the École normale, proposed a structuralist reading of Marx, highlighting the "epistemological break" between Marx's early work on alienation and the "theoretical antihumanism" of *Capital*. Another lecturer at the École normale, Jacques Derrida, read works of linguists and philosophers of language in order to establish a "grammatology"—an early version of his philosophy of "deconstruction." Similarly confronted with the expanding and allegedly new "human sciences," Michel Foucault outsmarted them all with *The Order of Things* (1966), a study that uncovered such profound epistemic structures of the human sciences that even their most accomplished practitioners had been unaware of them.

Rooted in a generational, demographic, and institutional shift from the classical humanities to the contemporary human and social sciences, it is quite telling that virtually none of the leading structuralists had a university position. They were employed by research institutions (Braudel, Lévi-Strauss) or had a subaltern position as tutor or lecturer—but not full professor—in elite schools (Althusser, Derrida), if they weren't entirely outside of the academic system (Lacan). Only Foucault, who had been abroad for many years, held a university position for a short time, but part of it was in Vincennes, the experimental post-1968 university.[6] Being deprived of, or liberated from, the powers and privileges of the ordinary professor, many of them entertained strong connections with the intellectual world, especially with avant-garde reviews (*Tel Quel, Critique*) and with journalism and the publishing industry.[7]

Aside from some of these common features and shared affinities, "structuralism" in reality designated a plurality of rather different programs and practices. Following Lévi-Strauss's example, the label could refer to the theoretical promises of linguistics for other human sciences, it could designate "new" theoretical projects such as semiology or structuralist versions of Marxism and psychoanalysis, while it could also be associated with proto- or quasi-disciplines like Derrida's "grammatology" and Foucault's "archaeological" or "genealogical" study of discourse. While the underlying tendency was the break with the subject-centrism of existentialism combined with a quest for the new and the newest, some of the structuralist writings did not go beyond the conventional practice of "reading" classical texts while simultaneously reviving philosophical resistance to the tedious craftsmanship of empirical research. In the name of a kind of theoretical grandeur, Althusser and his followers denigrated the empirical inquiries of the "so-called" social sciences, considering their version of Marxism far superior to disciplines like sociology, which had an air of trivial empiricism.[8] The psychoanalytic theories of Lacan were another favorite topic of philosophers, no doubt because they opposed the "so-called sciences" of psychology and psychiatry in a similar manner.

The resistance to empirical social science was rooted, furthermore, in quite conventional pedagogical practices. Both Althusser's "symptomatic reading" of Marx and Derrida's method of text "deconstruction" originated in their task of preparing students at the École normale for the *agrégation* exam in philosophy, that is, in the training of reading classical texts and teasing out an interpretation as virtuosic and brilliant as possible.[9] What is described as "structuralism" was thus at once a research program in certain disciplines (linguistics, anthropology), a series of structural interpretations of classical authors proposed by philosophers like Althusser, and a more general intellectual mood, which was nourished by philosophers, publicists, and commentators in a "flirtation" with scientificity and objectivism.[10] "Structuralism to me meant the idea that everything has an underlying structure waiting to be discovered. It was fantastic. I read, on the one hand, *The Elementary Structures of Kinship* and *Structural Anthropology* of Lévi-Strauss, and, on the other hand, Barthes's *Mythologies*, which was an application to our societies. It was like we were going to construct a kind of periodic system of Mendeleev for all possible situations (interview)."

In sociology the rapid institutional expansion led to the establishment of a new infrastructure. Many members of the postwar generation were able to organize their own research group, develop its own research agenda, and the opportunities in turn attracted growing numbers of aspiring sociologists. The fashion of structuralism had little direct impact in sociology. Sociology depended more on funds from contract research and on the balance of power within the Faculty of Letters than on the vicissitudes of the intellectual field. The generation that had entered the discipline in the 1950s was not particularly attentive to grand theory anyway. The main exception were members of Gurvitch's network like Georges Balandier and Jean Duvignaud, who together with the Marxist sociologist Lucien Goldmann founded the journal *L'homme et la société* (1966), which united antistructuralist social theorists. In the newly founded *Revue française de sociologie* (1960), Sartre's *Critique de la raison dialectique* (1960) was criticized for being "utterly foreign" to a scientific study; some of Lévi-Strauss's work was courteously reviewed, but the theoretical controversies structuralism provoked were rather peripheral in sociology.[11] Younger and theoretically more articulate sociologists responded in more elaborate ways, but they were critical as well. Pierre Bourdieu, who attended the seminar of Lévi-Strauss and whose interests included structural anthropology and linguistics, was a constructive critic. He rejected its fashionable aspects and entered into a constructive critique of structuralist models, recalling that the structural mode of analysis, in fact, went back to the quite unfashion-able Durkheimian program of treating "social facts as things."[12] Robert Castel similarly wished to dissociate the "structural method" from "struc-turalist ideology."[13] Raymond Boudon, trained in the school of quantitative research of Lazarsfeld and Stoetzel, was more dismissive. There was no such thing as a "structural method," he argued, in the sense that there is an "experimental method." Structuralists, it seemed to him, lacked an adequate methodology; in the absence of techniques to bring rain for crops, they "sang for rain as some tribes do."[14]

The mood of professional optimism that reigned in sociology came to an end during the events of May '68. The student revolt had started in the sociology department of the new University of Nanterre, where one of the leaders of the movement, Daniel Cohn-Bendit, was a student and where several well-known sociologists had just accepted a position (Bourricaud, Crozier, Lefebvre, Touraine). The two months of student manifestations and a nation-wide movement of mass strikes came as a surprise and a shock and inaugurated a period of intense politicization in sociology. May '68 destroyed the working consensus that had characterized the discipline in the 1960s, and the events would both politically and scientifically divide the sociological community for years to come. But because research fund-ing and academic positions continued to expand for a number of years, many younger sociologists were able to find an academic position and to create their own group. May '68 accelerated a generational succession con-ferring important institutional and other responsibilities to members of the younger generations.[15]

When in the course of the 1970s economic prospects deteriorated, France, like other Western countries, entered a decade of slow economic growth, rising inflation, and eventually a deep economic recession. The *trente glorieuses*, the thirty years of high economic growth, low unemploy-ment, and a continuously expanding public sector were over. International economic competition increased and following the British and American response to the economic downturn, most Western countries adopted neo-liberal policies, cutting back on the welfare state, deregulating markets, and privatizing state enterprises. In 1981 the left-wing government under the presidency of François Mitterrand started out with a different political agenda. It included a large-scale consultation of the scientific community to restore the confidence in the government after years of political suspi-cion with regard to the social sciences. Given the difficult economic times, however, the left-wing government soon imposed budget cuts and French political elites gradually adopted neoliberal policies as well.[16]

After a decade of lower levels of funding, disillusionment with the grand intellectual projects of the 1960s, and a stagnating research sector, the social sciences went through a second cycle of expansion after 1985. This time, however, expansion took place in quite different circumstances and was restricted to the universities. The research sector no longer profited from the expansion, which implied a steadily aging research population and increased competition for fewer research jobs. Due to the government policy of stimulating a demand-driven growth of higher education, which was related to European educational policies, student numbers and university positions expanded again from the mid-1980s onward. Between 1985 and 1995, the percentage of pupils with a high school degree (the *baccalauréat*) allowing entry into the university rose from 35 to 65 percent of the age group. Since many of new students preferred vocational studies over classical disciplines, the social sciences now had to compete with a broad range of studies that were more attuned to the labor market. Aside from economics, which became the dominant social science in academia as well as in policy circles, this concerned a host of vocational disciplines that promised students chances on the labor market, which the classical social sciences lacked.

The transformation of the intellectual field during the 1980s and 1990s was related to the political changes after 1968, the economic downturn of the late 1970s and early 1980s, and the subsequent rise of neoliberalism. With the continuing growth of educated readers, popular media came to play an ever more active role in the intellectual debate. The daily newspaper *Libération* (1973), the television program *Apostrophes* (1975–90), and weeklies such as the *Nouvel observateur* and *L'express* continuously selected books, portrayed and ranked their authors, and commented on their meaning.[17] The blurring of the distinction between scholars, journalists, and television personalities became a major issue with the appearance of the "new philosophers" in the latter half of the 1970s. After the French translation of Solzhenitsyn's *The Gulag Archipelago*, young former left-wing philosophers conquered the media with an assault on "totalitarianism" in all its guises, including the totalitarianism of intellectuals and their all-embracing theories. The appearance of these "new philosophers" was part of the political reaction against May '68 and the proliferation of leftist groups as well as against the coalition of socialists and communists around their "common program."[18] The reaction against the old and the new Left found an intellectual basis in liberal journals like *Contrepoint* (1970–76) and *Commentaire* (1978–), which were founded by members of the circle around Raymond Aron.[19] The decline of Gaullism and the traditional Right was accompanied by a revival of classical liberalism, a resurgence of political philosophy, and a marked skepticism with regard to planned change and the ambitions of the social sciences in that respect. On the basis of a diffuse "antitotalitarian" alliance, a convergence occurred of major intellectual journals (*Esprit, Le débat, Commentaire*) and week-lies (*Nouvel observateur, L'express*) around the themes of human rights, individualism, and democratic pluralism. The change included the rehabil-itation of Raymond Aron and the rediscovery of Tocqueville, but it lacked the intellectual excitement that had been characteristic of the period of "structuralism."[20]

The changing sensibilities were carried by a generational shift that coincided with the extension of the intellectual field in the direction of the market sector, the emergence of vocational disciplines in the universi-ties, and the growth of applied research. The proliferation of economics in higher education and the rise of business schools are significant exam-ples.[21] No less typical was the rise in prominence of public administration and political science, *science po*.[22] For a long time peripheral in univer-sities and the research sector alike, the "political sciences" expanded swiftly from the 1970s onward. For recruiting university professors a national *agrégation* exam in political science was created (1971), an autonomous section for political science was established in the CNRS (1983), and the Fondation nationale des sciences politiques (FNSP) was recognized as a *grand établissement scientifique* (1985). During the 1990s, *science po* expanded further, among other ways by internation-alizing its curriculum. In the course of the process, the political sciences obtained a recognizable role outside of their own institutional sphere as well. Political philosophers, for example, entered the École des hautes études (EHESS), where they found an institutional basis in the Centre Raymond Aron (1982).

As a consequence of the diversification of higher education and a stag-nating research sector the role of intellectuals came under scrutiny once again.[23] Historians from the EHESS played a pivotal role in this reorien-tation. Pierre Nora, who taught at the EHESS and was a publisher at the prestigious publishing house Gallimard, launched a new journal, *Le débat* (1980), which obtained a central position in the intellectual field. Accord-ing to the brief editorial, *Le débat* no longer wished to "impose a system," had "no message" to deliver, and no "ultimate explanations to provide." Treating "history, politics and society," as the subtitle indicated, the journal wished to provide a platform for discussion and exchange of ideas.[24] While excluding old-fashioned Marxists and irresponsible *gauchistes*, the jour-nal extended the network of its contributors to enlightened entrepreneurs, policy specialists, and other experts. Another way of reaching out beyond the traditional boundaries of the intellectual field and widening the cir-cles of exchange was by organizing clubs that explicitly aimed at bridging traditional cleavages. The historian François Furet, then president of the EHESS, cofounded a think tank, the Fondation Saint-Simon (1982–99), which united intellectuals, businessmen, and journalists to reflect on the major obstacles for the "modernization" of France.[25]

A different response to the diversification of the intellectual field and the disintegration of the role of grand intellectuals came from Michel Foucault. Arguing that the idea of the "universal intellectual," who acted as the spokesman for universal causes, had to be abandoned, Foucault advocated "specific intellectuals." Depending on their particular knowledge and capacities, they should work on well-defined topics, collaborate with laypeople, and jointly prepare public interventions. Foucault's own work on prisons and his Groupe d'information sur les prisons (GIP, 1971–72) was a case in point. But in spite of Foucault's prominence, the intellectual agenda during the 1980s was not set by Foucauldian "specific intellectuals" but by members of the network around Le débat and Esprit, which represented the liberal center. The intellectual ceremonies of the bicentennial of the French Revolution in 1989, for example, were dominated by François Furet, who coedited a Critical Dictionary of the French Revolution (1988) and labored to replace the social history of the Revolution by an account in which the history of political ideas was given pride of place.

When during the 1990s a growing opposition manifested itself against neoliberal policies, it was accompanied by a reflection on the demise of the critical role of intellectuals. Pierre Bourdieu, who, like Foucault, had rejected the figure of the "total intellectual" that Sartre epitomized, nonetheless wanted to preserve a critical function of intellectuals. His notion of the "collective intellectual" referred to more or less specialized scholarly groups that would work together on public issues. A collective around Bourdieu thus produced a widely discussed study on social suffering in contemporary society, The Weight of the World (1993). The book became a best-seller, parts of it were turned into theater plays and documentaries, and it inspired analogous projects in other European countries. Two years later a proposal of the right-wing government to reform the Social Security system provoked the largest worker mobilization the country had known since 1968 and split the intellectuals into opposite camps. The governmental plan was supported by a petition of publicists who were close to the journal Esprit, the Fondation Saint-Simon, and the reform-minded trade union (CFDT); they were opposed by those who supported the workers' strike.[26] Sociologists were not merely divided between Left and Right but within the Left as well: some publicly supported the plan (Donzelot, Dubet, Paugam, Touraine, Wieviorka), whereas others espoused the cause of the workers (Bourdieu, Baudelot, Boltanski, Dubar, Lahire, Thevenot, Topalov). Although the "silence of the intellectuals" had been a catch phrase in the 1980s, the 1990s saw a movement of renewed commitment and a quest for public engagement in the social sciences. Pierre Bourdieu, who

after Foucault's death in 1984 became the central figure in this movement for "committed scholarship," launched a European review of books,
Liber (1989–98), which was published in many languages (but not in
English). In the wake of the social movement of 1995, he founded a publishing house, Raisons d'agir, which publishes a series of small and inexpensive books on a wide variety of topics. Its first volume, Bourdieu's *On
Television* (1995), provoked a heated debate about the functioning of the
media and sold over two hundred thousand copies. Several subsequent
titles ended up on the best-seller lists as well. The successful enterprise
was emulated by the historian Pierre Rosanvallon, who in 2002 started
a similar series of small books, *La république des idées*. Although at the
end of the twentieth century the social sciences formed more autonomous
and more specialized disciplines than in the 1960s, they had not simply retreated in their academic compartments. New forms of intellectual
commitment were explored and "public social science," as Michael Burawoy later called it, had become a major concern, in France earlier than in
other countries.[27]

Research Policy and the Research Sector

In order to gain a more precise understanding of these two cycles of
expansion, the related transformation of the intellectual field, and the
consequences for sociology, it is necessary to distinguish clearly between
the research sector and the universities, although for a while both went
through a phase of strong growth. The establishment of the Fifth Republic
in 1958 under the presidency of de Gaulle inaugurated a period of greater
political stability, especially after the independence of Algeria in 1962, and
of strong growth in scientific research and higher education. Science policy had become a governmental concern in the Third Plan (1958–61) and
the promotion of scientific research was a central feature of the Fourth
Plan (1962–65). Enhancing investment in research explicitly included the
social sciences in both the Fifth (1966–70) and the Sixth Plan (1971–75).[28]
As a result of these policies the expenses for research and development
increased spectacularly: from 0.9 percent of GDP in 1958 to 2.4 percent in
1968. After 1968 the percentage slightly decreased and stabilized around
1.7 percent during the second half of the 1970s, but the growth of research
funding in the social sciences continued until the mid-1970s.[29] From 1960
to 1968, the budget of the CNRS grew some 25 percent every year (after
discounting for inflation).[30] During the 1980s and 1990s the expenses for
research and development slightly went up again, but as compared with
other countries France slid from a third place worldwide in 1968 to a four-
teenth position in 2010.

This exceptionally strong growth of public investments in research had a twofold effect in the social sciences. First it led to the rapid growth of research groups and research positions, in particular within the framework of the two main research institutions: the CNRS and the Sixth Section of the EPHE. The growth of both institutions was concentrated in the 1960s and 1970s, a period that was followed by two decades of stagnation, and in the case of sociology of a certain contraction. The other consequence of the expansive research policy between 1960 and 1975 was that contract research expanded, creating a growing pool of temporarily employed researchers. When the programs for contract research started to diminish after the first oil crisis (1973) and many of the temporary researchers risked losing their livelihood, those with more than five years of research experience, so-called *hors-statut*, were given a chance to obtain a permanent position.[31] As a consequence of this integration policy, the sociology section of the CNRS more than doubled between 1975 and the beginning of the 1980s, virtually blocking any regular recruitment. This integration policy, however, which was devised for social reasons, couldn't mask the fact that the social sciences were increasingly under attack. Since May '68, policy experts considered the social sciences to be overly politicized, insufficiently scientific, and not useful enough for public policy.[32] When these criticisms were accompanied by the economic downturn, research funding dropped considerably and plans were devised for removing the social sciences from the national research organization, the CNRS.[33] Against the background of declining funding and divisive political confrontations, several reports about sociology around 1980 evoke a deep crisis of the discipline.[34]

Whereas CNRS researchers in sociology increased from about 50 (1960) to 130 (1975), their number more than doubled the following five years, reaching a high of 340 researchers by 1983 (figure 6.1). In the years after,

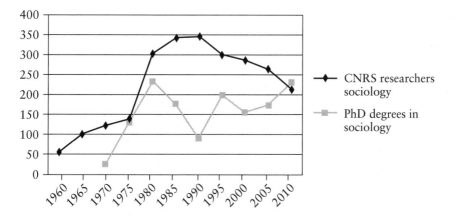

FIGURE 6.1
CNRS researchers and PhD degrees in sociology (1960–2010)

the number of researchers stabilized, but after 1990 it declined eventually, reaching a level of around 200 in 2013. Both the strong increase between 1975 and 1982 and the decline after 1990 were more pronounced in sociology than in other disciplines, although the overall trend of CNRS positions in the social and human sciences was not fundamentally different: the strong growth between 1960 and 1980 was followed by stagnation or decline between 1980 and 2000. Another indicator of the level of research activity, the number of PhD degrees, shows a roughly similar trend. In sociology, there was a strong growth in PhD degrees from 1965 to about 1980, when job prospect in higher education and research improved. The 1980s saw a sharp drop in PhD degrees, which increased again only during the first half of the 1990s in the course of the second cycle of expansion. From the mid-1990s to 2005 there is no clear trend but strong fluctuations, between roughly 100 and 200 PhD degrees per year, a significant proportion of which (between 40 and 50 percent) concerns foreign students, who commonly return to their home country after obtaining their degree.

The other major research institution, the Sixth Section of the EPHE, although much smaller than the CNRS, evolved in a similar manner. It went through a phase of strong growth from 1960 to the mid-1970s, followed by a period of overall stagnation (see figure 6.2). By 1975 its teaching staff had more than tripled, going up from 86 positions (1960) to 271 (1975); the number of junior positions grew at an even faster rate: from 10 (1960) to 158 (1975). By 1975 the majority of the "directors of study" had a full-time position at the Sixth Section, which was a qualitative change from the early years of the school when a majority had a position elsewhere as well. Since 1975, when the Sixth Section was officially renamed École des

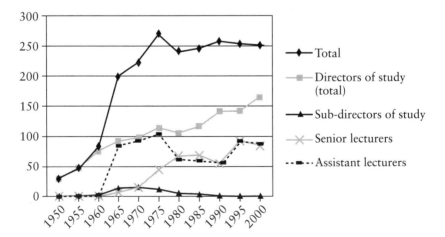

FIGURE 6.2
Teaching staff of the École des hautes études en sciences sociales (1950–2000)

hautes études en sciences sociales, the teaching staff has remained stable. The stagnation in the overall number of positions was accompanied by a process of internal promotions and a certain institutional closure: almost half of the recruitments during the period 1986–2005 were internal promotions.[35] With the disappearance of certain subaltern categories (assistant lecturer, *chef de travaux*, and "subdirector of study"), many of them were promoted to senior lecturer (*maître de conferences*) or "director of study." Another indication of the relative closure of the school is that about 60 percent of the senior lecturers recruited between 1991 and 2005 had obtained their PhD at the EHESS, succeeding about three times more often than external candidates.[36]

In addition to this pattern of strong growth followed by stagnation and a certain institutional closure, sociology lost some of its prominence within the EHESS. Whereas sociology had been one of the central disciplines in the school—together with history, economics, and anthropology—its position declined after about 1980. During the 1970s almost a third of the PhD degrees awarded by the school were in sociology; after 1980 this proportion diminished and stabilized at about 18 percent during the two decades up to 2005.[37]

The core institutions of the research sector, CNRS and EHESS, thus exhibit an exceptionally strong growth between 1960 and 1975, favoring members of the generations born in the 1930s and 1940s, whereas those who were born somewhat later faced both diminishing job openings in research and increased competition. As a consequence of this uneven pattern of growth, many of the social science research centers and journals were established during the first cycle of expansion (1960–75). After the mid-1970s the pace of renewal slowed down and the average age of the population of researchers went up. The stagnating research sector of the 1980s and 1990s thus helps to explain shifts in career strategies and intellectual reorientations. Since research positions stagnated, but the audience of educated readers and student numbers continued to expand, media activities and teaching became more important components in the work of many researchers. Writing textbooks, introductory overviews, and reference works (dictionaries, encyclopedias) became more prominent, as did editing large synthetic projects aimed at audiences outside of the restricted sphere of the research community. The historians of the *Annales* school were particularly successful in these undertakings. Prior to the 1970s their books tended to be large and detailed volumes, discretely published by the press of the ÉPHÉ or the publisher Armand Colin. Le Roy Ladurie's *Montaillou* (1975) was one of the first best-sellers of what was now labeled "new history"; it was followed by others that were similarly published by prestigious general publishing houses (Gallimard, Seuil, Fayard, Flammarion) and could be reviewed in the press by colleagues, who had started writing for dailies and weekly magazines. Successful multivolume projects were launched on the "new history," the history of women, urban France, rural France, private life, and the book and publishing industry. Pierre Nora's book series on collective memory, *Lieux de mémoire* (1984–92) eventually encompassed seven volumes, including chapters on virtually every realm of "remembrance" that touched on the French nation and national identity.

Although these "new" historical studies gained an enormous popularity in the press and publishing world, the leading scholarly journal of the *Annales* group had difficulties in redefining its position. In 1987 it proclaimed a "critical turn," which had become necessary given the "general crisis of the social sciences."[38] No social science, the editors wrote, could claim "intellectual" or "institutional hegemony" and the ambition to "unify" the social sciences, even to "federate" them, had to be abandoned. None of the defining ingredients of the *Annales* program (long-term processes, quantitative history, the critique of political and narrative history), furthermore, could be upheld as they once were. Levels of analysis, time horizons, and writing styles were complementary rather than contradictory, and their articulation no longer corresponded to any clear-cut principle. Interdisciplinarity had to be redefined, not in a theoretical sense but as a problem of day-to-day historical practice. As a consequence of these reconsiderations, the subtitle of the journal—economies, societies, civilizations—which had indicated a hierarchical order of increasing scale and scope, was dropped and replaced by a factual and more modest one: "history, social sciences."

Teaching Sociology

The expansion of social science teaching displays two distinct cycles as well. The first cycle of the 1960s and the beginning of the 1970s included the establishment of two-year (DEUG), three-year (*licence*), and four-year (*maîtrise*) undergraduate degrees for nearly all social science disciplines. In addition to these university degrees, the "economic and social sciences"— basically economics and sociology—were in 1966 introduced in secondary education, for which in 1976 a selective, national *agrégation* exam was established to recruit the upper layer of their teaching staff. Sociology degrees show a particularly strong growth during both two cycles of expansion, between 1960 and 1975, and again between 1985 and 2000 (see figure 6.3).[39] The development of university positions follows the same pattern. University positions started to increase once sociology had become a major in 1958. The number of full professors and associate professors went up from 7 (1963) to 93 (1981), while different categories of nontenured lecturers increased from 27 (1963) to 327 (1981).[40] Due to a reform in the position of university personnel in 1984, there are no figures that are strictly comparable for the second cycle of expansion, but the number of tenured, junior, and senior positions in sociology went up from 290 (1986) to 670 (2000).[41] From being above all a research endeavor, sociology in the last two decades of the twentieth century increasingly became a teaching discipline (see figure 6.4).

The differences between both cycles of growth become all the more salient when the field structure as a whole is taken into account. The expansion during the first cycle was part of the process in which the social sciences emerged as challengers to the humanities. During much of the 1960s, for example, philosophy and classical letters continued to produce more

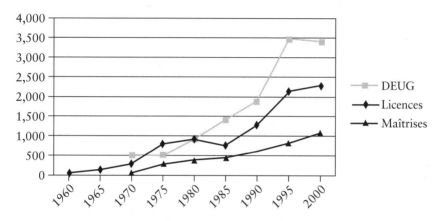

FIGURE 6.3
Sociology degrees (1960–2000)

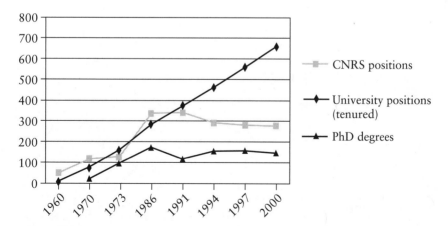

FIGURE 6.4
Academic positions and PhD degrees in sociology (1960–2000)

bachelor (*licence*) degrees than new disciplines like psychology and sociology. In quantitative terms the relations shifted in favor of the social sciences only during the 1970s when more *licence* degrees were awarded in economics and psychology, and to a lesser extent in sociology, than in philosophy and in classical letters (see table 6.1). During the second growth phase, from 1985 to 2005, the shift from the classical humanities toward the social sciences continued, but it was accompanied by another change: students now massively preferred vocational, transdisciplinary studies such as "management science," "educational sciences," "information and communication studies," or "physical education and sport." As is well indicated by the growth of associate professors (*maîtres de conferences*), the second cycle was concentrated in universities in which vocational and applied studies were becoming the largest disciplines. The growth rate of teaching positions was highest in departments like "management" and "information and communication sciences" and lowest in the classical disciplines (philosophy, history); the social sciences occupied an intermediary position (see table 6.2).

The social sciences in the 1980s and 1990s, then, did not merely go through a relative shift from research to teaching, but within the teaching institutions they were now also competing less with philosophy than with vocational disciplines and applied fields. Instead of intellectual competition other issues prevailed, in particular labor market considerations and contract research. The conditions under which Bourdieu and Foucault had developed their work during the 1960s were thus radically different from the conditions under which young philosophers and social scientists started their careers in the last decades of the twentieth century. Intangibles such as the "intellectual mood" of both periods, or the exceptional intellectual excitement of the 1960s, are conditioned by such largely invisible factors.

TABLE 6.1
Licence degrees in classical and new disciplines (1960–80)

	1960	1965	1970	1975	1980
Philosophy	180	411	802	779	575
Classical letters	513	726	1,005	861	477
History	332	565	2,175	2,432	1,848
Psychology	123	263	860	2,112	2,690
Economics	?	751	3,662	4,340	4,046
Sociology	27	132	286	809	849

Sources: Statistiques des enseignements et informations, Les examens et diplômes (1967, 1970, 1975, 1977); INSEE, *Annuaire rétrospectif de la France* (1948–1988); O. Piriou, "Que deviennent les diplômés de sociologie?," *Socio-logos* 3, 2008, http://socio-logos.revues.org/1622; L. Pinto, *La vocation et le métier de philosophe*, Paris, Seuil, 2007.

TABLE 6.2
Associate professors (tenured) in the human and social sciences (1986–2005)

	1986	1990	1995	2000	2005	Growth Rate
Philosophy	192	202	190	216	259	1.35
History	521	630	722	1,000	1,079	2.07
Anthropology	45	66	63	88	109	2.42
Sociology	163	271	348	479	571	3.50
Political science	53	91	123	153	205	3.87
Psychology	229	414	568	787	903	3.94
Educational sciences	95	174	280	361	414	4.36
Economic sciences	255	595	809	1,067	1,239	4.86
Information/ communication	82	184	263	381	519	6.33
Management sciences	182	362	539	903	1,278	7.02
Physical education/ sport	12	64	149	341	529	44.10

Source: Unpublished documents of the Conseil national des universités (CNU).

But the growth of sociology students during these two growth cycles was not merely a quantitative phenomenon. The social composition of the student population changed as well. During the 1960s, sociology attracted students with a relatively high social background, who in comparison with students in classical and more selective disciplines had less educational capital. In Bourdieu and Passeron's analysis, sociology offered underselected upper-class students a "refuge": sociology combined the advantages of a soft option with the glamour of a fashionable and general subject, which, unlike disciplines leading to a teaching degree, did not sully their intellectual aspirations with the "vulgarity of vocational training."[42] When sociology continued to attract more and more students, however, upper-class males abandoned the discipline. During the 1980s and 1990s, sociology attracted a more female population with relatively low social backgrounds. Sociology became a discipline with a very low proportion of students from elite backgrounds and one of the highest rates of students from working-class families, many of them being the first in their family to enter university. Especially in provincial universities, where research facilities are scarce, undergraduate students tend to view sociology not so much in intellectual terms, but rather as a not very selective form of vocational training, useful for becoming a social worker or primary school teacher.[43]

The expansion of the discipline also implied that sociology gradually spread from Paris to the major provincial cities. There had been a few chairs outside of Paris ever since Durkheim started teaching in Bordeaux, but research remained a Parisian affair for a long time. Only when sociology spread to the provinces did research centers emerge in major university cities throughout the country. Although none of these regional centers could compete with the capital, some succeeded in specializing in certain areas and gaining a reputation in their field of expertise. The Laboratoire d'économie et de sociologie du travail (LEST, 1969) in Aix-en-Provence, for example, united economists and sociologists of work and developed a comparative approach to labor markets. Similar examples from other cities could be quoted. The best-known and most prominent work, however, remained concentrated in Paris, where the most prestigious scientific institutions and schools are located, the best libraries are housed, and where both the funding institutions and the publishing industry are concentrated. In 2001, three out of four CNRS sociological research centers were still located in Paris and its immediate surroundings.[44] During the 1980s and 1990s between two-thirds to three-fourths of all PhD degrees in sociology were awarded by Parisian institutions.[45]

If the growth of the discipline had not threatened the hegemony of Parisian institutions and the dominance of elite schools, it did contribute to a strong thematic differentiation. Sociologists in the 1950s had been primarily concerned with the sociology of work. Although this has remained a core area of French sociology, the main emerging domains during the 1960s and 1970s were the sociology of education, the sociology of culture, and urban sociology; the sociology of religion and rural sociology became more peripheral. The new research domains were directly linked to funds that the planning agencies made available through programs for contract research.[46] During the 1980s and 1990s contract research for central planning agencies declined. Contract research became more decentralized and generally an affair of specific ministries, regions, and cities. It gradually also restricted the autonomy of researchers. In comparison with the 1960s and the beginning of the 1970s, contract research became more narrowly defined, more closely bound to specific policy aims, and more instrumental.[47] As a consequence, it was far more difficult to use funds from contract research for developing a more general program of the kind that Bourdieu or Touraine had pursued in the 1960s and early 1970s.

The intellectually most prominent new areas of research during the last decades of the twentieth century were probably economic and political sociology.[48] Both were linked to changes in the power relations between disciplines. The reemergence of economic sociology was a response to the dominance of economics and the spread of neoliberal policies. French scholars developed original approaches to economic sociology, which were partly independent from the North American currents that were concentrated on economic networks and economic organizations.[49] The emergence of political sociology was related to the expansion of public administration, *science po*, which belatedly became a significant research pole and attracted some of the most ardent supporters of a policy-oriented sociology. Michel Crozier's group joined *science po* in the 1970s; after having directed the group of rural sociology for many years, Henri Mendras founded the Sociological Observatory of Change (OSC, 1988).

Publishing Sociology

The market for social science books and journals displays a somewhat similar pattern as the development of higher education: the strong growth between 1960 and 1975 was followed by a period of consolidation and reorientation. The first period has been described as the "golden years" of publishing in the human sciences.[50] Prior to 1960 social science studies were usually published by specialized, scholarly presses like the Presses Universitaires de France and were printed in small numbers. That Levi-Strauss's *Tristes tropiques* (1955) was well received and sold well was, in part, because it was read as a literary work. During the 1960s and 1970s the most prestigious general publishing houses (Gallimard, Seuil, Minuit, Flammarion, Fayard), which had traditionally published literature, essays, and work from the humanities, created special book series for the human sciences. In the French publishing system such series are often directed by well-known academics, who are in charge of selecting books and authors. Gurvitch created a sociological book series with the Presses Universitaires de France in 1950, which he directed until his death in 1965. In the 1960s and 1970s general publishers followed: Braudel directed the series *Nouvelle bibliothèque scientifique* (1962, Flammarion), Bourdieu *Le sens commun* (1965, Minuit), Pierre Nora the *Bibliothèque des sciences humaines* (1966) and the *Bibliothèque des histoires* (1971), both with Gallimard. The introduction of pocket books extended the market further. Among the most prominent ones were the series *10/18* (1962), *Idées* (1962), *Petite collection Maspéro* (1967), and *Points* (1970).

During the 1980s and 1990s publishing underwent changes that roughly corresponded with the transformations that were indicated above. In line with growing student numbers the market for textbooks and reference works continued to expand, whereas the market for theoretical writings and scholarly monographs contracted. François Maspéro, who had founded his publishing house during the war in Algeria in 1959 and published political and theoretical writings of the Left (Althusser, Castoriadis, Lefebvre), quit the publishing business in 1982. The sales of his books had "suddenly collapsed" between 1978 and 1981, which were years of a severe economic recession and a vivid political reaction against the post-1968 radicalism.[51] Maspéro's publishing house was renamed La Découverte, most of the older book series disappeared, and the publisher typically survived thanks to a successful series of small, high-quality textbooks (*Repères*). Due to increasing academic specialization, a lack of grand and vivacious theorizing, and the rise of vocational disciplines, the market for scholarly monographs went through a marked change as well. The average number of printed copies of scholarly monographs fell, eventually reaching levels where general publishers became far less interested in publishing original studies and translations.[52] In some cases newly founded small publishers took over the role of the bigger publishers.[53] But young authors were increasingly relegated to a publishing house like L'Harmattan, which publishes books in small numbers, offering neither editorial services nor serious distribution, and instead of paying royalties asks authors to buy a number of copies of their own work. In terms of its publishing volume, L'Harmattan became a major publisher in the human sciences, producing 120 titles in 1980 and 2,000 in 2010.[54]

Scholarly journals tend to have more restricted audiences than books. After Gurvitch's *Cahiers internationaux de sociologie* (1946) and the new series of the *Année sociologique* (1949), a host of new journals was founded around 1960. The two new Sorbonne professors, Jean Stoetzel and Raymond Aron, both appointed in 1955, each launched their own journal. Stoetzel the *Revue française de sociologie* (1960), which was an outlet for mainly empirical studies, based at the Centre d'études sociologiques (CES), and intended to compete with Gurvitch's theoretically oriented journal. Two-thirds of the articles in Gurvitch's journal were theoretical papers, whereas this proportion was barely a fourth in the *Revue française de sociologie*. Whereas the *Cahiers internationaux* published hardly anything on "methodology," methodological papers alone represented 16 percent of the articles in the *Revue française*.[55] Stoetzel's Sorbonne colleague and rival Raymond Aron launched a general sociology journal as well, the *Archives européennes de sociologie* (1960). Together with Ralf Dahrendorf (then in Hamburg) and Tom Bottomore (London), the trilingual journal was based at Aron's Centre of European Sociology (1960) and aimed at reviving the European tradition of historical and comparative social science. Aside from these general journals, several more specialized ones appeared: *Archives de sociologie des religions*

(1956), *Sociologie du travail* (1959), *Communications* (1960), and *Études rurales* (1960). At the end of the first cycle of expansion, Pierre Bourdieu founded *Actes de la recherche en sciences sociales* (1975), which was a new type of journal that had considerable impact well beyond sociology. Focused on a specific theme, each issue contained articles that made use of varied forms of documentation (historical documents, images, statistical tables, ethnographic observations, interview fragments) and often drew on perspectives from different disciplines and approaches. The journal had a large format, might contain long articles but also brief notes, and consistently published important foreign authors. Opposed to Parisian fads and intellectual verbalism, it was thoroughly rooted in empirical research while being critically attuned to important questions in both public and scientific debates.

The journals that appeared on the scene during the second cycle of expansion were commonly more specialized, although a host of interdisciplinary journals appeared as well. Several of these incorporated elements of Bourdieu's *Actes*, such as a preference for thematic issues and the use of more varied documentation and writing styles. Among them were *Sciences sociales et santé* (1982), *Espaces et sociétés* (1983), *Droit et sociétiés* (1985), *Politix* (1988), *Genèses* (1990), and *Travail, genre et sociétés* (1999). The *Revue du Mauss* (1982) was an interdisciplinary platform for anti-utilitarian approaches, *Terrain* (1983) a thematic journal for European ethnography, *Raisons pratiques* (1990) an interdisciplinary journal focused on the study of action and interaction. More general sociology journals also saw the light of day: *Sociétés contemporaines* (1990) and *Sociologie* (2010). In terms of diffusion, however, the new generation of journals had significantly fewer subscriptions than the older journals.[56]

A comparison of sociology journals with journals in other disciplines provides some additional insight into the academic position of sociology as compared with other disciplines. Comparing the reference pattern in the major journals, it is possible to specify the intellectual profile of various disciplines. In a bibliometric study, citations were examined for the "core journals" of each discipline.[57] For these "core journals," a ranking was established of the most cited journals during the last decade of the twentieth century. These lists of most frequently cited journals per discipline can be compared along two dimensions: the *disciplinary openness* they exhibit and their *international openness*. The first can be measured by the relative weight of references to journals belonging to other disciplines, the latter by the relative weight of references to non-French journals (that is, to journals of which a clear majority of the editors work outside of France and French-speaking countries). The result of the comparison shows that the human sciences in France include three types of disciplines. Disciplines like economics/management, political science, and philosophy are strongly monodisciplinary as well as highly international in their reference pattern. A discipline like law is monodisciplinary as well, but unlike economics and political science, predominantly nationally oriented, since the core journals contain a high proportion of references to French journals. Sociology represents a third type of discipline: it is most strongly interdisciplinary in its references, but rather similar to law in its predominantly national orientation (see figure 6.5).[58] Within this triangular structure, history and anthropology occupy intermediary positions. Although sociology is a pluralistic discipline with a relatively dispersed intellectual profile, its strong interdisciplinary orientation is in France accompanied by a relatively high level of national closure.

Sociology's high level of disciplinary openness, furthermore, is not a one-sided affair because sociology's core journals are more frequently quoted outside of the discipline than the core journals of other disciplines. In this sense sociology has the characteristics of an interdiscipline; its ambition of investigating social relations in every domain implies that—more than other disciplines—it is embedded in multiple exchanges with other

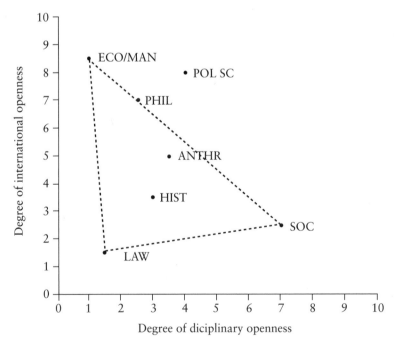

FIGURE 6.5
Degree of disciplinary and international openness of the human sciences (1991–2001)

human sciences, although these tend to be restricted to the French or Francophone context. Its comparatively low level of international orientation is confirmed by other data. PhD degrees in sociology, for example, are often about France and its regions, and in comparison to political science, history, and anthropology, more rarely about other European countries.[59] Participation of French sociologists in world congresses of sociology has been limited and declined significantly during the 1990s, whereas international meetings and associations were, on the contrary, expanding.[60] French contributions to the European Sociological Association (1992) were also disproportionally slight.[61]

Rhetoric and Reality of Professionalization

The position sociology obtained in the academic field eventually required another mode of professional association. The Institut français de sociologie (IFS) that the Durkheimians had founded in 1924 had been a learned and "exclusively scientific" society. It served as a meeting place for intra- and interdisciplinary debate and exchange, but consciously refused to fulfill other functions; it steadily declined after the Second World War.[62] The plea for more professional training and a different mode of certification came from researchers at the CES. In 1953, Georges Friedmann and Jean-René Tréanton had argued that it was necessary to break with the "speculative orientation" of Durkheim and his successors and to reorient sociological reflection toward the "economic and social problems of the twentieth century." Sociological research had to be focused on empirical investigations in the service of "practical action." As such, sociologists had to acquire a reputation of professionalism and objectivity, for which the demographic studies conducted by the national institute for demography could serve as example.[63] But when in 1958 the bachelor degree (*licence*) in sociology was created, this was a general academic and not in any sense a "professional" degree. It consisted of four certificates (general sociology, social psychology, political economy, and one optional) and included neither research training nor any form of specialization. Because of its general character, the degree was qualified as "deceitful" by the group of sociology students at the Sorbonne. The teaching for the bachelor, they argued, was merely "rhetorical" and "encyclopedic" and did not provide any preparation for research. The group repeatedly expressed its concern about the lack of job prospects and in 1966 pleaded again for a more "technical and specialized" curriculum, which would prepare for a sociological "profession" based on proper scientific training and research skills and be regulated by a professional code of conduct.[64]

The most tangible step taken in the direction of more professional training was the proposition to create an "expert degree" in sociology. The proposal was presented in 1964 by Jean-René Tréanton at a meeting of the newly founded Société française de sociologie (SFS, 1962). The degree would be intermediary between the bachelor (*licence*) and the PhD degree and was modeled on existing expert degrees in demography and psychology. But the proposal was rejected because the most powerful university patrons privileged existing academic hierarchies over new forms of professional education. They considered it more important to recruit graduates from the selective École normale supérieure with an *agrégation* degree in philosophy than to set up training programs for professional sociologists. Jean Stoetzel, for example, himself a *normalien* philosopher, who founded the first institute for public opinion polls in France and was a staunch defender of quantitative research, did not think it was of much use to have an expert degree. The *agrégation* exam in philosophy, after all, "guarantees" a "high-quality recruitment" of sociological personnel.[65]

The refusal to improve professional training at the expense of traditional criteria of academic excellence was curiously at odds with the rhetoric of the SFS. The newly founded society officially declared that it wanted to unite "all French sociologists" and organize the "profession of sociologist."[66] Whereas this objective was regularly repeated and professional interests were discussed during the first meetings of the SFS, the new professional organization primarily served to organize the discipline's public relations. Sociologists and their association presented themselves as professional partners for state agencies and other organizations willing to provide research funds. In 1963 Raymond Aron presided over a "debate dinner" about the relations between industry and sociology. Some sixty industrialists and sociologists exchanged views on the question how sociology could contribute to the improvement of industrial organization.[67] Similar meetings were held about a variety of other topics as well, commonly related to state planning agencies that were increasingly interested in the social aspects of economic modernization. The first national congress of the SFS in 1965 was about the "social transformations of French society." It was intended as a public demonstration that sociologists produced studies that were indispensable to understand and manage the ongoing social and economic changes. Two of the six presidents of the sessions, for example, were high civil servants engaged in developing new forms of state planning (Claude Gruson, Pierre Massé). The book that came out of the conference employed a language that was quite close to that of the modernization views of planning officials. Its three parts treated "attitudes of the French with regard to change," "change in relation to economic growth," and the "management of change."[68] Characteristic of this convergence of interests was that not all the papers presented were included in the book. Several were considered to be too far removed from the issues of planned change and too critical or too pessimistic in tone to be of use in the rapprochement of sociologists and planning officials. Relegated to the *Revue française de sociologie*, the rejected papers were typically concerned with the "conservative school" (Bourdieu), the "rigidity of an institution" (Isambert-Jamati), and "regional closure" (Tréanton).[69]

Although there were obviously dividing lines of various kinds, the discipline as a whole was characterized by a fairly generally shared working consensus. A good illustration is Raymond Aron's project to publish a sociological encyclopedia in the prestigious *Pléiade* book series. Aron, who was the most authoritative sociologist since he belatedly had arrived at the Sorbonne in 1955, would write the introduction and the conclusion. Bourdieu elaborated the table of contents, which included virtually all the major figures of the discipline. Passeron would write a sociological account of the history of the discipline, Boudon was responsible for the part on methods, Touraine and Crozier would write on firms and organizations, Bourdieu himself on education, and Balandier on the development of traditional societies.[70]

May '68, however, put an abrupt end to broad collaborative ventures like Aron's encyclopedia. Although research and teaching continued to expand and many groups profited from the expansion, the professionalization rhetoric ended abruptly. The second congress of the SFS was held in 1969 to discuss "crises and conflicts of French society." But the different views expressed were so conflict ridden that the proceedings were never published. Two years later, in 1971, another attempt was made, but the congress never took place because members of the Group of Anti-Sociological Struggles (GLAS) prevented it.[71] Accompanied by rock music, some sixty activists wearing carnival masks disrupted the conference, which had not even officially started, denouncing sociology's role as a mere "lubricant" for the state planning machinery. After the mid-1970s, the SFS continued to organize meetings, but they took place in provincial cities, no longer in Paris, and were much smaller.

The issue of professionalization was eventually taken up again in a more restricted manner by two other organizations. Since sociology after 1980 expanded primarily within universities and outside academic institutions, specific associations were founded for both sectors. Sociology teachers in higher education founded the Association des sociologues enseignants du supérieur (ASES, 1989). The association regularly examined teaching programs, recruitment practices, and evaluation procedures. Another association united "professional sociologists," that is, sociologists who worked outside of the academic sector. For a number of years this Association professionnelle des sociologues (APS, 1982) investigated emerging forms of "practical sociology" and coordinated activities of its practitioners. Although the activities declined after a number of years, "practical sociologists" have continued to manifest themselves. Many were trained in the sociology of organizations and their work as consultants or practitioners of policy research raised questions that were not properly addressed in academic settings. A specific association was created in 1998 for sociologists who work for firms, and a journal, *Sociologies pratiques* (1999), was founded to serve as a platform for all those who are employed outside of academia. Because of the growing importance of these forms of "practical sociology," some observers have signaled a "practical turn" that would characterize the discipline at the beginning of the twenty-first century.[72]

Since the SFS (1962) was no longer very active after 1971, it was eventually replaced by a new association, the Association française de sociologie (2004), which was intended to unite all sociologists in a single organization. The new association was presented explicitly as a professional association and no longer as a learned society. About half of its members were academic sociologists, a quarter were PhD students and postdocs, another quarter consisted of "practical" sociologists. Its first national conference in 2004 brought together more than a thousand sociologists, distributed over forty-one research committees. Professional integration, however, is still relatively weak and the two categories most frequently used in 2003 for describing the state of the discipline were indeed its "dispersion" and organization in "clans."[73]

Conclusion

The decades after 1960 were a period of unprecedented growth for all of the social sciences. From being a small and divided subfield, sociology transformed into an organized academic discipline. The structural dynamics of this process of expansion displays two cycles of growth. The first one was concentrated in the 1960s and the first half of the 1970s when the opportunities to do social scientific work improved enormously and the human sciences gained considerable public visibility and a higher intellectual status while simultaneously securing considerable funding from policy institutes. For a while everything seemed to improve. After a decade of lower levels of funding and a politically and scientifically divided social science community between 1975 and 1985, the social sciences went through a second phase of growth between 1985 and 2000. This time, however, the expansion was in the universities, whereas the research sector stagnated or contracted. Instead of primarily challenging the classical humanities, as had been the case in the 1960s and 1970s, the social sciences now competed with disciplines that were more attuned to the market sector, like economics and a host of vocational disciplines, which promised students chances on the labor market that the classical social sciences lacked.

These two phases of growth were separated by two crises: the political crisis of May '68 and its aftermath and the economic crisis of the latter half of the 1970s and beginning of the 1980s. The first cycle is generally remembered as the "golden years" of the social sciences when funding was abundant, growth continuous, and the social sciences miraculously combined a high level of intellectual legitimacy with considerable demand from policymakers. As Alain Touraine ironically remarked in 1966: "A French sociologist today tries to keep in touch with both the state planning agencies and *Les temps modernes*."[74] These various factors combined produced a mood of confidence and optimism at which many look back with a certain amazement, as did this interviewee: "I remember that in 1967 or so I proposed a research project together with A., it worked, and it was fantastic: at twenty-six or twenty-seven years old I had more resources than I have ever had since, I had a technical collaborator, a secretary. . . ."

Although sociology was intellectually more peripheral during the period of structuralism than anthropology and perhaps linguistics, the discipline was also affected by the intellectual excitement of these years and the uncommon amount of daring work that was done. Some of it had started in the periphery of the academic system during the 1940s and 1950s (Dumézil, Lévi-Strauss), but came to fruition and found a much larger audience during the 1960s when it was joined by a range of newcomers, including Roland Barthes, Michel Foucault, Jacques Derrida, and Pierre Bourdieu.

After the crisis of May '68, political support for the social sciences diminished, internal struggles came to the fore, and much of the "working consensus" that had characterized the 1960s collapsed. Self-confidence and optimism suffered a second blow from the economic downturn of the years around 1980, which eventually led to a neoliberal reorientation in the policy realm that produced a reconfiguration of the social sciences. During the last decades of the twentieth century sociologists, individually as well as collectively, grappled with three contradictory tendencies. One was between expanding university teaching and declining positions in research, the second was between a shrinking sector for "academic" sociology and a rising one for "practical" sociology, the third was between a predominantly national orientation and an internationalizing social science practice in Europe and beyond.

Although the discipline's growth was accompanied by new journals and a professional association, one of the peculiarities of the institutional expansion was that sociology did not become a discipline quite like others. Several attempts to create a professional sociology degree and to improve the functioning of the national sociological association did not produce the desired results. Sociology lacks not only a prestigious national teaching degree (*agrégation*), which exists in all major teaching disciplines, but it also lacks a recognized form of practitioners' training and certification (like in psychology). Having succeeded in becoming an organized academic discipline, sociology still enjoys a relatively low degree of intellectual and professional autonomy. Representing a basis for heteronomous movements of various kinds, this weak autonomy is regularly deplored. But discouraging the closure and routinization that academic and other specialties tend to characterize, it is perhaps also a blessing in disguise. Much of the vitality of sociology in France is indeed related to its multiple connections to other disciplines, to the inflow of talent from other fields, and to its fluctuating but ongoing orientation toward both the intellectual field and public debate.

Having at the end of the twentieth century become more of a teaching than a research discipline, with a stronger tendency to secure its usefulness in extra-academic endeavors and a relatively strong national focus, sociology is at the same time the most interdisciplinary discipline among the human sciences. Significant parts of the discipline have not retreated within the boundaries of university departments or specific research specialties. Sociology was a vital ingredient in numerous transdisciplinary enterprises. Pierre Bourdieu's journal *Actes de la recherche en sciences sociales* (1975) broke with the standard format of a scientific journal, was organized around well-chosen themes, incorporated visual material, and reflexively combined different methods and points of view. *Actes* served as the example for a host of other multidisciplinary ventures. Ethnographic studies have found a new outlet in the journal *Terrain* (1983), historically oriented social scientists created *Genèses* (1990), the social scientific study of politics and the state is the center of attention of *Politix* (1988), and the varieties of action and interaction are dissected and discussed in the *Revue du MAUSS* (1981) and *Raisons pratiques* (1990).

Part of this new wave of multidisciplinary initiatives was a renewed engagement with public affairs. Some of this work has taken the form of more sustained policy commitments and a variety of "practical sociologies." But others have redefined their relation to public debate and civic institutions. Touraine's group entered into interactions with new social movements and frequently participated in public debates. Pierre Bourdieu's conception of "committed scholarship" and the "collective intellectual" inspired undertakings as varied as a European review of books, *Liber*; the collective book project on suffering in contemporary societies, *The Weight of the World* (1993); and a small publishing house. As was the case in the new transdisciplinary ventures, the significance of these new public initiatives was in no way restricted to sociology and generally concerned the public role of social science and the intellectual field at large.

CHAPTER 7

※※※

Intellectual Styles and the Dynamics
of Research Groups

The pattern of expansion documented in the previous chapter offered both established and aspiring sociologists a broadening space of possibilities. The work that sociologists undertook under these conditions can be understood as the result of the encounter between their specific resources and dispositions and the (im)possibilities offered by the expanding field. Following this principle, I will in this final chapter consider the work of four sociologists who each represented a distinct style of practicing sociology. Research practices in the expanding discipline obviously became enormously varied and only a full-fledged field analysis could properly capture the main tendencies and their underlying principles of differentiation. But field structures can be approached through case studies as well, and enterprises that occupy a strategic position can clarify significant parts of the field dynamics as a whole.

The figures selected for this chapter—Touraine, Crozier, Boudon, Bourdieu—all produced a body of work that went significantly beyond the specific research domain(s) in which they started and that acquired international recognition as being of more general sociological interest. With Durkheim and Mauss they have, for example, become the most cited French sociologists in the United States between 1970 and 2010.[1] Spanning a period of four or more decades, each one of them not only published major individual studies but in the 1960s and 1970s built up a productive research group as well. Histories of science are conventionally about exceptional, more or less heroic individuals, but considering their achievements in more detail, they are nearly always brought about in groups or circles.

Outstanding individual accomplishments become possible because they are embedded in two types of social processes.[2] The first one is the socialization process through which members of the older generation transmit skills and resources to their students. Particularly productive scientists tend to be students of other particularly productive scientists, who successfully transmit both formal and tacit knowledge as well as positions and network connections (membership to journals and committees, relations to people that matter).[3] The second process is related to the group, circle, or school that ambitious scholars build up themselves. As compared with purely individual work, such collectives have vital advantages. They enable a pooling of resources, allow for a division of labor, and accelerate and intensify the learning process. Groups also provide the benefit of covering more areas and issues than any individual ever can, and therefore have particularly significance for generalizing insights. Regular interactions in well-functioning groups are, furthermore, known to be invigorating and tend to produce high levels of emotional and intellectual energy.[4]

Unlike most of their colleagues, the sociologists selected for this chapter profited from both of these dynamics. Not only did they have a privileged connection to the most centrally located patrons and mentors (Friedmann for Touraine and Crozier, Stoetzel and Lazarsfeld for Boudon, Aron for Bourdieu), but they all built up a leading research group as well. Representing a particular style of work, these groups have had a defining significance for the discipline as a whole. Developed in mutual competition, the work of these groups thus reveals major structuring principles of the discipline as a whole. This significance is not restricted to a certain approach to sociology, which can be summarized in textbooks, but is inseparable from the fact that these groups have been responsible for supervising dissertations, producing textbooks, editing journals, publishing book series, and organizing workshops, conferences, exchange programs, and the like. The totality of these activities and the specific group dynamics would require a separate and more detailed analysis than I can present here. But the four sociologists founded and directed such a group and their activities defined the elective affinities by which these groups were held together.

Alain Touraine and Michel Crozier belong to the postwar generation. Starting out in very similar circumstances and belonging to the circle of Friedmann, their publications went well beyond the sociology of work, which formed its starting point. Over the years their work diverged and crystallized into two opposed ways of practicing sociology. Starting from his early inquiries on industrial workers and working-class movements, Touraine developed a sociology of social action and social change, which was closely related to his sustained engagement with contemporary political issues. In keeping with this orientation, Touraine and his closest collaborators have been among the most visible sociologists in France, publishing regularly in newspapers, magazines, and nonspecialist journals, and whose books tends to be part of the public debate.[5] Touraine's work can be seen as a form of public sociology, rooted in a historically informed theory of social action and focused on sociopolitical issues in postindustrial societies. Michel Crozier soon identified with the opposite pole of the spectrum. Critical of French intellectuals and their philosophical debates and political engagements, he became the leading proponent of policy sociology.[6] Fundamentally oriented not so much toward academic endeavors or the public debate, Crozier defined his work as a response to, and in interaction with, the managerial demands of large organizations, initially public organizations, later including private companies as well. Much of it focused on the institutional sclerosis of bureaucratic institutions, which Crozier highlighted in his publications and in the reforms he advocated.

Sociologists of the next generation entered the field after 1958, when the discipline was rapidly expanding and the human sciences enjoyed a much wider acclaim. Raymond Boudon and Pierre Bourdieu are arguably the most prominent figures of their generation and, similar to Touraine and Crozier, represent rival ways of conceiving of and practicing sociology. Entering a field that was in a process of academic institutionalization, both were more intensely preoccupied with the scientific status and academic credibility of the discipline than any member of the previous generation. Since Bourdieu and Boudon—unlike Crozier and Touraine—were philosophers by training, they were predisposed to tackle the theoretical challenges the discipline was confronted with. Boudon started out by working on methodology and later became the most prominent spokesmen of "methodological individualism" in France. A critic of the French intellectual scene, Boudon's career has taken place for the most part neither in research nor in policy institutions, but in the university and represents a particular form of academic sociology. Building on a variety of research projects and theoretical sources, Pierre Bourdieu's work cut across the existing forms of sociology and is best described as a reflexive sociology, which he elaborated in major studies and combined with a selective and critical engagement with more broadly intellectual and public issues. Like Touraine, Bourdieu's career was primarily in the research sector.

Beyond the Sociology of Work

Postwar French sociology emerged around empirical studies of the labor process. The successive development of this core area of research can be described in terms of a growing differentiation into various specialties (labor, professions, leisure, firms, organizations), and more specifically, as a divergence between more intellectual or academic and more applied or policy-related approaches.[7] The former remained primarily embedded in the intellectual and academic field and was based in research institutions, whereas the latter was part of the movement for "applied" or "practical sociology" that developed in close interaction with policy institutions, public administration, and management. Touraine was the most authoritative representative of the former tendency, Crozier of the latter. Although the separation of the two deepened after 1968, its origins are older and are not merely related to the polarization of the academic field after 1968, but also to the specific resources and dispositions of the protagonists.

Alain Touraine came from an academic Parisian family—his father was an eminent physician and president of the Academy of Medicine—that was close to public institutions and its ethos of public service, while being rather "foreign" to the business world.[8] He went to the country's intellectual elite school, the École normale, where his training was in history. The years after the Liberation, when the collaborationist Vichy regime as well as the prewar elites had been discredited and Communists were part of the government, had "changed everything" for him. Like many others, Touraine was convinced that industrialism, the laboring classes, and their "collective action" would lead to radical change and a "new society."[9] By family background, training, and inclination, Touraine was close to the concerns that dominated the intellectual field. He considered the work of Georges Friedmann the best guide to the changes he witnessed and from the outset distinguished clearly between scientific understanding and applied research. American sociology was ambiguous in that respect; it was "social science" and "social technology" at the same time.[10] French sociology, the young Touraine argued, should be limited to scientific diagnostics and refrain from proposing solutions for the social adjustment of workers and employees. Although the predominant philosophy of the time left very little space for empirical social science, Touraine was sympathetic to the themes of existentialism, to issues of choice, action, and commitment. In the sociology of action he elaborated, with its insistence on the active role of a historical subject, Touraine remained close to the intellectual sensibilities of his formative years.

Belonging to the same generation and starting his career in the same research group, Michel Crozier's work developed in the direction of a sociology of organizations and organizational reform. In his commitment to a sociology that would be useful for managing large organizations, Crozier explicitly broke with the codes and conventions of the Parisian intelligentsia. Born in a calm Parisian suburb to a father who ran a small business, he received his training at a business school, the École des hautes études commerciales (HEC). But Crozier was not quite at ease, neither in the business school he attended nor in the intellectual circles into which he was drawn. He had cherished literary ambitions and was a man of the Left—for a while was close to some Trotskyites—but his intellectual orientation would increasingly come from American sociology. For a study of American trade unions, Crozier made an early journey to the United States in 1947 and 1948. Not unlike Touraine and other members of their generation, he was initially rather critical about the American social sciences and the corporate uses of "human engineering" and other forms of applied social science. In one of his first articles, he urged European intellectuals to stand up against this "deceit" that under the guise of science was aimed at social adjustment and normalization.[11] But it was nevertheless important, he argued, to carefully study American corporations and the way the labor force was organized and managed. For the young Crozier, this called for a break with the habits of the Parisian intelligentsia. Instead of philosophical faultfinding and moralizing debates, there was an urgent need for "practical knowledge." Painters like Picasso, fashion designers, existentialist philosophers, and other members of the cultural elite belonged to a civilization in decline. Their refined cultural preoccupations obscured the fact that among industrial nations, France was lagging behind. It was time for French intellectuals to dedicate themselves to "very simple and concrete projects," similar to the ones carried out by technical specialists: "Why can't our great moralists and profound philosophers tell us how to organize the Renault plants or the community of Bagnolet or the neighborhood of Saint-Quentin?"[12]

The direction of thought expressed by Touraine and Crozier, rooted in their family background and educational training, and shaped by the demand for studies about industrial modernization, differed not only in the way they related to intellectuals and policymakers but also in their perception of American social science. Touraine was critical of several aspects of American sociology, notably its lack of historical grounding and the absence of a critical reflection on social issues. Although Crozier initially voiced similar reservations, his experience had been fundamentally different. Having a greater distance to French intellectuals and technocratic elites, Crozier found an alternative model of intellectual commitment and social organization in the United States. Remembering his first stay there, his reservations could not mask the fact that he was profoundly impressed. "I was won by the then general belief in unlimited progress, merely by the force of sincere dialogue. I was also touched by the generous, universalist élan that . . . enabled the Marshall Plan and the reconstruction of Europe."[13] Digesting the lessons of his first stay in the United States and developing his relations with Daniel Bell and other members of the Parisian branch of the anticommunist Congress for Cultural Freedom, Crozier considered himself something of a "left-wing American."[14]

Social Action and Public Sociology

After his study on the evolution of work in the car manufacturing plants of Renault, Alain Touraine founded his own Laboratory of Industrial Sociology (1958) at the École des hautes études. Like a range of other centers established in the 1960s, Touraine's group grew rapidly, profiting from the combined growth of research funds and positions in the research sector. Beyond empirical studies of the labor process, Touraine's more specific focus was on social action, on the collective attempts of people to resist the constraints of the system of which they are part, gain some measure of control over their own work and life, and provoke historical change. He presented his thoughts on such a form of sociology in his *Sociologie de l'action* (1965), which was an ambitious attempt to define a theoretical position of his own. Following a general analysis of the development of "industrial civilization," Touraine proposed a sociology of action that would critically complement functionalist and structuralist theories. Functionalism was concerned with the differentiation of social systems and processes of socialization required for people to fulfill the functions attributed to them. Structuralism was concerned with symbolic systems by which people communicate. The primary objective for a sociology of action is to understand historical change. Its core notions, Touraine argued, are those of a "historical subject" and "project." Social groups go beyond the social and cultural structures they are embedded in by following a "project" of their own; by doing so they constitute themselves as a historical subject, that is, as a collective agent of change. Touraine's book, which was one of the first major general statements by a member of the younger generation, provoked a harsh reaction from the members of his dissertation committee. The defense of his two-volume *Thèse d'État*, expected to be a tribute to this upcoming talent and attended by a large crowd, became a legendary and painful confrontation.

Raymond Aron, who since 1955 occupied the main sociology chair at the Sorbonne and had himself lectured and published on industrial society, seems to have been slightly irritated by the grand airs with which Touraine presented his work. Unimpressed, Aron reproached Touraine for having launched himself in a more philosophical than sociological analysis and for having neither the training nor the conceptual mastery to accomplish that. His fellow committee members Friedmann and Stoetzel were hardly less critical, and Touraine nearly left the defense, which he experienced as a "ceremonial execution"; he was happy to leave for Chile shortly afterward, but was plagued by nightmares weeks after.[15]

The revolt of May 1968 gave Touraine's work a new twist and his group a new impulse. The student movement, Touraine argued, was not so much indicative of the crisis of old institutions; it represented a new type of social conflict, carried by a new social movement. Instead of considering the student movement as opposing industrial civilization, it made much more sense to see it as the vanguard of a new, "postindustrial" society. The main contradiction of postindustrial societies was no longer between labor and capital, but between technocratically managed decision centers and those subjected to "dependent participation." Not exploitation but alienation is central, and new social movements express and explore historically significant ways to escape this condition and thus help to reshape and reinvent social relations. Since the emphasis was on creativity and invention against the background of a broad historical transformation, Touraine's approach to social movements was quite different from the one that was later developed in the United States by Charles Tilly and others, where resources and mobilization processes within an opportunity structure were the central notions.

After 1968 Touraine's center at the École des hautes études became the Center for the Study of Social Movements (1970) and was rebaptized a decade later the Center for Sociological Analysis and Intervention (1981). With his main collaborators—François Dubet, Zsuzsa Hegedus, and Michel Wievorka—Touraine launched projects on new social movements such as the antinuclear movement, feminism, regionalist movements, and the Polish Solidarity movement. Much of it was a response to the question Touraine had already raised in his *Sociologie de l'action* (1965) but had not been able to answer. One of the aims of the book had been to reflect on the "great problem" of which "type of social movement would play the role the workers movement had played during the development of the capitalist economy?"[16] For studying new social movements, Touraine designed a method of inquiry that was not just a way to register, observe, or measure social action, but also allowed sociologists to actively intervene in the movement they studied. This "sociological intervention" implied bringing activists and sociologists together in a sequence of meetings. During the initial phase activists are confronted with researchers' questions about the objectives, meaning, and perspective of their struggle. It is followed by a "self-analysis" of the activists, acknowledging a plurality of interpretations, to which the researchers subsequently add their own analysis. This confrontation leads to a change of perspective among the activists, a "conversion," the aim of which is to arrive at the most "elevated meaning of their action."[17] Parallel to a series of case studies, Touraine returned to his action theory in *Production de la société* (1973) and *Le retour de l'acteur* (1984). Societies, he underlined, have the essential capacity to produce and not merely to reproduce themselves, that is, to acknowledge that social relations are the result of social action and to incorporate that insight. This principle of "historicity" was central in studying new social movements and Touraine spelled out some of its political consequences as well, among others in a much-debated book essay on the death of socialism (1980).

Faced with the subsequent decline of social movements during the 1980s and 1990s, Touraine reengaged with the issue of historical transformation and tackled questions of modernity and postmodernity in *Critique de la modernité* (1992) and *Pourrons-nous vivre ensemble, égaux et différent* (1997). As in his earlier work, Touraine presented a broad historical sketch of contemporary transformations (decline of macroinstitutions, globalization, individualization), which he and his collaborators combined with empirical case studies and a regular flow of essays. Much of this work was premised on what Touraine saw as the fundamental loss of unity of modern societies. Liberalized global markets have "desocialized" producers and consumers alike, just as the globalization of exchange networks has considerably weakened the power of nation-states and other institutions. Between economic and technological globalization on the one hand, and the cultural realm on the other, between the world of instrumentality and the world of identity, many if not all forms of social and political mediation have broken down. This "demodernization" has far-reaching consequences for the task of sociologists. Sociology must acknowledge the "death of human beings as social beings": people are no longer defined by their social roles or social positions and the idea of "society" had lost its meaning.[18] This "end of the social" led to institutional disintegration, manifest in social exclusion, racism, terrorism, and other forms of violence, as well as to a new quest for meaning. Although new social movements were defined in similar opposition to institutional control, this quest for meaning is increasingly defined in terms of individuality and self-identity.[19] Central in this process of individuation is the effort of individuals to transform their behavior into a meaningful experience and self-identity. The aspiration to become a "subject," to create one's own "individuation," is common to all individuals and can be recognized collectively as a moral right. But this process of subjectivation can take place only by—at least partly—liberating the individual from market forces and communitarian control. Sociology is thus redefined as the study of the initiatives and conditions of existence of individual actors, that is, "real individuals, different from all others, but as much as they succeed in building themselves as Subjects, all of them equal."[20]

Without entirely abandoning the study of social movements, the research topics of Touraine's group shifted to other themes in the course of the 1980s and 1990s. Some were concerned with the decomposition of institutional control in education, urban planning, or health care, others with individualism and cultural diversity in contemporary democracies. Issues of "subjectivation" and the conditions under which this takes place were a shared interest. Much of this later work is part of a broader movement among French sociologists toward more microsociological inquiries and focused on contemporary forms of individuality, individualism, and the immediate social settings in which these take shape. This change was accompanied by vivid debates about currents such as pragmatism, ethnomethodology, symbolic interactionism, and social constructivism, among others, in the journal *Raisons pratiques* (1990), which was one of the new interdisciplinary journals.[21]

Organizational Analysis and Policy Sociology

Whereas the central figures of French sociology have regularly been graduates of the École normale supérieure, predisposed to occupy positions in the intellectual and academic world, Michel Crozier's background and training were different. From his early work onward, his inquiries were guided by a critical distance to the state nobility, as Bourdieu has called it, both to the intellectual and to the technocratic elites of the country. Recalling his formative years in his memoirs, Crozier explains his predilection for American social science by his position of relative outsider in the circles he was part of: "I had neither the credibility of a former member of the resistance nor that of a *normalien*, nor a proper philosophical training, nor sufficient expertise in Marxism, and I had never really been a Trotskyite either. I had only one ticket of entry and that was my knowledge of America."[22]

While Crozier regularly denounced Parisian intellectuals and academics, he simultaneously voiced criticisms of the ruling groups within the state apparatus, that is, members of the *grands corps*, trained at the elite schools for engineering and public administration. Crozier's trajectory can thus be located in this twofold opposition to the intellectual as well as to the administrative elite of the country. While American social science provided him with the intellectual means and models to define a position of his own, his entrepreneurial background and business training shaped his drive to actively pursue and realize that ambition.

The starting point for Crozier's career was a series of empirical inquiries of white-collar work, among others in a postal bank service, an insurance company, and factories of the French tobacco monopoly. They were intended to lead to a dissertation on the French middle class, to be supervised by Georges Gurvitch, and directly or indirectly financed by planning agencies concerned with modernizing the French economy. In the course of these early inquiries Crozier's attention shifted from labor relations to organizational arrangements. Problems of organizing the labor process seemed "more practical, more dynamical, easier to get at, and, ultimately, more relevant than that of social classes."[23] Crozier thus came to define his work as belonging to the—in France relatively unknown—sociology of organizations. After a short trip to the United States in 1956, he spent the year 1959–60 at the Center for Advanced Study in the Behavioral Sciences in Palo Alto in California, where he continued reading organization studies (Selznick, Merton, Gouldner, March, and Simon) and started writing his dissertation.

Upon his return to France he joined Raymond Aron's newly founded Center of European Sociology (1960), where in 1961 he formed his own research group. It obtained an independent status in 1966, after a conflict with Aron, later becoming the Center for the Sociology of Organizations (1976). In his memoirs Crozier typically speaks about his group as a "small research firm," recalling that he founded it when he had turned the same age as his father was when he started his business. More important for Crozier's enterprise than Aron's Center of European Sociology, where he unsuccessfully rivaled with Bourdieu for Aron's support, were the exchanges in the Jean Moulin Club and the circle around the journal *Esprit*. In the Jean Moulin Club (1958–70) Crozier met reform-minded younger civil servants; around the journal *Esprit* he interacted with publicists like Jean-Marie Domenach, who had similar interests. For Crozier these experiences were part of what he in 1964 prophetically called a "cultural revolution." In the French administration, he noted, the fashion was no longer for central control and authority, but for "reform by concrete commitment," improving participation and extending responsibility. On the side of the intellectuals, the social sciences were finally taken seriously, and Lévi-Strauss, although in Crozier's view an old-style *philosophe*, had done much for this belated recognition. For Crozier the social sciences owed their significance to the fact that they were a vital link between these two universes, between the intellectual tradition "seeking to reform itself and the world of action, which is trying to renew itself through a process of more scientific reasoning."[24]

Crozier's 1964 text on the cultural revolution was at once a diagnostic of the situation, a prediction about the direction of change, and a profession of faith: "I was no longer a man of the left in the usual sense of the word. I was a pragmatic, a reformer and happy at last to be one, and to claim my responsibility."[25] While the French administration opened up to new forms of expertise and research funding and positions increased, Crozier's group obtained a central position in the process of administrative reform.[26]

As much as Touraine's concern was social action and historical change, Crozier's focus was on understanding and reforming the French bureaucracy. The analytical underpinnings of these efforts are presented in *The Bureaucratic Phenomenon* (1964), which was published simultaneously in English and French, and which he defended as the main part of his *Thèse d'Etat*. The six-hour defense ceremony was perhaps less dramatic than in Touraine's case, but Crozier too felt attacked and humiliated. Among the Sorbonne professors, Stoetzel started out by giving him a lesson about proper French and punctuation. When Aron followed about the translation of certain terms and proposing a general sociology of France merely on the basis of two case studies, Crozier—exceptionally—interrupted him twice, inevitably causing a *brouille* between the two men.[27] Based on his case studies from the 1950s, Crozier showed that in bureaucracies hierarchical and formal relations are predominant and different strata are separated from one another. The observed anonymity and routine have a cultural component in the fear of face-to-face communication. These bureaucratic features, however, cannot be merely understood as dysfunctional. They are the outcome of more or less rational strategies in the struggle of different strata for power and status. A clear-cut hierarchy and well-established routines liberate people from personal dependencies and limit their struggle to uncertainty zones. Since such struggles tend to produce new regulations, they do not lead to change, but only to minor adaptations and vicious circles. Instead of adapting progressively to new circumstances, bureaucratic organizations change only as a consequence of an acute crisis. In the last part of his book Crozier depicted the cultural traditions, which particularly in France support and sustain bureaucratic modes of organization.[28]

Although Crozier, like many others, was bewildered by the events of May 1968 and, like Aron, Boudon, and Bourricaud, opposed the movement, he interpreted them as a protest against bureaucratic formalism and fear of personal contact. May '68 was not simply a psychodrama, as Aron had written, but a sudden crisis, typical of a bureaucratic system in which change is stalled. The events were at once a "festival of face-to-face relations" and a massive call for change.

In sociology the years after 1968 saw a general movement of reorientation and repositioning, which affected Crozier's group as well. For intellectual, political, and personal reasons old centers split up, new ones were created, and various realignments took place. In the overly politicized atmosphere, the academic field became strongly marked by political oppositions. Touraine, Bourdieu, and the École des hautes études represented the leading pole on the left, the network around Raymond Aron and the journals *Contrepoint* (1970–76) and *Commentaire* (1978–) represented the principal pole on the right. Within this polarized structure, Crozier and his group became the driving force in effectively institutionalizing a pole for policy sociology. After an affiliation with the Kennedy School of Government at Harvard and a brief passage at the new university of Nanterre (1967–68), Crozier returned to his research position at the CNRS and in the decade after publishing his post-1968 essay *The Stalled Society* (1970) repositioned himself. He reelaborated his views in a new book coauthored with his younger colleague Erhard Friedberg, proposing a more general "strategic analysis of organizations." The book, which was not restricted to bureaucracies, formed the core of his subsequent teaching, research, and consulting.

Together with two other members of the postwar generation, Henri Mendras and Jean-Daniel Reynaud, Crozier first created the Association for the Development of Applied Social Sciences (ADSSA, 1971). A short teaching program (six to eight weeks) was targeted at managers, a longer teaching program (fifteen months) at younger students. Crozier obtained support from leading politicians and associated civil servants, consultants, and a few professors (Boudon, Bourricaud).[29] The master program (DEA) in the sociology of organizations at Science Po explicitly broke with the classical academic model. Following his American experiences, seminars and tutorials were the main pedagogical forms and case studies were privileged over theory and academic erudition.[30]

Due to his involvement with the Enterprise Institute (1975), a think tank that worked for large companies, Crozier extended his research to private firms as well. A new essay, *You Can't Change a Society by Decree* (1979), was a warning for the Left, and in 1980, owing to his relations with the presidency of Giscard d'Estaing, Crozier founded an institute for training a new class of state managers. Barely a year after, however, when the socialist Mitterrand won the presidential elections, Crozier's institute was suppressed. But aside from such political volatility, Crozier's work went through a more profound change during the 1970s and 1980s, shifting from participating in commissions within or closely linked to the state administration to building up expertise in private consulting ventures outside of it. Directly related to this shift was a conceptual change: old notions of public service were replaced by organizational models from the private sector. What was called "new public management" was developed by management consultants who transferred organizational tools from private enterprises to public administration. In this transfer, which was slower in France than in Britain and the United States, Crozier played an important role, both as the director of a master program and research group in the sociology of organizations and as a publicist and consultant.[31] His plea for a modest state in *État modeste, état moderne* (1987), however, failed to win the support of Raymond Barre and other politicians he was close to, and during the presidential elections of 1988 Mitterrand was reelected.

Crozier's activities developed in close interaction with the demand for managing public and later also private organizations. By positioning himself early on in an intermediary position between policymaking and sociological research, and between American organizational analysis and academic French social science, Crozier's work evolved from a reform-oriented analysis of bureaucratic systems into a more general form of organizational analysis and management consulting. At the end of his career Crozier was recognized not only as a prominent sociologist and reformer, but as a founding figure of management as well. That all this work was undertaken while steadily remaining within the bureaucracy of the public research system is perhaps not the least irony of his career.

The Methodological Imperative

The different approaches represented by the leading sociologists are manifest in their theoretical statements, research monographs, and public engagements, but no less in the way they have accounted for their own careers. Crozier and Touraine both published comprehensive memoirs narrating their "life and work," as the formula has it, recalling major events and encounters and retrospectively restaging their own performances. Deliberately refusing the genre of the autobiographical memoir, Bourdieu published *Sketch for a Self-Analysis*, applying his reflexive conception of social sciences to various activities and to his own trajectory. Raymond Boudon has been more reluctant in this respect. He has not turned his own career into an object of sociological scrutiny and the autobiographical texts he published follow his main publications chronologically from the point of view of his latest views but do not provide much detail about the circumstances in which they were written. The colleagues who put together the *Festschrift* in his honor, *Raymond Boudon, a Life in Sociology* (2009), adopted the same attitude because—with the exception of an autobiographical text by Boudon himself—they did not include testimonies or historical chapters on Boudon as a student, teacher, guest professor, academician, or director of a research group. The four-volume *Festschrift* informs the reader about numerous aspects of "methodological individualism" but—paradoxically—does not contain very much information about the individual who so meticulously elaborated this individualist view. Since Boudon was neither a public sociologist nor a policy analyst, the tone of his semi-autobiographical booklet is more neutral and academic than in

Crozier's and Touraine's memoirs, up to the point of concealing its auto-biographical character by entitling it *Sociology as a Science* (2010).

Born in Paris, where his father reached a senior position in a commer-cial firm, Boudon studied philosophy at the École normale in the 1950s.[32] While reading the classical philosophers and doing some work on Hegel's correspondence, he was more attracted to the social sciences, in particular to economics and sociology. Gurvitch's teachings bored him, Aron seemed more a "grand intellectual" than a social scientist, but the discovery of Paul Lazarsfeld's and Morris Rosenberg's anthology of methodological writings, *Language of Social Research* (1955), triggered his interest in methodology. Boudon did not like the fieldwork he briefly did in the early 1960s, he con-sidered it too time-consuming, never repeated the experience, and instead focused on methodology.[33] After spending a year at the Bureau of Applied Social Research at Columbia University (1961–62), where he worked with Lazarsfeld and Robert Merton, Boudon acted as Lazarsfeld's assistant when he was guest professor at the Sorbonne (1962–63, 1966–67). The collaboration led to the coedition of three anthologies on methodology.[34] Boudon's dissertation was a reasoned inventory of the relations between mathematics and sociology. Following up on a suggestion of Lazarsfeld, his complementary thesis was a methodological critique of structuralism. In the same year as he defended his dissertation, in 1967, when he was just thirty-three, a chair for methodology and social science was created for him at the Sorbonne.

After the turmoil of 1968 Boudon published several articles trying to account for the university crisis. He spent the year 1972–73 in the United States, returning to France with *L'inégalité des chances* (1973), in which he gave an alternative explanation for educational inequality. Against Bourdieu and others, Boudon argued that for explaining the correlations between social background and educational attainment, "cultural heri-tage" was of limited explanatory value, and that interpretations according to which people "interiorize" social chances have to be rejected because they would deny that they make their own choices. Sociological analysis should focus on the decisions people deliberately make at various moments in their school career. Correlations between social class and schooling no longer appear as the outcome of different "factors" (income and/or educa-tional level of the parents), the weight of which is to be assessed by multi-variate analysis, but as the aggregate effect of successive individual choices. Individuals chose rationally for the most "useful combination of cost, risk, and benefit" and the parameters of that choice are set by their social posi-tion.[35] Although the book was immediately translated into English and did more for his scientific reputation than any other, Boudon did not continue in the sociology of education and social mobility. For himself the book marked the transition from a Lazarsfeldian approach to research methodology to a broader program. Although the first part of *L'inégalité des chances* announced a "systemic perspective," the latter part moves toward a theory of individual choice and decision making. Methodological individualism indeed became the core of Boudon's later work.

After having briefly directed the Centre d'études sociologiques (1968–71), he founded his own group, the Groupe d'étude des méthodes de l'analyse sociologique (GEMAS, 1971). Although still Lazarsfeldian in name, the group became primarily involved in developing, discussing, and diffusing the perspective of methodological individualism. Boudon's *La logique du social* (1979) offered a systematic introduction, the *Dictionnaire critique de la sociologie* (1982), coauthored with his Sorbonne colleague François Bourricaud, codified the approach, and various studies elaborated specific aspects. In *La place du désordre* (1984), for example, Boudon critically reviews theories of change and historical causality and proposes a methodological individualist alternative.

Boudon's general orientation and his group were intended to form an academic niche that was defined by a twofold opposition. Against the political and intellectual revolts of the 1970s, Boudon incarnated a classical academic program, one that wanted to preserve the "grand classical tradition" of Tocqueville, Weber, Durkheim, and others, and that opposed the multiplication of rapid essays and fashionable radicalism.[36] Boudon had been aghast by the proliferation of essayism and was deeply troubled by the writings of Foucault, Derrida, and other (post)structuralist thinkers. The problem, as he saw it, was that after 1968 academic personnel had turned their backs on their respective departments and addressed the intellectual public at large, trading academic recognition for media attention. Just as the old university produced mandarins, the new academic system produced gurus.[37]

The academic virtues Boudon defended implied a return to the classics of the discipline, a rehabilitation of erudition and classical norms of reasoning and composition, and, more generally, a defense of rationalism in the face of relativism and postmodernist nihilism. Much of his individual and collaborative work was concerned with canonical figures, publishing overviews, textbooks, commentary, and (re)interpretation, as well as translations and anthologies.[38] Whereas May '68 has stimulated Bourdieu to launch a new and experimental journal, *Actes de la recherche en sciences sociales*, it incited Boudon to return to a more classical mode of academic work.

This classic academic style that developed in reaction to the decomposition of the university after 1968 was more specifically opposed to "holist" approaches. The most fundamental opposition in the social sciences, according to Boudon, was between individualism and holism. While claiming that many analyses of classical authors—not just Tocqueville or Weber, but surprisingly also Marx and even Durkheim—follow an individualist method, Boudon was far more critical of his contemporaries. Holism, in which he included structuralism, functionalism, and Marxism, had, in fact, become the dominant methodology in sociology. Its crucial flaw was that it assumed an oversocialized actor who had no choice but to fulfill a social function or obey the imaginary dictates of classes, cultures, or societies.[39] The methodological postulates Boudon opposed to this view were that the "individual actor is the logical atom of sociological analysis," that this actor is "rational," and that social phenomena have to be understood as aggregated and often unintended or "perverse" effects of individual action.[40] Since the mid-1970s Boudon elaborated, refined, and illustrated these principles, not by undertaking major research projects himself but primarily by theorizing on the basis of classical and contemporary work of others.

The strand of methodological individualism he developed differs sensibly from that of his American counterpart James Coleman. A student of Lazarsfeld as well, Coleman had similarly moved from mathematical sociology to rational choice theory. But whereas Coleman, who was originally trained as an engineer, developed his version of rational choice theory in the context of the University of Chicago, Boudon, who was trained as a philosopher, elaborated his work from a position at the Sorbonne. Based on the microeconomics of Chicago economists, Coleman understood behavior in terms of expected utility. Rather than being a simple extension of the microeconomic model to social phenomena, Boudon's approach was a generalization based on a broader variety of sources. For Boudon utility maximization was a special case of a more general theory of rationality. This theory incorporated not only Herbert Simon's arguments about "bounded rationality" and Weber's notion of "value rationality" but it also took into account the work of cognitive psychologists who had documented cognitive biases and other deviations from the rational choice model.[41] This led Boudon in a series of books on collective beliefs and values to a theory of "ordinary rationality": individual behavior is rational in the sense that people have reasons for their action and they consider these reasons to be well grounded. Whether such reasons are personal or impersonal, instrumental or normative, people think of them as "good reasons" to decide one thing and not the other.[42] These reasons and systems of reasons depend on the actor's context, which defines the parameters of choice, and they evolve historically in the direction of a "diffuse rationalization." Rationalization entails a process of both innovation and "rational selection" of what has been invented.

As compared with the work of the other sociologists discussed in this chapter, very few of Boudon's studies are research monographs, policy inquiries, or intellectual interventions in the public debate. His work consists mostly of typically academic books: studies on classical sociologists and general sociological theory, accompanied by a steady flow of textbooks, treatises, reference works, dictionaries, and anthologies. The preferred answer he gave to the question "what is good sociology" was that a good article or book is what allows teaching an interesting course.[43] Boudon was attached to teaching, transmitting, and maintaining a form of classical social science. Instead of painstaking fieldwork, policy research, or giving in to the seductions of the media, sociologists should, according to Boudon, focus on specific and well-circumscribed phenomena ("methodological singularism"). For explaining such phenomena, "methodological individualism" and the theory of "ordinary rationality" provide the most satisfactory approach; in short: the "macro should be explained by the micro, and the micro by the actor's reasons."[44]

Raymond Aron once called Boudon an American island on French territory. But since Boudon's sources ranged from Austrian economics (Menger, Hayek) and German sociology (Weber, Simmel) to cognitive psychology and American rational choice theorizing, it would probably be more accurate to portray him as the French version of an international strand of social science thinking. Boudon hasn't followed any French tradition in particular, neither that of Montesquieu and Tocqueville (as Aron did) nor that of Tarde, let alone that of Durkheim. He was closer to Lazarsfeld and Merton, and has, indeed, continued this affiliation by his insistence on combining theories of the "middle range" within a strong methodological framework for which "analytical sociology" is but the most recent name. But his work is just as much shaped by an academic classicism that has deep roots in the French educational system and that is distinct from the more departmentalized forms of American social science. Boudon himself would probably not have been very appreciative of such an interpretation because it does not evoke the "good reasons" he had for doing what he did. But then again wasn't his French upbringing, training, and academic position an important parameter of his choices?

Reflexive Sociology

Much of the distinctiveness of Pierre Bourdieu's work is rooted in his specific trajectory. Raised in a remote mountain village in the southwest of France, where his father had become a postal employee, the young Bourdieu made it all the way up to the Parisian École normale. In his self-analysis, he identified the contrast between his provincial and popular upbringing and the long years of "scholastic confinement" in boarding schools in Pau and Paris, from his eleventh to his twenty-fourth year, as the formative tension of his career. This dual experience was at the root of his feelings of ambiguity toward the world of Parisian intellectuals and academics and constituted what he called his "cleft habitus": his inclination to play the intellectual game at a high level and his persistent revolt against its pretentiousness, its illusions, its lack of realism and responsibility.[45]

Studying philosophy at the end of the 1940s and the beginning of the 1950s, Bourdieu's intellectual universe was inevitably marked by the towering figure of Sartre and existentialism and phenomenology. But although interested in more scientifically oriented forms of phenomenology, Bourdieu was more fundamentally attracted to the philosophers who worked on conceptual questions in the history of science and philosophy, to the scrupulous historical epistemology of Georges Canguilhem, who was also a well-known *résistant,* and to the rigorous history of philosophy. While planning to write his PhD on "the temporal structures of affective life" to be supervised by Canguilhem, his Algerian experiences profoundly changed the course of his life. Bourdieu was sent to Algeria in 1955 for his military service; in 1960, after an intervention by Raymond Aron, he was urgently flown back to France because his name had appeared on the "red list," implying that he was in danger.

Since these Algerian years have received less attention than his later ventures and several of his Algerian studies are not available in English, it is worth recalling their importance in some detail. It was in the context of Algeria at war that Bourdieu developed an unorthodox way of doing research. It was this mode of inquiry that he subsequently transposed to metropolitan France and that formed the immediate context in which he developed his concepts. Emerging in a specific research project, these concepts were subsequently used in other research ventures as well, thus enriching and generalizing their meaning, and they were put together during the 1970s in the model that underlies all of his major studies, from *Distinction* (1979) and *The Logic of Practice* (1980) to *Homo Academicus* (1984) and *The State Nobility* (1989) up to *The Rules of Art* (1992) and *The Social Structures of the Economy* (2000).[46]

If one were to condense this model into a sort of analytical formula, however artificial that may be, one might say, first, that Bourdieu conceptualized sociology as a science of social practices, that is, as a science concerned with structured regularities, which are neither completely systemic nor entirely random, and the logic of which is fundamentally at odds with the dominant paradigms in the social sciences, whether centered on human action, rational choice, or on social systems. In order to account for these practices, they need to be understood as located in relatively autonomous social spaces (fields), which are defined by struggles over specific stakes between agents that are characterized by the volume and composition of their resources (capital) and by the dispositions by which they are inclined to use these resources (habitus). The indicated terms (practice, field, capital, habitus) are not the only concepts of Bourdieu's approach, but they do constitute the basic model.

Bourdieu's first book, *Sociology of Algeria* (1958), offered a sober overview of the country, its different groups of inhabitants, and colonial politics and society. It was written at a moment when the war for national liberation was spreading from the countryside to the urban centers, simultaneously becoming a cause among French intellectuals.[47] In Bourdieu's perception many intellectuals were ill informed; they ignored the complexities of the situation and some of them, particularly Sartre and Fanon, held unrealistic and "irresponsible" views.[48] After finishing his military service and shortly after the "battle of Algiers" (1957), Bourdieu joined the University of Algiers, teaching philosophy and sociology and initiating fieldwork with the help of students, continuing to work on his PhD in his spare time. A major part of his field research was undertaken within in a research association, the ARDES, which provided the funding and gave the inquiries their social and scientific legitimacy. Out of this collaborative work came his first articles and two additional books. Realized with a team of Algerian researchers and coauthored with three young statisticians from the Algerian office of the French Bureau of Statistics (INSEE), Bourdieu produced a detailed inquiry into the functioning of the urban economy in *Travail et travailleurs en Algérie* (Work and workers in Algeria, 1963). With his former student Abdelmalek Sayad and the help of other Algerian students, he also studied the resettlement camps that the French military had imposed on more than two million Algerian peasants, and which are analyzed in *Le déracinement* (The uprooting, 1964). The ethnological work on Kabyle ritual and kinship started at about the same time and was related to the rising figure of Claude Lévi-Strauss and the promise of structural anthropology.

The first characteristic of Bourdieu's Algerian research was the intense fieldwork itself. Bourdieu was one of the few intellectuals who considered that his presence in Algeria and his political sympathies had to imply a serious scholarly effort. Not content with "reading left-wing newspapers or signing petitions; I had to do something as a scientist."[49] This commitment through research distinguished Bourdieu from most of his schoolmates and fellow academics, both in Algeria and France. Undertaken in unusually difficult circumstances, the research did not resemble the sedentary existence of academic life to which he was accustomed. It developed through a heterogeneous network of collaborations, which included his students, who were his first informants and some of whom became research associates and collaborators, a few independent scholars, various Algerian intellectuals, members of the Social Secretariat that resided under the bishop of Algiers, as well as the statisticians of the Algerian office of the INSEE.

The research dealt with questions about the unity and diversity of traditional Algerian society, the consequences of colonialism, the transition from a precapitalist to a capitalist market economy, and the social and economic conditions for organized political action. But this enumeration pertains more to the outcome of the research than to the research process itself. The predominant characteristic of the research process itself was that nothing of it was self-evident, since none of the intellectual routines applied, neither Bourdieu's own working habits as a philosopher nor any of the standard research procedures. The war made philosophical issues and procedures seem irrelevant, and applying standard methods of anthropological fieldwork or statistical analysis was highly problematic. The statisticians, for example, quickly found out that the categories they intended to use for their survey of the labor market were inadequate. To have "a job" or to be "unemployed" designated something quite different in Algeria at war than in metropolitan France. Bourdieu's research group was thus forced to confront questions for which there were no standard answers. The collaboration with the statisticians led to a rethinking of both the design and the way of organizing the research.[50] Anthropological fieldwork was also far from self-evident. It was suspect in the eyes of many Algerian intellectuals because it was bound up with colonial rule and because issues of myth, ritual, and kinship seemed irrelevant for the political struggle. More broadly conceived ethnographic studies were more appropriate, but they raised scientific problems that the statisticians were all too familiar with, problems of selection bias and generalization (how to generalize on the basis of qualitative case studies).

In *Travail et travailleurs en Algérie*, Bourdieu explicitly addresses these issues. He does so in a critical analysis of the predominant "ideologies of science," which he considers to be obstacles for an effective research practice. Bourdieu discusses the "conflict of methods," especially of statistical and ethnographic methods, which he interprets sociologically as being rooted in the separation of scientific and literary training and in the status anxieties of its practitioners. Instead of ignoring or denying the competence of one another, Bourdieu argues that the reality of the situation calls for the "collaboration of methods." Various arguments are given why the reciprocal relationship between statistical and interpretive procedures, and the permanent *va-et-vient* between two, is a vital necessity: "Statistical regularities have sociological value only if they can be comprehended. And, the other way around, subjectively comprehensible relations constitute sociological models of real processes only if they can be observed empirically with a significant degree of confidence."[51] In the fieldwork different methods were combined: observations and interviews went along with distributing standardized questionnaires, which had to be filled in, allowing quantification and statistical treatment. Transcending the cleavage between ethnographic fieldwork and survey research was—and would remain—the hallmark of Bourdieu's research work.

In *Travail et travailleurs*, Bourdieu takes up other themes as well. He ironizes grand proclamations and moralizing judgments, recalling with Parmenides that no object, however reprehensible politically or morally, is unworthy of scientific scrutiny. While vigorously defending scientific inquiry, he does not claim any scientific neutrality: "What one may demand in all rigor of the anthropologist is that he strives to restore to other people the meaning of their behaviors, of which the colonial system has, among other things, dispossessed them."[52] Significantly, Bourdieu continues to discuss several aspects of the research process that he considers crucial but that are absent from the standard discussions of research methodology (paying attention to the role of women in the research process and insisting on the necessity of having a mixed Algerian-French research team).[53]

This practical and sociologically grounded reflexivity, which is at odds with the routinized compartmentalization of academic tasks, had its origins in the research collaboration that emerged in the exceptional circumstances in Algeria. The separation of methods, the divorce between scholarly questions and political issues, and the lack of reflexive awareness that tends to characterize academic work were radically called into question. The young Bourdieu responded to these challenges by conceiving research as a collective effort guided by the need of orchestrating a plurality of researchers, methods of inquiry (observations, interviews, statistical analysis), and scholarly resources (dissolving the boundaries between anthropology, sociology, and labor economics), and by reflexively facing the problems that came up instead of following standard rules and established precepts. This style, which became typical of all of Bourdieu's research undertakings, also provided him with a fundamental theoretical problem: How does the knowledge of objective structures, indicated by statistical frequencies or structures of myth and ritual, relate to the lived experience of the actors? How do objectivist modes of knowledge relate to subjective understandings? Whereas this question pervades his early research, it is elaborated theoretically for the first time in the introduction to the book on photography (1965), and more fully in his first major theoretical statement *Esquisse d'une théorie de la pratique* (1972). Bourdieu's research experiences in Algeria were, in short, not merely the beginning of his oeuvre but its very foundation.

The conceptual innovations for which Bourdieu's work is known can be located in a variety of research projects that he finished or undertook after returning to France. When he came back in 1960, the auspices for the social sciences in France were favorable. Starting as Aron's assistant at the Sorbonne, Bourdieu taught in Lille (1961–64), gave the first sociology course at the National School of Statistics (ENSAE, from 1964), and assured a seminar at École normale supérieure (1964–1984). His main position was at the École des hautes études, where in 1962 he became general secretary of Aron's Center of European Sociology (1959) and was elected director of studies two years later.[54]

The new research projects he undertook continued the dynamics of his Algerian inquiries. Organized as a collective enterprise in an unbureaucratic, partly improvised and open-ended manner, they typically combined ethnographic and survey methods. The theoretical aspirations, which were especially present among those who, like Bourdieu and Passeron, were trained in philosophy, functioned in research projects in which not only different research methods were combined but which built on divergent theoretical traditions as well. Weberian ideas on legitimacy and ideal types were interwoven with Marxian notions of class and Durkheimian reflections on social morphology and symbolic classifications. The work of Bourdieu's research group was not conceived in terms of any particular theory, specific method, or research specialty, but in a language that was borrowed from the French epistemological tradition. This tradition, represented by Bachelard and Canguilhem, had redefined philosophy as an epistemological reflection on scientific work. In *The Craft of Sociology* (1968), Bourdieu, Chamboredon, and Passeron used this epistemological tradition to define social science research as a rigorous scientific endeavor that was not fundamentally different from research in the natural sciences and that was critical and unorthodox precisely because it was rigorously scientific (breaking with "common sense," "ideologies," and other "preconceived notions" of the social world). This conception allowed the integration of different research methods as well as of concepts that belonged to rival theoretical traditions (Marx, Weber, Durkheim). In the context of French social science, this research style simultaneously opposed the "empty theories" of general theorists like Georges Gurvitch, the empiricism that had been prevalent in the previous generation of French sociologists, as well as the more recent conceptions of quantitative "methodology" (represented by Lazarsfeld and Boudon).

The projects Bourdieu undertook in a similarly exploratory and collaborative style as he had done in Algeria concerned topics ranging from the social transformation of his native village, the unequal access to higher education and art institutions, banks and their clientele, and the practice of photography and the dynamics of cultural production fields. The study on the social uses of photography is a good example. It concerned an apparently minor topic that hardly existed as an object of scholarly attention and that didn't carry much cultural prestige. But it allowed one to raise fundamental questions about cultural practices because there were few economic or technical obstacles for its practice and because the practitioners who were interviewed expressed their views and cultural preferences more frankly than when they were asked about high culture (painting, classical music). The organization of the research was typical as well. The final book, of which Bourdieu is the editor and main author, was based on twenty different research operations over a period of four years. Starting in Aron's seminar on the role of images in industrial society and partly financed by Kodak, the project included exploratory studies, ethnographic fieldwork, surveys, and case studies, involving some twenty people in various capacities (students, aspiring sociologists, occasional collaborators, colleagues).

These varied and intensive collaborative projects constituted the primary activity of Bourdieu's research group during the 1960s and much of the 1970s. It was in the course of these projects that Bourdieu's central notions appeared. The first conceptual issue was related to understanding the complexities of social behavior. In his Algerian work about the contradictions between the traditional peasant economy and contemporary market exchange, Bourdieu's analysis focused on differences in economic ethos and diverging attitudes toward time and the future. In the research on celibacy in the Béarn, he encountered a similar issue. There, the traditional mode of inheritance and reproduction was in crisis as well, as was apparent at the yearly village Christmas ball, where city folk danced with the local girls while bachelor peasants looked on. How could these men, who had inherited the land and the house, have become "unmarriageable"? The notion of "habitus" that Bourdieu introduced in this project referred to the bodily dispositions that disqualified the peasants in comparison with the increasingly present city dwellers. Bourdieu used the term *habitus* or *hexis* for the set of acquired characteristics that have become second nature, designating inclinations that are beyond the reach of conscious decisions.[55] In *Le déracinement* (1964) Bourdieu used the notion in a more general manner, not only for bodily postures but also as a "permanent and general disposition with regard to the world and others."[56] A more systematic use of the term appears in the postscript to two essays by Erwin Panofsky, which Bourdieu brought together and translated. Panofsky comments on the similarities between Gothic architecture and scholastic treatises. Both seem to derive from the same construction principles and Panofsky explains the similarity by observing that architects and theologians went to the same school, thus acquiring the same mental habits. The concept of habitus is here used in a more active sense, as a principle of invention, a way of handling and organizing very different material, rooted in the socialization of the producers.[57] Bourdieu presents this explanation as having a general meaning at odds with other explanatory strategies: with the cult of the individual genius, with unspecified references to the *Zeitgeist*, as well as with structuralist analysis à la Lévi-Strauss, Althusser, or Foucault, all of whom radically eliminated the actors and abstracted from a theory of action.

By its subsequent use in different research projects, the "habitus" notion emerged as a general concept for a theory of action. The progressive conceptualization draws on various research experiences and emerged as a generalization: it is produced neither by sudden intuition nor by an exercise of theoretical exegesis, but, first and foremost, as a conceptual account of successive research experiences. Informed by his theoretical training and driven by his propensity to find an alternative for subjectivist theories of action and objectivist accounts of structures, Bourdieu characterizes habitus as a "generative grammar" of action and a mediating structure between objective conditions and actual conduct.

The origins of the notion of "cultural capital," which originated in research on higher education, display a similar dynamics. In *The Inheritors* (1964), Bourdieu and Passeron argued that cultural inequalities represent a crucial yet largely unacknowledged selection mechanism in education. The knowledge of, the taste for, and the attitudes toward culture were the most important hidden factors in the elimination of pupils from the working classes. In the context of a dialogue with statisticians and economists, Bourdieu reformulated this analysis in terms of "cultural capital."[58] Just as culture functioned as capital, "prestige" and "honor" could be conceived as symbolic capital. They thus became ingredients in the critical theory of culture that Bourdieu intended to develop, while simultaneously giving rise to a new issue. In the introduction to the photography book, Bourdieu states that sociologists should not leave "anthropological questions" to philosophy. Since a proper theory of human action should include both the objective chances and the lived experience of the agents, it was necessary to leave the "fictitious opposition" of objectivism and subjectivism to philosophers and recognize that the analysis of objective probabilities, subjective experiences, and their intermediary mechanisms are "inseparable moments" of scientific analysis. From there on Bourdieu moved toward a more unified approach, combining his notions of "habitus" and "capital" in relation to specific practices, culminating in *Esquisse d'une théorie de la pratique* (1972).

In trying to overcome the opposition between "objectivism" and "subjectivism," Bourdieu considered these theoretical approaches to be different moments or types of analysis. Transcending or combining the two required a reflection on the status of the old as well as the new theory. Bourdieu thus called for a "theory of sociological theory."[59] This metatheoretical reflection was required not only for an adequate understanding of objectivist and subjectivist theories but also for defining an alternative theoretical program. In consciously addressing the issue, Bourdieu displays a form of reflexivity that was undoubtedly rooted in the fact that he was unwilling to take the theoretical game for granted, just as he had not taken empirical research for granted either. Instead of elaborating some kind of academic synthesis, Bourdieu typically steps back and first reflects on the act of theorizing and on the very notion of "theory."

Out of this reflection came his project for a "theory of practice," which was the result not so much of his wish to overcome the "dichotomy of objectivism and subjectivism," but more specifically of his sociological understanding of "objectivism" and "subjectivism" as particular modes of relating to the world. In his sociological understanding of theorizing, Bourdieu observes that objectivist theories are produced from the perspective of the outside observer, describing actual behavior as the result of following "rules" or as the "realization" of laws. In his research on kinship, however, Bourdieu found that what anthropologists consider to be widespread rules of matrimonial exchange were actually very infrequent. Instead of uniform rules that people would "obey," actual practices are the result of the strategic uses of probabilities attached to social positions. Although the subjectivist mode of knowledge produces an opposite distortion by understanding behavior as the outcome of conscious intentions or rational choices, it is equally rooted in an intellectualist understanding of human behavior. Both the structuralist and the subjectivist mode of understanding suffer from a similar ethnocentric bias.

After sociologically interpreting subjectivism and objectivism as forms of intellectual ethnocentrism, Bourdieu calls the "third type" of knowledge he intends to develop "praxeological." The theory of practice is characterized as a contribution to the "unification of the human sciences by destroying all the false alternatives that it suspends or interdicts, such as the opposition between objectivism and subjectivism."[60] It is added that the theory of practice includes a "theory of theory." Unlike other theories, the theory of practice tries to account for the cognitive effects of the various theoretical postures on the objects they try to understand. Although the expression "reflexive theory" is not used yet, that is clearly intended.

Esquisse d'une théorie de la pratique (1972) contains a theoretical account of the social world based on the notions of "habitus" and different forms of "capital" (economic, cultural, symbolic, and social capital), and it is simultaneously a reflection on theorizing as a particular relationship to the world, a relationship that engenders biases and distortions that represent fundamental obstacles for an adequate understanding of social practices. Bourdieu systematically elaborated this view in subsequent work on "scholastic biases," primarily in *The Logic of Practice* (1980, 1990) and *Pascalian Meditations* (1997, 2000). This dual character of the *Esquisse*, presenting a theory of social action as well as a theory of theorizing, was related to the reflexive inclination that is already present in Bourdieu's work on Algeria as well as to the institutional and political changes occurring after 1968. The student revolt and political mass movements had led to a break between Aron and Bourdieu; Aron and a few collaborators quit the Center of European Sociology, thus leaving Bourdieu in charge and giving him greater liberty to develop his own program.

Esquisse d'une theorie de la pratique was a provisional synthesis, among other reasons because the field concept, which had been emerged in another line of research, was still barely used. The concept had first appeared in an article on the intellectual and cultural field, in which Bourdieu argued that "creative projects" can be understood only when situated in the specific set of social relations in which they emerge. The title of the article, "Intellectual Field and Creative Project" (1966), expresses the intention of bridging the opposition between a structural analysis of intellectual production and a quasi-Sartrean understanding of creative acts. One of the ideas was to use Weber's analysis of religious specialists and its differentiation between priests, prophets, and magicians to understand the cultural and intellectual field.[61] Two years later, Bourdieu characterizes Weber's analysis as a paradigmatic example of a relational approach to the social world, which he considers to be the most significant property of structural analysis.[62] In redefining structuralism in this manner, it becomes compatible with a theory of action, and the field concept thus obtains a more general significance. Somewhat later again, Bourdieu returns to the issue more systematically. By rethinking Max Weber's sociology of religion, he proposes the first systematic formulation of his field theory. The notion of "field" allows the analysis of structural similarities of different social universes and the reflection on such analogies, for which Weber's sociology of the religious field provides a model.[63] In the course of the 1970s, the concept is applied to the religious field, the field of power, and the scientific field; it is then, in a second movement of synthesis, combined with the "anthropological" approach outlined in the *Esquisse*. Replacing the notion of "system," which had been used in the work on education, the field concept thus serves the purpose of contextualizing the analysis of social practices presented in the *Esquisse*.

Bourdieu's work was embedded in a highly distinctive type of research practice, which owed its characteristics to his Algerian experiences. Much can be said about how Bourdieu's familiarity with phenomenology and other theoretical traditions shaped his work, but the actual uses he made of these modes of thinking were consistently rooted in the particular dynamics of his research enterprise. Bourdieu's research-based conceptualizations, furthermore, obtained a more general meaning by domain switching, that is, by their use in a research project in which the concepts were to account for different issues that, seen from a more general point of view, could be treated as similar. Instead of the more common strategy of increasing specialization, the multiple domains Bourdieu and his group explored allowed him to transfer insights and experiences from one domain to the next, thus favoring empirically grounded generalizations. Crossing disciplinary and institutional boundaries worked in a similar manner. Instead of a predominantly monodisciplinary and intra-academic orientation, Bourdieu's group and collaborative research practice included a plurality of resources, thus stimulating the mobilization of ideas and points of view from a variety of disciplines (philosophy, anthropology, sociology, economics, linguistics, art history) and research practices (statistics, ethnography). If innovation results from "new combinations," as Schumpeter held, it requires a variety that Bourdieu not merely encountered, but that he consciously sought and organized.

But the variety that allows for new combinations merely leads to fragmentation or eclecticism unless there are mechanisms to keep them in check. Bourdieu's case is interesting in this respect as well because his research practice displayed three such countervailing mechanisms. The first one was the presence of a general scientific ambition, a common style of work and a shared conception of research among members of his research group. The sense of a common purpose that defines a group or a school stimulates exchange and collaboration among its members, discourages fragmentation, and promotes what may be called focused variation. For Bourdieu himself, as for many other French social scientists, this general ambition was rooted in his training in philosophy.

A second, more distinctive principle in dealing with variety is the reflexivity that Bourdieu acquired in the exceptional circumstances in Algeria, and that he was probably inclined to elaborate because of his atypical trajectory. Since he was not spontaneously at ease in the Parisian intellectual world into which his school success had brought him, he could not take its mode of operation for granted. The reflexive mode of working he developed was a way of coping with this situation, allowing him to rethink and reframe the problems he faced, and leading him to move beyond major oppositions and dichotomies. The most crucial result of this reflexive posture was probably his theory of practice itself, which he conceived as a fundamental break with the various forms of intellectualism.

A third and final device that contained the potentially centrifugal effects of research variety was the habit of regularly returning to his initial objects of study so as to exploit newly won insights for rethinking previous work and deepening his grasp on the issues at stake. *The Bachelor's Ball* (2003) is a good example. It contains three successive analyses of celibacy in the Béarn. Whereas the initial text (1962) was analytically centered on observable bodily dispositions, the second text, ten years later, focused more broadly on the way peasant families manage the stock of their economic and symbolic capital, and the last text, published in 1989, adds yet another dimension captured by field analysis, that is, the fact that local marriage patterns had become increasingly embedded in a unified national social space, which had the effect of devaluing local resources. A similar movement of progression can be documented for his work on higher education or for his studies of cultural production fields. As a consequence of combining his practice of reflexively monitored domain switching and boundary crossing with an "eternal return" to his previous objects of study, Bourdieu avoided the partition between sociological generalists and research specialists.

Bourdieu's work has been qualified in various ways—"genetic structuralism" being one of them. "Reflexive sociology" is perhaps less articulate, but it has the advantage of not being limited to a particular scientific program. Pierre Bourdieu was not just a scholar, he was a committed scholar whose activities have included a range of other activities than teaching and research, all of them marked by this reflexive sociological posture. Holding very few administrative and bureaucratic positions, Bourdieu was all the more active in public roles, not so much by signing petitions or writing in newspapers but by activities that were related to scholarship and research. He directed the book series *Le sens commun* (1964–92) and *Liber* (1997–2002); established his own publishing house, Raisons d'agir (1996), which, among other things, publishes a series of small, accessible, and inexpensive books; founded the European Review of Books, *Liber* (1989–98); and initiated or was involved in public manifestations and initiatives of various kinds. During more than a quarter of a century Bourdieu led one of the most innovative social science journals, *Actes de la recherche en sciences sociales* (1975). Owing to linguistic and other barriers, most of these activities have remained invisible to Anglo-American audiences. *Liber* was published in many languages, but not in English; the journal *Actes* is largely ignored outside the Francophone world. But as this enumeration indicates, Bourdieu's commitment was never merely a matter of taking sides or speaking out, it was above all a search for probing new ways—new genres of publication, media, modes of organizing—to combine scholarly work with civic commitment.

Conclusion

✖✖✖

"Knowing what one is doing when one does science . . .
presupposes knowing how the problems, tools, methods and
concepts that one uses have been historically formed."
—Pierre Bourdieu

Rather than understanding ideas, texts, or discourses independently of their producers and conditions of production, I have throughout this book tried to account for their formation as an inseparably intellectual and social process. Generating ideas is related to other ideas, to contesting certain ways of thinking while relying on others, and the intellectual dynamics that can be reconstructed historically is itself a social process. Thinking and elaborating thoughts is a fundamentally relational activity that can be understood as a process of position taking within an intellectual field. As such it depends on the actual or anticipated position within this field, on the resources that are (in)available to the person or group in question, and on their dispositions, that is, on the way the person or group is (dis)inclined to mobilize the resources they dispose of in the struggle in which they take part. This sociological field approach, also when used as a heuristic framework rather than as a model to be rigorously applied, has advantages over more traditional macroperspectives as well as over contemporary approaches that privilege local practices and small-scale interactions. Macroperspectives in terms of classes, nations, or social systems tend to ignore the relatively autonomous and specific dynamics of intellectual activity. Microapproaches tend to neglect the structural conditions under which local practices function, evolve, or dissolve.

If a field approach has significant advantages over both *systemic* and *interactionist* accounts of knowledge production, it also has certain benefits as compared with *institutionalist* accounts. Reducing field structures to organizational environments limits the explanatory value of the approach, and the same goes for conceptions that restrict the relevant context to norms or to formal and informal rules. The academic field has a relatively high level of institutionalization as compared with the literary or artistic field, but in accounting for intellectual work and its outcomes, more or less subtle differences in resources and dispositions are no less important to take into account than institutional structures. Understanding "Durkheimian sociology" required an assessment of the institutional characteristics of the academic field at the time, but since that doesn't represent more than a space of possibles, an opportunity structure, the intellectual strategy that Durkheim actually pursued was simultaneously dependent on the specific resources and propensities that he and the members of his group disposed of as compared with those of their chief competitors.

Using a field perspective in this sense for understanding the long-term trajectory of sociology in France first implied identifying its main episodes from the early nineteenth until the late twentieth century. For each one of these I tried to reconstruct the sociological production as an integral part of the expanding intellectual field. The intellectual field represents a structured set of constraints and opportunities for all those who wish to take part in the competition for obtaining or maintaining an intellectual position. Sociologists and their work have therefore been located in a setting that is much broader than that of a single discipline or a specific institution. This broader space, which is itself part of the inquiry, is subject to change, relatively short-term and more or less incremental change as well as more structural, transformative, and long-term change.

As an organized branch of scientific inquiry the social sciences emerged during the democratic revolutions of the late eighteenth and early nineteenth centuries. Their intellectual roots can be traced much further back in time, but it was only when the institutions of the old regime were swept away that this relatively new type of inquiry obtained its place as a distinct and organized scientific endeavor. The predominant conception was that the social sciences were *sciences of government*, instituted to provide guidance to national elites that could no longer rely on the dogma of divine right and the structures of absolutist rule. After a short-lived institute during the revolutionary years, a more enduring institution was established with the Academy of Moral and Political Sciences (1832). Founded and supported by members of the liberal political elite, the national Academy played a pivotal but largely forgotten role in the development of the social sciences. Integrating political specialties (law, political economy, statistics) with history and philosophy, the Academy functioned on the basis of the view that the social sciences were branches of an overarching "moral science," which would provide indirect but useful support to the government and other factions of the ruling elite. Opposed to the methods and models of the natural sciences, the "moral sciences" were thought to be concerned with regulating the behavior of free and morally responsible human beings. Within this framework the Academy organized prize contests on pressing issues, commissioned empirical inquiries into poverty, crime, and other threats to the public order, and took up more historical and theoretical questions about the postrevolutionary government of the nation.

French social science thus followed an institutional trajectory that is quite similar to that of other cultural and scholarly domains. The national Academy monopolized the legitimate production and tried to control the uses of the knowledge it produced, commissioned, or rewarded. After the revolutionary upheavals of 1848 in various parts of Europe, the Academy lost part of its legitimacy, but its pioneering role was followed by the creation of national organizations for the social sciences in other countries. Operating in a more decentralized and associative manner, British and American associations were similarly guided by a conception of social science that focused on issues of governance and policymaking, especially regarding the "social question."

Although the Academy of Moral and Political Sciences was never uncontested, neither from the conservative Right nor from the republican Left, it was only with the expanding research university during the Third Republic (1870–1940) that the center of the social sciences shifted to university faculties. From being part of a monopolistic academic regime, carried by more liberal factions of the notables, the social sciences now became a more autonomous and scholarly field. The centrally administered and relatively unified group of moral and political sciences split into more autonomous disciplines, each with its own chairs, scholarly journals, and professional associations. Disciplinary social science now became the predominant mode of teaching, research, and publishing. University disciplines gained a greater degree of autonomy not only with regard to the official Academy but also vis-à-vis governmental agencies and lay audiences. Establishing professional autonomy in its different guises—conceptually, socially, and institutionally—was the main preoccupation of the leading representatives of university disciplines, in classical (philosophy, history) as well as in newer domains (psychology, economics, sociology).

The emerging field of the social sciences was organized in France as a tripartite structure. Political studies moved to a school for public administration outside of the university, located at the periphery of the academic field yet obtaining a central role in the formation of administrative and political elites. Economics entered the Faculty of Law, while sociology and psychology were instituted in the Faculty of Letters, thus engendering an enduring dependence on philosophy and the humanities.

Seen from a comparative perspective, the conflicts between older academicians and aspiring members the professoriate were not specific for France. In other advanced nation-states a comparable opposition manifested itself between an older generation of policy-oriented gentleman scholars close to governmental elites and a younger generation of university professors. Although there were no national academies quite like in France, the British National Association for the Promotion of Social Science (1857), the American Social Science Association (1867), and the German Verein für Socialpolitik (1873) experienced a similar decline as the Academy of Moral and Political Sciences, giving way to more scholarly university disciplines, on the one hand, and to new ameliorative initiatives and policy agencies on the other.

In this intellectual and institutional constellation sociology occupied a very peculiar position. Unlike other disciplines sociology had no clear historical antecedents in moral philosophy or political theory, and emerged outside of the realm of the official academies. As conceived by Auguste Comte during the 1830s, sociology was neither a moral science nor a derivative of any of the natural sciences. Comte's differential theory of science allowed him to rethink the relations among the sciences and to redefine the aims and claims of social science accordingly. Instead of following a uniform model and a single method, Comte argued that each fundamental science has its own methods and research procedures, and necessarily so because the degree of complexity of its object-matter varies significantly. The sciences constitute a series of increasing complexity and decreasing generality. The laws of physics are relatively simple and are valid for all natural phenomena, large and small, animate and inanimate. The laws of biology are more complicated and their validity is restricted to living organisms. Human societies are still more complex and less general; human beings represent the smallest subset of natural phenomena. Following this scheme of increasing complexity and decreasing generality, Comte's *Cours de philosophy positive* (1830–42) explained in great detail how and why different methods prevail in the various sciences: the experimental method in physics, the comparative method in biology, the historical method in sociology. The new science of sociology was conceived as the "positive study of the totality of fundamental laws that are specific of social phenomena." As such it would integrate the study of politics, morals, and economics into a new and fundamentally historical science of human society.

However original and far-reaching it may have been, Comte's work had little or no impact in academic circles. He lacked a recognized position, his theory of the sciences was too broad for the increasingly specialized scientists at the Academy of Sciences, and too scientific for proponents of the moral sciences. Gradually turning away from the academic establishment, Comte's interests shifted to issues of morality and social reform. Although his theory would eventually have considerable impact in the social as well as in the life sciences, sociology virtually disappeared after Comte had completed his *Cours de philosophie positive*. Migrating to Britain, its resurgence in France occurred during the last third of the nineteenth century in the context of expanding universities and as a response to sociology's more favorable reception in Britain. This response was carried primarily by young philosophers from the university elite. Building on the work of Herbert Spencer in particular, they succeeded in transforming sociology from a stigmatized extra-academic enterprise into a legitimate university endeavor.

The work of the aspiring members of the professoriate can be understood as a two-front struggle. On the one hand, they opposed the official Academy of Moral and Political Sciences and its assumptions about moral philosophy and moral science. This critical stance was articulated in the name of a more demanding conception of science and scholarship. The aspiring professors were, on the other hand, equally critical of the intellectual representatives of various reform movements that—especially since 1848—had developed outside of the university (positivists, socialists, Catholic reformers like Le Play). Here they similarly opposed a more scholarly ethos to the doctrinaire character of reform movements, insisting on their uncritical combination of normative commitment and intellectual pretension. The main vehicle for the scholarly claims of the new generation were university-based disciplinary journals, which relied heavily on contemporary foreign scholarship, essentially British and German, and elaborated more systematic and methodical approaches to their domain of inquiry.

Following the work of university pioneers like Espinas and Fouillée, sociological studies multiplied rapidly between the 1880s and the outbreak of the First World War. Being part of the expanding university system, sociology became a subfield of its own, with separate journals and associations, and shaped by ardent competition between two rival networks: one led by Émile Durkheim, the other by René Worms. Out of this competition Durkheimian sociology emerged as the preeminent form of sociology. Durkheim critically elaborated a basically Comtean conception of social science. Similar in that respect to Comte, it allowed him to break away from the philosophical idealism (Fouillée) that was associated with the Academy of Moral and Political Sciences as well as from the organicism that had become its most important rival both in Britain (Spencer) and in France (Espinas, Worms). But unlike Comte's precepts, Durkheim transformed the idea of a relative autonomous social science into a well-defined research program and built up a productive group around his journal the *Année sociologique* (1898–1912).

While the Durkheimians eclipsed their competitors and became known as the "French school of sociology," sociology did not fare well institutionally. For almost half a century, from 1910 to approximately 1960, its university position remained limited to four chairs. More important for the development of the discipline in France were research positions outside of the university. They were concentrated in a small school like the École pratique des hautes études (EPHE), and after the Second World War, in institutes of the Centre national de recherche scientifique (CNRS). Corresponding to this institutional dualism of teaching and research, sociological work followed two separate tracks, one in the Faculty of Letters, where it was closely bound to philosophy and the teaching of philosophy students, the other in research schools and research institutes, in which sociology evolved within and across more specialized research areas.

Corresponding to this dual structure, the Durkheimian group after the First World War bifurcated into two distinct networks, one around university professors like Célestin Bouglé, the other carried by research scholars such as Marcel Mauss, Henri Hubert, François Simiand, and Marcel Granet. Through the work of the last group sociology entered various scholarly domains and contributed to a broad range of scholarly renewals. The university professors (Bouglé, Bayet, Davy), who represented the more official brand of sociology, were close to the dominant forms of philosophy, and although their successors (Gurvitch, Aron, Stoetzel) rejected Durkheimianism, one of their chief aims was to redefine the relations of sociology to philosophy. That Durkheimianism continued as a scientific tradition was due to the research wing of the network, but as such it survived in scholarly fields other than sociology (anthropology, social psychology, economics, historical studies, various "area studies"), most often without being perceived as related to the sociological tradition.

After the Second World War, the growth of sociology took off at a newly founded institute for empirical research, the Centre d'études sociologiques (1945). Here nearly all the members of the postwar generation started their careers, and empirical research on contemporary issues provided a new basis for the discipline. Engaging with American social science and responding to the demand for studies about economic reconstruction and industrial modernization, the sociology of work around Georges Friedmann became the leading sector. But to understand this research work as it was actually carried out, broader field structures need to be taken into account. Sociology after 1945 was caught up in a configuration that was defined by two antagonistic poles: an intellectual pole dominated by existentialist philosophy and a pole of policy research in state institutes. In the theoretical and political concerns that dominated the intellectual field and were defined by philosophers around Jean-Paul Sartre and the journal *Les temps modernes*, sociology was considered a suspicious enterprise associated with American-style empiricism. On the other hand, sociology had no established position in the emerging sector of policy research either. Since sociologists could ignore neither the intellectual field nor the empirical research in policy institutes, they were caught in a double bind. Many of the research projects were a hesitant response to the practically insurmountable tensions between Sartre and statistics, between politically committed intellectuals on the one hand and professional research experts on the other.

The period between 1960 and 2000 may be seen as the second institutional breakthrough of the discipline. The first had occurred at the end of the nineteenth century with the establishment of the first chairs, journals, and learned societies in the context of an expanding university under the more democratic and secular regime of the Third Republic (1870–1940). The second breakthrough took place during a period of unprecedented growth of higher education in general and of the social sciences in particular. For each of the disciplines involved, the expansion implied that they became more autonomous universes, with their own degrees, career structures, publication outlets, and modes of professional association. From being a small and divided subfield, sociology became an organized academic discipline.

This long wave of growth was marked more particularly by two cycles of expansion separated from each other by a period of crisis, stagnation, and intellectual reorientation. The first cycle was concentrated in the 1960s and early 1970s when the chances to do social scientific work improved drastically and the human sciences rather suddenly gained considerable intellectual and public acclaim. In France this was a period of high economic growth, an expanding system of state planning and Gaullist politics that favored public investment in research and education. Intellectually it was the era of "structuralism" and the flowering of new theoretical programs ranging from structural anthropology and semiotics and structuralist versions of Marxism and psychoanalysis to Foucault's archaeological or genealogical studies of discourse. In sociology it was a period of more self-conscious and original enterprises as well, some of them carried by members of the postwar generation (Crozier, Reynaud, Touraine), others by newcomers like Pierre Bourdieu and Raymond Boudon.

This first cycle of exceptionally rapid growth was followed by a decade of lower levels of research funding, declining recruitments, and a politically and scientifically divided academic community. From 1985 to the beginning of 2000 the social sciences went through another cycle of expansion; this time, however, expansion was limited to the universities, to a national policy of broadening access to higher education, whereas the research sector stagnated or declined and the social sciences were both intellectually and institutionally more severely challenged. Instead of primarily defying the classical humanities, as had been the case in the 1960s and early 1970s, the social sciences now had to compete with disciplines that were more attuned to the market sector, that is, with economics, which became the dominant social science in academia as well as in policy circles, and with a host of vocational disciplines (management, communication, educational sciences, physical education, and sports), which promised students chances on the labor market that the classical social sciences seemed to lack.

In the course of this long but discontinuous phase of expansion a multitude of new centers, research groups, and journals were established. Numerous new research specialties emerged, a few declined (rural sociology), and the sociology of work branched out in different directions (specializing in organizations, professions, firms, or social movements). In addition to an increasing number of specialist areas, some leading groups developed more general sociological perspectives as well. Crozier's analysis of organizations represented the predominant program for sociology as a policy science and entered programs of public administration and business schools. Touraine's work on new social movements developed into a sociology of collective action and social change in postindustrial societies, and simultaneously represented a new form of public social science. Raymond Boudon's interest in methodology evolved into a theoretical program for methodological individualism and an enlarged conception of rational choice. And Pierre Bourdieu's work in various research areas lead to a conception of reflexive social science and a distinct approach to social practices. Occupying different positions in the academic field and developed in mutual competition, these groups not only had a defining significance for the discipline in France, but following earlier figures like Comte, Durkheim, and Mauss, they gained considerable international recognition as well.

Having around 2000 become more of a teaching discipline with a shrinking number of research positions, a relatively strong national orientation in its research topics and references, and a rising demand for "practical sociologies," significant parts of the discipline did not retreat within the narrow boundaries of university departments and either academic or applied research specialties. As an heir of the Comtean conception of social science, sociology is in France still the most interdisciplinary-oriented discipline among the human sciences. As such it has remained a vital ingredient in numerous transdisciplinary enterprises that have shifted the boundaries between the disciplines. Pierre Bourdieu's journal *Actes de la recherche en sciences sociales* (1975), which broke with the standard format of an academic journal, was organized around well-chosen theme issues, incorporated visual material, and reflexively combined different methods and points of view. In France *Actes* served as the example for a host of new multidisciplinary ventures. Ethnographic studies found a new outlet in the journal *Terrain* (1983), historically oriented social scientists created *Genèses* (1990), the study of politics and the state has become the focus of *Politix* (1988), and the varieties of action and interaction are dissected and discussed in journals like the *Revue du MAUSS* (1981) and *Raisons pratiques* (1990).

These multidisciplinary initiatives were accompanied by a renewed engagement with public affairs. Going well beyond the practices of policy research, Touraine's group entered into sustained interactions with representatives of new social movements, and the members of his group are frequent participants in public debates. Pierre Bourdieu's conception of "committed scholarship" and the "collective intellectual" inspired undertakings such as a European Review of Books, *Liber*, and the founding of a publishing house. Most of these initiatives, however, have remained invisible outside of France. Although Bourdieu is one of the most cited social scientists in the world, the journal he created, *Actes de la recherche en sciences sociales*, is virtually absent from mainstream sociology. Although the *American Journal of Sociology* and *American Sociological Review* cited more than twenty-two thousand journal articles in the decade between 1992 and 2001, only two of these references were to *Actes de la recherche en sciences sociales*; more than six hundred journals were cited more often.[1] Quite exceptionally the journal *Liber* was published in many other languages than French as well, but not in English. In spite of what the rhetoric of internationalization suggests, sociology is still quite strongly bound to national systems of higher education, research, and publishing. Much of what is or might be of interest to the international community remains trapped within the borders within which it is produced, and a truly international social science remains a challenge for the French as well as for social scientists from other countries.

Epilogue: What Is French about Sociology in France?

At various occasions in the preceding chapters, references were made to "national traditions," French traditions, or, by way of comparison, other national traditions. Although a "national tradition" is easily evoked, in sociology as well as in other domains, the precise meaning and analytical significance of the notion are controversial.[1] The more common uses of the expression are uncomfortably close to common sense perceptions of nations and their peculiarities, and they often carry normative and polemical overtones ("French theory," "British empiricism"). A considerable part of the discourse on national traditions is indeed bound up with historic rivalries between nation-states and the national stereotypes that have accompanied them. Since there is a great dearth of more rigorous inquiries, the very idea of national intellectual traditions is contested. Joseph Schumpeter, author of the celebrated *History of Economic Analysis*, stated that it makes no sense to speak of "national schools" and that attempts to write the history of economics as a history of national traditions was about the "worst way to write the history of economics that can be imagined."[2] In spite of this strong rejection, however, Schumpeter himself acknowledged that national contexts, at least during certain periods, can be quite relevant. He described the physiocrats, for example, as an undeniably "French school" and referred to the "British tradition" of political economy stretching from Adam Smith's *Wealth of Nations* (1776) to at least John Stuart Mill's *Principles of Political Economy* (1848).

Schumpeter's rejection of "national traditions" was in fact less based on historical evidence than on normative grounds. Science, as he explained, "is of no country and does not bear any homogeneous national traits." The first part of this statement is empirically contestable, as he implicitly admitted himself, and is at least partly normative; the second half of the statement is too general a criterion for examining the possible impact of national conditions. Why should the lack of *general* homogeneity in national scientific practices oblige us to ignore its partial significance?

Reconsidering the issue, it may, first, be recalled that the social sciences have in various ways been shaped by their national contexts. It is well documented, for example, that patterns of institutionalization are related to differences in state structures.[3] In a politically centralized country such as France, the social sciences were first instituted in the form of a national academy, whereas its British counterpart, the British National Association for the Promotion of Social Science (1857), operated on a more decentralized and associative basis. When around the turn of the twentieth century the social sciences became university disciplines and scholarly work gained more autonomy from the state, this occurred in a political context characterized by the exacerbation of state rivalries and the advent of nationalist mass movements. In the countries at the forefront of this development—Germany, England, France, the United States, Italy—national particularities were often evoked to justify certain conceptions of social science and to discredit others. Durkheim increasingly presented sociology as a "French science" capable of strengthening and enhancing the moral and civic foundations of the secular and democratic Republic. Representatives of the social sciences in Germany like Max Weber were confronted with quite different national lineages: one in which the social sciences were thought of as interpretative and not nomothetic disciplines, the other in which they were conceived as belonging to the broader category of state sciences, *Staatswissenschaften*. None of these two issues was central in Britain or France. In the same period, as Dorothy Ross has shown, the social sciences in North America took shape in close association with the tradition of "American exceptionalism," which implied yet again different modes of questioning and conceptualization.[4] Such national structures continued to play a significant role in the years between the two world wars, a period marked by both rising international tensions and the emergence of American social science as the dominant pole of the international field. Yet however strong the resonance of American social science may have been, it was not uncontested, and its preeminence varied significantly, among others, by country.

Specific national conditions and rivalries between nations thus seem to represent a significant dimension of the social sciences, and they cannot be ignored if we are to understand their modes of conceptualization and how these have (not) circulated across national borders. Examining national patterns, furthermore, is not in any way contradictory to the importance of transnational exchange and international circulation. Historically, international social science arrangements were constructed on the basis of existing national structures; internationalization has in effect denationalized research practices, but it has, at times, also reinforced national loyalties and strengthened national specificities.[5]

Reconceptualizing National Traditions

Although there are indeed good reasons to take the national context of the social sciences into account, the notion of "national traditions" has so far remained diffuse and imprecise. It is quite common to evoke a national tradition or "national style" without explaining how these national traditions can be identified and how a possible explanation can be provided for both their emergence and their continuity.[6] If the notion of "national traditions" is used in this manner, it becomes a transhistorical entity, traditionally thought of as the "character" or "soul" of a nation, which makes it difficult to examine empirically and understand sociologically. For a reconceptualization, different meanings of the expression should be disentangled. When Durkheim's sociology is said to be French, this statement can, in fact, have several meanings. Each one of these is situated at a specific level of analysis and the possible outcome of a distinct kind of social process.[7] First, national traditions exist at the level of specific research domains or disciplines, in which case it designates a more or less coherent way of thinking and working that has spread beyond the people who inaugurated them and acquired some kind of national significance. A national tradition in this sense then refers to the work of a local group or circle, which has somehow become a central, even predominant way of practicing a specialty or discipline in a certain country (and not in others). Durkheim's sociology can be said to be French in this sense; it emerged in France, was partly constructed on the basis of indigenous sources, and was for many decades the country's predominant sociological school. In his study of psychological research, Kurt Danziger similarly compares the research practices of local groups—Wundt in Leipzig, Galton in London, Charcot and others in Paris—showing how their studies were inspired by indigenous intellectual traditions and how each of these developed in ways consistent with its specific national context.[8] Lavoisier and "French" chemistry or the group of economists in Vienna that came to be known as the "Austrian school" are examples of this kind of national tradition. In all these cases, a practice that first developed locally took on a national dimension before becoming categorized as a "national tradition." Comparative research is the most effective—though rarely used—means of understanding such national variations in research domains and disciplines.[9]

National traditions, second, designate more or less coherent ways of thinking that go beyond a single discipline or research specialty and that are related to nationally specific structures of the academic and the intellectual field. Typical examples include the German conception of the sciences of the state, the *Staatswissenschaften*, or, more recently, the North American notion of "behavioral sciences."[10] Both categories exemplify specific ways of defining and dividing the social and human sciences, which have far-reaching consequences for the way in which problems are posed and research is carried out. These supradisciplinary categories are overarching categories that can be empirically studied and sociologically understood by examining their genesis, functioning, and impact. The level of analysis here, in other words, is that of the academic or intellectual field at large. As discussed in chapter 1, this field in France was initially unified and controlled by a national academy before it came to be structured as a tripartite field structure at the end of the nineteenth century. Durkheim's sociology can be said to have been French in this second sense of the term as well because the Durkheimian conception of sociology was shaped by this particularly French structure of the academic field, in which, for example, philosophy had a preeminent position, whereas political science lacked academic legitimacy. The structure of national academic fields comes into play not only in producing certain conceptions of social science but also in the reception of foreign authors and the selective ways these are incorporated in national fields.[11]

The notion of national traditions can, finally, also refer to postures and practices on an even more general level. In contrasting British with French physics, Pierre Duhem famously drew a distinction between two modes of thinking, the "broad mind" and the "deep mind," which he found operative not only in physics but in other sciences as well, and even in literature. Poincaré's mathematical physics stood in direct contrast to Maxwell's, just as Descartes's thought had contrasted with Bacon's, and Corneille's work with Shakespeare's. According to Duhem, the English mind was "broad," meaning that it could readily "imagine extremely complicated sets of concrete facts," whereas it had difficulty in "conceiving abstract notions and formulating general principles."[12] By contrast, the French sought to construct a logical system in which rigorous deductions would unite the set of hypotheses on which theories were founded. The "deep mind" was oriented toward abstraction and generalization, and was therefore too narrow to "imagine anything complex before fitting it into a perfect order."

These two modes of thinking, also designated by the cursory notions of "British empiricism" and "French rationalism," have since Montesquieu, Hume, and Herder, been linked to notions of "national character" or "national spirit." Throughout the nineteenth century, the notion of "national character" was widely used and even became the focus of projects for disciplines such as "political ethology" (John Stuart Mill), "political psychology," or *Völkerpsychologie*.[13] But despite the cursory nature of Duhem's analysis and the failure to construct separate disciplines for studying national character, national traditions are identifiable at this third, most general level too. And Durkheim's sociology can also be said to have been French in this sense. Rather than assuming the existence of immutable national characters or "minds," however, it is more fruitful to identify the social processes that have—to a certain degree—unified intellectual habits and ways of thinking at the national level.

Norbert Elias's analysis of the notions of *civilisation* and *Kultur* provides an exemplary way to understand such processes.[14] Whereas the notion of "civilization" and "civilized behavior" had its roots in the etiquette of the court society, the concept of *Kultur* originated in an urban, bourgeois setting in which "depth" and "interiority" were valued. These contrasting notions of *civilisation* and *Kultur* gradually became national categories, and Elias emphasized the continuity with which such "specific patterns of thinking, acting and feeling recur, with characteristic adaptations to new developments, in one and the same society over many generations. It is almost certain that the meaning of certain key-words and particularly the emotional undertones embedded in them, which are handed on from one generation to another unexamined and often unchanged, plays a part in the flexible continuity of what one otherwise conceptualizes as 'national character.'"[15]

One of the reasons why these cultural and cognitive complexes can retain their significance is that the values and practices associated with them are institutionalized in national school systems. Elias's analysis of state formation can here be fruitfully combined with Bourdieu's work on education. Bourdieu has shown how criteria of excellence and the values transmitted by the school system reproduce distinct intellectual styles, which can be observed across very different intellectual domains. Bourdieu thus called for sociological study of "the institutionalized transmission of culture," defining it as "one path—and not the least significant—that the sociology of knowledge might take."[16] Citing Durkheim's studies of the French educational system, Bourdieu recalled that in advanced societies the school system tends to produce a "general disposition that then generates particular schemata likely to be applied in different areas of thought and action." Bourdieu called this disposition the learned habitus (*habitus cultivé*). Intellectual peculiarities traditionally described as part of a "national character" can in this way be linked to the "academic traditions of different nations," and more specifically, to the way in which each intellectual relates to his or her national academic tradition.[17] Bourdieu did not elaborate these points in separate studies, but he often returned to the issue, for example, in a short digression on common sense in *Pascalian Meditations*, insisting that common sense is "to a large extent national because most of the major principles of division have been inculcated or reinforced by educational institutions, one of the main missions of which is to construct the nation as a population endowed with the same categories and therefore of the same common sense."[18]

This common sense, or national "habitus," to use Elias's term, operates in ways that actors are not usually conscious of, but that they experience immediately when trying to accommodate to a different national context, where their dispositions and categories of thinking are no longer spontaneously adapted. In his analysis of German scientists in exile in the United States, Jonathan Harwood documents the astonishment of German scholars confronted with American researchers' high degree of specialization and their utter indifference to what Germans considered obvious components of *Bildung*.[19]

There is, then, no good reason to ban the idea of national traditions from the history of the social sciences. Once different meanings of the expression are disentangled and each of them is connected to identifiable social processes, the objections to its use can be overcome. National traditions represent a significant dimension of the development of the social sciences and of the particular ways ideas circulate beyond their national borders. Gaining a better insight into how national traditions emerge, function, and evolve may, in fact, be an effective way to counter the relativism that worried Schumpeter and others who have rejected the notion altogether.

Notes

Introduction

1. Based on the Social Science Citation Index (SSCI) and the Arts and Humanities Citation Index (AGCI), this study was published in the *Times Higher Education Supplement*, March 26, 2009.

2. Étienne Ollion and Andrew Abbott, "Quarante ans de sociologie française aux États-Unis: Notes bibliométriques sur la réception des sociologues français aux États-Unis," in D. Demaziere, D. Lorrain and C. Paradeise (dir.), *Transmissions, une communauté en héritage*, Rennes, Presses Universitaires de Rennes (in press).

3. On translations in the United States, see Gisèle Sapiro, "Quoi de neuf après la French Theory?: Les traductions sur le marché du livre académique aux États-Unis," in G. Sapiro (dir.), *Sciences humaines en traduction: Les livres français aux Etats-Unis, au Royaume-Uni et en Argentine*, Paris, Institut français/CESSP, 2014, pp. 14–48.

4. François Cusset, *French Theory: How Foucault, Derrida, and Deleuze, & Cie Transformed the Intellectual Life of the United States*, Minneapolis, University of Minnesota Press, 2008.

5. On the intellectual consequences of European integration, see Gisèle Sapiro (ed.), *L'espace intellectuel en Europe*, Paris, La Découverte, 2009; Johan Heilbron, "European Social Science as a Transnational Field of Research," in Sokratis Koniordos and Alexander Kyrtsis (eds.), *Handbook of European Sociology*, London, Sage, 2014, pp. 67–79. On globalizing social science, see Sébastien Mosbah-Natanson and Yves Gingras, "The Globalization of Social Sciences?: Evidence from a Quantitative Analysis of 30 Years of Production, Collaboration, and Citations in the Social Sciences (1980–2009)," *Current Sociology* 62, no. 5, 2014, 626–646; and Johan Heilbron, "The Social Sciences as an Emerging Global Field," *Current Sociology* 62, no. 5, 2014, 685–703.

6. For different yet partly overlapping approaches to the study of the social sciences, see Johan Heilbron, Rémi Lenoir, and Gisèle Sapiro (eds.), *Pour une histoire des sciences sociales*, Paris, Fayard, 2004; Charles Camic, Neil Gross, and Michèle Lamont (eds.), *Social Knowledge in the Making*, Chicago, Chicago University Press, 2011; Charles Camic and Neil Gross, "The New Sociology of Ideas," in Judith Blau (ed.), *The Blackwell Companion to Sociology*, London, Blackwell, 2010, pp. 236–249.

7. Pierre Bourdieu, *Homo Academicus*, Cambridge, Polity Press, 1988, p. xvii. For a field approach to the sociology of science, see Pierre Bourdieu, *Science of Science and Reflexivity*, Cambridge, Polity Press, 2004; Terry Shinn and Pascal Ragouet, *Controverses sur la science*, Paris, Raisons d'agir, 2005; Yves Gingras, *Sociologie des sciences*, Paris, Presses Universitaires de France, 2013.

8. For a reflection on this issue, see Norbert Elias, "Social Process Models on Multiple Levels," in Norbert Elias, *Essays III*, in *Collected Works*, vol. 16, Dublin, UCDP, 2009, pp. 40–43.

9. The *agrégation* is a highly competitive, national examination that on a yearly basis recruits professors. The *agrégés* form the teaching elite in secondary schools as well as in some university disciplines (law, political science, economics, business administration, medicine). Most secondary school subjects have an *agrégation* (philosophy, languages, history, natural sciences, social sciences).

10. Johan Heilbron, Nicolas Guilhot, and Laurent Jeanpierre, "Toward a Transnational History of the Social Sciences," *Journal of the History of the Behavioral Sciences* 44, no. 2, 2008, 146–160.

1. The Establishment of Organized Social Science

1. Peter Wagner, "Certainty and Order, Liberty and Contingency: The Birth of Social Science as Empirical Political Philosophy," in J. Heilbron, L. Magnusson, and B. Wittrock (eds.), *The Rise of the Social Sciences and the Formation of Modernity*, Dordrecht, Kluwer Academic Publications, 1998–2001, pp. 241–63; Peter Wagner, *A Sociology of Modernity*, London, Routledge, 1994.

2. Wolf Lepenies, *Between Literature and Science: The Rise of Sociology*, Cambridge, Cambridge University Press, 1988.

3. Daniel Roche, *Le siècle des lumières en province: Académies et académiciens provinciaux, 1680–1789*, Paris, Mouton, 1978, vol. 1, p. 102.

4. A rare and partial exception was the tacitly permitted but short-lived "Club de l'Entresol." See Nick Childs, *A Political Academy in Paris, 1724–1731*, Oxford, Voltaire Foundation, 2000.

5. Entry on *académicien* in J. B. R. Robinet, *Dictionnaire universel des sciences morale, économique, politique et diplomatique*, 30 vols., London, 1777–83.

6. For a more extensive treatment, see Johan Heilbron, *The Rise of Social Theory*, Cambridge, Polity Press, 1995; and the special issue "Naissances de la science sociale, 1750–1850," *Revue d'histoire des sciences humaines*, no. 15, 2006.

7. Brian Head, "The Origins of 'la science sociale' in France, 1770–1800," *Australian Journal of French Studies* 19, 1982, 115–32; Jean-Luc Chappey, "De la science de l'homme aux sciences humaines: Enjeux politiques d'une configuration de savoir (1770–1808)," *Revue d'histoire des sciences humaines*, no. 15, 2006, 43–68; Philippe Steiner, "La science de l'économie et les sciences sociales en France (1750–1830)," *Revue d'histoire des sciences humaines*, no. 15, 2006, 15–42.

8. Martin S. Staum, *Minerva's Message: Stabilizing the French Revolution*, Montreal, McGill-Queen's University Press, 1996.

9. The Belgian Royal Academy created a class for the "moral and political sciences" in 1843; an Academy of Moral Sciences was established in Madrid in 1857, followed in 1861 by an Academy of Moral and Political Sciences as part of the Royal Society of Naples. See Julien Vincent, "Les sciences morales de la gloire à l'oubli," *Revue pour l'histoire du CNRS*, no. 18, 2007, 38–43.

10. Lawrence Goldman, *Science, Reform, and Politics in Victorian Britain: The Social Science Association, 1857–1886*, Cambridge, Cambridge University Press, 2002.

11. Ibid. For the German and American associations, see Irmela Gorges, *Sozialforschung in Deutschland, 1872–1914*, Königstein, Anton Hain, 1980; Thomas Haskell, *The Emergence of Professional Social Science*, Urbana, University of Illinois Press, 1977. For comparative perspectives, see Peter Wagner, *Sozialwissenschaften und Staat*, Frankfurt am

Main, Campus, 1990; Peter Wagner, Carol Weiss, Björn Wittrock, and Hellmut Wollmann (eds.), *Social Sciences and Modern States*, Cambridge, Cambridge University Press, 1991; Dietrich Rueschemeyer and Theda Skocpol (eds.), *States, Social Knowledge, and the Origins of Modern Social Policies*, Princeton, NJ, Princeton University Press, 1996.

12. Lucien Jaume, *L'individu effacé, ou le paradoxe du libéralisme français*, Paris, Fayard, 1997; Aurelian Craiutu, *Liberalism under Siege*, Lanham, MD, Lexington Books, 2003.

13. Christophe Charle, *Histoire sociale de la France au XIXᵉ siècle*, Paris, Seuil, 1991, pp. 41–50.

14. François Guizot, "Ordonnance du Roi qui rétablit dans le sein de l'Institut royal de France l'ancienne Classe des sciences morales et politiques (1832)," in Académie des sciences morales et politiques, *Notices biographiques et bibliographiques*, Paris, 1981, pp. xv–xviii.

15. For the pivotal period at the end of the eighteenth century, see Éric Brian, *La mesure de l'État: Géomètres et administrateurs au XVIIIᵉ siècle*, Paris, Albin Michel, 1994; Charles Coulston Gillispie, *Science and Polity in France: The Revolutionary and Napoleonic Years*, Princeton, NJ, Princeton University Press, 2004.

16. For these and the following data, see Corinne Delmas, *Instituer des savoirs d'État: L'Académie des sciences morales et politiques au XIXᵉ siècle*, Paris, L'Harmattan, 2006.

17. Nearly all members had published at least one book before being elected, which seems to have been a scholarly precondition for membership.

18. Delmas, *Instituer des savoirs d'État*; Sophie-Anne Leterrier, *L'institution des sciences morales et politiques, 1795–1850*, Paris, L'Harmattan, 1995. For a useful bibliography, see R. de Lasteyrie, *Bibliographie générale des travaux historiques et archéologiques publiés par les sociétés savantes de la France*, Paris, Imprimerie Nationale, 1901, vol. 3, pp. 536–89. On the archives, see Elise Feller and Jean-Claude Goery, "Les archives de l'Académie des sciences morales et politiques, 1832–1848, " *Annales de la révolution française*, no. 222, 1975, 567–83.

19. For the sociogenesis of local and national welfare arrangements from this perspective, see Abram de Swaan, *In Care of the State: Health Care, Education, and Welfare in Europe and the USA in the Modern Era*, Cambridge, Polity Press, 1988.

20. Doris S. Goldstein, "Official Philosophies in France: The Example of Victor Cousin," *Journal of Social History* 1, 1967–68, 259–79; Patrice Vermeren, *Victor Cousin, le jeu de la philosophie et de l'État*, Paris, L'Harmattan, 1995; Xavier Landrin, "L'eclecticisme spiritualiste au XIXᵉ siècle: Sociologie d'une philosophie transnationale," in Louis Pinto (éd.), *Le commerce des idées philosophiques*, Broissieux, Éditions du Croquant, 2009, pp. 29–65.

21. Tocqueville was of the same persuasion, sharply condemning materialism and urging his readers to "rehabilitate the spiritual dimension in politics." See his letter to Louis de Kergorlay, September 28, 1834, quoted in Richard Swedberg, *Tocqueville's Political Economy*, Princeton, NJ, Princeton University Press, 2009, p. 3.

22. Stanley Mellon, *The Political Uses of History: A Study of Historians in the French Restauration*, Stanford, CA, Stanford University Press, 1958; Yvonne Knibiehler, *Naissance des sciences humaines: Mignet et l'histoire philosophique*, Paris, Flammarion, 1973; Pim den Boer, *History as a Profession: The Study of History in France, 1818–1914*, Princeton, NJ, Princeton University Press, 1998.

23. Académie des sciences morales et politiques, *Concours de l'Académie, 1834–1900*, Paris, Imprimerie Nationale, 1901, p. 5.

24. On these early forms of what was later named "social research," see Michelle Perrot, *Enquêtes sur la condition ouvrière en France au XIXᵉ siècle*, Paris, Hachette, 1972; Louis Chevalier, *Classes laborieuses et classes dangereuses à Paris pendant la première moitié du 19ᵉ siècle*, Paris, Plon, 1958; B. Ratcliffe, "Classes laborieuses et classes dangereuses à Paris pendant la première moitié du XIXᵉ siècle?: The Chevalier Thesis Reexamined," *French Historical Studies* 17, no. 2, 1991, 542–74; Marc Renneville, *Crime et folie: Deux siècles d'enquêtes médicales et judiciaires*, Paris, Fayard, 2003; Judith Lyon-Caen, "Enquêtes, littérature et savoir sur le monde social en France dans les années 1840," *Revue d'histoire*

des sciences humaines 17, 2007, 99–118. For the public opinion surveys that were similarly preoccupied with the threats to public order, see Pierre Karila-Cohen, *L'État des esprits: L'invention de l'enquête politique en France (1814–1848)*, Rennes, Presses Universitaires de Rennes, 2008.

25. For a critical analysis of Villermé's assumptions and categories of observation, see William Reddy, *The Rise of Market Culture*, Cambridge, Cambridge University Press, 1984, pp. 171–84.

26. William Coleman, *Death Is a Social Disease: Public Health and Political Economy in Early Industrial France*, Madison, University of Wisconsin Press, 1982; Bernard-Pierre Lécuyer, "Démographie, statistique et hygiène publique sous la monarchie censitaire," *Annales de démographie historique*, 1977, 215–45.

27. Giovanna Procacci, *Gouverner la misère: La question sociale en France 1789–1848*, Paris, Seuil, 1993; Robert Castel, *Les métamorphoses de la question sociale*, Paris, Fayard, 1995, esp. chap. 5.

28. Tocqueville, "Mémoire sur le pauperisme," in *Oeuvres*, Paris, Gallimard, 1991, vol. 1, pp. 1155–97; E. Keslassy, *Le libéralisme de Tocqueville à l'épreuve du paupérisme*, Paris, L'Harmattan, 2000.

29. Quoted in Alain Alcouffe, "The Institutionalization of Political Economy in French Universities: 1819–1896," *History of Political Economy* 21, 1989, 322.

30. Evelyne Laurent and Luc Marco, "Le *Journal des économistes* ou l'apologie du libéralisme 1841–1940," in Luc Marco (éd.), *Les revues d'économie politique en France (1751–1994)*, Paris, L'Harmattan, 1996, pp. 79–120.

31. Joseph Schumpeter, *History of Economic Analysis* (1954), New York, Oxford University Press, 1978, p. 497; Lucette Le Van-Lemesle, *Le juste ou le riche: L'enseignement de l'économie politique, 1815–1950*, Paris, Comité pour l'histoire économique et financière de la France, 2004.

32. It is rarely acknowledged that well before Dilthey elaborated the dichotomy of *Geisteswissenschaften* and natural sciences, the Cousin school had already proposed a similar conception. The term *Geisteswissenschaften* was coined in a German translation of John Stuart Mill's logic as an equivalent of "moral sciences." See Alwin Diemer, "Die Differenzierung der Wissenschaften in die Natur- und Geisteswissenschaften," in A. Diemer (Hrsg.), *Beiträge zur Entwicklung der Wissenschaftstheorie im 19. Jahrhundert*, Meisenheim am Glan, A. Hain, 1968, pp. 182–83.

33. *Dictionnaire des sciences philosophiques*, Paris, Hachette, 1844–52, vol. 6, pp. 672–73.

34. M. Le Comte Portalis, "Discours sur la marche et les progrès des sciences morales et politiques," *Séances et travaux de l'Académie des sciences morales et politiques*, 1843, vol. 3, pp. 331–54.

35. Tocqueville, *L'ancien régime et la révolution* (1856), Paris, Gallimard, 1967, p. 237. On Tocqueville, see Hugh Brogan, *Alexis de Tocqueville*, London, Profile Books, 2006.

36. For anecdotical evidence, see Adolphe Lair, *L'Institut de France et le Second Empire*, Paris, Plon, 1908.

37. See part 2 of Gisèle Sapiro, *La responsabilité de l'écrivain*, Paris, Seuil, 2011.

38. François Guizot, *Mémoires pour servir à l'histoire de mon temps*, Paris, Michel Lévy, 1858–67, vol. 6, pp. 345–46.

39. See especially Ernest Renan, "La métaphysique et son avenir" (1860), in *Oeuvres complètes*, Paris, Callmann-Lévy, 1947, vol. 1, pp. 680–714.

40. See especially H. Taine, *Philosophie de l'art* (1865), Paris, Hachette, 1917, chap. 1.

41. On Taine's ascendency as a "total intellectual," covering the intellectual field as a whole, see Christophe Charle, *Paris, fin de siècle*, Paris, Seuil, 1998, pp. 97–123.

42. As compared with Cousin and Caro, for example, Taine, Renan, and Littré were far more frequently discussed in the newspaper *Le temps*. See *Tables du journal Le Temps*, Paris, CNRS Éditions, 1966.

43. On Littré and his circle, see Johan Heilbron, "Sociology and Positivism in the Nineteenth Century: The Vicissitudes of the Société de sociologie (1872–1874)," *History of the Human Sciences* 22, no. 4, 2009, 30–62.

44. Émile Littré, *Conservation, révolution et positivisme* (1852), Paris, Aux Bureaux de la Philosophie Positive, 1879, p. 160.

45. Elme Caro, *Problèmes de morale sociale*, Paris, Hachette, 1876, p. 4.

46. Paul Janet, *La crise philosophique: Mm. Taine, Renan, Littré, Vacherot*, Paris, Baillière, 1865, pp. 6–7.

47. Claude Blanckaert (ed.), *Les politiques de l'anthropologie*, Paris, L'Harmattan, 2001; Jennifer M. Hecht, *The End of the Soul: Scientific Modernity, Atheism, and Anthropology in France*, New York, Columbia University Press, 2003; Carole Reynaud Paligot, *La République raciale*, Paris, Presses Universitaires de France, 2006.

48. Philip Nord, *The Republican Moment: Struggles for Democracy in Nineteenth-Century France*, Cambridge, MA, Harvard University Press, 1995.

49. Christophe Charle, *Les élites de la République (1880–1900)*, Paris, Fayard, 1987; for a comparative perspective, see Christophe Charle, *La crise des sociétés impériales: Allemagne, France, Grande-Bretagne 1900–1940*, Paris, Seuil, 2001.

50. Eugen Weber, *The Nationalist Revival in France, 1905–1914*, Berkeley, University of California Press, 1959.

51. Emile Zola, *Le roman expérimental* (1880), quoted in Claude Digeon, *La crise allemande de la pensée française (1870–1914)*, Paris, Presses Universitaires de France, 1959, p. 273.

52. Claude Nicolet, *L'idée républicaine en France*, Paris, Gallimard, 1982, pp. 258 and 374.

53. On French higher education, see Victor Karady, "Les universités françaises de Napoléon à la Deuxième Guerre Mondiale, " in Jacques Verger (éd.), *Histoire des universités en France*, Toulouse, Privat, 1986, pp. 261–365; George Weisz, *The Emergence of Modern Universities in France, 1863–1914*, Princeton, NJ, Princeton University Press, 1983; Christophe Charle, *La république des universitaires, 1870–1940*, Paris, Seuil, 1994.

54. Hélène Gispert (ed.), *Par la science, pour la patrie—L'association française pour l'avancement des sciences (1872–1914)*, Rennes, Presses Universitaires de Rennes, 2009.

55. Weisz, *Emergence of Modern Universities in France*, p. 69.

56. Victor Karady, "Educational Qualifications and University Careers in Nineteenth-Century France," in Robert Fox and George Weisz (eds.), *The Organization of Science and Technology in France, 1808–1914*, Cambridge, Cambridge University Press, 1980, pp. 95–124.

57. On scholarly publishing, see Valérie Tesnière, *Le Quadrige: Un siècle d'édition universitaire 1860–1968*, Paris, Presses Universitaires de France, 2001.

58. Charle, *Élites de la République*, pp. 410–11.

59. Jean-Louis Fabiani, *Les philosophes de la République*, Paris, Minuit, 1988, pp. 111–18.

60. George Weisz, *Emergence of Modern Universities in France*, p. 314.

61. Lucien Mercier, *Les universités populaires: 1899–1914*, Paris, Les Éditions Ouvrières, 1986.

62. On disciplines, see Johan Heilbron, "A Regime of Disciplines: Toward a Historical Sociology of Disciplinary Knowledge," in Charles Camic and Hans Joas (eds.), *The Dialogical Turn: New Roles for Sociology in the Postdisciplinary Age*, Lanham, MD, Rowman & Littlefield, 2004, pp. 23–42. For social science disciplines, see Peter Wagner, Björn Wittrock, and Richard Whitley (eds.), *Discourses on Society: The Shaping of the Social Science Disciplines*, Dordrecht, Kluwer Academic Publishers, 1991.

63. This shift from a monopolistic regime dominated by a national academy to a more differentiated and competitive field structure is quite similar to what happed in the arts and literature. See Pierre Bourdieu, *Manet, une révolution symbolique*, Paris, Raisons d'agir/Seuil, 2013. For the transnational dimension, see Johan Heilbron, Nicolas Guilhot, and Laurent Jeanpierre, "Toward a Transnational History of the Social Sciences," *Journal of the History of the Behavioral Sciences* 44, no. 2, 2008, 146–60.

64. On international organizations, see John Boli and George M. Thomas (eds.), *Constructing World Culture: International Nongovernmental Organizations since 1875*, Stanford, CA, Stanford University Press, 1999; Anne Rasmussen, *L'internationale scientifique*

(1890–1914), Thèse de doctorat, 2 vols., Paris, École des hautes Éétudes en sciences sociales, 1995.

65. Eric Brian, "Transactions statistiques au XIXᵉ siècle," *Actes de la recherche en sciences sociales* 145, 2002, 34–46.

66. For the neglected connections between sociology and empire, see George Steinmetz (ed.), *Sociology and Empire: The Imperial Entanglements of a Disciplne*, Durham, NC, Duke University Press, 2013.

67. Johan Heilbron, "The Tripartite Division of French Social Science," in P. Wagner, B. Wittrock, and R. Whitley (eds.), *Discourses on Society: The Shaping of the Social Sciences Disciplines*, Dordrecht, Kluwer Academic Publishers, 1991, pp. 73–92.

68. Pierre Favre, "Les sciences de l'État entre déterminisme et libéralisme: Émile Boutmy (1835–1906) et la création de l'École libre des sciences politiques," *Revue française de sociologie* 22, 1981, 429–65; Dominique Damamme, "Genèse sociale d'une institution scolaire: l'École libre des sciences politiques," *Actes de la recherche en sciences sociales* 70, 1987, 31–46.

69. Pierre Favre, *Naissances de la science politique en France, 1870–1914*, Paris, Fayard, 1989.

70. Françoise Mélonio, *Tocqueville et les français*, Paris, Aubier, 1993, p. 235.

71. Pierre Bourdieu, *La noblesse d'État*, Paris, Éditions de Minuit, 1989, pp. 183–264.

72. Fernand Braudel, *Écrits sur l'histoire*, Paris, Flammarion, 1968, p. 7.

73. Jean Leca, "La science politique dans le champ intellectuel français," *Revue française de science politique* 32, 1982, 653–78; Jean Leca, "French Political Science and Its Subfields," in D. Easton, J. Gunnell, and L. Graziano (eds.), *The Development of Political Science: A Comparative Survey*, London, Routledge, 1991, pp. 147–86.

74. Alcouffe, Institutionalization of Political Economy in French Universities, p. 328.

75. Marc Pénin, "La *Revue d'économie politique*, ou l'essor d'une grande devancière (1887–1936)," in Marco, *Revues d'économie en France*, pp. 157–96.

76. Walras's notes are quite revealing about the internal functioning of the group of orthodox economists and the concentration of their academic and other powers. See Léon Walras, "Pensées et réflexions," *Cahiers Vilfredo Pareto*, no. 11, 1967, 103–40.

77. Frédéric Lebaron, *La croyance économique: Les économistes entre science et politique*, Paris, Seuil, 2000; Marion Fourcade, *Economists and Societies: Discipline and Profession in the United States, Britain and France, 1890s to 1990s*, Princeton, NJ, Princeton University Press, 2009.

78. Claire-Françoise Bompaire-Evesque, *Un débat sur l'université au temps de la Troisième République: La lutte contre la nouvelle Sorbonne*, Paris, Aux Amateurs de Livres, 1988.

79. Frédéric Gugelot, *La conversion des intellectuels au catholicisme en France 1885–1935*, Paris, CNRS Éditions, 1998; Hervé Serry, *Naissance de l'intellectuel catholique*, Paris, La Découverte, 2004.

80. Antoine Compagnon, *La Troisième République des lettres*, Paris, Seuil, 1983.

81. Harry W. Paul, "The Debate over the Bankruptcy of Science," *French Historical Studies* 5, 1968, 299–327.

82. Richard Griffiths, *The Reactionary Revolution: The Catholic Revival in French Literature, 1870–1914*, London, Constable, 1966, p. 263. For this cultural revolt as an early phase of fascism, see Zeev Sternhell, *The Birth of Fascist Ideology*, Princeton, NJ, Princeton University Press, 1994. For "Catholic sociology," see Hervé Serry, "Saint Thomas sociologue?: Les enjeux clericaux d'une sociologie catholique dans les années 1880–1920," *Actes de la recherche en sciences sociales* 153, 2004, 28–39.

83. Louis Pinto, "La vocation de l'universel: La formation de la représentation de l'intellectuel vers 1900," *Actes de la recherche en sciences sociales* 55, 1984, 23–32.

84. Christophe Charle, *Naissance des intellectuels 1880–1900*, Paris, Minuit, 1990; and for a comparative perspective, Christophe Charle, *Les intellectuels en Europe au XIXᵉ siècle: Essai d'histoire comparée*, Paris, Seuil, 1996.

85. Lepenies, *Between Literature and Science*; Fritz Ringer, *Fields of Knowledge: French Academic Culture in Comparative Perspective, 1890–1920*, Cambridge, Cambridge

University Press/Éditions de la MSH, 1992, pp. 237–47; Gisèle Sapiro, "Défense et illustration de l'honnête homme," *Actes de la recherche en sciences sociales* 154, 2004, 11–27.

86. See R. C. Grogin, *The Bergsonian Controversy in France, 1900–1914*, Calgary, University of Calgary Press, 1988; François Azouvi, *La gloire de Bergson*, Paris, Gallimard, 2007.

87. Louis Pinto, *Les neveux de Zarathoustra: La réception de Nietzsche en France*, Paris, Seuil, 1995.

88. On these oppositions, see Sapiro, "Défense et illustration de l'honnête homme," 11–27.

89. Émile Durkheim, "L'individualisme et les intellectuels (1898)," in Émile Durkheim, *La science sociale et l'action*, Paris, Presses Universitaires de France, 1987, pp. 261–78.

2. An Improbable Science

1. Comte introduced the term in lesson 47 of his *Cours*, which was originally part of volume 4 (1839); see Auguste Comte, *Cours de philosophie positive*, Paris, Hermann, 1975, vol. 2, p. 88.

2. Johan Goudsblom, "On the Development of the Concept of Society," in *Sociology in the Balance*, Oxford, Blackwell, 1977, pp. 15–18; Keith Michael Baker, "Enlightenment and the Institution of Society: Notes for a Conceptual History," in *Main Trends in Cultural History*, ed. Willem Melching and Wyger Velema, Amsterdam, Rodopi, 1994, pp. 95–120; Johan Heilbron, *The Rise of Social Theory*, Cambridge, Polity Press, 1995, part 1.

3. Brian W. Head, "The Origins of 'la science sociale' in France, 1770–1800," *Australian Journal of French Studies* 19, 1982, 115–32.

4. Gregory Claeys, " 'Individualism,' 'Socialism,' and 'Social Science,' " *Journal of the History of Ideas* 47, 1986, 81–93.

5. L. H. Adolph Geck, *Über das Eindringen des Wortes 'sozial' in die deutsche Sprache*, Göttingen, Otto Schwartz & Co., 1963; Eckart Pankoke, *Sociale Bewegung, Sociale Frage, Sociale Politik: Grundfragen der deutschen 'Socialwissenschaft' im 19. Jahrhundert*, Stuttgart, Ernst Klett, 1970.

6. Jacques Guilhaumou, "Sieyès et le non-dit de la sociologie: Du mot à la chose," *Revue d'histoire des sciences humaines*, no. 15, 2006, 117–34.

7. Auguste Comte, "De la division qui a existé jusqu'à présent entre la morale et la politique," in *Écrits de jeunesse, 1816–1828*, Paris, Mouton, 1970, pp. 469–71.

8. The fact that the Belgian statistician and astronomer Adolphe Quételet had also spoken of "social physics" undoubtedly reinforced Comte's determination to find a new term, but given the general change in his vocabulary, it is unlikely that this was the main reason for dropping the expression "social physics."

9. Comte, *Cours de philosophie positive* (lesson 47), vol. 2, p. 88.

10. For an incisive early statement, see Auguste Comte, "Fragments sur les tentatives qui ont été faites pour fonder la science sociale sur la physiologie et sur quelques autres sciences (1819)," in Comte, *Écrits de jeunesse, 1816–1828*, pp. 473–82.

11. See Johan Heilbron, "Social Thought and Natural Science," in *The Cambridge History of Science*, vol. 7, ed. Theodore Porter and Dorothy Ross, Cambridge, Cambridge University Press, 2003, pp. 40–56. On positivism and biology, see especially Georges Canguilhem, *Études d'histoire et de philosophie des sciences*, Paris, Vrin, 1983.

12. For more details on discipline formation, see the second part of Heilbron, *Rise of Social Theory*. The notion of a second scientific revolution has occasionally been used by historians of science since the early 1960s, but its meaning hasn't been properly specified and elaborated, and neither the expression nor the idea behind it have caught on. See I. Bernard Cohen, *Revolution in Science*, Cambridge, MA, The Belknap Press, 1985, pp. 91–101.

13. See Johan Heilbron, "A Regime of Disciplines: Toward a Historical Sociology of Disciplinary Knowledge," in C. Camic and H. Joas (eds.), *The Dialogical Turn: New Roles for Sociology in the Postdisciplinary Age*, Lanham, MD, Rowman & Littlefield, 2004, pp. 23–42.

14. For a more elaborate discussion, see part three of Heilbron, *Rise of Social Theory*. On Comte more generally, see Mary Pickering, *Auguste Comte: An Intellectual Biography*, 3 vols., Cambridge, Cambridge University Press, 1993 and 2009.

15. On Laplacian physics, see Robert Fox, "The Rise and Fall of Laplacian Physics," *Historical Studies in the Physical Sciences* 4, 1974, 89–136.

16. Comte, *Cours de philosophie positive* (lesson 3), vol. 1, pp. 78–79.

17. Émile Littré, Letter to Comte, March 29, 1852, quoted in Mirella Larizza, *Bandiera verde contro bandiera rossa: Auguste Comte e gli inizi della Société positiviste (1848–1852)*, Bologna, Il Mulino, 1999, p. 569.

18. On the positivist movement, see W. M. Simon, *European Positivism in the Nineteenth Century*, Ithaca, NY, Cornell University Press, 1963; Bernhard Plé, *Die 'Welt' aus den Wissenschaften: Der Positivismus in Frankreich, England und Italien von 1848 bis ins zweite Jahrzehnt des 20. Jahrhunderts*, Stuttgart, Klett-Cotta, 1996; Annie Petit, *Heurs et malheurs du positivisme: Philosophie des sciences et politique scientifique chez Auguste Comte et ses premiers disciples (1820–1900)*, Doctoral thesis, Université de Paris I, 1993.

19. Émile Durkheim, "La sociologie en France au XIXᵉ siècle (1900)," in *La science sociale et l'action*, Paris, Presses Universitaires de France, 1970, pp. 111–36.

20. Wolf Lepenies, *Das Ende der Naturgeschichte*, Frankfurt, Suhrkamp, 1978.

21. J. D. Y. Peel, *Herbert Spencer: The Evolution of a Sociologist*, London, Heineman, 1971; Mark Francis, *Herbert Spencer and the Invention of Modern Life*, Ithaca, NY, Cornell University Press, 2007; Mike Hawkins, *Social Darwinism in European and American Thought, 1860–1945*, Cambridge: Cambridge University Press, 1997.

22. For one of the earliest uses of the term in the latter sense, see François Barrier, *Principes de sociologie*, 2 vols., Paris, Noirot, 1867. Barrier was a medical doctor specializing in childhood diseases who became a follower of Fourier and edited the Fourierist journal *La science sociale* (1867–70). Another of the earliest sociological book publications is Charles de Laval d'Arlempde, *Essai de sociologie*, Roanne, Imprimerie Vignal, 1872, which is a philosophical essay arguing that liberty and authority presuppose each other.

23. On the reception of Spencer in France, see Daniel Becquemont and Laurent Mucchielli, *Le cas Spencer*, Paris, Presses Universitaires de France, 1998.

24. This corpus of publications, based on the bibliographical catalogue of Otto Lorenz, is analyzed in Sébastien Mosbah-Natanson, *La sociologie est à la mode: Productions et producteurs de sociologie autour de 1900*, Thèse de doctorat, Université Paris-Dauphine, 2007.

25. Émile Littré, "De la condition essentielle qui sépare la sociologie de la biologie (1868)," in *La science au point de vue philosophique*, Paris, Didier, 1873, pp. 348–75.

26. Émile Littré, "Plan d'un traité de sociologie," in *La philosophie positive*, 1872, vol. 9, pp. 153–60.

27. Starting like Comte from the distinction between statics and dynamics, Littré divided sociology into two main branches, *sociodynamie* (dynamics) and *sociomérie* (statics). *Sociodynamie* was further divided into two parts, one concerned with maintaining society (*socioergie*), the other with its evolution (*sociauxie*). These subdivisions, which corresponded to chapters and chapter subheadings in the treatise he announced, were themselves subdivided once more. At the end of the outline, he added a third main branch—on social disturbances or pathology, to be called *sociotaraxie*—to the fundamental distinction between *sociodynamie* and *sociomérie*.

28. On Littré's network and his Société de sociologie, see Johan Heilbron, "Sociology and Positivism in the Nineteenth Century: The Vicissitudes of the Société de sociologie (1872–1874)," *History of the Human Sciences* 22, no. 4, 2009, 30–62.

29. Émile Littré, "De la méthode en sociologie," in *La philosophie positive*, 1870, vol. 6, pp. 291–301.

30. Claude Nicolet, *L'idée républicaine en France 1792–1924*, Paris, Gallimard, 1982, p. 225; and Nicolet, "Littré et la République," *Revue de synthèse*, nos. 106–8, 1982, 463–96.

31. Christian Topalov (ed.), *Laboratoires du nouveau siècle: La nébuleuse réformatrice et ses réseaux en France, 1880–1914*, Paris, Éditions de l'EHESS, 1999.

32. Marie-Claude Blais, *La solidarité: Histoire d'une idée*, Paris, Gallimard, 2007.

33. Frédéric Le Play, "Instruction sur la méthode d'observation dite des monographies de famille (1862)," republished in *Les études sociales*, nos. 131–32, 2000, 203–21.

34. F. Le Play, *Les ouvriers européens: Études sur les travaux, la vie domestique et la condition morale des populations ouvrières de l'Europe*, Paris, Imprimerie Impériale, 1855, pp. 293–94.

35. Ibid., p. 294.

36. Anthony Lorry, "Les monographies des *Ouvriers européens* (1855 et 1877–79) et des *Ouvriers des deux mondes* (1857–1930)," *Les études sociales*, nos. 131–133, 2000, 93–145; Stéphane Baciocchi and Jérôme David (éd.), "Frédéric Le Play, anthologie et correspondance," *Les études sociales*, nos. 142–144, 2005–2006; Antoine Savoye and Fabien Cardoni (éd), *Frédéric Le Play: Parcours, audience, héritage*, Paris, Mines Presses, 2007; Antoine Savoye and Frédéric Audren (éd.), *Naissance de l'ingénieur social: Frédéric Le Play et ses élèves*, Paris, Presses de l'École des mines, 2008.

37. Antoine Savoye, "Les paroles et les actes: Les dirigeants de la Société d'économie sociale, 1883–1914," in Christian Topalov (éd.), *Laboratoires du nouveau siècle*, Paris, Éditions de l'ÉHESS, 1999, pp. 61–87.

38. Antoine, Savoye, "Les continuateurs de Le Play au tournant du siècle," *Revue française de sociologie* 22, no. 3, 1981, 315–44.

39. Marie Ymonet, "Les héritiers du Capital: L'invention du marxisme en France au lendemain de la Commune," *Actes de la recherche en sciences sociales* 55, 1984, 3–14; and the special issue "Réceptions de Marx en Europe avant 1914," *Cahiers d'histoire: Revue d'histoire critique*, no. 114, 2011.

40. Joseph Llobera, "Marx's Social Theory and the Durkheimian School," *Études durkheimiennes* 6, 1981, 7–16.

41. Janet Horne, *A Social Laboratory for Modern France: The Musée Social and the Rise of the Welfare State*, Durham, NC, Duke University Press, 2002.

42. Vincent Goulet, "'Transformer la société par l'enseignement social': La trajectoire de Dick May entre littérature, sociologie et journalism," *Revue d'histoire des sciences humaines*, no. 19, 2008, 117–42.

3. Sociology and Other Disciplines in the Making

1. This analytical scheme of a two-front struggle of the younger members of the professoriate differs, for example, from Laurent Mucchielli's analysis. In his view physical anthropology was the dominant paradigm in the human sciences and sociology arose primarily as a critical reaction to that. Both assertions, however, can be questioned. It was the Academy of Moral and Political Sciences rather than the Academy or Faculty of Medicine that dominated the human sciences in the mid-nineteenth century, and the first university sociologists were not generally opposed to naturalist and organicist approaches (neither Espinas nor Worms were opposed). See Laurent Mucchielli, *La découverte du social*, Paris, La Découverte, 1998. On the notion of two-front strata that Elias uses in his analysis of the French nobility, see Norbert Elias, *The Court Society*, vol. 2 of the *Collected Works*, Dublin, UCD Press, pp. 280–82.

2. The philosopher Ribot typically presented his favorite British authors (Mill, Bain, Spencer) not merely as the most advanced but also as essentially independent of Comte and the French positivists, who in academic circles were hopelessly discredited. See L. Dugas, *La philosophie de Théodule Ribot*, Paris, Payot, 1924, pp. 41–42.

3. William Keylor, *Academy and Community: The Foundation of the French Historical Profession*, Cambridge, MA, Harvard University Press, 1975, p. 54; Pim den Boer, *History as a Profession: The Study of History in France, 1818–1914*, Princeton, NJ, Princeton University Press, 1998.

4. On philosophy, see Jean-Louis Fabiani, *Les philosophes de la République*, Paris, Minuit, 1988.

5. Grégoire Wyrouboff, "Compte rendu de la *Revue philosophique*," *La philosophie positive*, vol. 16, 1876, pp. 468–69.

6. Théodule Ribot, "Philosophy in France," *Mind*, vol. 2, 1877, pp. 366–86. In a letter Ribot called his article a "pamphlet" in which spiritualism was "lashed." See Ribot's letter to Espinas, *Revue philosophique* 87, 1962, 338.

7. For the origins of Ribot's project, see his letters to Espinas (1867–1875) in the *Revue philosophique*, no. 1, 1957, 1–14; Jacqueline Thirard, "La fondation de la "Revue philosophique," *La Revue philosophique*, no. 4, 1976, 401–13; Laurent Mucchielli, "Les débuts de la psychologie universitaire," in Mucchielli, *Mythes et histoire des sciences humaines*, Paris, La Découverte, 2004, pp. 199–232.

8. Ribot letter to Espinas, February 26, 1880, *Revue philosophique* 95, 1970, 170.

9. Jacqueline Carroy, Annick Ohayon, and Régine Plas, *Histoire de la psychologie en France, XIXᵉ–XXᵉ siècles*, Paris, La Découverte, 2006.

10. The numerical values in these tables are no more than rough indications. What is indexed as sociology, for example, includes reviews of books about the social question as well as essays on issues of the day. The numbers illustrate that once sociology has become a legitimate scholarly category, many publications are categorized as "sociological" that would previously have been placed elsewhere. Although the presence of psychology and sociology in the *Revue philosophique* was quite significant, the subjects philosophers chose for their more career-sensitive doctorates were far more traditional: a bit less than 4 percent of the doctorates between 1870 and 1914 had a sociological theme and slightly less than 10 percent concerned experimental psychology. See Fabiani, *Philosophes de la République*, p. 85.

11. For this theme, see Fabiani, *Philosophes de la République*, pp. 119–57.

12. On Espinas, see John Brooks III, *The Eclectic Legacy: Academic Philosophy and the Human Sciences in Nineteenth-Century France*, Newark, University of Delaware Press, 1998, pp. 97–133.

13. Alfred Espinas, "Etre ou ne pas être, ou du postulat de la sociologie," *Revue philosophique* 51, 1901, 449–80.

14. Alfred Espinas, *Des sociétés animales: Essai de psychologie comparée*, Paris, Germer Ballière, 1878; Espinas, "Les études sociologiques en France," *Revue philosophique*, vol. 13, 1882, 565–607, and vol. 14, 1882, 337–67 and 509–28. The issue of social cohesion or "solidarity" was debated in both the life sciences and the human sciences. See Marie-Claude Blais, *La solidarité: Histoire d'une idée*, Paris, Gallimard, 2007.

15. Alfred Fouillée, "Vues synthétiques sur la sociologie," *Revue philosophique*, vol. 9, 1880, 369–96.

16. Alfred Fouillé, *La science sociale contemporaine*, Paris, Hachette, 1880.

17. Théodule Ribot, "Lettre à Espinas, le 17 juin 1880," *Revue philosophique* 95, 1970, 170. Letourneau was a financially independent doctor who never practiced medicine and became a prolific writer on the evolution of human customs and social institutions.

18. Alfred Espinas, review of Guarin de Vitry, *Revue philosophique*, vol. 1, 1876, 97–102; Ribot's reviews of Espinas, *Revue philosophique*, vol. 4, 1877, 327–34, and vol. 7, 1879, 88–90; C. H., review of P. von Lilienfeld, *Revue philosophique*, vol. 6, 1878, 93–105; E. Colsenet's review of Roberty, *Revue philosophique*, vol. 11, 1881, 68–77; F. Paulhan on Letourneau, *Revue philosophique*, vol. 11, 1881, 546–55; P.T. on Bresson, *Revue philosophique*, vol. 12, 1881, 92–94; J. Delboeuf on Le Bon, *Revue philosophique*, vol. 12, 1881, 433–37.

19. Letter of Ribot to Espinas, March 15, 1873, in *Revue philosophique* 82, 1957, 10.

20. Daniel Becquemont and Laurent Mucchielli, *Le cas Spencer*, Paris, Presses Universitaires de France, 1998, pp. 239–42.

21. For academic support of Fouillée's position, see E. Beaussire, "La morale laïque, examen de la morale évolutionniste de M. Herbert Spencer," in *Séances et travaux de l'Académie des sciences morales et politiques*, 1881, 491–540.

22. Académie des sciences morales et politiques, *Concours de l'Académie*, Paris, Imprimerie nationale, 1901, p. 121.

23. *Séances et travaux de l'Académie des sciences morales et politiques* 122, 1884, 905.

24. L. Wuarin, *Examen critique des principes et des fondements sur lesquels reposent les théories désignées de nos jours sous le nom de sociologie*, 1885, manuscript, 443 pages, carton 93, Manuscrits des concours, Archives de l'Institut de France.

25. Dr. Bazalgette, Review of A. Espinas, *Des sociétés animales*, in *Revue occidentale* 2, 1879, 260–76.

26. Charles Robin and Grégoire Wyrouboff, "Déclaration," *La philosophie positive*, vol. 31, 1883, pp. 321–33.

27. Jean-Marie Guyau, who was Fouillée's stepson, died prematurely in 1888 at the age of thirty-three. He published widely noted studies on art and religion, coined the term "anomie," and was about the only sociologist Nietzsche appreciated.

28. On the journal and the group around it, see Stéphan Soulié, *Les philosophes en République*, Rennes, Presses Universitaires de Rennes, 2009.

29. Mucchielli, *Découverte du social*, p. 111.

30. In addition to Mucchielli's book, see Victor Karady, "Durkheim, les sciences socials et l'université," *Revue française de sociologie* 17, no. 2, 1976, 267–311; Terry N. Clark, *Prophets and Patrons: The French University and the Emergence of the Social Sciences*, Cambridge, MA, Harvard University Press, 1973; Roger Geiger, "The Development of French Sociology, 1871–1905," PhD thesis, University of Michigan, 1972.

31. The articles on "belief and desire" (1880) were republished in *Essais et mélanges sociologiques*, Lyon, A. Storck, 1895, pp. 235–308; his work on economic psychology became *La psychologie économique*, Paris, Alcan, 1902.

32. Gabriel Tarde, "Qu'est-ce qu'une société?," *Revue philosophique*, vol. 18, 1884, 489–510, republished as the second chapter of *Les lois de l'imitation*, Paris, Alcan, 1890. On Tarde, see Jean Milet, *Gabriel Tarde et la philosophie de l'histoire*, Paris, Vrin, 1970; Ian Lubek, "Histoire de psychologies perdues: Le cas de Gabriel Tarde," *Revue française de sociologie* 22, no. 3, 1981, 361–95.

33. Tarde, *Lois de l'imitation*, p. 55.

34. Gabriel Tarde, "Darwinisme naturel et darwinisme social," *Revue philosophique*, vol. 17, 1884, 607–37.

35. Louise Salomon, "Gabriel Tarde et la société parisienne à la fin du XIXe siècle," *Revue d'histoire des sciences humaines*, no. 13, 2005, 127–40. On Tarde's lesser reputation in university circles, see Philippe Besnard, "The *Année sociologique* Team," in Philippe Besnard (ed.), *The Sociological Domain: The Durkheimians and the Founding of French Sociology*, Cambridge, Cambridge University Press, Paris, Éditions de la MSH, 1983, p. 21.

36. See the 1903 public debate between Durkheim and Tarde in Émile Durkheim, *Textes*, Paris, Minuit, 1975, vol. 1, pp. 160–65. On their controversy, see Steven Lukes, *Emile Durkheim: His Life and Work*, Harmondsworth, UK, Penguin Books, 1973, pp. 302–13; Philippe Besnard, "Durkheim critique de Tarde," in Massimo Borlandi and Laurent Mucchielli (eds.), *La sociologie et sa methode: Les Règles de Durkheim un siècle après*, Paris, L'Harmattan, 1995, pp. 221–43.

37. See the judgments in Dirk Käsler, *Sociological Adventures: Earle Edward Eubank's Visits with European Sociologists*, New Brunswick, NJ, Transaction Publishers, 1991, pp. 116 and 124.

38. After having entered the École normale in 1887, Worms obtained the *agrégation* in philosophy (1890) and political economy (1897), and acquired PhDs in law (1891), political economy (1896), and philosophy (1896), to which he later added a doctorate in the life sciences, *sciences naturelles* (1912).

39. Rachel Vanneuville, "Le droit administratif comme savoir de gouvernement?: René Worms et le conseil d'État," *Revue française de science politique* 53, no. 2, 2003, 219–35.

40. Käsler, *Sociological Adventures*, p. 135.

41. Jean Milet, *Gabriel Tarde et la philosophie de l'histoire*, Paris, Vrin, 1970, p. 33.

42. René Worms, "Après dix ans," *Revue internationale de sociologie* 11, no. 1, 1903, 2.

43. On Worms's enterprises, see Roger Geiger, "René Worms, l'organicisme et l'organisation de la sociologie," *Revue française de sociologie* 22, no. 3, 1981, 345–60; Terry Clark, *Prophets and Patrons*, pp. 147–54.

44. "Notre programme," *Revue internationale de sociologie* 1, no. 1, 1893, 1–3.

45. Of the 135 authors who during the first decade contributed at least one article to the *Revue internationale de sociologie*, 63 percent were French. See Sébastien Mosbah-Natanson,

"Internationalisme et tradition nationale: Le cas de la constitution de la sociologie française autour de 1900," *Revue d'histoire des sciences humaines*, no. 18, 2008, 35–62.

46. Marcel Bernès didn't write a PhD dissertation and continued to teach philosophy in secondary education; Guillaume Duprat became a professor of sociology in Geneva in 1922. See Geiger, "René Worms."

47. Whereas the majority of contributors to Worms's journal were French (63 percent), Frenchmen represented only a minority (16.6 percent) among the members of the Institut international. The 229 members of the association up to the First World War came from France (38), Britain (34), Italy (33), Germany (19), Russia (15), United States (14), Belgium (14), Spain (13), Austria (9), Hungary (7), Switzerland (6), other European countries (16), South America (9), and Asia Minor (2). See Christian Fleck, *Transatlantische Bereicherungen: Zur Erfindung der empirischen Sozialforschung*, Frankfurt, Suhrkamp, 2007, p. 49.

48. Ulrike Schuerkens, "Les congrès de l'Institut international de sociologie de 1894 à 1930 et l'internationalisation de la sociologie," *International Review of Sociology* 6, no. 1, 1996, 7–24.

49. Quoted in Geiger, "René Worms," p. 354.

50. Robert Michels, "Le 2ᵉ congrès des sociologues allemands à Berlin," *Revue internationale de sociologie*, décembre 1912, 827–31.

51. The Institut international published fourteen volumes of the *Annales de l'Institut international de sociologie* between 1895 and 1913.

52. Anne Rasmussen, *L'internationale scientifique (1890–1914)*, Thèse de doctorat, 2 vols., Paris, École des hautes études en sciences sociales, 1995, p. 410.

53. Clark, *Prophets and Patrons*, p. 153.

54. On Durkheim, see Lukes, *Émile Durkheim*; and Marcel Fournier, *Émile Durkheim (1858–1917)*, Paris, Fayard, 2007.

55. On Renouvier, see Marie-Claude Blais, *Au principe de la République: Le cas Renouvier*, Paris, Gallimard, 2000.

56. For Durkheim's program, see Johan Heilbron, "Ce que Durkheim doit à Comte," in Philippe Besnard, Massimo Borlandi, and Paul Vogt (eds.), *Division du travail et lien social: La thèse de Durkheim un siècle après*, Paris: Presses Universitaires de France, 1993, pp. 59–66. For some of the ill-defined issues of his early work, see Lukes, *Émile Durkheim*, pp. 93–94.

57. Émile Durkheim, "Organisation et vie du corps social selon Schaeffle (1885)," in Durkheim, *Textes*, vol. 1, pp. 355–77.

58. Giovanni Paoletti, *Durkheim et la philosophie*, Paris, Garnier, 2012, pp. 401–21. On the centrality of Boutroux in the network of philosophers, see Randall Collins, *The Sociology of Philosophies*, Cambridge, MA, The Belknap Press, 1998, pp. 759–63.

59. Émile Durkheim, "Cours de science sociale (1887)," in Émile Durkheim, *La science sociale et l'action*, Paris, Presses Universitaires de France, 1970, p. 83.

60. Émile Durkheim, "Lettre au Directeur de la Revue néo-scolastique (1907)," in Durkheim, *Textes*, vol. 1, pp. 402–5.

61. Durkheim, "Cours de science sociale (1887)," pp. 89–90.

62. Émile Durkheim, "La science sociale selon De Greef (1886)," in Durkheim, *Textes*, vol. 1, p. 39.

63. Durkheim, "Cours de science sociale (1887)," p. 106.

64. For positive as well as critical judgments of early sociologists, see Lukes, *Émile Durkheim*, pp. 82–90. Durkheim's call for empirically investigating well-defined sociological problems was encouraged, in particular, by Claude Bernard's work on the experimental method in medicine and by Ribot's writings on experimental psychology. Durkheim characteristically advised Mauss in 1890 to read the books Ribot published in the 1870s about experimental psychology in Britain and Germany: "As Durkheim had been between 1881 and 1886, I was conquered." See Marcel Mauss, "Th. Ribot et les sociologies (1939)," in M. Mauss, Oeuvres, Paris, Minuit, 1969, vol. 3, pp. 565–67.

65. Durkheim's use of terms and arguments from organicist theories, therefore, is insufficient proof that he was an organicist. His appreciation is always conditional and premised

on his more fundamental argument about the sui generis character of human societies and the corresponding autonomy of sociology.

66. Émile Durkheim, "La sociologie en France au XIXᵉ siècle (1900)," in Durkheim, *Science sociale et l'action*, p. 130.

67. Émile Durkheim, "Les études de science sociale (1886)," in Durkheim, *Science sociale et l'action*, p. 214.

68. Durkheim used these last terms in his preface to the *Année sociologique*. See Émile Durkheim, "Préface (1898)," in Émile Durkheim, *Journal sociologique*, Paris, Presses Universitaires de France, 1969, p. 36.

69. Émile Durkheim, *Montesquieu et Rousseau, précurseurs de la sociologie* (1892), Paris, Rivière, 1966, p. 25.

70. Émile Durkheim, "La sociologie en France au XIXe siècle (1900)," in Durkheim, *Science sociale et l'action*, pp. 111–36. See also Mosbah-Natanson, "Internationalisme et tradition nationale," pp. 35–62.

71. On his Bordeaux courses, see Fournier, *Émile Durkheim*, pp. 124–25.

72. For a guide through the secondary literature on Durkheim, see the journal *Durkheimian Studies/Études durkheimiennes*, published since 1995 by the Oxford Centre of Durkheimian Studies. The original *Études durkheimiennes* was founded by Philippe Besnard in 1977 and taken over by Robert Alan Jones in 1987. For a recent overview in English of contemporary debates, see Jeffrey Alexander and Philip Smith (eds.), *The Cambridge Companion to Durkheim*, Cambridge, Cambridge University Press, 2005.

73. Yves Goudineau, "Évolution sociale, histoire, et études des sociétés anciennes dans la tradition durkheimienne," in *Historiens et sociologues aujourd'hui: Journées d'études annuelles de la Société française de sociologie 1984*, Paris, Éditions du Centre national de la recherche scientifique, 1986, pp. 37–48.

74. Émile Durkheim, "Lettre à Marcel Mauss, le 18 juin 1894," in Émile Durkheim, *Lettres à Marcel Mauss*, Paris, Presses Universitaires de France, 1998, pp. 34–36.

75. Émile Durkheim, "Lettre à Gabriel Tarde, le 31 mars 1895," *Durkheimian Studies/Études durkheimiennes*, vol. 6, 1994, p. 11.

76. The first issue of the *Année* opened with a learned, 70-page article by Durkheim on the origins of the prohibition of incest. The debate about the rupture in Durkheim's work has, I think, too one-sidedly focused on the consequences of Durkheim's 1894–1895 lecture course on religion. On this new role of religion and Durkheim's redefinition of sociology, see Bernard Lacroix, *Durkheim et le politique*, Paris, Presses de la Fondation national des sciences politiques, 1981; Philippe Besnard, *L'anomie, ses usages et ses fonctions*, Paris, Presses Universitaires de France, 1987, pp. 132–39.

77. Louis Pinto, *La théorie souveraine*, Paris, Éditions du Cerf, 2009, p. 48.

78. Émile Durkheim, *The Rules of Sociological Method*, London, The MacMillan Press, 1982, p. 48. On the origins, interpretation, and reception of the *Rules*, see Borlandi and Mucchielli, *Sociologie et sa méthode*.

79. Émile Durkheim, *On Suicide* (1897), London, Penguin Books, 2006, p. 143.

80. On integration and regulation as independent variables, see Besnard, *L'anomie*, pp. 70–74.

81. Durkheim, *Lettres à Marcel Mauss*, p. 77.

82. Ibid., p. 78.

83. Gaston Richard, Review of "É. Durkheim, *Le suicide*," *Année sociologique* 1, 1998, 397–406.

84. Philippe Besnard, "La destinée du *Suicide*," in Massimo Borlandi and Mohamed Cherkaoui (eds.), *"Le suicide," un siècle après Durkheim*, Paris, Presses Universitaires de France, 2000, pp. 185–218; W. S. F. Pickering and Geoffrey Walford (eds.), *Durkheim's "Suicide": A Century of Research and Debate*, New York, Routledge, 2000.

85. Dominique Merllié, "L'enquête autour de 1900: La non-participation des durkheimiens à une mode intellectuelle," *Mil neuf cent*, no. 22, 2005, 133–54.

86. Durkheim, *Rules*, p. 163.

87. Émile Durkheim, *De la division du travail social* (1893), Paris, Presses Universitaires de France, 1973, p. xxxix.

88. Gérard Noiriel considers Durkheim the first great "specific intellectual" in France; see G. Noiriel, *Les fils maudits de la République*, Paris, Fayard, 2005, p. 209.

89. Émile Durkheim, "L'individualisme et les intellectuels (1898)," in Durkheim, *Science sociale et l'action*, pp. 261–78.

90. On the *Année*, see Besnard, "*Année sociologique* Team," pp. 11–39; See also Fournier, *Émile Durkheim*, pp. 329–63. On the Durkheim school as a social movement, see Randall Collins, "The Durkheimian Movement in France and in World Sociology," in Alexander and Smith, *Cambridge Companion to Durkheim*, pp. 101–35.

91. Émile Durkheim, "Lettre au Président de la Sociological Society de Londres (1904)," in Durkheim, *Textes*, vol. 1, p. 169.

92. Émile Durkheim, "Letter to Bouglé, 24 March 1896," in Besnard, *Sociological Domain*, p. 42.

93. The nineteen most productive collaborators (out of a total of forty-six) comprise all those who contributed 1 percent or more of the reviews. See Philippe Steiner, *La sociologie de Durkheim*, Paris, La Découverte, 1994, p. 11.

94. On the comparative properties of these networks, see Victor Karady, *Stratification intellectuelle, rapports sociaux et institutionnalisation: Enquête socio-historique sur la naissance de la discipline sociologique en France*, Paris, Centre de sociologie européenne, 1974; Karady, "Durkheim, les sciences sociales et l'université: Bilan d'un semi-échec," *Revue française de sociologie* 17, no. 2, 1976, 267–311. Clark's data indicate an even lower percentage of the collaborators of Worms's journal at the Faculty of Letters. See Terry N. Clark, "Marginality, Eclecticism, and Innovation: René Worms and the *Revue internationale de sociologie* from 1893 to 1914," *Revue internationale de sociologie*, series 2, no. 3, 1967, 12–27.

95. Durkheim's remark that "sociology should be done sociologically" is reported by Lapie; see Paul Lapie, "Letter to Bouglé, 14 March 1897," in Besnard, *Sociological Domain*, p. 63.

96. On the various socialist groups, see Christophe Prochasson, *Les intellectuels, le socialisme et la guerre, 1900–1938*, Paris, Seuil, 1993.

97. Durkheim, *Lettres à Marcel Mauss*, p. 87.

98. Durkheim, "Préface (1898)," pp. 31–36.

99. Émile Durkheim, "Lettres à Henri Hubert," *Revue française de sociologie* 28, 1987, 483–534 (p. 513). For similar instructions to Mauss, see Durkheim, *Lettres à Marcel Mauss*, pp. 57–58, 68, 75.

100. Durkheim, "Lettres à Henri Hubert," p. 514.

101. In addition to Besnard, *Sociological Domain*, see Victor Karady, "Stratégies de réussite et modes de faire-valoir de la sociologie chez les durkheimiens," *Revue française de sociologie* 20, no. 1, 1979, 49–82; and Philippe Besnard (ed.), "Le centenaire de *l'Année sociologique*," *Année sociologique* 48, no. 1, 1998, 9–25.

102. Victor Karady, "Durkheim et les débuts de l'ethnologie universitaire," *Actes de la recherche en sciences sociales* 74, 1988, 23–32.

103. Pierre Favre, "The Absence of Political Sociology in the Durkheimian Classifications of the Social Sciences," in Besnard, *Sociological Domain*, pp. 199–216. The virtual absence of physical anthropology in the *Année sociologique* was another significant feature of the *Année*. See Mucchielli, *Mythes et histoire des sciences humaines*, pp. 163–98.

104. Victor Karady, "The Durkheimians in Academe," in Besnard, *Sociological Domain*, pp. 71–89.

105. Jennifer Mergy, "On Durkheim and *Notes critiques*," *Durkheimian Studies/Études durkheimiennes* 4, 1998, 1–7.

106. Besnard, "*Année sociologique* Team," p. 32.

107. Victor Karady, *Stratification intellectuelle*, p. 92.

108. Émile Durkheim and Marcel Mauss, "Note sur la notion de civilisation (1913)," in Durkheim, *Journal sociologique*, pp. 681–85.

109. Émile Durkheim, "Letter to François Simiand, 15 February 1902," in Besnard, *Sociological Domain*, p. 56.

110. Marcel Mauss, "An Intellectual Self-Portrait," in Besnard, *Sociological Domain*, p. 139.

111. George Weisz, "The Republican Ideology and the Social Sciences," in Besnard, *Sociological Domain*, pp. 90–119.

112. For the relations of Durkheimian sociology to philosophy, history and economics, see Jean-Louis Fabiani, "Métaphysique, morale, sociologie," *Revue de métaphysique et de morale*, nos. 1–2, 1993, 175–91; Louis Pinto, *La théorie souveraine: Les philosophes français et la sociologie au XXe siècle*, Paris, Éditions du CERF, 2009; Robert Leroux, *Histoire et sociologie en France*, Paris, Presses Universitaires de France, 1998; Philippe Steiner, *L'école durkheimienne et l'économie*, Genève, Droz, 2005.

113. Émile Worms, "Le tellurisme social," *Séances et travaux de l'Académie des sciences morales et politiques*, 1899, 409–55 (p. 433).

114. Lester Ward, "Sociology at the Paris Exposition of 1900," quoted in *International Encyclopedia of the Social Sciences*, Second edition, ed. by David Sills, "sociology."

115. See *International Encyclopedia of the Social and Behavioral Sciences*, 2nd edition, ed. by James Wright, "sociology, history of."

4. The Metamorphoses of Durkheimian Scholarship

1. Marcel Mauss, "An Intellectual Self-Portrait," in Philippe Besnard (ed.), *The Sociological Domain*, Cambridge, Cambridge University Press, 1983, p. 141.

2. On the Granet's exemplary role, see Georges Dumézil, "Préface," in Marcel Granet, *La religion des chinois*, Paris, Payot, 1980, pp. v–viii; Claude Lévi-Strauss, *De près et de loin*, Paris, Seuil, 1990, pp. 140–41.

3. Victor Karady, "Durkheim, les sciences sociales et l'université: Bilan d'un semi-échec," *Revue française de sociologie* 17, no. 2, 1976, 267–311. The present chapter is an updated and abridged version of Johan Heilbron, "Les métamorphoses du durkheimisme, 1920–1940," *Revue française de sociologie* 26, no. 2, 1985, 203–37.

4. To be more precise: the Bordeaux chair was held by Gaston Richard (to 1930), Max Bonnafous (1930–40), and Jean Stoetzel (1945–55); the Strasbourg chair by Maurice Halbwachs (1919–35), Georges Gurvitch (1935–40, 1944–48), and Georges Duveau (1948–58). One of the Sorbonne chairs was held by Paul Fauconnet (1921–38), Halbwachs (1939–40), and Albert Bayet (1940, 1944–48), the other by Bouglé (1908–15, 1919–35, 1937–39), Halbwachs (1935–37), Bayet (1939–40), Halbwachs (1940–44), and Georges Davy (1944–55). The Strasbourg chair was created to compensate for the loss of the "social philosophy" chair in Toulouse, held first by Bouglé (1898–1908), then Paul Fauconnet (1908–21), then changed into a chair of "moral philosophy and education."

5. Roger Lacombe, *La méthode sociologique de Durkheim*, Paris, Alcan, 1926, p. 1.

6. Guillaume Duprat, "Rôle de l'Institut international de sociologie dans la coopération intellectuelle," in C. Bouglé et al., *Les convergences des sciences sociales et l'esprit international*, Paris, P. Hartmann, 1938, pp. 48–55.

7. Achille Ouy, "Les sociologies et les sociologues: Des querelles d'écoles à l'unité de la science, *Revue internationale de sociologie* 46, 1938, 595–642; 47, 1939, 245–75 and 463–91.

8. On the Institut français de sociologie, see Johan Heilbron, "Note sur l'Institut français de sociologie (1924–1962)," *Études durkheimiennes* 9, 1983, 9–14.

9. Lucien Lévy-Bruhl, *History of Modern Philosophy in France*, Chicago, Open Court Publishing, 1899, p. 463.

10. Dominique Parodi, *La philosophie contemporaine en France: Essai de classification des doctrines*, Paris, Alcan, 1919, p. 495.

11. Ibid., p. 157.

12. Ibid., p. 160.

13. Émile Bréhier, *Transformation de la philosophie française*, Paris, Flammarion, 1950, p. 49.

14. Célestin Bouglé, *Les maîtres de la philosophie universitaire en France*, Paris, Maloine, 1937, p. 98.

15. H.-C. Puech and P. Vignaux, "La science des religions," in C. Bouglé et al., *Les sciences sociales en France: Enseignement et recherche*, Paris, P. Hartmann, 1937, pp. 134–62.

16. J. Lambert, "Les relations internationales," in Bouglé et al., *Sciences sociales en France*, pp. 302–23.

17. "Notre programme," *Année politique française et étrangère* 1, 1925, 1–13.

18. See Serge Berstein, *Histoire du parti radical*, 2 vols., Paris, Presses de la Fondation nationale des sciences politiques, 1980, 1982.

19. Célestin Bouglé, "Comment étudier la sociologie à Paris?," *Annales de l'Université de Paris* 2, 1927, 313–24.

20. Célestin Bouglé, "Introduction," in Bouglé et al., *Convergences des sciences sociales*, pp. 11–29.

21. Fourteen of Halbwachs's other articles were published in philosophy journals, five in history journals, four in statistical periodicals, and two in psychology reviews; distribution established on the basis of V. Karady and A. Thiébart's bibliography in M. Halbwachs, *Classes sociales et morphologie*, Paris, Éditions de Minuit, 1972, pp. 411–44; supplementary information in John Craig, "Maurice Halbwachs à Strasbourg," *Revue française de sociologie* 20, no. 2, 1979, 292. See also the special issue on Halbwachs of the *Revue d'histoire des sciences humaines*, no. 1, 1999.

22. Heilbron, "Note sur l'Institut français," 9–14.

23. Most of these reviews have now been published in Jennifer Mergy (ed.), "Mauss et les durkheimiens," *Année sociologique* 54, no. 1, 2004, 75–269.

24. Marcel Mauss, "La sociologie en France depuis 1914" (1933), in *Oeuvres*, vol. 3, Paris, Éditions de Minuit, 1969, p. 438.

25. Granet was one of Mauss's closest companions. See Philippe Besnard, "Un conflit au sein du groupe durkheimien," *Revue française de sociologie* 26, no. 2, 1985, 247–55.

26. Parodi was inspector general of education (1919–38) and president of the *agrégation* jury in philosophy. René Hubert was dean of the Faculty of Letters at Lille, rector of the University of Poitiers, and rector of the University of Strasbourg after World War II. Lapie was rector of the Academy of Toulouse before being appointed director of primary education in 1914. Davy not only taught at Dijon but was also dean of the faculty there (1922–30) and later became rector of the Academy of Rennes (1931–38), inspector general of public education (1938–44), and dean of the Sorbonne (1950–55); he remained president of the *agrégation* jury in philosophy for a record seventeen years (1940–56). Lastly, Bouglé was an extraordinary university administrator who simultaneously held numerous positions within and outside the university, the most important of which were vice director (1927) then director (1935–40) of the École normale supérieure.

27. Quotations are from the following accounts: Hubert Bourgin, *De Jaurès à Léon Blum: l'Ecole normale et la politique*, Paris, Fayard, 1938, pp. 468–70; *Bouglé, 1870–1940* (booklet published by the ENS shortly after his death, no date or editor); G. Davy, "Célestin Bouglé, 1870–1940," *Revue française de sociologie* 8, no. 1, 1967, 3–13; C. Rist, "C. Bouglé," *Revue d'économie politique* 54, 1940, 1–3; M. Halbwachs, "Célestin Bouglé, sociologue," *Revue de métaphysique et de morale* 48, 1941, 24–47.

28. Letter from E. Milhaud to M. Mauss (February 20, 1939); Archives of the Institut français d'histoire sociale (code 14 AS 388). My thanks to Bruce Thompson for making a copy of the letter available to me.

29. Quotations are from the following accounts: Bourgin, *De Jaurès à Léon Blum*, pp. 347–65; Maurice Halbwachs, "François Simiand," *Journal de la Société statistique de Paris* 76, 1935, 252–56; Charles Rist, "François Simiand (1875–1935)," *Revue d'économie politique* 49, 1935, 241–46. On Simiand, see Ludovic Frobert, *Le travail de François Simiand*, Paris, Economica, 2000.

30. Rist, "François Simiand (1875–1935)," p. 242.

31. Lucien Febvre, "François Simiand (1873–1935)," *Annales d'histoire économique et sociale* 7, 1935, 391.

32. For detailed accounts of the work of several Durkheimians, see Jean-Christophe Marcel, *Le durkheimisme dans l'entre-deux-guerres*, Paris, Presses Universitaires de France, 1987; Laurent Mucchielli, *Mythes et histories des sciences humaines*, Paris, La Découverte, 2004; Philippe Steiner, *Durkheim and the Birth of Economic Sociology*, Princeton, NJ, Princeton University Press, 2010.

33. Maurice Halbwachs, "La doctrine d'Émile Durkheim," *Revue philosophique*, vol. 43, 1918, 353–411 (354).

34. Marcel Mauss, "In memoriam (1925)," in *Oeuvres*, vol. 3, p. 477.

35. Marcel Granet, "La sociologie religieuse de Durkheim," *Europe* 86, 1930, 287–92.

36. Halbwachs, "Doctrine d'Émile Durkheim," p. 408.

37. Ibid., p. 407.

38. Marcel Mauss, "Rapports réels et pratiques de la psychologie et de la sociologie (1924)," in Mauss, *Sociologie et anthropologie*, Paris, Presses Universitaires de France, 1950, p. 284.

39. Marcel Mauss, "Fragment d'un plan de sociologie générale descriptive (1934)," in *Oeuvres*, vol. 3, p. 303.

40. Mauss, "In memoriam," p. 477.

41. Mauss, "Rapports réels et pratiques," p. 283.

42. Marcel Mauss, "Mentalité primitive et participation (1923)," in *Oeuvres*, vol. 2, pp. 126–27.

43. Mauss, "Fragment d'un plan de sociologie générale descriptive," p. 354.

44. Georges Davy, "Sur Durkheim," *Europe* 86, 1930, 284–87.

45. Georges Davy, *Emile Durkheim: Choix de textes avec une étude du système sociologique*, Paris, Louis-Michaud, 1911, p. 12.

46. Georges Davy, *Sociologues d'hier et d'aujourd'hui*, Paris, Alcan, 1931, p. 3.

47. Célestin Bouglé, "Préface," in E. Durkheim, *Sociologie and philosophie* (1924), Paris, Presses Universitaires de France, 1951, p. xv.

48. Parodi, *Philosophie contemporaine en France*, p. 452.

49. The discussion was published in full in the *Bulletin de la Société française de philosophie*, 1906, pp. 169–212.

50. Bouglé, "Préface," p. vi.

51. Célestin Bouglé, "Quelques souvenirs," *Europe* 86, 1930, 283.

52. Georges Davy, "Émile Durkheim: L'homme," *Revue de métaphysique et de morale* 26, 1919, 181–98 (198).

53. Halbwachs, "Doctrine d'Émile Durkheim," p. 392.

54. Georges Davy, "Émile Durkheim: L'oeuvre," *Revue de métaphysique et de morale* 27, 1920, 71–112.

55. Davy, "Célestin Bouglé, 1870–1940," pp. 3–13.

56. Paul Lapie, "Avant-propos," in Lapie, *Morale et science: Conférences faites à la Sorbonne*, Paris, F. Nathan, 1923, p. 30.

57. Célestin Bouglé, "La sociologie française et l'éducation nationale (1936)," in Bouglé, *Qu'est-ce que la sociologie?*, 7th ed., Paris, Alcan, 1939, pp. 163–74; Paul Fauconnet, "Introduction: L'oeuvre pédagogique de Durkheim," in É. Durkheim, *Education and sociologie*, Paris, Alcan, 1926, pp. 1–33 (p. 15).

58. This "resolution" (1926), is cited in the *Bulletin de l'Institut français de sociologie*, 1932, vol. 2, p. 95.

59. Mauss, "Note de méthode sur l'extention de la sociologie (1927)," in *Oeuvres*, vol. 3, p. 294. On the question of teaching sociology in the *écoles normales primaires*, cf. R. Geiger, "La sociologie dans les écoles normales primaires: Histoire d'une controverse," *Revue française de sociologie* 20, no. 2, 1979, 257–67. Contrary to Geiger's indications, however, not all the Durkheimians saw the undertaking in the same way, as is also indicated by the following comment by Henri Hubert: "Don't be overly concerned . . . about the difficulties that the new study program may involve. In the end, it all comes down to presenting the old traditional notions of family and civic morality in a new form" (see the account by Max Lazard in the *Bulletin de l'Institut français de sociologie*, 1932, col. 2, p. 119).

60. Raymond Lenoir, in *Bulletin de l'Institut français de sociologie*, 1932, vol. 2, p. 96.

61. Marcel Granet, in *Bulletin de l'Institut français de sociologie*, 1932, vol. 2, pp. 98–107.

62. Parodi, *Philosophie contemporaine en France*, p. 384.

63. Davy, *Sociologues d'hier et d'aujourd'hui*, p. 12.

64. Célestin Bouglé, *Leçons de sociologie sur l'évolution des valeurs*, Paris, A. Colin, 1922, p. 242.

65. Célestin Bouglé, "Sur les rapports de la sociologie avec la morale," *Revue pédagogique* 83, 1923, 157–77.

66. See Bouglé, *Leçons de sociologie sur l'évolution des valeurs*, p. 236; Albert Bayet, *La morale de la science*, Paris, Alcan, 1931; and Parodi's rejection of pragmatism in *Du positivisme à l'idéalisme*, Paris, Vrin, 1930, pp. 48–87.

67. On Lévi-Strauss's debt to Granet, see Yves Goudineau, "Lévi-Strauss, la Chine de Granet, l'ombre de Durkheim," *Cahiers de l'Herne*, Special issue on Lévi-Strauss, Paris, 2004, 165–78; François Héran, *Figures de la parenté*, Paris, Presses Universitaires de France, 2009.

68. The average age of the contributors rose continually—from forty-four (1905) to sixty (1935) for the *Revue philosophique* and from forty-three (1905) to sixty-two (1935) for the *Revue de métaphysique et de morale*. See W. P. Vogt, "Identifying Scholarly and Intellectual Communities: A Note on French Philosophy, 1900–1939," *History and Theory* 21, 1982, 267–78.

69. "La génération de 1930 est la génération du refus." See Michel Winock, *Histoire politique de la revue "Esprit," 1930–1950*, Paris, Seuil, 1975, p. 19; Jean-Louis Loubet del Bayle, *Les non-conformistes des années trente*, Paris, Seuil, 1969.

70. Denis de Rougemont, "Cahier de revendications," *Nouvelle revue française* 20, 1932, 51. See also J. Touchard, "L'esprit des années trente: Une tentative de renouvellement de la pensée politique française," in *Tendances politiques de la vie française depuis 1789*, Paris, Hachette, 1960, pp. 89–120. On the intellectual elite, see Jean-François Sirinelli, *Génération intellectuelle*, Paris, Presses Universitaires de France, 1994.

71. Roland Weil, *Le chômage de la jeunesse intellectuelle diplômée*, Paris, Recueil Sirey, 1937, p. 119.

72. On the import of phenomenology, see Louis Pinto, *La théorie souveraine*, Paris, Éditions du CERF, 2009, pp. 57–112; on Marxism, see Isabelle Gouarné, *L'introduction du marxisme en France: Philosoviétisme et sciences humaines, 1920–1939*, Rennes, Presses Universitaires de Rennes, 2013.

73. Isabelle Gouarné, "Engagement philosoviétique et posture sociologique dans l'entre-deux-guerres: Le rôle politico-intellectuel de Georges Friedmann," *Sociologie du travail* 54, 2012, 356–74.

74. Loïc Blondiaux, *La fabrique de l'opinion: Une histoire sociale des sondages*, Paris, Seuil, 1998.

75. Max Bonnafous and Marcel Déat were *normalien* philosophers who collaborated on the *Année sociologique* in 1925. Bonnafous planned to write a thesis on suicide. Although he was appointed to the Bordeaux chair in 1930, which he officially held until 1940, he did not produce significant sociological work and instead was cabinet secretary to government ministers in 1934, 1938, and 1940, and became a member of the Vichy government during the war. Déat published two textbooks, *Notions de sociologie* (1925) and, together with Bouglé, a *Guide de l'étudiant en sociologie* (1921), but didn't finish his PhD either and was primarily engaged in politics. After the Second World War he was sentenced to death for collaboration and fled to Italy. See Mathieu Desan and Johan Heilbron, "Young Durkheimians and the Temptation of Fascism: The Case of Marcel Déat" (working paper). For sociology under the Vichy regime, see Francine Muel-Dreyfus, "La rééducation de la sociologie sous Vichy," *Actes de la recherche en sciences sociales* 153, 2004, 65–77; and the special issue "Les sociologues sous Vichy," *Anamnèse*, no. 7, 2012.

76. Alexander Riley, "'Renegade Durkheimianism' and the Transgressive Left Sacred," in J. Alexander and P. Smith (eds.), *The Cambridge Companion to Durkheim*, Cambridge, Cambridge University Press, 2005, pp. 274–301.

77. Raymond Aron, *La sociologie allemande contemporaine*, Paris, PUF, 1950 (1935), p. 97.

78. "Keep in mind that the veterans were demanding positions, honors, compensations, glory, women . . . and that what they threw into the scales along with their demands for recognition of their suffering was the most narrow-minded type of patriotism, the most ridiculous conformism. Our hatred for the *Anciens Combattants* knew no bounds. . . ." H. Lefèbvre, *La somme et le reste* (1959), Lausanne, Bélibaste, 1973, p. 32.

79. Bouglé, *Leçons de sociologie sur l'évolution des valeurs*, p. 124.

80. Paul Nizan, *Les chiens de garde* (1932), Paris, François Maspero, 1976, p. 37.

81. On such a process of synchronisation, see Pierre Bourdieu, *La distinction: Critique sociale du jugement*, Paris, Editions de Minuit, 1979, p. 530.

82. Nizan, *Chiens de garde*, p. 97. Raymond Aron typically explained his "allergy" to Durkheimian sociology in similar terms; see R. Aron, *Mémoires: 50 ans de réflexion politique*, Paris, Julliard, 1983, p. 71.

83. Marcel Fournier, *Marcel Mauss*, Paris, Fayard, 1994.

84. Benoît de l'Estoile, *Le goût des autres: De l'exposition coloniale aux arts premiers*, Paris, Flammarion, 2007; Alice Conklin, *In the Museum of Man: Race, Anthropology, and Empire in France, 1850–1950*, Ithaca, NY, Cornell University Press, 2013.

85. J. E. Craig, "Maurice Halbwachs à Strasbourg," *Revue française de sociologie* 20, no. 1, 1979, 273–92 (288). A colleague of Halbwachs at the Sorbonne described him as "a very discreet man, not a good professor. He was very scholarly, very conscientious, but didn't have much success with students; he spoke rather slowly, in a low voice" (philosophy professor).

86. For the shifting choices of Sorbonne students, see the table in Johan Heilbron, "Les métamorphoses du durkheimisme," *Revue française de sociologie* 26, no. 2, 1985, 237.

87. Victor Karady, *Stratégie de carrière et hiérarchie des études chez les universitaires littéraires sous la Troisième République*, Paris, Centre de sociologie européenne, 1973, p. 31 (mimeographed).

88. Nizan, *Chiens de garde*, p. 95.

89. A hundred or so journals were available in the reading room, while the library supplied Bouglé with materials according to his interests. On the CDS, see Brigitte Mazon, "La création du Centre de documentation sociale," *Études durkheimiennes* 9, 1983, 15–20; Jean-Christophe Marcel, *Le durkheimisme dans l'entre-deux-guerres*, Paris, PUF, pp. 223–55.

90. On Rockefeller Foundation, see Brigitte Mazon, "L'intervention de la Fondation Rockefeller," *Revue française de sociologie* 26, 1985, 203–37; Ludovic Tournès, "La Fondation Rockefeller et la construction d'une politique des sciences sociales en France (1918–1940)," *Annales* 63, no. 8, 2008, 1371–1402.

91. E. Halévy et al., *Inventaires: La crise sociale et les idéologies nationales*, Paris, Alcan, 1936; R. Aron et al., *Inventaires II: L'économique et le politique*, Paris, Alcan, 1937; R. Aron et al., *Inventaires III: Classes moyennes*, Paris, Alcan, 1939.

92. Christophe Charle, *La république des universitaires, 1870–1940*, Paris, Seuil, pp. 355–57.

93. Letter from T. B. Kittredge to C. Bouglé, May 10, 1932 (Archives Nationales N 61 AJ 97).

94. Excerpt from report on first year of activity of the Conseil universitaire de la recherche sociale (Archives Nationales 61 AJ 100). See also P. Vaucher, "Le Conseil universitaire de la recherche sociale," *Annales de l'Université de Paris*, 1937, 58–65.

95. *Entretiens sur les sciences de l'homme*, Paris, Herman et Cie, 1937, pp. 1–3. On the ideas about economic planning and their criticism, see François Denord, *Néo-libéralisme version française*, Paris, Demopolis, 2007. On new forms of economic expertise, see Odile Henry, *Les guérisseurs de l'économie: Sociogenèse du métier de consultant (1900–1944)*, Paris, CNRS Éditions, 2012.

96. G. Friedmann, *Problèmes du machinisme en URSS et dans les pays capitalistes*, Paris, Éditions Sociales Internationales, 1934; R. Mauduit, *La réclame: Étude de sociologie économique*, Paris, Alcan, 1933; R. Polin and J.-G. Charon, *Les coopératives rurales et*

l'Etat en Tchécoslovaquie et en Roumanie, Paris, Alcan, 1934; R. Marjolin, *L'évolution du syndicalisme aux Etats-Unis: De Washington à Roosevelt*, Paris, Alcan, 1936.

97. Gabriel Le Bras, among several others, mentions the necessity of "local monographs" and "numerous collaborations" in his "Les transformations religieuses des campagnes françaises depuis la fin du XVIIe siècle," *Annales sociologiques*, E series, 1937, vol. 2, 15–70.

98. See, for example, Aron's review of P. Descamps, *La sociologie expérimentale* (1933), *Annales sociologiques*, A series, 1936, vol. 2, 90–92; the relevant paragraph by Bouglé in *Sciences sociales en France*, p. 24; R. Polin, "Monographie et synthèse d'après Le Play," in Bouglé et al., *Convergences des sciences sociales et l'esprit international*, pp. 246–51.

99. H. Mougin, "Un projet d'enquête sur les classes moyennes en France," *Inventaires III*, Paris, Alcan, 1939, p. 294.

100. René König, "Bilanz der französischen Soziologie um 1930 (1931-32)," republished in R. König, *Émile Durkheim zur Diskussion: Jenseits von Dogmatismus und Skepsis*, München, Carl Hanser Verlag, 1978, pp. 56–103.

101. Robert Merton, "Recent French Sociology," *Social Forces* 12, 1934, 537–45.

102. Patricia Madoo Lengermann, "The Founding of the *American Sociological Review*: The Anatomy of a Rebellion," *American Sociological Review* 44, 1979, 185–98; George Steinmetz, "American Sociology before and after World War Two: The (Temporary) Settling of a Disciplinary Field," in Craig Calhoun (ed.), *Sociology in America*, Chicago, University of Chicago Press, pp. 314–66.

103. Talcott Parsons, "The Prospects of Sociological Theory," *American Sociological Review* 15, 1950, 3–16.

5. Pioneers by Default?

1. For an early and very consistent expression of this view, see Jean Stoetzel, "Sociology in France: An Empiricist View," in H. Becker and A. Boskoff (eds.), *Modern Sociological Theory in Continuity and Change*, New York, The Dryden Press, 1957, pp. 623–57. On Stoetzel's own role in this process, see Loïc Blondiaux, *La fabrique de l'opinion*, Paris, Seuil, 1998; and Guillaume Stankiewicz, "Comment en finir avec une tradition dominante?: Rupture et continuité dans la trajectoire de Jean Stoetzel," *Revue d'histoire des sciences humaines* 18, 2008, 137–58.

2. This paragraph stems partly from an unpublished paper of mine written in Dutch, which was translated by Beverly Jackson.

3. J. W. Lapierre, "Vers une sociologie concrète?" *Esprit* 19, 1951, 720–30.

4. Jean-Marie Domenach, "Les intellectuels et le communisme," *Esprit* 23, 1955, 1200–1214.

5. Alain Touraine, *Un désir d'histoire*, Paris, Stock, 1977, p. 45.

6. Jean-Paul Sartre, *Situations* II, Paris, Gallimard, 1948, p. 45.

7. Pierre Bourdieu, *Sketch for a Self-Analysis*, Cambridge, Polity Press, 2007, p. 24.

8. Ibid.

9. Anna Boschetti, *Sartre et Les temps modernes*, Paris, Minuit, 1985, p. 18. On the literary field, see Gisèle Sapiro, *The French Writer's War, 1940–1953*, Durham, NC, Duke University Press, 2014.

10. Marvin Faber (ed.), *L'activité philosophique contemporaine en France et aux États-Unis*, Paris, Presses Universitaires de France, 1950.

11. Sartre, *Situations* II, p. 257.

12. Ibid., p. 13.

13. For these intellectual journals, see Boschetti, *Sartre et Les temps modernes*, pp. 185–220.

14. Jeannine Verdès-Leroux, *Au service du parti*, Paris, Fayard, 1983; Frédéric Matonti, *Intellectuels communistes*, Paris, La Découverte, 2005.

15. Sylvie Patron, *Critique (1946–1996), une encyclopédie de l'esprit moderne*, Paris, IMEC, 2000.

16. Sartre, *Situations* II, p. 26.

17. Jean-Paul Sartre, *Situations* III, Paris, Gallimard, 1949, p. 163.

18. Jean-Paul Sartre, *Situations* I, Paris, Gallimard, 1947, p. 186.

19. François Goguel, "L'orientation des sciences humaines en France," *Esprit* 15, 1946, 872–75; Anne-Marie Goguel, "Orientations des sciences sociales aux Etats-Unis," *Esprit* 21, 1953, 840–51.

20. Jeanine Verdes-Leroux, *Au service du parti*, Paris, Fayard, 1983, p. 252.

21. For this overview, I have relied on the analytical index of *Le monde*.

22. Jean Lacroix, "De la technocratie," *Le monde*, January 7, 1950.

23. On French planning, see François Fourquet, *Les comptes de la puissance*, Paris, Encres, 1980.

24. Dominique Barjot (ed.), *Catching Up with America: Productivity Missions and the Diffusion of American Economic and Technological Influence after the Second World War*, Paris, Presses de l'Université de Paris-Sorbonne, 2002.

25. Robert Paxton, *Vichy France: Old Guard and the New Order*, New York, Alfred Knopf, 1972, pp. 330–52.

26. Michael Pollak, "La planification des sciences sociales," *Actes de la recherche en sciences sociales*, nos. 2–3, 1976, 105–21; Marion Fourcade, *Economists and Societies*, Princeton, NJ, Princeton University Press, 2009.

27. Paul-André Rosental, *L'intelligence démographique: Sciences et politiques des populations en France (1930–1960)*, Paris, Odile Jacob, 2003.

28. Frederic C. Lane, Diary, December 2, 1952, Archives of the Rockefeller Foundation. Document kindly communicated by Brigitte Mazon.

29. Viviane Isambert-Jamati, "La "résurrection" de *l'Année sociologique* après la seconde guerre mondiale," *Année sociologique* 48, no. 1, 1998, 229–48.

30. See the minutes of the Institut français de sociologie, April 24, 1947, Archives of the IFS.

31. Colin Nettelbeck, *Forever French: Exile in the United States, 1939–1945*, New York, Berg, 1991; Laurent Jeanpierre, "Une opposition structurante pour l'anthropologie structurale: Lévi-Strauss contre Gurvitch, la guerre de deux exilés français aux Etats-Unis," *Revue d'histoire des sciences humaines*, no. 11, 2004, 13–43.

32. Georges Gurvitch, *La vocation actuelle de la sociologie*, Paris, Presses Universitaires de France, 1957.

33. Jean-Christophe Marcel, *Éléments pour une analyse de la réception de la sociologie américaine en France (1945–1959)*, Université de Paris—Sorbonne, Mémoire pour l'habilitation à diriger des recherches en sociologie, le 24 novembre 2010, pp. 27 and 128.

34. Jean-Christophe Marcel, "Georges Gurvitch: Les raisons d'un succès," *Cahiers internationaux de sociologie* 110, 2001, 97–119.

35. Among many testimonies, see, for example, Jean Cazeneuve, *Les hasards d'une vie*, Paris, Buchet-Chastel, 1989, p. 77.

36. Quoted in Georges Balandier, *Georges Gurvitch*, Paris, Presses Universitaires de France, 1957, p. 60.

37. Gurvitch, *Vocation actuelle de la sociologie*, p. 4.

38. Georges Gurvitch, "La crise de l'explication en sociologie," *Cahiers internationaux de sociologie* 21, 1956, 3–18.

39. Jean Cazeneuve was Gurvitch's successor at the Sorbonne. Balandier took over the editorship of the *Cahiers internationaux de sociologie* (the journal stopped publication in 2010).

40. On the CNRS, see Jean-François Picard, *La république des savants: La recherche française et le CNRS*, Paris, Flammarion, 1990; Denis Guthleben, *Histoire du CNRS, de 1939 à nos jours*, Paris, Armand Colin, 2013.

41. This chapter is aside from primary and secondary publications based on official documents of the Centre national de la recherche scientifique (CNRS) and Centre d'études sociologiques (CNRS archives 78305/11 and 78309/36). I have freely drawn on my article "Pionniers par défaut: Les débuts de la recherche au Centre d'Études Sociologiques," *Revue française de sociologie* 32, no. 3, 1991, 365–79. See, furthermore, Jean-Michel Chapoulie,

"La seconde fondation de la sociologie française, les États-Unis et la classe ouvrière," *Revue française de sociologie* 32, no. 3, 1991, 321–64; Jean-Michel Chapoulie, "Le travail de terrain, l'observation des actions et des interactions, et la sociologie," *Sociétés contemporaines* 40, 2011, 5–27; Jean-René Tréanton, "Les premières années du Centre d'études sociologiques," *Revue française de sociologie* 32, no. 3, 1991, 381–404, and 33, no. 3, 1992, 487–95; Jean-Christophe Marcel, "Le déploiement de la recherche au Centre d'études sociologiques (1945–1960)," *Revue pour l'histoire du CNRS* 13, 2005, 1–15; Patricia Vannier, *Un laboratoire pour la sociologie?: Le Centre d'Études Sociologiques (1946–1968)*, Thèse de sociologie, Université Paris V, le 8 janvier 1999.

42. Henri Lévy-Bruhl, "Le Centre d'études sociologiques," *Synthèse*, no. 5, 1946, 130–32.

43. Charles Bettelheim and Suzanne Frère, *Une ville française moyenne: Auxerre en 1950*, Paris, A. Colin, 1950.

44. This assessment is based on the social background of thirty-two of the thirty-seven researchers I have been able to identify.

45. One-quarter of the researchers at the CES between 1946 and 1956 were at some point members of the Communist Party. See Vannier, *Un laboratoire pour la sociologie?*, p. 262. "Worker-priests" formed a movement that emerged during the Second World War to reach the group of workers that the Catholic Church could no longer reach otherwise. The "Économie et humanisme" movement was—similar to the Le Play movement—concerned with descriptive monographs inspired by strong Catholic commitments. See Denis Pelletier, *Économie et humanisme: De l'utopie communautaire au combat pour le tiers-monde, 1941–1966*, Paris, Éditions du Cerf, 1996.

46. Vannier, *Un laboratoire pour la sociologie?*, p. 389.

47. Paul-Henri Chombart de Lauwe, "Contribution to the Roundtable Debate," in Alain Drouard (ed.), *Le développement des sciences sociales en France au tournant des années soixante*, Paris, Éditions du CNRS, 1983, pp. 33–37. See also Chombart de Lauwe's autobiographical account in *Un anthropologue dans le siècle*, Paris, Descartes & Cie, 1996.

48. Henri Mendras, *Comment devenir sociologue: Souvenir d'un vieux mandarin*, Arles, Actes Sud, 1995, p. 41.

49. Alain Touraine, "Ambiguïté de la sociologie industrielle américaine," *Cahiers internationaux de sociologie*, no. 12, 1952, 131–46.

50. Picard, *République des savants*, p. 190.

51. Edgar Morin, "Les activités du Centre d'études sociologiques," *Année sociologique* 5, 1953, 555–59.

52. Alain Touraine, "Sur l'organisation des recherches au Centre d'études sociologiques," *Recherches sociologiques*, no. 1, 1955, 42–47.

53. See Gwenaëlle Rot and François Vatin, "L'enquête des Gaston ou les sociologues au travail," *Actes de la recherche en sciences sociales*, no. 175, 2008, 62–81.

54. Jacques Dofny, Claude Durand, Jean-Daniel Reynaud, and Alain Touraine, *Les ouvriers et le progrès technique*, Paris, Armand Colin, 1966.

55. Paul-Henri Maucorps, "Nécessité et conditions de la recherche collective," *Recherches sociologiques*, nos. 3–4, 1955, 55–67. On Maucorps and others (Naville, Stoetzel) with a background in psychology, see Olivier Martin and Patricia Vannier, "La sociologie française après 1945: Place et rôles des méthodes issues de la psychologie," *Revue d'histoire des sciences humaines*, no. 6, 2002, 95–122. On Naville, see Françoise Blum (ed.), *Les vies de Pierre Naville*, Villeneuve d'Ascq, Presses Universitaires du Septentrion, 2007.

56. L. Tanguy, *La sociologie du travail en France*, Paris, La Découverte, 2011, pp. 67–68.

57. As the rural sociologist Mendras noted: "Of course I had a car. More important, I had a horse." See Henri Mendras, "On Being French in Chicago, 1950–51," *La Revue Tocqueville/The Tocqueville Review* 21, no. 1, 2000, 33–40.

58. Alain Chenu, "U.S. Sociology through the Mirror of French Translation," *Contemporary Sociology* 30, no. 2, 2001, 105–9.

59. Chapoulie, "Seconde fondation de la sociologie française," pp. 342–49; Jean-Christophe Marcel, *Éléments*.

60. Touraine, *Désir d'histoire*, pp. 66–67.

61. Michel Crozier, *Ma belle époque*, Paris, Fayard, 2002, pp. 79 and 159.

62. François Bourricaud, "La sociologie française," in *Transactions of the Forth World Congress of Sociology*, vol. 1, 1959, pp. 23–32.

63. Françoise d'Eaubonne, *Le temps d'apprendre à vivre*, Paris, Albin Michel, 1960, p. 362.

64. See, for example, *Rapport sur l'activité générale du CNRS* (October 1951–October 1952), p. 42. On the demand for social science research, see Michael Pollak, "La planification des sciences sociales," *Actes de la recherche en sciences sociales*, nos. 2–3, 1976, 105–21.

65. On the history of major empirical research projects after 1945, see Philippe Masson, *Faire de la sociologie: Les grandes enquêtes françaises depuis 1945*, Paris, La Découverte, 2008.

66. Paul-Henri Chombart de Lauwe, *La vie quotidienne des familles ouvrières*, Paris, Éditions du CNRS, vol. 1, p. 25.

67. Ibid., p. 8.

68. Gabriel Le Bras, *Études de sociologie religieuse*, 2 vols., Paris, Presses Universitaires de France, 1955, 1956. On Le Bras, see D. Julia, "Un passeur de frontières: Gabriel Le Bras et l'enquête sur la pratique religieuse en France," *Revue d'histoire de l'Église de France* 92, 2006, 381–413.

69. Le Bras, *Études*, vol. 1, pp. 324–25.

70. For a comparative analysis of American, French, and German industrial sociology, see Jörg Oetterli, *Betriebssoziologie und Gesellschaftsbild*, Berlin, Walter de Gruyter, 1971, esp. pp. 23–26. For two foreign perspectives on French sociology of work, see Michael Rose, *Servants of Post-Industrial Power?: Sociologie du travail in Modern France*, London, MacMillan Press, 1973; Klaus Düll, *Industriesoziologie in Frankreich*, Frankfurt am Main, Europäische Verlagsanstalt, 1973. The last two studies are critically discussed in *Sociologie du travail* 22, no. 1, 1980, 55–75.

71. Alain Touraine, in Anni Borzeix and Gwenaëlle Rot, *Genèse d'une discipline, naissance d'une revue: Sociologie du travail*, Nanterre, Presses Universitaires de Paris Ouest, 2010, p. 67.

72. On "technological determinism" in French sociology of work, see Marc Maurice, "Le déterminisme technologique dans la sociologie du travail (1955–1980)," *Sociologie du travail* 22, no. 1, 1980, 22–37. On Friedmann, see Pierre Grémion and Françoise Piotet (eds.), *Georges Friedmann, un sociologue dans le siècle 1902–1977*, Paris, CNRS Éditions, 2004; Gwenaële Rot and François Vatin, "Les avatars du 'travail à la chaîne' dans l'œuvre de Georges Friedmann (1931–1966)," *Genèses*, no. 57, 2005, 23–40. For a general overview, Tanguy, *Sociologie du travail en France*.

73. Edgar Morin, "A propos de la formation des sociologies en France," in International Sociological Association, *Papers*, Congress of Liège, 1953, vol. 1 (stenciled).

74. Alain Touraine, *Sociologie de l'action*, Paris, Seuil, 1965, p. 15.

75. Chapoulie, "Seconde fondation de la sociologie française," pp. 354–55.

76. Morin, "Activités du Centre d'études sociologiques," pp. 555–59.

77. Touraine, "Sur l'organisation," pp. 42–47.

78. Philippe Besnard, *Études durkheimiennes*, Genève, Droz, 2003, pp. 363–68.

79. Pierre Bourdieu, *In Other Words*, Cambridge, Polity Press, 1990, pp. 5–6.

80. Pierre Bourdieu and Jean-Claude Passeron, "Sociology and Philosophy in France since 1945: Death and Resurrection of a Philosophy without Subject," *Social Research* 34, no. 1, 1967, 162–212.

81. Mendras, "On Being French in Chicago, 1950–51," pp. 33–40.

82. Brigitte Mazon, *Aux Origines de l'EHESS: Le rôle du mécénat américain (1920–1960)*, Paris, Éditions du CERF, 1988; Jacques Revel and Nathan Wachtel (eds.), *Une école pour les sciences sociales*, Paris, CERF/Éditions de l'EHESS, 1996.

83. Fernand Braudel, "Foreword," in Traian Stoianovitch, *French Historical Method*, Ithaca, NY, Cornell University Press, 1976, p. 15.

84. For the position of the school within the French academic field, see Pierre Bourdieu, *Homo Academicus*, Cambridge, Polity Press, 1988, pp. 105–12.

85. On the *Annales* school, see Peter Burke, *The French Historical Revolution: The Annales School, 1929–89*, Cambridge, Polity Press, 1990; André Burguière, *The Annales School*, Ithaca, NY, Cornell University Press, 2009. On the *Annales* school and sociology, see Jérôme Lamy and Arnaud Saint-Martin, "La frontière comme enjeu: Les *Annales* et la sociologie," *Revue de synthèse* 131, no. 1, 2010, 1–29.

86. Braudel, "Foreword," p. 12.

87. Ibid.

88. *International Encyclopedia of the Social Sciences*, second edition, edited by D. Sills, 1968 "Lucien Febvre."

89. Jean Leca, "French Political Science and Its Subfields," in D. Easton, J. G. Gunnell, and L. Graziano (eds.), *The Development of Political Science*, London, Routledge, 1991, pp. 147–86.

90. Eric Hobsbawm, *Interesting Times*, London, Allen Lane, 2002, p. 331; Maurice Aymard, "In Memoriam Clemens Heller," *Social Science Information* 42, 2003, 283–87.

91. Mazon, *Aux origines de l'EHESS*, pp. 119–135; Ludovic Tournès, *Sciences de l'homme et politique: Les fondations philanthropiques américaines en France au XXᵉ siècle*, Paris, Garnier, 2011, pp. 216–43.

92. Lucien Febvre, "Vieilles années, nouvelle *Année*," *Annales ESC*, 8, 1953, 106–7.

93. Fernand Braudel, *Écrits sur l'histoire*, Paris, Flammarion, 1969, p. 60.

94. Fernand Braudel, "Chez les sociologues: Georges Gurvitch ou la discontinuité du social," *Annales ESC* 8, 1953, 347–61.

95. Fernand Braudel, *The Wheels of Commerce*, London, Collins, 1982, p. 458.

96. See Bertrand Müller, *Lucien Febvre, lecteur et critique*, Paris, Albin Michel, 2003.

97. Lucien Febvre, "Débats autour de la sociologie," *Annales ESC* 9, 1954, 524–26.

6. Cycles of Expansion and Field Transformations

1. Tenured university positions in sociology include a small number of demographers. See Brice Le Gall and Charles Soulié, "Note démographique: Sociologie et philosophie, étude comparée," *Regards sociologiques* 36, 2008, 43–52. For a rich institutional account, see Alain Chenu, "Une institution sans intention: La sociologie en France depuis l'après-guerre," *Actes de la recherche en sciences sociales*, nos. 141–42, 2002, 46–59.

2. Maria Vasconcellos, *L'enseignement supérieur en France*, Paris, La Découverte, 2006; Brice Le Gall and Charles Soulié, "Massification, professionnalisation et réforme du gouvernement des universités," in C. Charle and C. Soulié (eds.), *Les ravages de la "modernisation" universitaire en Europe*, Paris, Syllepse, 2008.

3. For the prototypical conflict between the challenger Roland Barthes and the academic authority Raymond Picard, see Pierre Bourdieu, *Homo Academicus*, Cambridge, Polity Press, 1988, pp. 112–18.

4. For an inventory of structuralist themes and figures, see François Dosse, *History of Structuralism*, Minneapolis, University of Minnesota Press, 1997; Anna Boschetti, *Ismes, du réalisme au postmodernisme*, Paris, CNRS Éditions, 2014.

5. Bourdieu, *Homo Academicus*; Louis Pinto, *La théorie souveraine*, Paris, Éditions du Cerf, 2009, pp. 183–293.

6. Charles Soulié (ed.), *Un mythe à détruire?: Origines et destin du Centre universitaire experimental de Vincennes*, Vincennes, Presses Universitaires de Vincennes, 2012.

7. Bourdieu, *Homo Academicus*, p. xix.

8. See Pierre Bourdieu, "Le discours d'importance," in *Language et pouvoir symbolique*, Paris, Fayard, 2001, pp. 379–96 (chapter not included in the English edition).

9. See Edward Baring, *The Young Derrida and French Philosophy, 1945–1968*, Cambridge, Cambridge University Press, 2011.

10. Jean-Louis Fabiani, *Qu'est-ce qu'un philosophe français?* Paris, Éditions de l'EHESS, 2010, p. 120.

11. Jean-Daniel Reynaud, "Sociologie et 'raison dialectique,'" *Revue française de sociologie* 2, no. 1, 1961, 50–66; M. Mataresso, "Lecture de Claude Lévi-Strauss," *Revue française de sociologie* 4, no. 2, 1963, 195–205.

12. Pierre Bourdieu and Jean-Claude Passeron, "Sociology and Philosophy in France since 1945: Death and Resurrection of a Philosophy without Subject," *Social Research* 34, no. 1, 1967, 162–212.

13. Robert Castel, "Méthode structurale et idéologies structuralistes," *Critique*, no. 210, November 1964, 963–78.

14. Raymond Boudon, *The Uses of Structuralism*, London, Heinemann, 1971, pp. 51 and 140.

15. Marc Joly, *Devenir Norbert Elias*, Paris, Fayard, 2012, p. 187.

16. François Denord, *Néo-libéralisme version française*, Paris, Demopolis, 2007; Monica Prasad, *The Politics of Free Markets: The Rise of Neoliberal Economic Policies in Britain, France, Germany, and the United States*, Chicago, University of Chicago Press, 2006.

17. On the *Nouvel observateur*, see Louis Pinto, *L'intelligence en action: Le nouvel observateur*, Paris, Métailié, 1984.

18. Bernard Brillant, *Les clercs de 68*, Paris, Presses Universitaires de France, 2003; Michael Scott Christofferson, *French Intellectuals against the Left*, New York, Berghahn Books, 2004; Serge Audier, *La pensée anti-68: Essai sur les origines d'une restauration intellectuelle*, Paris, La Découverte, 2008.

19. Rémy Rieffel, *La tribu des clercs*, Paris, Calmann-Lévy, 1993, pp. 225–60.

20. Claire Le Strat, Willy Pelletier, *La canonisation libérale de Tocqueville*, Paris, Éditions Syllepse, 2006.

21. Marion Fourcade, *Economists and Societies*, Princeton, NJ, Princeton University Press, 2009; Frédéric Lebaron, *La croyance économique*, Paris, Seuil, 2000.

22. Yves Déloye and Bernard Voutat (eds.), *Faire la science politique*, Paris, Belin, 2002; Gérard Grunberg, "La recherche à science po," *Revue pour l'histoire du CNRS*, no. 11, 2004, http://histoire-cnrs.revues.org/680.

23. Vincent Gayon, "Jeu critique: La 'fin des intellectuels' (1975–1985)," *Le mouvement social*, no. 239, 2012, 25–44.

24. *Le débat*, no. 1, 1980, 1. See also Pierre Nora's opening essay "Que peuvent les intellectuels?" 3–19.

25. For a perceptive essay on the French intellectual scene during the last two decades of the twentieth century, see Perry Anderson's articles in the *London Review of Books* (September 2 and 23, 2004), republished with a reply by Pierre Nora in P. Anderson, *La pensée tiède*, Paris, Seuil, 2005.

26. J. Duval, C. Gaubert, F. Lebaron, D. Marchetti, and F. Pavis, *Le "décembre" des intellectuels*, Paris, Éditions Raisons d'agir, 1998.

27. Michael Burawoy, "For Public Sociology," *American Sociological Review* 70, 2005, 4–28.

28. Philippe Bezes et al. (éd.), *L'État à l'épreuve des sciences sociales*, Paris, La Découverte, 2005; Alain Chatriot and Vincent Duclert (eds.), *Le gouvernement de la recherche*, Paris, La Découverte, 2006. For the consequences of these policies for various research groups, see Philippe Masson, "Le financement de la sociologie française: Les conventions de recherche de la DGRST dans les années soixante," *Genèses* 62, 2006, 110–28.

29. DGRST, *La recherche scientifique et technique dans le budget de l'État, 1958–1967*, Paris, 1976, p. 72; Jean-François Picard, *La république des savants*, Paris, Flammarion, 1990, p. 252.

30. Denis Guthleben, *Histoire du CNRS, de 1939 à nos jours*, Paris, Armand Colin, 2013, p. 225.

31. The integration of *hors-statut* concerned more than 400 researchers, including 171 in sociology, 72 in economics, 45 in anthropology, 28 in history, 20 in psychology, and 20 in the political science. See R. Boudon, Y. Freville, and L. Guieysse, "Rapport sur la politique contractuelle en sciences sociales," *Le progrès scientifique*, nos. 199–200, 1979, 45–53.

250 NOTES TO PAGES 163–171

32. Philippe Bezes and Nicole de Montricher, "Le moment CORDES (1966–1979)," in Bezes et al., *L'État à l'épreuve des sciences sociales*, pp. 37–71.

33. Olivier Martin (ed.), "Dossier: Menaces sur les sciences sociales vers 1980," *Revue pour l'histoire du CNRS*, no. 7, 2007, http://histoire-cnrs.revues.org/541.

34. See especially Jean-Claude Passeron, "Sociologie, bilan et perspectives," in Maurice Godelier (ed.), *Les sciences de l'homme et de la société en France*, Paris, La Documentation française, 1982, pp. 185–219. The data about CNRS researchers used in figure 6.1 is based on *Rapports d'activité du CNRS* (1959–1969), Documents of the Service central du personnel (1970–1980), and various issues of the *Bilan social* of the CNRS (since 1984).

35. Isabelle Backouche and Christian Topalov (eds.), *Vingt ans d'élections à l'École des hautes études en sciences sociales (1986–2005)*, Paris, EHESS, 2008, p. 24. The data about the teaching staff of the École des hautes études used in figure 6.2 is based on documents of the Archival service of the EHESS and the *Annuaires* de l'EHESS (since 1975).

36. Olivier Godechot and Alexandra Louvet, "Academic Inbreeding: An Evaluation," http://www.laviedesidees.fr/Academic-Inbreeding-An-Evaluation.html.

37. Backouche and Topalov, *Vingt ans d'élections*, pp. 30–31.

38. See "Histoire et sciences sociales: Un tournant critique?," *Annales ESC*, no. 2, 1988, 291–93; "Histoire et sciences sociales: Tentons l'expérience," *Annales ESC*, no. 6, 1989, 1317–23. On the reorientation of the historians at the École des hautes études, see the reflections in Bernard Lepetit (ed.), *Les formes de l'expériences*, Paris, Albin Michel, 1995.

39. For degrees in sociology see Odile Piriou, "Que deviennent les diplômés de sociologie?" *Socio-logos* 3, 2008, http://socio-logos.revues.org/1622.

40. Bourdieu, *Homo Academicus*, pp. 252–53; unpublished documents of the Service des études informatiques et statistiques (SEIS) of the Ministry of Education.

41. Le Gall and Soulié, "Note démographique, pp. 43–52.

42. Pierre Bourdieu and Jean-Claude Passeron, *Reproduction in Education, Society, and Culture*, London, Sage, 1977, pp. 94–97; Yvette Delsaut, "Les opinions politiques dans le système des attitudes: Les étudiants en lettres et la politique," *Revue française de sociologie* 11, 1970, 45–64.

43. Gérard Mauger and Charles Soulié, "Le recrutement des étudiants et lettres et en sciences humaines et leurs objets de recherche," *Regards sociologiques* 22, 2001, 23–40; Bernard Convert, "Espace de l'enseignement supérieur et stratégies étudiantes," *Actes de la recherche en sciences sociales*, no. 183, 2010, 14–31.

44. Claude Dubar, *La recherche sociologique en Ile de France* (unpublished report), Paris, 2004, p. 11.

45. Jean-Michel Chapoulie and Claude Dubar, "La recherche en sociologie dans les universités," Paris, IRESCO, 1991, p. 32; Bruno Auerbach, "Production universitaire et sanctions éditoriales," *Sociétés contemporaines*, no. 74, 2009, 123–45.

46. Passeron, "Sociologie, bilan et perspectives," pp. 185–219. On urban sociology, see Michel Amiot, *Contre l'État, les sociologues: Éléments pour une histoire de la sociologie urbaine en France (1900–1980)*, Paris, Éditions de l'EHESS, 1986. On research in the domain of culture since the founding the Ministry of Cultural Affairs in 1959, see Vincent Dubois, *La politique culturelle*, Paris, Belin, 1999.

47. Ph. Bezes, M. Chauvière, J. Chevallier, N. de Montricher, and F. Ocqueteau, "Introduction," in Bezes et al., *L'État à l'épreuve des sciences sociales*, pp. 14–17; Franck Poupeau, *Une sociologie d'État: L'école et ses experts en France*, Paris, Raisons d'agir, 2003.

48. For a ranking of research themes as they appear in conference papers and PhD dissertations, see Dubar, *Recherche sociologique en Ile de France*, pp. 19–20; Auerbach, "Production universitaire et sanctions éditoriales," pp. 123–45.

49. Johan Heilbron, "Economic Sociology in France," *European Societies* 3, no. 1, 2001, 41–67; Philippe Steiner, "Pourquoi la sociologie économique est-elle si développée en France?," *L'Année sociologique* 55, no. 2, 2005, 391–416.

50. Rémy Rieffel, "L'édition de sciences humaines et sociales," in Pascal Fouché (ed.), *L'édition française depuis 1945*, Paris, Éditions du Cercle de la Librairie, 1998, pp. 88–108.

51. Interview with François Gèze, *Libération*, February 1, 2007; interview with Christian Bourgois in *Les nouvelles littéraires*, no. 2753, September 11–18, 1980; Camille Joseph, *Les éditions La Découverte*, Thèse de doctorat, Paris, EHESS, 2010, pp. 361–89.

52. Bruno Auerbach, "Publish and Perish," *Actes de la recherche en sciences sociales*, no. 164, 2006, 74–92; see also the interview with the publisher Prigent "Sur la politique de traduction: Entretien avec Michel Prigent," *Le débat* 93, 1997, 96–101.

53. Sophie Noël, *L'édition indépendante critique: Engagements politiques et intellectuels*, Villeurbanne, Presses de l'Enssib, 2012.

54. According to the article "Autant en rapporte L'Harmattan," *Libération*, March 6, 1995.

55. In addition, both journals published a comparable proportion of synthetic papers (about 8 percent). See Patricia Vannier, *Un laboratoire pour la sociologie?: Le Centre d'études sociologiques (1946–1968)*, Thèse de sociologie, Université Paris V, le 8 janvier 1999, pp. 369–70.

56. Of the general sociology journals, *Actes de la recherche en sciences sociales* has the highest number of subscriptions. It is—in decreasing order—followed by the *Revue française de sociologie, Cahiers internationaux de sociologie, Archives européennes de sociologie*, and the *Année sociologique* (based on data for 2003).

57. The "core journals" in sociology were *Actes de la recherche en sciences sociales, Cahiers internationaux de sociologie, Revue française de sociologie*, and *Sociologie du travail*. For more details, see Johan Heilbron and Anaïs Bokobza, "Transgresser les frontières en sciences humaines et sociales en France" (working paper).

58. The values on both dimensions of figure 6.5 are derived from the relative weight of references in the core journals of each of the seven disciplines. The degree of disciplinary openness is indicated by the relative weight (on a scale from 0 to 10) of references to extradisciplinary journals among the twenty most cited journals. The degree of international openness is indicated by the relative weight of references to foreign journals among the twenty most cited journals. The qualification and coding of the cited journals is my own. It may be noted that the fourth type of discipline, one that is strongly interdisciplinary as well as predominantly internationally oriented, does not seem to exist.

59. According to data for 1993 and 1994. See Charles Soulié, "Des déterminants sociaux des pratiques scientifiques: Étude des sujets de recherche des docteurs en sciences sociales en France au début des années 1990," *Regards sociologiques*, no. 31, 2006, 91–105.

60. French membership of the International Sociological Association (ISA) declined from two hundred (1990) to ninety-eight (2002). Data kindly provided by Robert van Krieken.

61. Claude Dubar, *La recherche sociologique en Ile de France*, Paris, 2004, p. 24.

62. See Johan Heilbron, "Note sur l'Institut français de sociologie (1924–1962)," *Études durkheimiennes*, 9, 1983, 9–14.

63. Georges Friedmann and Jean-René Tréanton, "Remarques sur les activités et responsabilités professionnelles des sociologues en France," in International Sociological Association (ISA), *Papers*, vol. 1, Liège, 1953.

64. See *Études sociologiques* (1958–68), the bulletin of the Groupe des étudiants en sociologie de l'Université de Paris (GESUP).

65. Jean Stoetzel, "La sociologie française d'aujourd'hui," *Revue des travaux de l'Académie des sciences morales et politiques*, 118, 1965, 254–60.

66. Johan Heilbron, "La 'professionnalisation' comme concept sociologique et comme stratégie des sociologues," in *Historiens et sociologues aujourd'hui*, Paris, Éditions du CNRS, 1986, pp. 61–73.

67. See the special issue "Sociologie et industrie: Une interrogation mutuelle," *L'expansion de la recherche scientifique*, no. 19, 1963.

68. Jean-Daniel Reynaud (ed.), *Tendances et volontés de la société française*, Paris, Sedeis, 1966.

69. The four papers, including another one by Emile Poulat on religion, were published together in the *Revue française de sociologie* 7, no. 3, 1966. For a skeptical commentary on

the rapprochement of planners and sociologists, see Edgar Morin, "Le droit à la réflexion," *Revue française de sociologie* 6, no. 1, 1965, 4–12; and Morin, "Note sur la transformation des colloques de sociologie," *Revue française de sociologie* 7, no. 1, 1966, 82–83.

70. Joly, *Devenir Norbert Elias*, p. 221.

71. For the declaration of the Group of Anti-Sociological Struggles (GLAS), see R. Lourau, *Le gai savoir des sociologues*, Paris, 1977, pp. 114–15.

72. Odile Piriou, "Que deviennent les diplômés de sociologie?," *Socio-logos* 3, 2008, http://socio-logos.revues.org/1622.

73. Gérard Houdeville, *Le métier de sociologue en France depuis 1945*, Rennes, Presses Universitaires de Rennes, 2007, p. 110.

74. Alain Touraine, "Unité et diversité de la sociologie," in International Sociological Association, *Transactions of the Sixth World Congress of Sociology*, Louvain, 1967, part 2, p. 130.

7. Intellectual Styles and the Dynamics of Research Groups

1. In recent years Bruno Latour has joined the group of most-cited French sociologists. See Etienne Ollion and Andrew Abbott, "Quarante ans de sociologie française aux États-Unis: Notes bibliométriques sur la réception des sociologues français aux États-Unis," in D. Demaziere, D. Lorrain and C. Paradeise (dir.), *Transmissions, une communauté en héritage*, Rennes, Presses Universitaires de Rennes (in press).

2. On these vertical and horizontal dimensions of intellectual networks, see Randall Collins, *The Sociology of Philosophies*, Cambridge, MA, Belknap Press of Harvard University, 1998.

3. Harriet Zuckerman, *Scientific Elite*, New York, The Free Press, 1977.

4. On microinteractions and creative collaboration, see Randall Collins, *Interaction Ritual Chains*, Princeton, NJ, Princeton University Press, 2004; Michael Farrell, *Collaborative Circles*, Chicago, Chicago University Press, 2001.

5. Of the twenty sociologists most frequently present in the press (1995–2002), five belong to Touraine's group. With Edgar Morin and Eric Fassin, Touraine himself is on top of the list; Bourdieu has a position near the bottom, whereas Boudon and Crozier are absent; Boudon's style is typically more academic, Crozier's more policy oriented. See Laurent Jeanpierre and Sébastien Mosbah-Natanson, "French Sociologists and the Public Space of the Press," in C. Fleck, A. Hess, and S. Lyon (eds.), *Intellectuals and Their Publics*, Farnham, UK, Ashgate, 2009, pp. 173–91.

6. This characteristic partly overlaps with Burawoy's distinction of four types of sociology: professional, public, policy, and critical sociology. See Michael Burawoy, "For Public Sociology," *American Sociological Review* 70, 2005, 4–28.

7. Anni Borzeix and Gwenaële Rot, *Genèse d'une discipline, naissance d'une revue: "Sociologie du travail,"* Nanterre, Presses Universitaires de Paris Ouest, 2010; Lucie Tanguy, *La sociologie du travail en France: Enquête sur le travail des sociologues, 1950–1990*, Paris, La Découverte, 2011.

8. See Alain Touraine, *Un désir d'histoire*, Paris, Stock, 1977.

9. Ibid., p. 45.

10. Alain Touraine, "Ambiguité de la sociologie industrielle américaine," *Cahiers internationaux de sociologie* 7, 1952, 131–47; Alain Touraine, *L'évolution du travail ouvrier aux usines Renault*, Paris, CNRS, 1955, p. 182.

11. Michel Crozier, "Human engineering," *Les temps modernes* 7, 1951, 44–75.

12. Michel Crozier, "Les intellectuels et la stagnation française," *Esprit* 21, 1953, 771–82.

13. Michel Crozier, *Le mal américain*, Paris, Fayard, 1980, p. 19.

14. Michel Crozier, *Ma belle époque*, Paris, Fayard, 2002, p. 75.

15. Touraine, *Un désir d'histoire*, p. 108; Raymond Aron, *Mémoires*, Paris, Julliard, 1983, p. 348. For the metaphysical overtones of Touraine's book, see the review by two of his philosophically trained colleagues, Jean-Daniel Reynaud and Pierre Bourdieu, "Une

sociologie de l'action est-elle possible?," *Revue française de sociologie* 7, no. 4, 1966, 508–17; Touraine's reply is in the same issue, 518–27.

16. Alain Touraine, *Sociologie de l'action*, Paris, Seuil, 1965, p. 469.

17. Centre d'études des mouvements sociaux, *Rapport sur les activités*, Paris, 1980, p. 59; Alain Touraine, *La voix et le regard*, Paris, Seuil, 1978. For a recent overview, see Michel Wieviorka, "Sociology's Interventions: Engaging the Media and Politics While Remaining a Social Scientist," *Current Sociology* 62, no. 2, 2014, 243–52.

18. Alain Touraine, "Sociology without Society," *Current Sociology* 46, no. 2, 1998, 119–43.

19. But Touraine also has a tendency to conflate the two. See Alain Touraine, *Critique de la modernité*, Paris, Fayard, 1992, p. 270.

20. Alain Touraine, "Can We Live Together, Equal and Different?," *European Journal of Social Theory* 1, no. 2, 1998, 165–78.

21. For a brief overview of these new sociologies, see Philippe Corcuff, *Les nouvelles sociologies*, Paris, Armand Colin, 1995.

22. Crozier, *Ma belle époque*, p. 79.

23. Ibid., p. 104.

24. M. Crozier, "The Cultural Revolution: Notes on the Change in the Intellectual Climate of France," *Daedalus*, winter 1964, 514–42.

25. Crozier, *Ma belle époque*, p. 202.

26. This is well documented in Philip Bezes, *Les réformes de l'administration française (1962–2008)*, Paris, Presses Universitaires de France, 2009.

27. On the dissertation ceremony and the *brouille* with Aron, see Crozier, *Ma belle époque*, pp. 256–59.

28. On Crozier's work, see Pierre Grémion, "Michel Crozier's Long March: The Making of *The Bureaucratic Phenomenon*," *Political Studies* 40, no. 1, 1992, 5–20; Francis Pavé (ed.), *L'analyse stratégique, sa genèse, ses applications et ses problèmes actuels*, Paris, Seuil, 1994.

29. For the post-1968 period, see Michel Crozier, *À contre-courant: Mémoires (1969–2000)*, Paris, Fayard, 2004.

30. Alexandre Paulange-Mirovic, " 'Nous avons réinventé la sociologie': L'Association pour le développement des sciences sociales appliquées: Genèse sociale d'une entreprise académique (1968–1975)," *Revue française de science politique* 63, no. 3, 2013, 545–67; M. Crozier and E. Friedberg, "L'expérience du DEA de sociologie de l'IEP de Paris," in J.-M. Chapoulie and C. Dubar, *La recherche en sociologie dans les universités*, Paris, Report for the Ministry of Education, 1991.

31. Isabelle Berrebi-Hoffman and Pierre Grémion, "Elites intelectuelles et réforme de l'État," *Cahiers internationaux de sociologie* 76, 2009, 39–59.

32. For some biographical information, see Raymond Boudon, *La sociologie comme science*, Paris, La Découverte, 2010; R. Boudon, *Y a-t-il encore une sociologie?* Paris, Odile Jacob, 2003.

33. Jean-Michel Morin, *Boudon, un sociologue classique*, Paris, L'Harmattan, 2006, p. 27.

34. On Lazarsfeld, see M. Pollak, "Paul Lazarsfeld, fondateur d'une multinationale scientifique," *Actes de la recherche en sciences sociales* 25, 1979, 45–60; J. Lautman and B.-P. Lécuyer (eds.), *Paul Lazarsfeld (1901–1976)*, Paris, L'Harmattan, 1998.

35. Raymond Boudon, *L'inégalité des chances*, Paris, Armand Colin, 1973, pp. 76–77.

36. Entretien avec Raymond Boudon par Brigitte Mazon, le 13 février 2012; see http://www.gemass.fr/spip.php?article3740&lang=fr.

37. Raymond Boudon, *Effets pervers et ordre social*, Paris, Presses Universitaires de France, 1977, pp. 88–92.

38. Boudon published numerous studies on classical authors, translated Simmel, and regularly coauthored and coedited dictionaries and anthologies.

39. R. Boudon, "Individualisme ou holisme: Un débat méthodologique fondamental," in H. Mendras and M. Verret (eds.), *Les champs de la sociologie française*, Paris, Armand Colin, 1988, pp. 31–45.

40. R. Boudon, *La logique du social* (1979), Paris, Hachette 1983, pp. 14, 51–52. On methodological individualism, see Lars Udehn, *Methodological Individualism: Background, History, and Meaning*, London, Routledge, 2001.

41. See R. Boudon, "Beyond Rational Choice Theory," *Annual Review of Sociology* 29, 2003, 1–21.

42. Although Boudon's theory of "ordinary rationality" significantly broadens the notion of "rational choice," it does not seem to overcome its intellectualist bias. The erroneous translation of a quote from Weber may illustrate that. In the introduction to "Die Wirtschaftsethik der Weltreligionen" (The economic ethic of world religions), Weber writes: "Interessen (materielle und ideelle), nicht: Ideen, beherrschen unmittelbar das Handeln der Menschen (Interests (material and ideal), not: ideas, dominate the immediate action of people)." Boudon's translation, however, says the opposite: "Ce ne sont pas les intérêts, mais les idées qui dominent en première instance l'action humaine." See Boudon, *Sociologie comme science*, p. 84.

43. Morin, *Boudon, un sociologue classique*, p. 326.

44. See Boudon, *Sociologie comme science*, pp. 90-93.

45. Pierre Bourdieu, *Sketch for a Self-Analysis*, Cambridge, Polity Press, 2008, p. 127. For an illuminating comparison of the trajectories of Bourdieu, Derrida, and Foucault, see Louis Pinto, "Volontés de savoir: Bourdieu, Derrida, Foucault," in L. Pinto, G. Sapiro, and P. Champagne (eds.), *Pierre Bourdieu, sociologue*, Paris, Fayard, 2004, pp. 19–48. On Foucault, see José Luis Morena Pestaña, *En devenant Foucault, sociogenèse d'un grand philosophe*, Broissieux, Éditions du Croquant, 2006.

46. For a more detailed analysis, see Johan Heilbron, "Practical Foundations of Theorizing in Sociology: The Case of Pierre Bourdieu," in C. Camic, N. Gross, and M. Lamont (eds.), *Social Knowledge in the Making*, Chicago: Chicago University Press, 2011, pp. 181–205.

47. For the Algerian years, see especially Abdelmalek Sayad, *Histoire et recherche identitaire*, Saint-Denis, Éditions Bouchene, 2002. See also the special journal issues Tassadit Yacine (ed.), "L'autre Bourdieu," *Awal. Cahier d'études berbères*, nos. 27–28, 2003, and Loïc Wacquant (ed.), "Following Pierre Bourdieu into the Field," *Ethnography* 5, no. 4, 2004.

48. See the texts republished in Pierre Bourdieu, *Interventions, 1961–2001: Science sociale et action politique*, Marseille, Agone, 2002. For Bourdieu's position in relation to that of other French intellectuals, see James Le Sueur, *Uncivil War: Intellectuals and Identity Politics during the Decolonization of Algeria*, Philadelphia, University of Pennsylvania Press, 2001.

49. Pierre Bourdieu, *In Other Words: Essays Towards a Reflexive Sociology*, Cambridge, Polity Press, 1990, p. 39.

50. Claude Seibel, "Les liens entre Pierre Bourdieu et les statisticiens à partir de son expérience algérienne," in J. Bouveresse and D. Roche (eds.), *La liberté par la connaissance: Pierre Bourdieu (1930–2002)*, Paris, Odile Jacob, pp. 105–19.

51. Pierre Bourdieu, Alain Darbel, Jean-Paul Rivet, and Claude Seibel, *Travail et travailleurs en Algérie*, Paris, La Haye, Mouton, 1963, p. 11.

52. Ibid., p. 259

53. Ibid., pp. 257–67.

54. On Aron, Bourdieu, and the Center of European Sociology, see Marc Joly, *Devenir Norbert Elias*, Paris, Fayard, 2012, pp. 187–243.

55. Pierre Bourdieu, *Le bal des célibataires: Crise de la société paysanne en Béarn* (1962), Paris, Seuil, 2002, p. 115.

56. P. Bourdieu and A. Sayad, *Le déracinement: La crise de l'agriculture traditionnelle en Algérie*, Paris, Minuit, 1964, p. 102.

57. P. Bourdieu, "Postface," in E. Panofsky, *Architecture gothique et pensée scolastique*, Paris, Minuit, 1967, 135–67.

58. P. Bourdieu, "La transmission de l'héritage culturel," in DARRAS, *Le Partage des bénéfices: Expansion et inégalités en France*, Paris, Minuit, 1966, p. 388.

59. P. Bourdieu, "Structuralism and the Theory of Sociological knowledge," *Social Research* 35, no. 4, 1968, 681–706.

60. Cover text of the first edition of Pierre Bourdieu, *Esquisse d'une théorie de la pratique*, Genève, Droz, 1972.

61. P. Bourdieu, "Champ intellectuel et projet créateur," *Les temps modernes* 22, 1966, 865–906.

62. Bourdieu, "Structuralism and the Theory of Sociological knowledge," p. 697.

63. P. Bourdieu, "Une interprétation de la théorie de la religion selon Max Weber," *Archives européennes de sociologie* 12, no. 1, 1971, 3–21; Bourdieu, "Genèse et structure du champ religieux," *Revue française de sociologie* 12, no. 3, 1971, 295–334; Bourdieu, "Champ du pouvoir, champ intellectuel, habitus de classe," *Scolies: Cahiers de recherche de l'École normale supérieure*, no. 1, 1971, 7–26.

Conclusion

1. The position of other French social science journals was quite similar: the *Annales* was cited once, *Sociologie du travail* once, the *Revue française de sociologie* did best with eight citations. See Johan Heilbron, "La sociologie européenne exist-t-elle?," in G. Sapiro (ed.), *L'espace intellectuel en Europe: De la formation des États-nations à la mondialisation XIXᵉ–XXᵉ siècles*, Paris, La Découverte, 2009, pp. 347–58. The translation into English of a yearly selection of articles of certain French journals hasn't improved the citation scores very much, indicating that the issue of national closure is more than a question of language barriers. See Yves Gingras and Sébastien Mosbah-Natanson, "La question de la traduction en sciences sociales: Les revues françaises entre visibilité internationale et ancrage national," *Archives européennes de sociologie* 51, no. 2, 2010, 305–21.

Epilogue: What Is French about Sociology in France?

1. For a history of sociology in terms of national traditions, see Donald Levine, *Visions of the Sociological Tradition*, Chicago, Chicago University Press, 1995.

2. Joseph Schumpeter, "Recent Developments of Political Economy (1931)," in J. Schumpeter, *The Economics and Sociology of Capitalism*, Princeton, NJ, Princeton University Press, 1991, 284–97.

3. On political structuring of the social sciences, see P. Wagner, C. Weiss, B. Wittrock, and H. Wollmann (eds.), *Social Sciences and Modern States: National Experiences and Theoretical Crossroads*, Cambridge, Cambridge University Press, 1991; D. Rueschemeyer and T. Skocpol (eds.), *States, Social Knowledge, and the Origins of Modern Social Policies*, Princeton, NJ, Princeton University Press; New York, Russell Sage Foundation, 1996; Peter Wagner, *Modernity as Experience and Interpretation*, Cambridge, Polity Press, 2008, esp. pp. 165–87.

4. Dorothy Ross, *The Origins of American Social Science*, Cambridge, Cambridge University Press, 1991.

5. On the internationalization of the sciences, see E. Crawford, T. Shinn, and S. Sverker (eds.), *Denationalizing Science: The Contexts of International Scientific Practice*, Dordrecht, Kluwer Academic Publishers, 1993; for the social sciences, see J. Heilbron, N. Guilhot, and L. Jeanpierre, "Toward a Transnational History of the Social Sciences," *Journal of the History of the Behavioral Sciences* 44, no. 2, 2008, 146–60; Yves Gingras, "Les formes spécifiques de l'internationalité du champ scientifique," *Actes de la recherche en sciences sociales*, no. 141–42, 2002, 31–45; Gisèle Sapiro, "Le champ est-il national?," *Actes de la recherche en sciences sociales* 200, 2013, 71–85.

6. For a typical example, see Johan Galtung, "Structure, Culture, and Intellectual Style: An Essay Comparing Saxonic, Teutonic, Gallic, and Nipponic Approaches," *Social Science Information* 20, 1981, 817–56.

7. For a more elaborate version of this argument, see Johan Heilbron, "Qu'est-ce qu'une tradition nationale en sciences sociales?," *Revue d'histoire des sciences humaines*, no. 18, 2008, 3–16.

8. K. Danziger, *Constructing the Subject: Historical Origins of Psychological Research*, Cambridge, Cambridge University Press, 1990.

9. For illuminating examples, see Marion Fourcade, *Economists and Societies*, Princeton, NJ, Princeton University Press, 2009; Libby Schweber, *Disciplining Statistics: Demography and Vital Statistics in France and England, 1830–1885*, Durham, NC, Duke University Press, 2006.

10. D. F. Lindenfeld, *The Practical Imagination: The German Sciences of State in the Nineteenth Century*, Chicago, Chicago University Press, 1997; Peter Senn, "What Is Behavioral Science?," *Journal of the History of the Behavioral Sciences* 2, no. 2, 1966, 107–22.

11. For comparative studies of intellectual and academic fields, see Christophe Charle, *Les intellectuels en Europe au XIXᵉ siècle*, Paris, Le Seuil, 1996; Fritz Ringer, *Fields of Knowledge: French Academic Culture in Comparative Perspective*, Cambridge, Cambridge University Press, 1992; Gisèle Sapiro (ed.), *L'espace intellectuel en Europe*, Paris, La Découverte, 2009.

12. Pierre Duhem, *La Théorie physique, son objet, sa structure* (1906), Paris, Vrin, 1981, pp. 91–92.

13. R. Romani, *National Character and Public Spirit in Britain and France, 1750–1914*, Cambridge, Cambridge University Press, 2002; C. Trautmann-Waller, *Aux origines d'une science allemande de la culture: Linguistique et psychologie des peuples chez Heymann Steinthal*, Paris, CNRS Éditions, 2006.

14. Norbert Elias, *On the Process of Civilisation* (1939), Dublin, UCD Press, 2012.

15. Norbert Elias, *Studies on the Germans: Power Struggles and the Development of Habitus in the Nineteenth and Twentieth Centuries*, in *Collected Works*, vol. 11, Dublin, University College Dublin Press, 2013, p. 139.

16. Pierre Bourdieu, "Systèmes d'enseignement et système de pensée," *Revue internationale des sciences sociales* 19, no. 3, 1967, 367–88, republished in F. Clément, M. Roca i Escoda, F. Schultheis, and M. Berclaz (eds.), *L'inconscient académique*, Genève, Éditions Seismo, 2006, pp. 21–46.

17. Ibid., p. 43.

18. Pierre Bourdieu, *Pascalian Meditations*, Cambridge, Polity Press, 2000, pp. 97–99.

19. Jonathan Harwood, "National Differences in Academic Culture: Science in Germany and the United States between the World Wars," in C. Charle, J. Schriewer, and P. Wagner (eds.), *Transnational Intellectual Networks: Forms of Academic Knowledge and the Search for Cultural Identities*, Berlin, Campus, 2004, pp. 53–79.

Index

Page numbers followed by *f* and *t* indicate figures and tables.